THE GOVERNMENT AND POLITICS OF FRANCE

The Government and Politics of France

Second Edition

Anne Stevens

St. Martin's Press
New York

THE GOVERNMENT AND POLITICS OF FRANCE
Copyright © 1992, 1996 by Anne Stevens
All rights reserved. No part of this book may be used or reproduced
in any manner whatsoever without written permission except in the
case of brief quotations embodied in critical articles or reviews.
For information, address:

St. Martin's Press, Scholarly and Reference Division,
175 Fifth Avenue, New York, N.Y. 10010

First edition (in the UK by Macmillan Press) 1992
First published in the United States of America in 1996

Printed in Great Britain

ISBN 0–312–16242–1 (cloth)
ISBN 0–312–16247–2 (paperback)

Library of Congress Cataloging-in-Publication Data
Stevens, Anne, 1942–
The government and politics of France
p.   cm.
Includes bibliographical references (p.) and index.
ISBN 0–312–16242–1. — ISBN 0–312–16247–2 (pbk.)
1. France—Politics and government—1789–   I. Title.
JN2451.S74   1996
320.944—dc20   96–18408
                                               CIP

For Helen

Contents

Part IV   France and Europe

List of Tables, Figures, Exhibits and Maps

Exhibits

Maps

Preface

Early in the 1950s my parents tired of summer holidays mostly spent on chilly wind-swept beaches and embarked, with hire car, tents and four young children, on what was, in the lingering climate of post-war austerity, a still unusual adventure – a tour through France. I still recall the vivid realisation, as the ferry approached Calais, that France looked different, and the even sharper shock of discovering that it really did sound different too. That journey took us from Calais to the Spanish border, and back along the Mediterranean coast. When the family turned towards the Channel again my twin sister and I stayed behind, to spend a further few weeks near Nîmes, in the Ardèche and in Marseilles with the French family with whom we had been corresponding.

That summer left its mark on both my twin and me. It was for both of us the start of a continuing interest in and affection for the country and the first of many visits. For me it was a beginning that, twenty years later, led me, through many changes and chances, to the study of contemporary France. My sister came earlier to the subject, as an undergraduate in Philip Williams' lectures when the Fifth Republic was still quite young. She retains her connections with France and French people, nowadays in part through the association that twins the Anglican cathedral of Manchester with the Roman Catholic basilica of Saint Sernin in Toulouse. This book is dedicated to her.

The book is intended as an introduction to the study of French government and politics for students in sixth forms, colleges and universities, and also as a guide for general readers with an interest in French affairs. I hope it enables those interested in and concerned with events in France to understand and analyse them with a clear understanding of their background and context. For this reason the emphasis is on long-term trends and on elements of continuity as well as on change. Nevertheless, the constitutional, governmental and political changes that have occurred since 1992 seemed to justify a second edition and, while much has remained unchanged, I have taken the opportunity to update and revise extensively. In this second edition I have tried to correct errors, adjust the emphasis where it has not stood the test of time, carry forward the story where appropriate and include some new material, especially in areas which reviewers quite rightly suggested were dealt with too sparingly in the first edition. I have reshaped Chapter 11, extending the discussion of France and Europe, which seems more than ever a crucial aspect of French government and politics, and placed the general conclusion in a separate chapter. I have been pleased to learn that readers found the first edition helpful, and am grateful to those students and their teachers whose comments have assisted the revisions for the second edition.

Teaching and research on aspects of French politics and administration have been at the centre of my working life for the past two decades, and I owe a great deal to the many colleagues, acquaintances and friends who make this area of study so congenial and stimulating. I should like particularly to mention my gratitude to the Association for the Study of Modern and Contemporary France, to the editors of *Modern and Contemporary France* and to the Maison Française at Oxford for all they do to make the study of contemporary France both pleasant and fruitful. Such merits as this book may have derive quite largely from successive generations of students on the course, 'The Politics of the Nation State: France', which I taught at the University of Sussex, and on 'The Politics and Government of France' and 'Politics in Contemporary Western Europe' at the University of Kent at Canterbury. I am grateful to them and to Nicholas Wrathall who read the first draft. Without Liz Davies, of the University of Sussex Computer Centre, much of the text could not have moved from Brighton to Canterbury with me. Chrissy Emms saw me through my first year in Canterbury and Sheila Holness has looked after me ever since.

I have accumulated many debts over the years I have worked in this field; as I look back I am particularly conscious of those to Dr Howard Machin, Professor John Gaffney, Professor Siân Reynolds and Dr Peter Holmes. Professor Clive Church and Professor Françoise Dreyfus both read the whole manuscript of the first edition and assisted with the second edition, the latter through her comments and the former by carrying additional burdens so that I could undertake the necessary revisions during part of a study term generously provided by the University of Kent at Canterbury. I am also grateful for comments from Dr Robert Elgie which assisted the revision. My family, Handley, Hilary, Lucy and Mary Stevens all believed in me and in the book, even when progress seemed difficult. So did a patient and supportive editor, Steven Kennedy. Without Vincent Wright there would have been no research, no teaching and no book at all. For the weaknesses and errors it contains I am alone responsible.

December 1995   ANNE STEVENS

Acknowledgements

The author and publishers are grateful to the following for permission to reproduce copyright material:

Longman Publishers USA for a figure from *The French Polity* by W. Safran. Copyright © 1995 by Longman Publishers USA (Table 4.1).
Frank Cass Publishers for a table from John Frears, 'The French Parliament: Loyal Workhorse, Poor Watchdog', *West European Politics*, 13 (2) July 1991 (Exhibit 7.4).
The Economist for a figure © The Economist, London, 30 September 1995 (Figure 3.1).
Methuen for a figure from M. Duverger, *Political Parties*, 1964 (Figure 8.1).

Every effort has been made to contact all copyright-holders, but if any have been inadvertently overlooked the publishers will be pleased to make the necessary arrangement at the earliest opportunity.

- ⊚   Regional prefecture

- ——   Regional boundaries

The Regions of France

Part I

Historical and Constitutional Framework

1

France: An Introduction

France is sometimes represented as a hexagon (see p. xvi). The coasts of the Channel and then the Atlantic, the Pyrenees and the Mediterranean sea, the Alps and the Jura, the Vosges and the Rhine and the long land frontier with Luxembourg and Belgium seem to outline a regular pattern. The shape of France is not, however, the consequence of some long and rational process of geometrical neatness. It emerged only slowly, as successive French kings extended their control from their heartland around Paris, conquering Normandy, driving the English out of the South West and the West (Calais, the last English outpost, fell to the French in January 1558) asserting their domination over Burgundy (1481) and Provence (1491), and incorporating Brittany into the kingdom (1532). At the beginning of the nineteenth century Napoleon extended the sphere of metropolitan French administration into the Low Countries and parts of Germany and Northern Italy. In 1815 the Treaty of Vienna redefined France's borders: Savoy and the town of Nice, which had been annexed during the Revolution were then lost. They were to return in 1860. The bitter history of Alsace (mostly incorporated into France in 1648) and Lorraine (incorporated in 1766) which were conquered and attached to the German Empire in 1870, regained by the Treaty of Versailles in 1919, conquered again in 1940 and liberated in 1945 left a deep mark on French historical consciousness.

As a result, perhaps, of this chequered history and a certain obsession with French territorial integrity which derives from it, the French constitutions of both 1946 and 1958 proclaim France as a secular, democratic, social, but also indivisible republic. Like many constitutional pronouncements this is a statement of will and inten-

3

tion as much as of fact. The intention is to bring together a country of great diversity and a contested and conflict-ridden political history into a united nation state. In the hope of setting the context for the more extended discussions of the state of French government and politics which follow, this chapter attempts to outline some of the main elements of that diversity. An examination of the geographical and historical diversity of France is followed by a consideration of some of the factors which have contributed to political change and development. The impact of the Revolution, the legacy of Napoleon, the rise of the Republic, relationships between state and church and the period of Liberation and reconstruction have all had their repercussions upon the political, economic and social structures of France today.

Geographical Diversity

France, with a land area of 212 919 square miles (543 965 square kilometres) is the third largest country in Europe, exceeded only by Russia and the Ukraine. North and west of a line from the mouth of the Gironde to the Ardennes the land only occasionally rises as high as 250 metres above sea level, and indeed much of North West France is less than 100 metres above sea level. South and east of this line the Massif Central which occupies about one sixth of the land area rises gradually southeastward with summits of over 1700 metres along the southern escarpment of the Cevennes. Its now extinct volcanoes were thrown up by the tectonic movements that produced the Alps. These, to the east, include the highest mountain in Europe, Mont Blanc (4807 metres). To the south of the Massif Central lie the undulating plains of Languedoc, separated by the valley of the Rhône from Provence, and from Spain by the mountain wall of the Pyrenees. North of the Alps are the wooded hills of the Jura, the Vosges and the Ardennes. More than 23 per cent of the land area of France is forested. The basins of the main rivers – Seine, Loire, Saône, Rhône, Garonne – shape and delineate the various regions.

The oceanic climate of the west of France with its moderate variations of temperature and its frequent and abundant rainfall gives way gradually to the east to a more continental type of climate, with greater extremes of temperature and lower rainfall. The south of France enjoys a mediterranean climate, with mild winters and hot dry summers. Weather patterns throughout France are generally moderate and stable, without seasonal extremes and without sudden marked fluctuations from day to day.

Geographical and climatic conditions help to account for the diversity of French landscapes, from the mountainous and pastoral landscape of the Alps, to the broad flat cereal fields of the plains of Northern France and the vineyards of Languedoc, themselves somewhat different in appearance from the greener, more hilly wine growing country of Burgundy. The coasts of Northern and Western Brittany are rocky and spectacular, further south the Atlantic coast is formed of dunes and marshes. 'Differing conditions of geology, morphology, climate, soil and vegetation are responsible for widely differing natural habitats. Out of these habitats man has made regions, accentuating natural diversity by differences of organisation and use' (Pinchemel, 1987, p. 13). So distinctive are the landscapes produced by certain conditions and types of agriculture, such as the lavender growing of Provence, that attempts are now made to ensure their preservation as part of France's environmental heritage.

At the 1992 census the population of metropolitan France was 57 218 000 people. This is similar to the populations of Italy (57.4 million) and the United Kingdom (56.8 million). In the middle of the eighteenth century, it is reckoned, France was the most densely populated country in Europe. Nowadays it is amongst the least densely populated. If France had the same average number of people per square kilometre as the United Kingdom it would have a population of 126 million (Pinchemel, 1987, p. 125). Since the beginning of the nineteenth century the population of France has almost doubled – but growth has not been at a steady rate. Population growth during the nineteenth century was slow, and the population actually declined not only during the First and Second World Wars, but also during the 1930s. Since 1945 the population has increased much more rapidly, growing since 1946 by some 14 million, a greater increase than that which had occurred over the previous century and a half. This increase is largely due to a marked, but fairly short-lived, rise in the birthrate during the babyboom years of 1945–55, combined with sharp reductions in the death rate, and particularly in infant mortality. Immigration, mostly from neighbouring countries, was an important cause of population growth throughout the nineteenth century and indeed up to the 1930s. During the 1950s and the 1960s immigration, chiefly from European countries and also from French-speaking Africa, accounted for about

40 per cent of the population growth. Around 7 per cent of the population do not possess French nationality. After 1962, the year of Algerian Independence, over 800 000 French people who had been resident in North Africa settled in France (Pinchemel, 1987, p. 124).

The population of France is far from being uniformly distributed within the country. The most striking feature is the concentration in and around Paris. The Ile-de-France region – Paris and the surrounding area – which contained less than 4 per cent of the national population at the beginning of the nineteenth century, 6.5 per cent at the beginning of the twentieth century, and just over 15 per cent at the end of the Second World War, is now inhabited by more than 18 per cent of the population of France (Pinchemel, 1987, pp. 129–30).

This concentration is an extreme example of a more general phenomenon of urban growth. Towards the end of the 1920s about half the inhabitants of France lived in areas categorised as rural; that is, in districts which contained no settlement of more than 2000 inhabitants. In the 1980s only just over one quarter do so. All types of towns have grown, but especially those which now have populations of between 100 000 and 1 million, of which there are now 38 in France. Only three towns exceed 1 million, however; they are Lyons, Marseilles and Paris, which, with over 2 million within its city boundaries, far outstrips the other two.

Modern France has lost much its earlier diversity of dialects and languages. In 1863 at least a quarter of the country's population lived in communes that did not speak French and nearly 450 000 out of just over 4 million school children between the ages of seven and thirteen spoke no French at all (Weber, 1979, p. 67). Breton and the Langue d'Oc of the south, being different languages rather than dialects, most effectively resisted the onslaught of Parisian French during the nineteenth and twentieth centuries and are now precariously maintained by bilingual speakers supported by vigorous regional cultural movements.

The regions are also economically diverse. In France the main force of the industrial revolution was not experienced until the second half of the nineteenth century. The economic geography of France that was established before the First World War and is the basis of the present-day pattern arose from several diverse factors. These included the presence of natural resources – coal in Central France and the Nord–Pas-de-Calais, iron ore in Lorraine – or of long established traditional industries – textiles in Lyons and in the North for example. The growth and shape of the railway system was another factor, as was the development of hydro-electric power. Between the wars and until the mid-1950s industrialisation was centred in Paris and to the North and East; indeed at that period over 50 per cent of industrial employment was located within the four regions of the Ile-de-France, the Nord–Pas-de-Calais, Lorraine and the Rhône–Alpes. Outside the Paris region this industrialisation was based upon long-standing textile, chemical, mining and iron and steel-based industries (Tuppen, 1983, p. 147).[1]

Since the 1950s the areas of traditional industrialisation have experienced the problems associated with decline whilst some formerly largely agricultural areas especially in the West, but also in the Alps, have seen the growth of advanced technology industries in a number of towns. Government policy in the 1950s and 1960s was aimed at encouraging industry to move out of Paris. This resulted in the movement out of some industrial activities, though many firms retained headquarters in Paris. Much of the movement was into the area immediately surrounding Paris – the Ile-de-France. From the early 1970s policy concentrated more on industrial reorganisation, concentration and adjustment than on decentralisation. Even today industrial activity is quite unevenly distributed across France and contrasts exist between regions in the level and nature of their industrial activity.

'At the micro level of *pays* or *arrondissement* France is almost certainly the most variegated [of European countries] in its landscapes and traditional ways of life. The mosaic of mountain, hill, scarpland or plain has been interpreted through a long history of rural and small town development. The late arrival of large scale industry and urbanisation has not had the effect of creating the greater uniformity in ways of life found, for example, in Britain' (House, 1978, p. 56). Distinctive landscapes, building styles, methods of farming, products, lifestyles, even cooking, from the butter, cream and cider of Normandy to the olives, tomatoes, herbs and wine of Provence, reinforce feelings of regional identity. The mobility of the population in the decades since the Second World War, commercial and industrial developments and the impact of genuinely mass media such as television have all helped to produce a greater uniformity of lifestyle and experience throughout France. However, many French people still have strong feelings for their own or their family's origins and a sense of belonging not only to the nation but also to the locality – of being French but also, perhaps chiefly, Breton, Alsatian, Provençal or Corsican.

The Impact of the French Revolution

The impact of the French Revolution upon the history of modern Europe lies not only in its social, economic and political consequences, but also in the perceptions, even the myths, which surrounded it and the strength of the political traditions and analyses which looked back to it as a crucial point of reference. These competing and contradictory traditions formed the basis for many of the conflicts and cleavages discussed below. Historians debate the causes and consequences of the Revolution; from its turbulent events stem many of the political and administrative currents, forces and patterns that shape modern France. Although continuities can also be traced, linking people, behaviour and institutions across the watershed of the Revolution, it was nevertheless an abrupt break with the pattern of what had gone before, a pattern that was very soon described as the old order (the *ancien regime*). That pattern was based in principle upon an absolute monarchy, upheld by a theory of divine right which assimilated royal authority and divine authority, making dissent from the royal government not simply a political choice but a sin, and by a hierarchical society which emphasised the existence of three separate orders, or estates, within society – the clergy, the nobility and the remainder, the third estate. Government consisted of the attempt by the King to manage a diverse and imperfectly unified country through a system of royal officials. This administration was chiefly concerned with the maintenance of public order, the levying of taxes and provision for military needs. However, since at least the seventeenth century the need for the government to be concerned with the commerce and industry of the country, as the economic basis for international wealth, prestige and power had been recognised. The name of Louis XIV's minister, Colbert, is particularly associated with attempts to encourage trade, foster economic development and introduce industries through governmental supervision and initiative.

Royal administration was seen as the affair of the King, not to be the subject of study or question. There was virtually no concept of a national political system, despite the King's effort to impose his authority everywhere. Local rights and interests took priority over national considerations. The country was a vast and complex patchwork of local customs, local laws, local rights, and local habits. Many traditional rights were vested in groups and bodies whose membership the King could not alter.

This pattern was swept away with great speed by the Revolution, swept away, moreover, in the name of rational philosophical uniform principles. The representatives of the three estates, summoned for the first time since 1614 to meet as the Estates General, and transformed into a National Assembly, voted in August 1789 for what is described as the abolition of feudalism – the ending of the old patterns of privileges and rights and the abolition of the sale of offices. These measures implied the restructuring of the systems of local administration, of justice and of taxation. The principles upon which this restructuring was to occur were set out in the Declaration of the Rights of Man, passed on 26 August 1789. This Declaration, which forms an integral part of the present-day French constitution, asserts the right of all men[2] to liberty, property, security and resistance to oppression. It insists that the law is the same for everyone, all citizens being equally entitled to avail themselves of its protection and equally subject to its sanctions, and that all citizens should be eligible for position and public employment on the sole criterion of ability. Political authority stems, according to Article 3, from the nation. The Declaration also includes an assertion of freedom of religious belief and of speech and publication.

With the abolition of the monarchy in 1792 Republicanism became an essential component of the Revolutionary tradition. War, initially against Austria and Prussia, which had begun earlier in 1792, was waged in the name of the defence of the revolutionary principles and of the liberation of the rest of Europe from what were seen as tyrannical and oppressive regimes. These aims eventually served as arguments to legitimate the conquests of Napoleon. From the events of the war sprang a powerful tradition of the nation in arms, defending, against reactionary enemies, not merely the country, but also the broad moral principles of liberty and equality which France was felt to embody.

The Revolution, however, left France deeply divided. There were divisions even within the revolutionary tradition. In popular mythology these have come to be symbolised by the divisions between Girondins – a group of members of the national assembly grouped around the representative from the Gironde, the area around Bordeaux – and the Jacobins – the party of Robespierre, named after the former Jacobin monastery where the group met. The Girondins are held to symbolise a more moderate, more participatory, form of republicanism, with an emphasis on local rights. The adjective 'jacobin' is applied to a tradition which insists firmly upon the power and the authority of the central institutions of the republic, upon the need for uniformity throughout the country and upon a strong and centralised direction of public affairs.

Opposed to the revolutionary republican tradition there was a monarchist tradition, seeking a return to a hierarchical and ordered society. The restoration of the monarchy in 1815 marked a brief ascendancy for this political tradition which was an important component of the 'Right' in French political life for much of the nineteenth century. In addition to this 'anti-revolutionary' current, it is possible, following David Thomson, to identify a 'counter-revolutionary' current. 'Common to all forms was the blunting of some consequences of the Revolution by accepting and turning against them some of its other consequences and implications' (Thomson, 1969, p. 80). The political manifestations of this current were liberal Orleanism, dominant during the constitutional monarchy of the Orleanist King Louis-Philippe between 1830 and 1848, and the Bonapartists, with their appeal to a strong leader supported by popular plebiscite. All these currents played important roles in the politics of the nineteenth century, and even when the dynasties to which they were attached died out or dwindled the political cleavages which they symbolised continued.

Church and State

The salience, and the bitterness, of the division between revolutionary and reactionary political traditions was enhanced by the fact that it was deeply entangled with another area of conflict, that over the place and role of the Roman Catholic church within society. Under the *ancien régime* the church held a particular place in society, for religious doctrine played an important role in legitimising the power of the monarch. The clergy constituted the first of the estates of the realm, and had important privileges, of social precedence, of determining their own level of taxation, which consequently bore less heavily upon them than upon the other estates, and of administering justice – the church had its own courts. The church was wealthy, through the levy which it raised on agricultural produce (tithes) and the fees that it charged, and through its landholdings. The church attempted to maintain religious uniformity – the Roman Catholic church was the only one permitted to hold services – and enjoyed powers of censorship. Much of the educational system was in its hands.

The initial period of the Revolution (see Exhibit 1.1, p. 12) saw the ending of the privileges which the clergy had enjoyed in their role as feudal landowners. Then, in 1790, as the need for money grew pressing, the National Assembly voted the Civil Constitution of the Clergy, which deprived the church of its landed possessions and its right to levy tithes and made the clergy salaried officials. The Pope condemned this move. From this time on resistance to the Revolution was increasingly identified with support for the church.

Equally, revolutionary principles came to appear incompatible with traditional religion and in 1793 a revolutionary calendar was introduced abolishing Sundays – weeks were replaced by 10-day periods – and removing traditional associations with the Christian year. A cult of reason was invented and a campaign of de-christianisation begun. This was short-lived, and Napoleon, facing a society in which Roman Catholicism was still deeply anchored, brought order and compromise through the conclusion, in 1801, of a Concordat with the papacy. This remained in force until 1905. The church's lands were not restored, the clergy were paid salaries by the government and the degree of religious toleration introduced by the Revolution through the recognition of Protestants and Jews was maintained.

The restored monarchy in 1815 did not abrogate the Concordat, but temporarily fostered a closer relationship between church and government. After the Revolution of 1830 the church became increasingly associated with reactionary political ideas. During the period of reaction to the Revolution of 1848 and under the Second Empire, when the preservation of a stable social order seemed important, governments supported the church, especially over the provision of help for Catholic schools.

By the end of the nineteenth century, the church was clearly identified with the forces of the reactionary Right, with conservatives who hankered for a return to an ordered hierarchical society. It had great difficulty accepting the principle of a republican regime, with all its implications of democracy and popular sovereignty, and only did so at all, and then partially, slowly and reluctantly, in a movement known as *ralliement*, at the urging of Pope Leo XIII in the 1890s.

Moreover, the Marxist origin of much socialism made it abhorrent to the church, so that even when partially reconciled to the Republic the church remained profoundly hostile to Socialism. The clash between clerical and anti-clerical forces was dramatically demonstrated at the time of the Dreyfus affair (see Exhibit 1.2), which linked together a whole series of complex themes, involving a large number of social and political groupings in taking sides and hence ranging themselves in virulent opposition to the proponents of the alternative view.

The identification of the church with reactionary and conservative principles and forces within society aroused fierce hostility to it amongst those who professed democratic and Republican traditions and looked back to the achievements of the Revolution, and amongst Socialists. Since the Republican principles of democracy and particularly of freedom of opinion and expression, seemed incompatible with the acknowledgement of any kind of role for the church in

---

EXHIBIT 1.1

Regimes in France since 1789

May–June 1789 Estates General meets at Versailles and declares itself a constituent national assembly.
August 1789 Adoption of the Declaration of the Rights of Man.
September 1789 New constitution; limited monarchy.
August 1792 Invasion of the Tuileries Palace; end of the monarchy.
September 1792 Meeting of the Convention.
January 1793 Execution of the King.
April 1793 Establishment of the Committee of Public Safety.
June 1793 Vote for 1793 Constitution; never implemented.
10 October 1793 Convention decides that government will be 'revolutionary' until peace is achieved.
April 1795 Directory constitution.
November 1799 (18 Brumaire an VIII) Coup d'état of Napoleon Bonaparte.
December 1799 Constitution of the Consulate.
May 1804 Establishment of the First Empire.
April 1814 Restoration of the monarchy; Constitutional Charter.
March 1815 Return of Napoleon. Imperial constitution amended by *Acte Additionnel*.
June 1815 Second abdication of Napoleon – return to monarchy and 1814 charter.
1830 Constitutional monarchy (July monarchy) under Louis-Philippe.
1848 Second Republic.
1852 Second Empire under Napoleon III.
1870 Provisional regime.
1875 'Wallon amendment' – consolidation of Third Republic.
1940 Occupation. 'Vichy' regime continued Third Republic constitution except where amended by Pétain's constitutional acts.
1944 Provisional Government.
1946 Fourth Republic.
1959 Fifth Republic.

society this hostility, known as anti-clericalism,[3] persisted as a major trend in French political life. *Laïcité* (secularism) was a particularly important plank in the platform of Republicans, and was shared by the Socialists, who had good Marxist reasons for their hostility. The field of education was a particularly hotly contested one, since this is a major way in which the church can impinge upon society. In 1905 the advocates of *laïcité* achieved the formal separation of churches and state, which no longer recognises any religion nor pays any clergy.

The 1905 separation of church and state did not, however, put an end to the problems of relationships between the church and the Republic. Church schools continued to exist, especially at secondary level, and the problem of the nature, level and organisation of state aid for these schools was a crucial and bitter issue in the politics of the Fourth republic. With the coming of the Fifth Republic a new settlement was achieved, which allowed for some state control over church schools in return for subsidies. The advent of the first Socialist government of the Fifth Republic in 1981 and the return of a strong majority of the Right in 1993 revived some of the old controversy (see Exhibit 10.4) – a reminder that, although often inextricably inter-twined with other issues, the old conflict between clerical and anti-clerical sentiments has not been entirely forgotten in France.

The Legacy of Napoleon

Napoleon Bonaparte, who came to power initially as one of three consuls in 1799, was crowned Emperor in 1804, and was finally defeated and exiled by the British in 1815, introduced a third strand of political tradition that evoked some of the aspects of the Revolution – chiefly the emphasis upon direct popular support – and allied them to administrative rationality, authoritarian institutions and an asser-tion of national grandeur. Bonapartism was not a return to the hierarchical privileged society of the *ancien régime*: nor was it a continuation of the democratic republican aspects of the period from 1791 to 1799.

The restoration of the monarchy in 1815 was followed in 1830 by a period of constitutionally limited monarchy under Louis–Philippe. In 1848 the short-lived Second Republic introduced the practice of manhood suffrage but Louis Napoleon, who was elected President in 1848, and became Emperor as Napoleon III in 1852, whilst fully accepting the suffrage, used it, initially at least, as a basis for authoritarian rule confirmed by plebiscite. The defeat and capture of Napoleon III by Prussian forces in 1870 entailed the replacement of the Empire by a republican government.

In political terms the legacy of Bonapartism was a political tradition which supported the idea of popular sovereignty as embodied within an empire and confirmed by plebiscite. It 'looked to an authoritarian government rather than to religion or the habit of deference to maintain order and social stability' (Anderson, 1977, p. 101). It can also be linked with the idea that a strong and charismatic leader may, especially at times of crisis, be required to override the incurable divisions of French society.

Perhaps more important than the political aspects of Bonapartism has been Napoleon's administrative legacy. He inherited the work of the Jacobins and the Directory, whose aim had been to give France a uniform administrative system and to organise militarily in order to win the war. Napoleon required a civil administration that would permit him to mobilise the resources that his campaigns required. He wished to see a well-organised country. He set about developing a pattern of local government based upon the territorial unit of the *département*. To supervise and control this local government he placed the prefectoral system upon a firm footing. A prefect was posted in each *département* as the local representative of the central government. Despite much hostility, for the prefect was often seen as the unacceptable and oppressive emanation of an authoritarian central power, especially given the early linkage of the system with Napoleon's need for a steady of flow of conscripts to his armies, the system survived the many changes of regime of the nineteenth and twentieth centuries. The administration of the French educational system also looks back to the Napoleonic division of the country into *académies*, under the overall control of a senior official appointed from Paris, grouping together state educational institutions at all levels.

Amongst the key principles upon which Napoleonic administration operated was, first, an insistence upon territorial and functional uniformity. All local authorities, whether large or small, affluent or impoverished, enjoyed the same legal and administrative powers as their counterparts elsewhere and the structures and functioning of all the public services were shaped to a uniform pattern. Secondly, the administrative institutions were not to be subject to the control and jurisdiction of Parliament or the Civil Courts. Control was, however, required, since the image and legitimacy of the state would suffer if irregularities and abuses occurred. Hence, important and powerful

---

EXHIBIT 1.2

The Dreyfus Affair

In 1894 a list, probably recovered from a waste-paper basket in the German Embassy, and detailing documents apparently handed over to the Germans by an officer of the French army acting as a spy for them, came into the hands of French counter-intelligence. Suspicion fell upon Captain Alfred Dreyfus, a Jewish officer from Alsace. The evidence was flimsy, but the military authorities were being harassed by the right-wing press who alleged that a traitor had been discovered, but would escape justice because he was Jewish and consequently had influential protectors. A secret court-martial was held, Dreyfus was found guilty and sentenced to life imprisonment in the tropical prison island, Devil's Island. Two years later, with information continuing to flow to the Germans, a new counter-intelligence chief re-examined the case. Although senior officers tried to suppress his opinions, and to bolster up the case against Dreyfus with additional forged evidence, the doubts became known. In the hope of quelling them another officer, to whom some evidence had pointed, was court-martialled, in 1898, and triumphantly acquitted. Two days later the novelist Emile Zola published his famous article *J'accuse* accusing the army of deliberate injustice.

France became very divided indeed. There were those who believed in the necessity of upholding the rights of every individual, and who called for justice. The League for the Defence of the Rights of Man was founded. Many of those arguing for Dreyfus were strongly anti-clerical and anti-militarist. They were supported by a number of left-wing politicians. On the other hand were those who were convinced that to question the army's proceedings was to undermine the state and subvert national strength. The church, the monarchists and the aristocracy came out in support of the army, and there were very strong currents of anti-semitism.

Eventually Dreyfus was brought back from Devil's Island. In 1899 another court-martial found him guilty but with extenuating circumstances, the nearest the army would come to admitting a mistake. Dreyfus was promptly pardoned by the President, and later completely exonerated by a civilian appeal court. But the divisions and passions which this extraordinary and melodramatic affair had aroused, and the myths it created, were not quickly forgotten.

---

control systems were created within the administration, including administrative courts and prestigious inspectorates.

To staff the administration Napoleon looked to a civil service which would, at the highest levels, be endowed with prestige and status. He wished, he said, to constitute the civil administration as a body with a certain autonomy and a standing in society to rival that of church or army. In order to rally representatives of influential groups to his regime he sought to attract able young men of suitable background to prestigious, rewarding and interesting administrative jobs. High salaries, impressive official residences and such marks of prestige and social status as titles and uniforms were provided as incentives to such recruitment.

The Napoleonic system was in some senses a system of checks and balances. A powerful, prestigious, able, efficient administration operating through centralised and authoritarian institutions would act as a counterweight to the elected assemblies. This dual tradition, of authoritarian administrative institutions and participatory assemblies, combining something of both the old royal aspirations to a unified and centralised and well-administered state, and of the democratic principles of the Revolution, can be traced throughout the subsequent history of French government. In its ideal of a highly structured rationally organised system, acting within a clear and codified legal framework, the French administration continues today to look back to Napoleon.

The Evolution of the Republic

In 1870 Napoleon III was defeated and captured by the invading Prussian armies and on 4 September the Third Republic was proclaimed. It was set up and consolidated in stages, rather than by a single constitutional act. Indeed, many of those who drew up the initial drafts of the laws which, in 1875, provided the constitutional framework for the Republic hoped they would prove to be temporary measures within which a constitutional monarchy could be restored. This did not occur. On 16 May 1877 the President, Marshal MacMahon, backed by monarchists and bonapartists, finding himself unable to create a government that would respect what he felt to be the proper balance of powers between Parliament and presidency, dissolved the National Assembly, which had a Republican majority. The subsequent election returned a majority who were clearly opposed to his views. MacMahon gave in and chose an acceptable Prime Minister. No President of the Third or Fourth Republics ever again felt able to use the dissolution of Parliament as a political weapon. MacMahon's experience marked the end of any inclination on the part of presidents of the Third Republic to exercise executive powers independently of Parliament (Anderson, 1977, p. 10).

The Third Republic survived many crises – the threat of a coup d'état by General Boulanger, the Dreyfus Affair (Exhibit 1.2), the Panama scandal, the Stavisky affair and the riots of 1934 being only some of the most serious and notorious – and the First World War. It collapsed only in 1940 under the force of invading German tanks. The balance of power within the institutions had tipped decisively towards Parliament. Its members knew that there would be no dissolution, and hence governments could be allowed to fall and new combinations to emerge. Between 1870 and 1914, for example, France had no fewer than 60 governments. The multiplicity of loosely organised party groupings within Parliament meant that all governments were combinations of political forces, based upon compromise and negotiation. There were, moreover, important political forces which did not accept the republican regime at all. Those on the extreme Right called for a return to monarchy or for 'strong' leadership. On the Left Marxist Socialists, including, after 1920, the Communists, condemned the Republic as bourgeois. When it collapsed, in 1940, under the overwhelming weight of the German invasion, its shortcomings were seized upon to provide at least part of the explanation for the rapid defeat.

The Third Republic was based upon direct manhood suffrage. Women did not obtain the vote until 1944.[4] However, the advent of manhood suffrage did not, under the Third Republic, entail the emergence of organised political parties. Local committees would be set up to support candidates at particular elections, but only gradually did they begin to have a continuous existence, and the labels adopted by particular candidates were not necessarily a very clear guide to how they would behave once within Parliament. Even by the end of the Third Republic the only broadly organised mass-based parties with a disciplined group of members of Parliament were on the Left.

The Rise of Socialism

The slow development of the industrial revolution in France was accompanied by a slow development of working-class politics. France throughout the nineteenth century produced highly influential socialist thinkers and leaders, and a tradition of participation in political life by working men that could look back to the Revolution. However, the event that marked the movement most deeply was the Paris Commune of 1871, both for its actual effects and for the powerful myths which it engendered.

The working-class Left as it emerged in France was marked by a number of features. First, within the trade union movement there were several varied and conflicting strands. Many of the early unions, especially, were chiefly concerned with appalling working conditions and immediate grievances (Hilden, 1986). There were others who saw unions as part of the wider struggle against exploitation and as instruments in the development of class consciousness. Anarchists and revolutionary syndicalists looked to strikes, and especially the general strike, as a means of direct action aimed at the revolutionary over-throw of capitalist society. The unions were relatively weak and underfunded. Although union developments and political develop-ments often went together, there was no close institutional connection between the socialist political parties and the union movement.

Secondly the mass-based socialist party, known from its formation in 1905 until 1971 as the French Section of the Workers' Interna-tional (*Section française de l'internationale ouvrière* – SFIO), contained within various strands of socialist thought. Its first great leader, Jean Jaurés, brought it to accept the possibility of reform through parlia-mentary institutions, but it long retained its revolutionary rhetoric.

Thirdly, in 1920 a majority of the SFIO's rank and file member-ship accepted Lenin's 21 conditions, devised to ensure the defence of the revolution in the Soviet Union, split off from the SFIO and formed the French Communist Party. Thereafter two organised parties existed to represent the Left.

Fourthly, whilst both parties claimed to be working-class parties, they were not necessarily strong in all the areas of the industrial working class and, conversely, they both enjoyed support from groups outside the main areas of industrialisation. For at least the first half century of its existence the SFIO drew much of its support from workers in small plants and secondary industries, and above all from public employees and minor civil servants. The Communist Party was strong not only in the industrial centres around Paris and in the Nord–Pas-de-Calais, but also in more rural areas, such as parts of the Massif Central and the Mediterranean coast, where it represented not so much the working-class struggle as the tradition of dissent from, and resistance to, domination and authority that derived from the Revolution (Williams, 1972, p. 79).

Occupation, Resistance, Liberation

Before the rapid advance of the German armies in 1940 the Third Republic crumbled and fell. Under Marshal Pétain, the military hero of the First World War, an armistice was concluded. France was initially split into a *zone annexée*, joined to Germany, a *zone occupée*, controlled by the German authorities, and a *zone libre*, within which a government was reconstituted at Vichy, in central France. It was effectively a dictatorship, for Pétain as head of the French State (not Republic) was given plenary powers pending a new constitution, which was never promulgated. Its orientation was authoritarian and traditionalist, symbolised by the slogan *Travail Famille Patrie* (work, family, country). In November 1942 German troops occupied the whole country. The Vichy government was increasingly subject to the demands of the German forces and identified with collaboration with the Germans.

On 18 June 1940 General de Gaulle, a junior general who had held a junior ministerial post as Minister of War for less than a month, broadcast from London an appeal to all French people to reject any armistice and, if they wanted to carry on the struggle, to contact him in London. Resistance in France was initially limited and spasmodic. It developed only slowly, growing particularly after the institution of a system of forced labour in Germany for many young men. Those involved in the Resistance represented many strands of political ideas – Socialist, Catholic and, after Hitler's invasion of the Soviet Union in 1941, Communist. In 1942 a National Council of the Resistance was set up in France, and de Gaulle came to be recognised as its leader. By 1944 he was the head of the French Committee for National Liberation, supported by a provisional consultative assembly, in Algiers, on which the National Council of the Resistance was represented. He succeeded in imposing the authority of this Provisional Government on each part of France as it was liberated, and in June 1944 triumphantly entered Paris.

The legacy of Occupation and Liberation was a bitter one. For many French people the first reaction to the trauma of defeat and occupation was a need to restore something like normality to everyday life (Paxton, 1972, pp. 16–18). Nevertheless, as the occupation continued, choices were made. The dilemmas and tragedies of these choices have formed the subject matter of telling works of literature and film. Times were hard for everyone. Average consumption levels fell to about 45 per cent of their pre-war level. Many people experienced the Nazi occupation as harsh and repressive, for example in the system of compulsory forced labour. France did not escape the anti-semitism of the Nazis, which found some echoes in anti-semitic views that had long been present within some sections of French society. Jews and others, especially those suspected of helping the

Resistance and the allies, were rounded up, executed or deported to the concentration camps, whence few returned. Attacks on Germans could mean the shooting of 50 hostages in reprisal. There were other outrages such as the burning of 642 women and children in the village of Oradour-sur-Glane in 1944. However, many French people, in fact the majority, accepted, and indeed some initially supported, the government established in Vichy under Marshal Pétain which co-operated with the Germans, becoming increasingly subservient, especially after the Germans occupied the whole of France in November 1942. In Paxton's words, 'Even Frenchmen of the best intentions, faced with the harsh alternative of doing one's job, whose risks were moral and abstract, or practising civil disobedience, whose risks were material and immediate, went on doing the job' (Paxton, 1972, p. 383).

The period of Liberation inevitably brought disorder and retribution. Whilst de Gaulle's government attempted to impose a degree of control and legality, there were widespread purges of actual and supposed collaborators, no doubt accompanied in some places by a good deal of personal rancour. There were about 10 000 executions, three-quarters of them while the fighting was going on and less than a thousand of them after due legal process. About 100 000 people suffered lesser legal penalties (Rioux, 1980, pp. 54–6).

These divisive events continue at times to cast long shadows over French life. The trial in 1987 of Klaus Barbie, for war crimes committed in Lyons, roused bitter memories, accusations and coun-ter-accusations, for example over the betrayal of the young prefect, Jean Moulin. Having joined de Gaulle in London he had returned to France to lead the National Council of the Resistance and bring it to acknowledge de Gaulle's leadership.

The history of the war years has presented difficulties for several leading French politicians. These include Georges Marchais, leader of the French Communist Party (PCF) from 1972 to 1994, who certainly spent a good deal of the war working in Germany. His ambiguous record exemplifies the difficulties faced by the PCF, for if their record of heroic resistance after the Nazi invasion of the Soviet Union in 1941 is extremely honourable, their attitude in the first days of the Occupation was less clear-cut. The ambiguities of the period and its aftermath are equally well illustrated in the case of Socialist President François Mitterrand. As a young man before the war he was active in an extreme right-wing political organisation. During the war, after escape from a prisoner of war camp, he was both a

sufficiently assiduous servant of the Vichy government to be deco-
rated by it, and courageously and dangerously active in the Resistance. After, or possibly even during, the war he befriended René
Bousquet who was eventually, but not until 1991 and then after
considerable delays, indicted for crimes against humanity committed
while he was a senior police official under Vichy (Tournier, 1995,
p. 257). Bousquet was murdered before he came to trial. Mitterrand
was unable to avoid the accusation that he allowed loyalty to a
supporter and friend – a friendship which he openly acknowledged in
1994, towards the end of his presidency – to cloud his judgement in
relation to a period where his own actions were highly contradictory.

Division and Instability

This traumatic period had a number of political effects. One was the
discrediting of the ideas of the Right, since so many of their adherents
had supported Vichy and collaboration. For the first decades after
the war no political movement was willing to admit to being situated
on the Right in politics. Right-wing and conservative political ideas
did not disappear: some resurfaced later within the Gaullist movement and others later still in the resurgent Extreme Right of the
1980s.

The Communist Party and the SFIO emerged from the war
strengthened by an honourable record of resistance, so that the
1946 general election marked a high point of the Communist vote.
More than one voter in every four voted for the PCF, some, no doubt,
seeking to assert their anti-collaborationist credentials by voting
conspicuously for a leading party of the Resistance. The strength of
the PCF, which was attracting by far the largest vote of any single
party, was a very marked feature of France in the post-war years. De
Gaulle had succeeded in bringing the PCF within the overall
Resistance framework and incorporating it into his Provisional
Government, and it remained within the government until the
increasing tensions of the Cold War forced it out in 1947.

In the context of the post-war world, especially the developments
in Eastern Europe, the strength of French Communism was striking.
It was easy for allegations that the Party was placing its members in
the key positions in the public sector and the governmental machine
to gain ground. Later assessments suggest that this occurred within
some sectors of the nationalised industries, but to a limited extent.

Real fears of a Communist take-over certainly help to explain the virulent anti-Communism of some groups in post-war French politics, fears which may have been magnified by the apparent political instability of the period from 1946 to 1958.

In the Provisional Government over which de Gaulle presided until early 1946 were representatives of the three parties which, in the elections held in 1945, proved to enjoy massive support; they were the Communists, the SFIO and the Christian Democrats. The Right disappeared almost completely and the centre Republican and Radical groups, too associated with what were felt to be the weaknesses of the Third Republic, also did poorly.

That the new regime should be a parliamentary republic was unquestioned. What the balance of power between the institutions should be was much more in dispute, and in early 1946 de Gaulle resigned over what he saw as the parties' insistence on returning to the bad old ways of the past and putting their own interests first. The Fourth Republic, based upon a constitution adopted in October 1946, lasted until 1958 (see Exhibit 1.3).

The Fourth Republic was dogged for most of its existence by the perception that it was an unstable and precarious regime. A number of features contributed to this. They included:

- the balance of power between the institutions that resulted from the 1946 constitution;
- the succession of coalition governments;
- the nature of the party system;
- the traumatic process of de-colonisation.

The 1946 constitution was the outcome of a turbulent process. De Gaulle, the head of the Provisional Government in 1945, viewing the strong representation of the traditional parties of the Left in the Assembly elected in 1945 with the task of producing a constitution 'gloomily assumed', in Maurice Larkin's words, that the Constitution that would emerge would fail to fulfil the needs of the country as he perceived them (Larkin, 1988, p. 139). He resigned in January 1946, undoubtedly in the hope that by so doing he would bring everyone to their senses. In fact a tripartite government of Communists, Socialists and Christian Democrats was formed. The first proposed constitution was rejected by referendum in May 1946. A new Constituent Assembly was elected, another tripartite government formed, and in October 1946 a constitution was approved by referendum. It bore

---

EXHIBIT 1.3

**Prime ministers of the Provisional Government
and the Fourth Republic**

Charles de Gaulle September 1944 – January 1946
Felix Gouin January 1946 – 23 June 1946
Georges Bidault June 1946 – December 1946
Léon Blum December 1946 – January 1947
Paul Ramadier January 1947 – November 1947
Robert Schuman November 1947 – July 1948
André Marie July 1948 – August 1948
Robert Schuman August 1948 – September 1948
Henri Queuille September 1948 – October 1949
Georges Bidault October 1949 – June 1950
Henri Queuille June 1950 – July 1950
René Pleven July 1950 – February 1951
Henri Queuille March 1951 – July 1951
René Pleven August 1951 – January 1952
Edgar Faure January 1952 – February 1952
Antoine Pinay March 1952 – December 1952
René Mayer January 1953 – May 1953
Joseph Laniel June 1953 – June 1954
Pierre Mendès France June 1954 – February 1955
Edgar Faure February 1955 – January 1956
Guy Mollet February 1956 – May 1957
Maurice Bourgès-Manoury June 1957 – September 1957
Félix Gaillard November 1957 – 15 April 1958
Pierre Pflimlin 13 May 1958 – 28 May 1958
Charles de Gaulle 1 June 1958 – January 1959

---

a 'depressing resemblance' (Larkin, 1988, p. 142) to the constitutional arrangements of the Third Republic.

Although attempts were made to limit the extent to which Parliament could control the government and force frequent changes, in fact earlier patterns of behaviour persisted (Williams, 1972, p. 428). Prime ministers had to devote a great deal of energy to putting together deals and agreements between the various political groups to ensure support for their programmes, and when they were not certain of doing so would often prefer to resign rather than risk formal defeat. The strength of the legal texts, which should have provided the basis for strong leadership, was never adequate to change the conciliatory and bargaining personalities and political habits of the men who were chosen as prime ministers. Parliament feared a strong leader, and even those prime ministers who wished to act firmly found themselves frustrated by the unwillingness of their fragmented following to support them, and by the likelihood that even if support could be called upon one time, it would not be forthcoming the next time it was needed (Williams, 1972, p. 207).

The weakness of the prime minister in the face of the members of Parliament, and the fragmentation of political groups led to a constant succession of coalition governments, for no single party group was strong enough to dominate the Assembly. In many respects the changes of government were more akin to reshuffles than to the replacement of a governmental team. Governments would retain a large proportion of the ministers of the preceding team, often in the same posts. Many prime ministers had been ministers in the previous government, and might take up another post in the succeeding cabinet. However, the fact that these reshuffles affected the leader as well as the members of the team meant that governmental authority suffered, for the position of prime minister was derived not from electoral choice but from political manoeuvres and seemed highly precarious. Continuity or legitimacy in the handling of contentious matters could not be assured.

The fragmented nature of the party system compounded these difficulties, which were exacerbated by the rejection of the whole nature of the regime by two of the major political groupings (see Table 1.1). The Communists had supported the first constitutional draft which had been rejected. They never fully accepted the rules of the game in the Fourth Republic, although they were willing to work within it and to return members of Parliament. Likewise, the Gaullists echoed de Gaulle's own virulent denunciations of the weaknesses of the regime. They too came to work within it, but the regime was fairly consistently to come under fire from both sides. Its respectability and credibility suffered in consequence. Moreover, at the point in the mid-1950s when the Gaullist movement seemed to be fading the challenge to the system vociferously expressed by Pierre Poujade and his followers grew rapidly (see Exhibit 8.3, p. 230).

Whether any regime, let alone the contested arrangements of the Fourth Republic, could have withstood the traumas that de-colonisation afflicted upon France is debatable. During the two decades after the end of the Second World War France, like other European nations, underwent a process of decolonisation. For France the process was frequently bloody and bitter. The independence of Indo-China was conceded after military defeat. The war for Algerian independence brought down the Fourth Republic in 1958, and caused bitter division within politics and society. Violence in Algeria

TABLE 1.1

**Support for the Fourth Republic:
votes cast in general elections, 1946–58, %**

	June 1946	November 1946	June 1951	January 1956
Parties supporting the regime				
Socialists	21.1	17.8	14.6	15.2
Radicals and allies	11.6	11.1	10	15.2
Christian democrats	28.2	25.9	12.6	11.1
Total	60.9	54.8	36.2	41.5
Parties opposing the regime				
Communists	25.9	28.2	26.9	25.9
Gaullists and allies		3.0	21.6	3.9*
Poujadists				11.6
Extreme Right				1.2
Total	25.9	31.2	48.5	42.6
Others	12.9	13.7	14.1	15.7

Note:
* The Gaullists split their support between a left-wing Republican Front alliance including the Socialist Party and some Radicals, and a more right-wing alliance including Christian Democrats.

on the part of those who sought independence began in 1954. Successive governments of the Fourth Republic remained committed to the retention of Algeria as an integral part of France – *Algérie Française* – and to the suppression of violence and terrorism. The parties were divided on the question of concessions to Algerian nationalism. There were also divisions provoked by the methods of the French authorities and the army, especially the use of torture. In February 1958 a bombing raid on a village (Sakhiet) over the border in Tunisia demonstrated the inability of the government to enforce its policies upon the military authorities in Algeria, for the army had acted without the backing of the civilian authorities in Algiers or Paris (Horne, 1979, p. 267). It also provoked international intervention, and much-resented attempts at mediation by an American mission. In the spring of 1958 the prospect of the advent of a prime minister who might be tempted, in the face of international pressure, the rising economic cost of the war and war-weariness in metropolitan France, to negotiate with the Algerian independence movement provoked the events in Algiers that led to the return of de Gaulle to power.

It took all de Gaulle's personal authority and powers of survival (he was the object of at least a dozen assassination attempts: Lacouture, 1986, p. 272) combined with a weary but widely-held view that a solution must be found to achieve the agreement that resulted in an independent Algeria in 1962, and in the settlement of over 800 000 French former inhabitants of Algeria in mainland France. The other African colonies were given the right to choose independence by the Constitution of 1958, and by 1962 all of them had done so.

All these factors contributed to a perception of a country whose deep and bitter divisions made the construction of a regime that would be widely accepted as legitimate and the maintenance of a government that would be capable of sustained and coherent policy seem at best improbable.

Reconstruction and Modernisation

Beneath the froth of governmental instability the period from 1944 to 1958 was in fact a period of immense recovery from the devastation of war time. There were many aspects to the economic and social transformation that France underwent in the three 'glorious' decades after the war (Fourastié, 1979). Underlying them were some broad areas of social and economic consensus that allowed many of the transformations to proceed more within the tradition of administrative action than that of political conflict.

In 1944 General de Gaulle's Provisional Government was faced with harsh choices about the nature of the reconstruction of the economy and the methods to be employed. Within the governmental team there was a degree of conflict about the aims and methods that would be desirable. The outcome of these conflicts had a good deal of influence upon the subsequent nature and development of the French economy.

De Gaulle appointed both a finance minister, René Pleven, and an economics minister, Pierre Mendès France. That the state had a role to play was evident to all concerned: the circumstances of the period, as well as longstanding habits and expectations of state activity in the economic sphere, made an important governmental contribution inevitable. Mendès France had proposed, in a report published in Algeria in February 1944, a policy of austerity. Restrictions on consumption, restraint on incomes, blocking of bank accounts, monetary reform and state control over production and exchange seemed to him the necessary conditions for the re-establishment of a healthy, vigorous and balanced economy (Lacouture, 1981, p. 168). Pleven disagreed; after the ordeals they had endured throughout the years 'the French had the right to breathe a little' (Lacouture, 1981, p. 169). The population was healthy, the country fertile, and some of its productive plant was still usable. From January 1945 it became obvious to Mendès France that his advice was not acceptable to de Gaulle and his government, and in April he resigned, leaving behind him a reputation for integrity and probity.

The French government had chosen an approach that recognised the virtues of a liberal and market-oriented approach to reconstruction. Capitalism should be allowed to work reasonably freely. However, it was clear to many of those around de Gaulle that this could not mean a return to the pre-war situation. During the 1930s small groups of officials and businessmen had analysed what they saw as the problems of the French economy and had prescribed solutions which involved forecasting, planning and consultation between government and industry. In the atmosphere of the Liberation their time had come (Kuisel, 1979, pp. 105–19 and chs 7–8). Their ideas were complemented by those of Jean Monnet who, having negotiated an American loan to 'see the French economy through the winter' (Monnet, 1978, p. 228) came back to France in November 1945 determined to contribute to the modernisation of an economy that he diagnosed as 'appallingly backward' (Monnet, 1978, p. 233).

Monnet's solution involved the creation of a framework which would permit, indeed encourage, the growth of private, entrepreneurial, competitive capitalism in France. There was a danger, past experience suggested, that France would be content with 'frugal mediocrity behind a protectionist shield' (Monnet, 1978, p. 238). The role of the state was, in effect, to create modern capitalism in France. The framework he proposed, and utilised in the work of the Planning Commission set up in January 1946, was a political framework for a de-politicised, agreed pattern of industrial growth. The planning mechanisms, much cited and occasionally copied elsewhere, worked best in a period of reconstruction when priorities were clear and external funding available, in the form of American Marshall Aid. The broader general attitudes were, however, more widely important.

The transformations of the three post-war decades were backed by steady economic growth. From 1950 to 1960 the average annual rate of growth of the economy was 5 per cent and from 1960 to 1970 5.8 per cent (Parodi, 1981, p. 48). These transformations included, first, a vast change in the employment structure of the country. Between 1946 and 1975 the proportion of the workforce employed in agriculture, forestry and fisheries declined from more than one in three workers (36.46 per cent) to less than one in ten (9.5 per cent) (Parodi, 1981, p. 80). Ten years later the proportion had declined to 8 per cent. About a third of the work force is nowadays employed in industry and the remaining majority mostly work in the service sector of the economy.

Another transformation was the development of the public sector in the economy. The first nationalisations took place under the Socialist Popular Front government of 1936, and in 1945–6 some of the main public utilities (electricity, gas, coal-mining) were nationalised, as were half the banking and insurance companies. The late 1940s was also the period of the consolidation of the institutions of the welfare state. Insurance schemes that provided old-age pensions and covered illness, disability and unemployment were set up, and the system of family allowances extended.

France was a founder member of the European Coal and Steel Community (ECSC), devised largely by Jean Monnet, and promulgated by a French minister, Robert Schuman, who originated from Luxembourg and had consequently fought on the German side in the First World War. It was largely intended to ensure that two of the major components required for the production of the weapons of war came under such supra-national control that never again could they be used to equip a 'European civil war'. France was also a founder member of the European Economic Community (EEC) in 1958. During the 1960s and 1970s many officials and their counterparts in big business, nationalised industry and banking were committed to a view that the advent of the EEC required an open economy with enterprises that could be competitive with foreign, especially American, companies. This involved state activity to promote rapid industrialisation, mergers and development. The result of these and other pressures was the encouragement of *grands projets* – the major endeavours which included the nuclear power programme that by the mid-1980s was producing two thirds of France's electricity needs; the high speed train system; the telecommunications development which increased the proportion of households with a telephone from only just over a quarter in 1975 to some three-quarters ten years later; and the Channel tunnel.

Conclusion

France today is built upon a number of conflicting and paradoxical traditions. Speaking of the first half of the twentieth century in words that still have relevance, Philip Williams said, 'In France three issues were fought out simultaneously: the eighteenth century conflict between rationalism and Catholicism, the nineteenth century struggle of democracy against authoritarian government, and the twentieth century dispute between employer and employed' (Williams, 1972, p. 4). Often these conflicts cut across each other, which helps to explain the fragmented nature of French politics, as do several other factors. First, rejection of the policies and actions of a particular government also frequently meant rejection of the whole political settlement upon which that government's power was based. From the point at which the King's unwillingness to operate within a constitution which he had himself accepted provoked the downfall of the monarchy opposition to a government was likely to imply opposition to the whole regime. The Revolution divided France deeply, and for over 150 years there was not the fundamental agreement about the rules of the political game that permits a stable constitutional settlement.

Secondly, the Revolution had combined an emphasis upon political rights and liberties with a set of centralised and uniform institutions far more powerful and pervasive than the monarchy had ever achieved. After the abolition of the feudal privileges and particularities that had made France a patchwork of administrative differences and set important limits upon the monarch's power, the legal and administrative systems were fully organised, codified and firmly established by Napoleon, as he sought to ensure effective resources to support his military ambitions. Much of the subsequent history of French government and politics can be seen as a struggle to find an acceptable and enduring balance between the democratic, participatory, representational strands of the Revolution's legacy, and its rational, organising, perhaps even authoritarian, administrative and institutional legacy.

On the one hand there have been areas where policy has been sound, effective and demonstrating a good deal of continuity. To phrase the matter in rather French terms, the administrative institutions of the state have operated well; political changes may at times have imposed limits upon administrative capacity, but within a quite broad and to some extent autonomous sphere policy has been made and applied. On the other hand political discussion has often been phrased in theoretical, idealist, intellectual and often divisive terms. 'We French,' an acute observer remarked, 'can have splendid political discussions: we don't know how to organise a discussion on policy.'

2

The Constitutional Framework

The constitution of the Fifth Republic is of fundamental importance in shaping present-day political life and governmental activity in France. Written constitutions, within any particular political society, at least when they are the product of a genuinely indigenous movement rather than being imposed from without, perform a range of functions. They are likely to embody a critique of the situation that existed previously; they are a distillation of the broad political values of the ruling groups within society, and also, within democratic regimes, of as wide a spectrum of political opinion as possible; they incorporate aspirations about the way in which the future political life of the society should develop and progress; they contain specific rules which determine the balance of political power within society and legitimise political activity; and if they survive for a certain length of time they may become points of reference which shape and determine social and political values and policy-making as well as reflecting them.

The 'profound restlessness' (Thomson, 1969, p. 11) of French political life in the two centuries since the Revolution has over that period frequently prevented the emergence of values that were sufficiently stable to ensure the longevity of constitutions. When the values of the constitution are so widely contested that to many it appears more as the programme of the ruling party or coalition than a statement of legitimising rules and a fair description of the balance of power, opposition is likely to take the form of a challenge to the whole constitutional regime as well as to the government of the day.[1] It is now clear that one of the main achievements of the current constitution, which instituted the Fifth Republic, has been to shift political discussion away from the nature of the regime. All the major political parties and the massive majority of public opinion now accept the constitutional framework, and its replacement is not on the political agenda.

The constitution matters and shapes political life because it lays down the ground rules within which the shifting balance of power between political forces is accommodated. It determines who may legitimately wield power. In France the political changes of the 1980s brought the constitution into sharper focus after nearly two decades when its importance had been largely ignored and the balance of political forces had enabled presidents and governments to use and abuse it. Since 1986 the political and governmental system has perforce had to revert to the principles which the constitution enunciated. Politicians have been reminded that, so long as the constitution broadly reflects the national consensus about how power should, ultimately, be distributed, its framework cannot be ignored and bypassed. It is no coincidence that the same period has seen a steadily increasing role for the Constitutional Council, the main guardian of constitutionality.

The present French constitution came into force on 4 October 1958. It had been approved on 28 September by a referendum which produced, in metropolitan France, a turn out of 84.6 per cent of the voters, 79.3 per cent of whom voted for it. This chapter describes the constitutional precedents for the Fifth Republic and the demand for a new constitution in 1958. It outlines the objectives of its authors and the main constitutional provisions. It goes on to discuss the nature of the regime which the 1958 constitution instituted, the way it has evolved and the impact of two major developments; first, the growth in the role of the Constitutional Council and, secondly, the periods of *cohabitation* between 1986 and 1988 and between 1993 and 1995.

The Constitutions of the Third and Fourth Republics

The first republican regime in France began with the fall of the monarchy in 1792 and was embodied in the constitution of 1793, which was never implemented. The Second Republic followed the 1848 revolution that overthrew King Louis-Philippe and lasted until Louis-Napoleon's coup-d'état in 1851 and his installation as Emperor Napoleon III in 1852. It was based on the principle of universal male suffrage. Its constitution provided for a single-chamber legislature, elected for a three year period, and a President, elected for four years. Both Parliament and President were seen as stemming from the expression of the popular will, and their relationship was unclear, until forcibly resolved by the actions of Louis-Napoleon who had been elected as the Second Republic's first President.

The Third Republic was the product of the defeat of France by the Prussians in 1870, of the Assembly (with a monarchist majority) that was hastily elected to fill the gap left by the collapse of the Empire, and of the constitutional laws passed in 1875 to provide a legal framework that might yet serve a constitutional monarchy. These laws provided for a two-chamber parliament, with a lower house directly elected by universal male suffrage for a maximum four year term and an upper house (the Senate) elected by an electoral college that chiefly represented the local councils in a way which ensured the over-representation of the small and rural authorities. The President was elected by a joint meeting of the two houses, of which the Senators formed about one-third and the lower house (the Chamber of Deputies) constituted about two-thirds.

After the experience of Marshal MacMahon in 1877 (see p. 16, above) members of the Chamber of Deputies knew that they were safe in their seats for four years, and could afford to let governments fall, whilst the presidency quite rapidly ceased to exercise any real political functions. The power of the Chamber of Deputies was predominant, for the members controlled the agenda of the house, and had the right to call short debates and a vote on any subject whilst the Chamber's committees, which examined legislation before it came before the full house, could so alter the drafts that the government might have a major struggle in the full debates to get the proposals back to their original intention. 'These procedures reflected a conception of politics which preferred a ministry safely subordinate to the representatives of the people to one strong and independent enough to govern effectively' (Williams, 1972, p. 186).

Like most constitutions, the constitution of the Fourth Republic contained within it an element of criticism of the arrangements it replaced; for example, it sought to limit the blocking powers of the Senate. As Philip Williams (1972) points out, however, its authors were 'neither willing nor able to erect a new structure and tried only to repair the faults that the old one had revealed in its years of decline'. They hoped that the dominance – and alliance – of a few organised political parties would continue and ensure sound majorities for disciplined parties, which would underpin effective government (Chapsal and Lancelot, 1979, p. 142; Williams, 1972, p. 190). In fact the old habits of the Third Republic rapidly reasserted themselves, with all the consequent difficulties of governmental ineffectiveness and instability.

The Demand for a New Constitution in 1958

To tell the full, and in parts highly dramatic, story of the advent of the Fifth Republic would involve recounting much of the political history of France since the 1930s. A necessarily brief version of the story may perhaps begin where, in a sense, it also ends, with the personality and actions of General Charles de Gaulle (see Exhibit 2.1).[2]

De Gaulle came into office as prime minister, for the second time, at the beginning of June 1958, at the height of the crisis caused by events in Algeria. France seemed to be on the brink of civil war, with the authorities in Paris incapable of exerting control over the army in Algiers, some of whose units had occupied Corsica and which was thought to be planning an invasion of metropolitan France. The National Assembly voted him into office and gave him, as he asked, authority to draw up a new constitution and submit it to a national referendum.

De Gaulle's insistence in 1958 that his return to office must involve the establishment of a new constitution was based on his repudiation of the principles underlying the arrangements of the Fourth Republic and his unrelenting hostility to the constitution which embodied them. He and his supporters were, however, not alone in their criticisms. Many political leaders were very conscious of the weaknesses of the Fourth Republic, and pressures for constitutional amendments had begun as early as 1950. The procedures for such amendments were difficult, but amendments had been made in 1954. By 1958 a large majority of the National Assembly were in favour of reform.[3] Diagnoses of the disease and prescriptions for its remedy varied, but several found an echo within the new constitution.

There were few formal limitations upon the drafters of the new constitution: Parliament, in voting, by a law of 3 June 1958, for the powers on which de Gaulle insisted to enable him to undertake the formulation of a new constitution, laid down five basic principles. They were:

EXHIBIT 2.1

Charles de Gaulle 1890–1970

Born in 1890 to a bourgeois Catholic family in Lille, de Gaulle was, from 1909 to 1940, a professional soldier. His ability and intellectual force, as well as his astonishing sense of his own capacity, marked him out. On 1 June 1940 he was promoted Brigadier-General, and on 6 June left his active command on his appointment as Under-Secretary of State (junior minister) for War in Paul Reynaud's government. He was involved in the intense consultation between the French and British governments during the disastrous days of the fall of France and it was thus that, following Reynaud's resignation on 16 June, de Gaulle was able to avail himself of a British plane that had brought him to the government headquarters in Bordeaux to escape back to London on 17 June. He knew that Marshal Pétain, whom President Lebrun had appointed as prime minister, would seek armistice terms. On 18 June the BBC broadcast, from London, de Gaulle's appeal for the continuation of resistance to the enemy.

In the absence of more senior figures the British government, by the end of June, recognised de Gaulle as the leader of the Free French. By 1944 he had succeeded in becoming the recognised leader of the Resistance within France and of the Provisional Government, based at first in Algiers, which took over in France as Liberation proceeded. In October 1945 a general election and a referendum returned an Assembly with constituent powers, dominated by three large organised political parties. In January 1946 de Gaulle resigned, thus marking his rejection of what he saw as the resurgence of purely party politics. In 1948 he created the Rally of the French People (*Rassemblement du Peuple Français*), launching it with massive meetings, but when it failed to sweep him into power and became like other parties he abandoned it. He returned to his country home at Colombey-les-Deux-Eglises to write his memoirs. He re-emerged dramatically onto the political stage in 1958 as the last prime minister of the Fourth Republic and then, from 1959 to 1969, the first President of the Fifth Republic. He resigned the presidency in 1969 and died in 1970.

De Gaulle had a distant, reserved, arrogant personality, dominating both by the 6 feet 4 inches of his physical presence, and by his unshakeable confidence in his destiny and mission. He could, when he chose, be courteous and charming. He was a brilliant communicator, using, indeed manipulating, language and image in radio and television broadcasts and set-piece press conferences.

In 1921 de Gaulle married Yvonne Vendroux. She succeeded, separately, in escaping to England, with their children, in 1940. De Gaulle was devoted to her and his family, especially to his handicapped younger daughter, who died young.

In his book on the qualities of leadership, *Le fil de l'épée* (The Edge of the Sword) published before the war, de Gaulle evokes three features essential to a leader – a doctrine, character and prestige. All these he possessed or acquired, but perhaps his doctrine or, rather, his single-minded vision of the greatness that France does and must represent, in the end remains his most influential and powerful characteristic.

- that all power must proceed from a system of direct suffrage;
- that both organisationally and operationally legislative and executive powers must be separated;
- that the government must be responsible to Parliament;
- that the independence of the judiciary must be guaranteed
- that the constitution must define the relationship between metropolitan France and 'her associated peoples'; that is, at that period, her overseas colonies and territories.

The law also specified that the draft constitution must be submitted for comment to a constitutional consultative committee consisting of sixteen members of the National Assembly, ten members of the upper house and thirteen members nominated by the government, assisted by representatives of the prime minister, the four senior ministers, and the minister of justice. In addition the Council of State, the senior governmental legal advisory body, was to be consulted. Since a referendum would follow this drafting and consultative process it can be said that effectively the constitution was the product of joint action between government and people, effectively by-passing parliamentary structures (Dreyfus and D'Arcy, 1993, p. 153).

The writing of the Fifth Republic's constitution had three further distinctive features:[4] first, it was very rapidly undertaken; work began in the middle of June and a completed working draft was ready on 15 July. The final version was published just over three weeks before the referendum, on 4 September. Secondly, the draft of the constitution was prepared, under the direction of Michel Debré, De Gaulle's minister of justice,[5] who was to become the first prime minister of the new regime, by a small working party. This working party was supervised by a cabinet committee which included De Gaulle, Debré, and the four senior ministers, who represented some of the major political forces within the National Assembly. Thirdly, since most of the discussions which surrounded the drafting process remained confidential until the publication of the archives at the end of the 1980s, it was for a long period difficult, in some areas, to gauge with any certainty the real intentions of the authors.

The Objectives of the Authors of the Constitution

De Gaulle himself outlined his own views on the requirements of a constitution for France in a speech in Bayeux in June 1946, six months after his resignation (see Exhibit 2.2). He spoke there of an old Gallic propensity for quarrelling and division, and for partisan rivalries beneath which, he said, the main interests of the country too often disappeared. The solution was a clear separation of legislative, executive and judicial powers. He argued for a bi-cameral legislature, whose upper house should consist of members elected by local councils but which might also include representatives of other organised groups. More importantly, he outlined a role for the head of state, who would be indirectly elected by a large electoral college. De Gaulle's elevated concept of the role of the President owed much, in Nicholas Wahl's words

> to all of de Gaulle's experience since 1940, not to mention his monarchist youth . . .: his peculiarly symbolic role as leader of the Free French; his almost absolute monarchic powers as President of the Provisional Government in 1944–1946; his frustration at seeing the customary weakness of the Third Republic's Presidency emerge again in the constitution of the Fourth Republic; his continuing expectation after 1945 that a continuing World War would again bring a catastrophe like that of 1940; his dismay at the liquidation of an overseas empire, the first to rally to Free France and then lost because no institution bound the territories to the Republic affectively as well as effectively; and finally his consideration of himself as 'national capital' to be drawn on as an ultimate recourse in time of crisis. (Wahl, 1959, p. 376)

The application of de Gaulle's ideas to the circumstances of 1958 produced the important constitutional provisions which define the role of the Head of State – the President of the Republic. The constitution attributes to the President all the powers traditionally enjoyed by French presidents, but substantially increases them (see Chapter 9).

De Gaulle's ideas about the shape that the constitution should take were elaborated during the 1940s and 1950s by some of his supporters, notably Michel Debré. As early as 1943 Debré had begun, on behalf of the National Council of the Resistance, to develop constitutional ideas. He did so from a background as a civil servant with a legal training and outlook, having been a member of the Council of State since 1935 and closely involved with proposals for reforms in governmental structures. Debré's analysis of France's constitutional problems stemmed from a conviction that the roles of the legislature and the executive were insufficiently separated. The parliamentary system as it developed under the Third and Fourth Republics had, he thought, produced weak and short-lived governments, insensitive to the responsibilities of the state, devoid of a sense of the general

EXHIBIT 2.2

Extracts from Charles de Gaulle's speech at Bayeux 16 June 1946

It is essential that our new democratic institutions themselves remedy the effects of our continual political effervescence. This is indeed, for us a question of life or death, given the world and the century in which we live, where the position, the independence and even the existence of our country and the French colonies is well and truly at stake. It is certainly central to democracy that opinions are expressed and that their proponents can try, through the vote, to achieve the policies and legislation they think right. But equally principles and experience all demand that the legislative, executive and judicial branches of government should be clearly separated and powerfully balanced, and that, over and above fleeting political circumstances, a national authority (*arbitrage*) should be established which can ensure continuity whatever happens.

Everyone agrees that the final voice on laws and budgets must be that of a directly elected Assembly. But the first instincts of such an Assembly are not always clear-sighted and untroubled. So a second Assembly, elected and constituted in a different way, needs to take on the task of publicly examining what the first house is doing . . .

Everything points to the creation of a second Chamber whose members would chiefly be elected by our local councils. It would be natural also to include representatives of the economic organisations, family associations and scholarly societies so that the voices of the principal interests of the country can be heard within the state institutions . . .

The executive branch cannot derive from this bicameral legislative Parliament. Otherwise there would be the risk of a confusion between the branches of government and the Government would soon be no more than a group of delegates . . . The unity, cohesion and internal discipline of the Government of France should be sacred, or the authority of the country rapidly becomes impotent and worthless. How could this unity . . . be maintained over time if the executive depended on another institution which it should balance and each of the members of the Government . . . was no more than a party's delegate?

The executive power must derive from the Head of State who is above the parties . . . In making appointments the Head of State must reconcile the general interest with the political tendency evident in Parliament. He must appoint ministers, and especially the Prime Minister who will direct the Government's policies and work. The Head of State must promulgate laws and enact regulations . . . He must preside over cabinet meetings . . . It should be his task to act as umpire (*arbitre*) over and above day-to-day politics, usually through his advice, and sometimes, in difficult periods, by inviting the country to exercise its sovereignty through a general election. Should it ever happen that our country is in danger, the Head of State should be the guarantor of national independence and of the treaties into which we have entered.

Source: De Gaulle (1959) pp. 649–52; author's translation.

interest, and lacking coherence, continuity and stability. Nor could the political system on its own, in his opinion, be relied on to produce the necessary qualities. An institutional framework was needed which would be a substitute for disciplined public behaviour and mechanistically enforce the required responses. It was in this light that he interpreted de Gaulle's views about the presidency, but he also brought to the 1958 constitution his support for a reform mooted some years previously, the idea that no-one should be allowed to continue as a member of Parliament following appointment as a minister. Ministers would have the right to attend and speak in the National Assembly and the Senate, but not to vote.

Moreover he ensured that the separation of powers was further enforced by the specific delineation, in Article 34, of those areas in which Parliament might legislate. According to Article 37 'matters other than those regulated by laws fall within the field of rule-making' which is the domain of the government. Debré insisted that a Constitutional Council should be created to determine whether laws respected the constitution, a function which would include policing the boundary between the legislative area of Parliament and the regulatory and executive area of the government.

De Gaulle and Debré had bitterly opposed the Fourth Republic's constitution, for it departed too far from the principles which they regarded as fundamental. However, by 1958, even amongst those who had supported it and worked within it criticisms had become pressing and attempts at reform had been initiated. These currents of ideas were represented in the process of formulating the constitution by the four ministers of state all of whom had been prominent in the political and parliamentary life of the Fourth Republic.[6] Their concern, in the words of one of them, Socialist Party leader and former prime minister Guy Mollet, was 'to put into operation a parliamentary system that would escape those defects of the previous regime that had been universally denounced: excessive control by the legislature over the executive and the consequent governmental instability' (Mollet, 1973, p. 33). All of those involved in drafting the constitution were, if, as Mollet admits, for varied motives, concerned to reinforce governmental authority. However, he continues, most of them wished to see this combined with the assertion of continued parliamentary powers which would ensure that Parliament could insist on its role, but without threatening or harassing the government (Mollet, 1973, pp. 32, 35, 38).

For those for whom such concerns were uppermost, the constitutional provisions which related to the requirement that the prime minister must tender the resignation of the government if defeated by a motion of censure or the rejection of the government's programme or a general statement of its policy, coupled with the precautions with which the procedures for votes of censure were surrounded, were of particular importance.

The Letter of the Constitution

The document that emerged from this complex drafting process has since been formally amended nine times. It now consists of 93 articles grouped in seventeen 'titles' and preceded by a preamble. The preamble incorporates within the scope of the constitution both the 1789 Declaration of the Rights of Man and Citizen and the principles contained within the preamble to the 1946 constitution (see Exhibit 2.3). Thus it attributes at least some continued existence to a document that it also replaces. The preamble to the 1946 constitution contains a statement of what it calls political, economic and social principles. Some of these principles involve civic rights: equal rights for women 'in all spheres'; the rights to belong to a trade union and undertake collective bargaining; the right 'within the framework of the laws which govern it' to strike; the right of asylum for refugees. Other principles envisage a role for the state in economic and social life: the public ownership of firms which are or become 'national public services' or monopolies; guarantees of the provision of free and secular education and of social protection which amount to a commitment to a welfare state and indeed to full employment. The 'Resistance–Liberation discourse'[7] of the period, with its criticisms of the old elites and the failures of the 1930s, was clearly reflected in this 1946 preamble, but in 1958 it could still be accepted as compatible with de Gaulle's vision of an economically and socially modernised France, which could unite behind the goal of rebuilding international status and respect.

The constitutional entrenchment of such rights may seem broad and general, and indeed specific mechanisms for enforcing them are not clearly provided; but, for example, in 1982 the Constitutional Council obliged the government substantially to revise the levels of compensation it proposed to offer to shareholders in companies that were to be nationalised, on the grounds that the government's initial scheme, by provided inadequate compensation, had infringed the shareholder's rights to property as embodied in the Declaration of the Rights of Man (see Exhibit 2.3).

EXHIBIT 2.3

The Declaration of the Rights of Man and Citizen 1789

1   Men are born and remain free and equal in rights; social distinction may be based only upon general usefulness.

2   The aim of every political association is the preservation of the natural and inalienable rights of man; these rights are liberty, property, security and resistance to oppression.

3   The source of all sovereignty resides essentially in the nation; no group, no individual may exercise authority not emanating expressly therefrom.

4   Liberty consists of the power to do what is not injurious to others . . .

5   The law has the right to forbid only actions which are injurious to society . . .

6   Law is the expression of the general will; all citizens have the right to concur personally, or through their representatives, in its formation; it must be the same for all, whether it protects or punishes. All citizens, being equal before it, are equally admissible to all public offices, positions and employments, according to their capacity, and without other distinction than that of virtues and talents.

7   No man may be accused, arrested or detained except in cases determined by law . . .

8   The law is to establish only penalties that are absolutely and obviously necessary; and no one may be punished except by virtue of a law established and promulgated prior to the offence and legally applied.

9   Since every man is presumed innocent until declared guilty, if arrest be deemed indispensable, all unnecessary severity for securing the person of the accused must be severely repressed by law.

10   No one is to be disquieted because of his opinions, even religious, provided their manifestation does not disturb the public order established by law.

11   Free communication of ideas and opinions is one of the most precious of the rights of man. Consequently, every citizen may speak, write and print freely, subject to responsibility for the abuse of such liberty in the cases determined by law.

12   The guarantee of the rights of man and citizen necessitates a public force; such a force, therefore, is instituted for the advantage of all and not for the particular benefit of those to whom it is entrusted.

13   For the maintenance of the public force and for the expenses of administration a common tax is indispensable; it must be assessed equally on all citizens in proportion to their means.

14   Citizens have a right to ascertain, by themselves or through their representatives, the necessity of the public tax, to consent to it freely, to supervise its use, and to determine its quota, assessment, payment and duration.

15   Society has the right to require of every public agent an accounting of his administration.

16   Every society in which the guarantee of rights is not assured or the separation of powers is not determined has no constitution at all.

17   Since property is a sacred and inviolable right, no one may be deprived thereof unless a legally established public necessity obviously requires it, and upon condition of a just and previous indemnity.

Source: Stewart (1951).

The constitution, in Title One, asserts the sovereignty of the French people and states, in a well-known phrase, that France is 'an indivisible, secular, democratic and social republic'. It also reflects another famous phrase, in asserting that the 'principle' of the Republic is 'government of the people, by the people, for the people'.[9] Since 1992 it has also stated that 'the language of the Republic is French', an amendment inserted in the context of the debates around the Maastricht Treaty of European Union as a symbolic reaffirmation of French national identity and status within Europe (Wilcox, 1994). Political parties are, in Article Four, given a specific constitutional status[10] but, in a phrase that attracted some attention when it was formulated, for it was widely held to be specifically directed against the French Communist Party, the constitution enjoins the parties to respect 'the principles of national sovereignty and of democracy'.

The structure of the constitution is set out in Exhibit 2.4. Many of its provisions are discussed in subsequent chapters, but a number of general points may be made here. First, the constitution clearly assigns sovereignty to the French people but, in contrast, for example, to the constitutional conventions of the United Kingdom, does not go on to infer from this the absolute sovereignty of the representatives of the people in Parliament. Indeed Article 34 specifies those areas in which parliament may legislate, and specifically precludes it from action in any other spheres, which are the domain of the government. Moreover, Article 55 provides that treaties duly approved and ratified take precedence over laws as long as they are observed by the other contracting parties. For many years this provision enabled France in principle to assimilate the legislation of the European communities into French law without undue difficulty. However, it proved inadequate to handle the rather more far-reaching changes required to conform with the Maastricht Treaty of European Union. A constitutional amendment in 1992 introduced a new Title 'The European Communities and the European Union', into the constitution, which recognised France's membership of the European Union and allowed for the transfer to it of certain powers.

The constitution instituted two bodies new to the French system: the Constitutional Council, which is more fully discussed below, and the Economic and Social Council. De Gaulle favoured representation not only along conventional electoral lines but also through the representation in the functions of the state of groups with economic and social interests. He saw this as a way of associating with the legislative process groups outside what he considered to be the

---

EXHIBIT 2.4

The structure of the constitution of the Fifth Republic*

Preamble	
Title One	Sovereignty
Title Two	The President
Title Three	The Government
Title Four	Parliament
Title Five	Parliament and Government
Title Six	Treaties
Title Seven	The Constitutional Council
Title Eight	The Judicial Authority
Title Nine	The High Court of Justice
Title Ten	Criminal liability of members of the government
Title Eleven	The Economic and Social Council
Title Twelve	Local Government
Title Thirteen	The French Community
Title Fourteen	Association Agreements
Title Fifteen	The European Communities and the European Union
Title Sixteen	Constitutional Amendment
Title Seventeen	Transitional Arrangements

*Following the constitutional amendments of 1993.

---

divisive and ideologically blinkered political parties (see Exhibit 2.5). His preference would probably have been, as he proposed at Bayeux and again in a reform put forward for referendum and defeated in 1969, the inclusion of such functional representation within the upper house of the legislature. However, the 1946 constitution had created a separate consultative economic committee, and an analogous solution was retained in 1958.

Two titles of the constitution are now completely obsolete, but the constitution has not been amended to remove them. Title Thirteen of the 1958 Constitution is concerned with the relationship of France's then overseas possessions, the states which were to form the 'Community'. The 1958 Constitution was a dual document. Formulated as it was in a period when the European nation states were rapidly divesting themselves of their colonial inheritance and as the problems and tensions of decolonisation, reflected internally, were producing a devastatingly acute internal crisis, the 1958 constitution not only outlined a new regime for France, but was intended to be the foundation 'charter' of a new set of relationships within her former Empire. Special institutions for the 'community' were envisaged as, in Article 85, was a special method for amending that part of the

---

EXHIBIT 2.5

The Economic and Social Council

Title Ten of the 1958 constitution institutes an Economic and Social Council, whose opinion the government may seek on proposed legislation, and must ask for on any bills of 'an economic or social character', the Council's composition is not specified by the constitution. It has, since 1984, consisted of 230 members, including 69 representatives of workers and employees, 72 of employers, and three of the 'liberal professions'. A further 19 members represent co-operatives and friendly societies and 17 come from family associations, housing associations, the mutual savings banks and similar bodies. Eight members represent the economic and social activities of the overseas territories, and two French nationals living abroad. Some of these representatives are elected by specified bodies – trade union confederations, for example – and others are appointed by the government at the suggestion or on the advice of various organisations. In addition 40 members are directly appointed by the government on the basis of their expertise in economic, social, scientific or cultural areas.

The Economic and Social Council has remained a rather marginal body. Although it has formally to be consulted on the five year plans that have been drawn up regularly since 1946 it has no role in the formulation of the plans, itself an increasingly marginalised process. The Council's views have carried little weight, and although it has occasionally produced interesting reports, largely on its own initiative, their impact has always been limited.

---

constitution (originally Title Twelve, now Title Thirteen) which comprised the 'charter'.[11] By 1962 all the territories concerned were fully independent, and the 'community' with its institutions, had ceased to exist. Title Thirteen is now as obsolete as Title Seventeen, originally Fifteen, which contains the temporary arrangements for the transition between the Fourth and the Fifth Republics.

Amending the Constitution

The constitution does contain within it a mechanism for its amendment, embodied in Title Sixteen, which consists of a single article, Article 89. President de Gaulle twice attempted to effect constitutional amendments by a procedure which bypassed Article 89, once successfully and once unsuccessfully (see Exhibit 2.6). Under Article 89, however, a bill to amend the constitution must be passed in both houses of Parliament in identical terms. A further stage is then required which may take one of two forms. The bill may then be approved by referendum. This was the procedure which President Mitterrand proposed to adopt in 1984 and again in 1990, but in 1984 the Senate rejected his bill and in 1990 the two houses of Parliament refused to adopt the necessary bill in identical terms, so both proposals lapsed.

Alternatively, but only in the case of a bill proposed by the government, it may be submitted to a joint meeting of both houses of Parliament, known as a Congress of Parliament, which must approve it unaltered by a three-fifths' majority. This mechanism for the revision of the constitution has been invoked for nine proposed revisions, seven of which succeeded. In 1963 it was used to amend the dates of the parliamentary sessions. In 1973 President Pompidou proposed to reduce the presidential term of office from seven to five years. The initial votes in the two houses separately suggested that the bill would not receive the necessary three-fifths' majority in the joint meeting and it was withdrawn. In 1974 President Giscard d'Estaing proposed two amendments; one, relating to the Constitutional Council, duly passed through all the stages, but the other, concerning the replacement in Parliament of members who had been obliged to resign because they had been appointed as ministers, was not put to the joint meeting, since again the separate votes had indicated that it would not pass. In 1976 another amendment, stemming from a recommendation by the Constitutional Council and setting out what was to be done if a duly nominated candidate died or became incapable during the period of an official presidential election campaign, successfully passed through all its stages.

Between 1992 and 1995 the Congress of Parliament met four times altogether. On the first occasion on 23 June 1992 the three-fifths majority was easily achieved for a constitutional amendment bill which created the new Title concerning the European Union, specified French as the language of the Republic and made amendments to articles concerning the French overseas territories and the Constitutional Council. The ease with which this amendment was achieved was notable, given the extent of the political divisions that were emerging over the ratification of the Maastricht Treaty and the closeness of the vote in the referendum three months later.

During his second term of office, as he increasingly stood back from much of the day-to-day political life of France, President Mitterrand placed a particular emphasis upon constitutional reform in his personal political programme. He launched a number of proposals, raising once again the possibility of reducing the presidential term of office, proposing much wider access to the Constitutional Council and suggesting a broadening of the powers of Parliament. An expert committee was set up to report on these proposals, but no action had been taken before the general election of 1993 overturned the Socialist government. Nevertheless, the new government took up two of the ideas that had been mooted, and a constitutional amendment of July 1993 made some reforms to the Article that sets up the High Council of the Judiciary (Conseil supérieur de la magistrature) and created a new Court of Justice of the Republic to impeach members of the government accused of criminal acts while in office. The second meeting of the Congress of Parliament in 1993 was caused by rather different circumstances. The government had introduced a bill which included a provision to give effect to that part of the Schengen agreement whereby an asylum-seeker who entered France from the territory of another state which was a party to the agreement could be returned forthwith to that state and his case examined there. The Constitutional Council declared such an arrangement to be unconstitutional. France could not pass over to another state the power to decide on requests for political asylum. The government decided that in order to achieve its objectives and fulfil its international obligations it was prepared to override the Constitutional Council by proposing a constitutional amendment. This was undertaken at considerable speed, and at a Congress of Parliament in November 1993 two new articles were added to the constitution, one allowing the Republic to make an agreement with another European state, provided that it respects human rights as France does, for that state to examine requests for asylum, and a second article that equally permits France, notwithstanding the first article, to accord asylum to any person. Following this amendment the bill that had previously been overturned was passed.

During his presidential campaign in 1995 Jacques Chirac did not show much interest in constitutional and institutional issues, marking himself out thereby from his second-round opponent, Lionel Jospin, who called for a five-year term for the president, more decentralisation and a stronger Parliament. It was, therefore, somewhat surprising that constitutional reform was one of the first major measures he undertook. In July 1995 the Congress of Parliament adopted amendments which extend the scope of the issues upon which a referendum may be called and which institute a single nine-month annual session for Parliament (see Chapter 7).

EXHIBIT 2.6

Constitutional amendments under de Gaulle

In 1962 the method of electing the President was changed from election by an electoral college to direct election by all voters. In 1969 a proposal to reform the Senate (the upper house of the legislature) which would be combined with the Economic and Social Council and to introduce a measure of regional government was defeated. The mechanism used for both these attempts was hotly disputed, for its constitutionality was questioned. In both cases de Gaulle invoked two articles of the constitution, Article 3 which says 'national sovereignty belongs to the people, who exercise it through their representatives or by way of referendum' and Article 11 which permits the President, on the proposal of the government, to submit to referendum 'any government bill dealing with the organisation of the public authorities'. These articles were held to provide a mechanism for constitutional revision which bypassed Parliament. Almost all the leading constitutional lawyers of the time took the view that Article 89 sets out the only valid amendment procedure. The government in 1962 consulted its highest legal advisory body, the Council of State, as is required for all draft legislation. The Council of State's opinions are always confidential, but a leak revealed that all but one of its members regarded the procedure as unconstitutional.[12]

The Constitutional Council was not formally able to give a view until after the referendum. At that point the President (Speaker) of the Senate, who had bitterly attacked de Gaulle for holding the referendum, referred the amendment to the Council. Although earlier unofficial soundings had shown the Council to be in agreement with the Council of State, once faced with a proposal approved by referendum it did not feel able to overturn the people's decision.[13] De Gaulle used a similar procedure in 1969, on the grounds that having approved his constitutional amendment in 1962 the people had also implicitly approved the procedure. The referendum resulted in the rejection of the proposed amendment and led directly to de Gaulle's resignation as President. No president since then has suggested bypassing parliament.

The Constitutional Balance: What Type of Regime?

The principal author of the constitution of the Fifth Republic was adamant that the system which it installed was what he called a parliamentary system. This system he contrasted with two other possible republican forms. One of these he called a *régime d'assemblée* – government by assembly – and the other was a presidential system.[14] The system that he characterised as 'government by assembly' had, in his view, been exemplified by the Third and Fourth Republics. Prime Ministers could not be appointed until the Assembly had approved them. Governments could relatively easily be overthrown by a hostile vote. The Assembly could control its own agenda. Initial discussion of proposed bills took place in committees of the Assembly, which could alter and reshape the proposals. The Assembly controlled the legality of elections and could thus to some extent determine its own membership. There was no system for determining whether laws were in conformity with the constitution. Debré saw the political stalemate that all too frequently arose from 'an assembly with the responsibility for choosing and sustaining a government, yet with a compulsion to check its action and a deep suspicion of its motives'[15] as an inevitable consequence, at least in France, of the concentration of powers within one institution. The changes which the Fifth Republic's constitution introduced, above all in the role of Parliament, clearly marked a decisive departure from the previous model.

The question whether the Fifth Republic is a presidential regime is harder to resolve. A great deal depends upon the definition employed. Some commentators take the constitution of the United States of America as providing the 'ideal type' of a presidential regime, against which the French situation may be measured (Quermonne and Chagnollaud, 1996, Ch. IX). Using such a definition, a presidential regime would be characterised by the following major features:

- a President who is both head of state and head of the government;
- a ministerial team chosen solely by the President, and not, consequently, responsible to or dismissible by the legislature;
- a President who is not answerable to the legislature and who can be removed only by a process of impeachment;
- a fixed term legislature; this means that crises within the legislature cannot be used to undermine the President or challenge his legitimacy.

Debré, in rejecting in 1958 the notion of a presidential regime for France, also assumed a fifth condition – that a President under such a system would have to be directly elected by universal suffrage, a condition which does not apply in the United States.

From a purely legalistic point of view it can be argued that only one of the American characteristics listed above – that the President is not answerable to Parliament – is found in France. Moreover, in 1958 direct election of the President was not envisaged. At the time the arguments which insisted that the new constitution would not impose a presidential regime had a specific political significance, even if they were couched in somewhat theoretical and legalistic terms. The circumstances in which de Gaulle had emerged as the 'providential' rescuer of France from crisis and even incipient civil war, combined with other traits evident in his political past – distrust of political parties, anti-communism, emphasis upon a strong state and international standing, the use of large and spectacular rallies and meetings as a means of political campaigning – all these gave rise to a degree of concern about possible fascist tendencies within his political approach. It was essential at the time to allay fears that the constitution necessarily involved an intolerable concentration of power in one person's hands.

A purely legalistic approach, however, does not give a clear picture of the way in which the political system under the constitution has evolved. Guy Mollet, who helped to persuade his own Socialist Party to support the constitution in 1958, wrote bitterly fifteen years later that it required an effort of the imagination to see how the constitution was intended to function; no effort had been made to apply it as it had been written, all that had happened was a succession of distortions (Mollet, 1973, pp. 39, 137). A noted French scholar, Jean-Louis Quermonne (Quermonne and Chagnollaud, 1996), concludes that the regime falls half way between a parliamentary and a presidential system and should not be regarded as analogous to other constitutional frameworks. Yet it has survived and receives broad approval, which suggests that so rapidly drafted a system expected, in the almost unanimous view of the political commentators of the time, to be strictly temporary, but embodying the aspirations of a broad spectrum of opinion, contained within it from the beginning potential for development and interpretation in a number of possible ways.

What becomes clear is that a written constitution, whilst it may provide a framework and a point of reference for political values in a particular society, is also, crucially, never neutral or external to political life in a country. Its application and interpretation depend upon the political values and the balance of political forces within the country at any time.

The Development of the Regime

In the period between 1958 and 1986 the balance of forces within the regime developed in a way which reinforced the power and position of the President to an extent which made it increasingly possible to speak of a 'presidential regime'. Many of the practices and factors which led to this will be considered in greater detail in later chapters. The crucial feature was the emergence of the President as not only head of state but also effectively as head of the government. This situation was reinforced by the institution, in 1962, of a system of direct election for the President.

By the end of the 1970s three of the four characteristics which were, in 1958, held to indicate the absence of a presidential regime – the separation of the headship of state from the headship of government; the choice by prime minister, not President, of the ministerial team; indirect election – had in practice been substantially eroded or disappeared. Moreover, although there is a maximum, rather than fixed, term for the legislature the right of dissolution has been sparingly used and always as a way of reinforcing the legitimacy of the president.

In 1962 de Gaulle dissolved Parliament as a response to a vote of censure against the government, a vote which, in criticising his proposed constitutional amendment procedure, was clearly directly aimed at him. He appealed to the popular vote against the 'politicians' of Parliament, and was rewarded by the return of an increased number of Gaullist members committed to unconditional support for the President. Equally in 1968 the early dissolution was a response to the events of May of that year, when student riots and workers' strikes put the authority of the government, and especially the personal status of the President, under great pressure (see Exhibit 10.3). De Gaulle appears to have been attracted to the notion of using a referendum to confirm his personal legitimacy. Prime Minister Pompidou and his government persuaded him that this purpose could be better served by an election. The outcome was increased representation for the Gaullists who gained an overall majority. In 1981 and 1988 Parliament was dissolved prematurely in order to allow the electors to re-affirm their presidential vote by returning to Parliament a majority that would support the policies of the newly elected President Mitterrand.

From the beginning discussions raged around the role of the President. They did so for two reasons; first, the difficulty of identifying from the language that was used about the role precisely what was involved. Article 5 provided a broad description of that role. In specifying the President's relationship to the 'public authorities' it used the phrase 'he provides, by his arbitration, for the regular functioning of the public authorities and the continuity of the

State'. *Arbitrage* can mean both arbitration, in a judicial sense, and umpiring. Although, as André Philip pointed out at the time, the umpire should not also be a player,[16] the phrase could also be taken to mean that the President should lay down the outlines and all the main directions of the governmental programme. And this, indeed, was what occurred.

The second reason for discussion about the role of the President arose from the difficulty of separating out the constitutional definition of the President's scope and the personal impact of de Gaulle himself. This was recognised at the time. Guy Mollet, anxious to preserve his notion of a constitutional balance that would retain the domination of the prime minister, attempted to persuade de Gaulle that he should not be a candidate for the presidency once the new republic was installed, but instead continue as prime minister, thereby ensuring the continued pre-eminence of that role. De Gaulle was clear however that his own place was not to be absorbed in the day to day details of government, still less to be implicated in the conflicts and hassle of party politics. He picked as his prime minister Michel Debré, a man with a minimal personal power base, even within the small group of long-term Gaullists, but with an immense loyalty to the President himself. De Gaulle did not intend to risk any challenges from the Prime Minister to his own dominant position at the top.

The 1958 election results reinforced this status. The constitutional referendum was widely recognised as being less a vote on a legal text than a national vote of confidence in de Gaulle. In the general election of November a rapidly organised group of Gaullists took 206 out of 536 National Assembly seats; and in the presidential elections of December 1958 78 per cent of the electoral college voted for de Gaulle. De Gaulle found himself, then, with a degree of popular and indeed organised political support that nothing in the history of the Fourth Republic foreshadowed. He owed it, initially, not to a broad political programme or to any kind of national organisation, but to the perception of the French people that he, and only he, could find and impose a solution to the problem of the future of Algeria. This he duly succeeded in doing. True to his emphasis on the need for direct national assent and for an assertion of the French people's confidence in his measures, he organised two referenda. They provided the assurances he required. In January 1961 75 per cent of voters in metropolitan France, and 71 per cent of a 59 per cent turn-out in Algeria approved the offer of self-determination to Algeria once peace could be re-established. In April 1962 91 per cent of those voting in metropolitan France approved the terms of his settlement which led to Algerian independence.

In some ways the early commentators were right; the political and constitutional balance instituted in 1958 was a provisional and temporary one. The degree of support enjoyed by de Gaulle had permitted the government, under his guidance coupled with the energetic action of Debré, to tackle a number of outstanding problems. But that support, while not limited to questions relating to Algeria, was nevertheless heavily dependent upon de Gaulle's indispensability as the peacemaker with Algeria. With that task accomplished he was likely to need a new base and possibly a redefined status. Those members of Parliament who defined their political position in terms of their loyalty to him were already organised as a political group. But de Gaulle was never willing to envisage himself as a party leader, or as dependent upon a particular and limited political power base.

In September 1962 de Gaulle announced that he proposed to submit to a referendum a constitutional modification that would provide for the direct election of the President, replacing the electoral college system. This proposal reflected the need to establish de Gaulle's personal position on a new basis, and also perhaps to ensure that the direction that the regime had taken since 1958 was embodied within its formal framework.

The provisions put forward, and approved by referendum, resulted in a two-ballot electoral system for the presidency.[17] Unless a candidate receives over 50 per cent of the vote at the first ballot, which has never occurred, the two candidates with highest number of votes go forward to the second ballot a fortnight later.

It may seem surprising that it was not envisaged from the start that the office would require the legitimacy and support that direct election would imply. Three factors apparently influenced the preference for an electoral college shown by the drafters of the text: they were alluded to by Debré in his speech to the Council of State. First, direct elections would have implied very specifically that the new regime was to be 'presidential', an implication that in the circumstances of the time would have been widely unacceptable. Secondly, the dual nature of the constitution meant that the president was also the head of the 'French Community'. It would have been difficult to exclude the inhabitants of the African states who belonged to that Community from the choice of their head of state, and even more difficult for the inhabitants of France to accept that they, on a 'one person one vote' system, might be outvoted in the choice of the head of state of France by people living outside metropolitan France. And finally, within metropolitan France the Communist Party, locked into a 'cold war' role and widely felt to owe its most fundamental loyalties to the Soviet Union – in Guy Mollet's famous gibe, 'not to the Left of the Socialist party but to its East' – nonetheless consistently polled the highest percentage of electoral votes of any party. On a simple plurality system of election a Communist candidate might win, a possibility which none of those involved in the formulation of the constitution was prepared to contemplate.

By 1962 these factors could all be differently perceived. De Gaulle's regime was widely supported and not generally regarded as fascist or intolerable. The 'Community' had disappeared and its institutions were obsolete. The Communist Party had not prospered, and the double ballot electoral system used for parliamentary elections had proved capable of ensuring that the proportion of votes it received was not reflected in actual electoral success. The 'spark'[18] which set off the process which led to the referendum was the assassination attempt against de Gaulle at Petit Clamart in August 1962. It came very close to succeeding, and the President's mind was then rapidly concentrated upon the need to provide a mechanism for ensuring that any successor to him could rely on the same broad measure of legitimacy and support that he enjoyed.

The outcome of the vote – just under 62 per cent of the voters approved direct election – has often been seen as the most crucial single event in the evolution of the regime. In terms of the balance of power its effect was to confer upon all future presidents a large measure of popular legitimacy and hence political pre-eminence. It precluded, as its opponents from amongst the political parties and the parliamentarians in 1962 had realised that it would, any return to a more Fourth Republican system of parliamentary predominance.[19] It gave a legal and democratic rationale to presidential practice and, precisely as de Gaulle intended, provided, at least in part, a mechanical institutional substitute for the particular circumstances which provided him with his initial legitimacy. He himself was then obliged to utilise this mechanism in 1965, when the election went into a second ballot, and it became apparent that the presidency would henceforth be as much political as charismatic. Indeed, the presidential election of 1965 may be seen as the consummation of the process begun in 1962. François Mitterrand, one of the most active and vocal opponents of the 1962 revision, was nonetheless prepared to campaign for the presidency in 1965 on the basis that the President should have a policy programme to offer. He said that if elected he would seek (as in fact he did in 1981 and 1988), through a general election, the parliamentary majority with which to implement it.

With the emergence of the notion of a 'presidential majority' the old dichotomy between presidential and parliamentary regimes lost some of its force; as the discussion of presidential practice in Chapter 3 helps to illustrate, 'presidential', at least within normal common-sense usages, is the appropriate description for the regime.

The Constitutional Council

The creation of the Constitutional Council has come to be recognised as the second major innovation in constitutional structure introduced by the Fifth Republic. In the case of the role of the presidency the full implications of the constitutional change only became clear after the 1962 amendment. Similarly, in the case of the Constitutional Council, it was the amendment of 1974 which clarified, confirmed and enlarged the scope of the new institution. Like the presidency, the Constitutional Council has moved well beyond the role envisaged for it by its creators (Avril and Gicquel, 1993, p.71).

The Constitutional Council consists of nine appointed members, three appointed personally by the President, three by the president (speaker) of the National Assembly, and three by the president of the Senate. Each appointed member serves for a non-renewable term of nine years, and one-third of the membership is replaced every three years. In addition any former President of the Republic has the right to sit as a member of the Council. Presidents Auriol and Coty exercised this right during the early years of the Fifth Republic but after his resignation President de Gaulle ignored the Council. Ex-President Giscard d'Estaing could have participated in the work of the Council during the period between 1981 and 1984 but declined to do so since he was still pursuing an active political career. In 1984 he was elected a member of Parliament, and in 1989 became a member of the European Parliament. In 1984 the Constitutional Council ruled that for ex officio members, as for others, holding a parliamentary seat was incompatible with participation in the work of the Council. Following his departure from office in 1995 President Mitterrand was able to sit as a member of the Council.

Membership of the Council is not confined to those with a legal background. Some members have been magistrates and lawyers, one the former president of the Court of Justice of the European Communities and several have been professors of law or of political science; others have been former senior officials, while well over half the total membership of the Council since its creation has comprised former members of Parliament and ministers. All the presidents of the Council have been drawn from this group of members. Charlot (1994, p. 200) argues that this has rendered the Council's independence more acceptable to successive governments. It cannot be held to be ignorant of the day-to-day realities of political life. Nevertheless, the appointments have not always proved uncontroversial, and President Mitterrand was criticised for the appointments of Robert Badinter in 1986 and Roland Dumas in 1995; both appointments being interpreted by some as an attempt to preserve left-wing influence in the Council and provide a suitable outlet for a presidential associate at a point where the political complexion of the government was likely to change very soon. The first woman to serve on the Council was Mme Noëlle Lenoir-Freaud in 1992.[20]

The Constitutional Council's role can be described under two headings: legal and advisory. The former is the major and dominant role, and itself falls into two main parts (see Exhibit 2.7).

The Constitutional Council judges the legality and validity of presidential, senatorial and National Assembly elections, and of referendums. It can therefore rule on cases where, following an election, the successful candidate is alleged to have been ineligible to stand, and on cases where a sitting member is alleged to have made him or herself ineligible to continue as a result of taking up an incompatible post. More importantly, it rules on the validity of elections, in cases where electoral malpractice or fraud is alleged. Following the 1993 general election the volume of cases referred to the Constitutional Council was much greater than after any previous election. The main reason for this was the new legislation controlling electoral expenses, which allowed the new National Committee (Commission nationale des comptes de campagne et des financements politiques) overseeing political party finances and electoral expenses to ask the Constitutional Council to consider cases. In all 648 cases were referred by the National Committee. Only six elections were annulled, one of them being that of the Socialist former minister of culture, Jack Lang.

The Council also rules on whether laws passed by the National Assembly are constitutional or not. The government may ask it to consider whether a bill under discussion falls within the scope of parliamentary law-making (see Chapter 7). Once a law which falls into the category of 'organic laws' – laws which provide for the detailed implementation of the constitution, for example by determining the electoral system – has been passed the Council must rule on whether it is constitutional. Other laws may be referred to the Council for a ruling before they are promulgated. If they are found to be unconstitutional they cannot enter into force.

A further legal function is the requirement that the Council approve the standing orders of both houses of Parliament and any amendment made to them.

The second activity which the Constitutional Council undertakes is an advisory one. It must be consulted if the President wishes to declare a state of emergency under Article 16 of the constitution. It is also consulted on the arrangements for presidential elections, and on the conduct of referendums.

The Council initially played a somewhat modest role but has now emerged as an important source of limitation and constraint upon the actions of the government. Some commentators have alleged that it has come to operate as part of the political process of making laws, in effect acting as a third chamber of the legislature. There are two main explanations for the nature of the Council's development. First, in its early years the Council, influenced by the extreme prudence of its first president (the Council was known to have held that the 1962 constitutional amendment was effected by unconstitutional means, but did not publicly say so) acted in ways which supported the new regime. Moreover, a major use to which the Council was put was to ensure that Parliament did not stray beyond the limits of its constitutionally ordained boundaries. The Council was seen at least in part as an element of the Gaullist system serving Gaullist ends (Keeler, 1985). Consequently, the willingness it showed in a decision in 1971 to take account of fundamental principles to protect certain civil liberties was largely discounted. The decision was crucial for two reasons, however. First, it established the principle that the rights set out in the documents referred to in the preamble to the Constitution (the Declaration of the Rights of Man and the Citizen and the preamble to the 1946 Constitution) were an integral part of the 1958 constitution and the rights they conferred could be relied on. Secondly, the decision (Decision 71-44 DC of 16 July 1971 relating to the right to set up an association) clearly indicated that the Council was willing to overturn laws proposed by the government when it was given the opportunity to do so.

Such opportunities arose very infrequently. For the first fifteen years of its existence bills could be referred for a ruling on their constitutionality only by the President, the prime minister and the presidents of the two houses of parliament. In the fifteen years before 1974 there were only nine references to the Constitutional Council.[21] Since during this period the government did not raise the question of the constitutionality of its own bills, and the President of the National Assembly belonged to the governing majority, the only source from which 'political' referrals were likely to arise at all was the president of the Senate. After Gaston Monnerville's unsuccessful referral of the 1962 constitutional amendment there was no further referral by the president of the Senate until the 1971 case described above. Alain Poher then waited until 1973 before making a further referral.

The second factor which explains the nature of the Consitutional Council's development is the impact of the 1974 reform which enlarged the circumstances under which the Constitutional Council can be asked to review the constitutionality of a law (see Exhibit 2.7). As the result of a constitutional amendment initiated by President Giscard d'Estaing in 1974 this possibility was extended to any 60 members of parliament. The effect was not expected to be very great (Avril and Gicquel 1993 p. 59). However, the number of references to the Council increased fivefold during the Giscard d'Estaing presidency, rising from nine in the first fourteen years of its existence to 47 in the subsequent seven years, of which 45 emanated from members of Parliament. During these years the Council began slowly to demonstrate that its potential powers could not be ignored and the political opposition began to realise that challenge to the constitutionality of laws could be a useful political weapon.[22] Only twelve of the 45 referrals between 1974 and 1981 resulted in a proposed law being held to be unconstitutional and, as John Keeler points out, up to 1981 no decision by the Council represented a major defeat for presidential or governmental policy (Keeler 1985). However, some of the decisions certainly caused embarrassment to a government, for example the 1977 annulment of a law which would have given the police a very wide-ranging right to search private vehicles. Fear of a reference to the Council might be enough to induce changes in certain proposals.

The complete change in the political orientation of President and government brought about a new situation in 1981. The members of the Constitutional Council had all been appointed under the previous political dispensation. It was possible that they might take a fairly rigorous line with the new government which was challenging a number of the ideological principles which had governed political life throughout the Fifth Republic. John Keeler notes that some opposition parliamentarians saw the Council as a last bulwark against revolutionary change. The number of references to the Council increased still further, to 66 in the period from 1981 to 1986, and the extent to which the Council could indeed hinder the implementation of presidential policy was demonstrated by an early decision over the bill to put into effect one of the major planks of Mitterrand's election platform, the nationalisation programme. The decision did not reject the principle of the government's right to nationalise, but did strike down some of the conditions under which this was to be achieved. The result was a political storm, but the government could do nothing but place another bill before Parliament, embodying the changes required in order to satisfy the Council.

The discovery by the political parties of the possibility of constitutional challenge to laws as a way of prolonging the political debate and reversing defeat in Parliament has continued to result in a substantial number of challenges to proposed laws. Moreover, a substantial proportion of the ordinary laws referred – since 1981 just over half – have been found to be, at least in part, unconstitutional.

Faced with a decision that a proposed law is unconstitutional a government has only three possible courses of action. It may abandon a bill altogether, an unusual but not unknown occurrence; it may, and usually does, revise the law in the light of the Constitutional Council's comments; or it may seek to revise the constitution itself in order subsequently to allow the implementation of the measures it was proposing. This has happened only once (see above pp. 46) in an instance related to the interaction between national law and France's obligations under international treaties or agreements: the Schengen agreements on immigration and the right of asylum.

There is, and will continue to be, a debate about the role of the Constitutional Council. Oppositions of both Left and Right use it, and will certainly continue to do so, as a means of obtaining changes in proposed laws that they have not been able to secure in Parliament although the outcome of a referral can never be predetermined. Governments are dissuaded from actions they might otherwise have favoured if they feel that there is a substantial likelihood that they may be overruled. Even when a government enjoys a considerable majority in Parliament it cannot act unchecked. The jurisprudence of the Constitutional Council provides a framework outside which it cannot stray. Equally, it is sometimes possible for a government to turn such constraints to its advantage. In 1990 Prime Minister Rocard submitted his bill on the financing of political parties to the Constitutional Council, presumably seeking to ensure that the bill, with its important implications for all parties, could not be held to be a purely partisan measure (Maus, 1991, p. 108). These considerations have led some to argue that the Constitutional Council has become a 'third chamber of the legislature' both in terms of its purely formal procedures, since, unlike a court, it intervenes before, not after, a bill becomes law, and because it applies essentially political considerations to the amendment of proposed legislation. Such arguments are strengthened, first, by a growing tendency by the Constitutional Council, since its 1971 decision, to use not merely the letter of the articles of the constitution but also general principles outlined in its preamble to guide its decisions. These general principles are, as Prime Minister Edouard Balladur pointed out to the special Congress of the two houses of Parliament called to pass the constitutional revision relating to the right of asylum, philosophical and political precepts, formulated in very different times. Put more positively, the point is that the application of some very general principles – the right to equality, for example – requires, and finds within the Constitutional Council, creative and carefully judged interpretations (Mény, 1993, pp. 151–2). Secondly, some of the Council's decisions are, as its jurisprudence develops, more detailed and more precise, and hence more constraining on the government. This is especially true when the Council recognises, as it has increasingly done, that, in the words of the proverb, 'the devil is in the details' and qualifies its declarations that a law is constitutional with directions about how it is to be applied if its constitutionality is to be preserved. The line between purely juridical and political interpretation is a a very fine one, and hard to discern. If the Constitutional Council is tending towards the political side, encouraged by the political provenance of its presidents and a proportion of its membership, then the hypothesis that the Council is a further stage in the political process becomes more plausible.

On the other side of the argument the following observations can be made.

- Only about a quarter of the Council's decisions on ordinary laws have been based on the general principles of the constitution (Charlot, 1994, pp. 203–40). The others have relied on the strict interpretation of the constitution's articles.
- The Council has not shown particular favour to either the political Left or Right, nor has there been a marked difference between periods when the Constitutional Council might be supposed to be broadly politically aligned with the government in power and those when, because of the differing timetables of Council appointments and electoral changes, it might not.
- The Constitutional Council can declare a proposed law unconstitutional. It can neither prevent a change in the constitution nor determine whether or how a government may act within the constitution. It certainly has not prevented governments of either political complexion carrying forward the major elements of their programmes, some of which – decentralisation, nationalisation, privatisation, changes in the law on immigration and citizenship – have major and far-reaching effects.

The development of the Constitutional Council since 1959 has given it a far greater role than was anticipated at its creation. It now plays a central role in restraining and constraining the legislative actions of French governments, both positively, by its decisions, and negatively, by inhibiting governments from advancing proposals that might not be sustained. The role of the Council might have become even more prominent had President Mitterrand's 1991 attempt to amend the constitution succeeded. The effect would have been to allow any citizen to plead the unconstitutionality of any law affecting human rights as a defence before a court of law. The Constitutional Council would then have had to rule whether or not the contested law was unconstitutional. The proposed amendment was unsuccessful.

Nevertheless, because it relies upon the constitution as the source of its decisions the Constitutional Council has also played an important role in securing general acceptance of the constitution and anchoring it within political life. The development of its role is one of the factors which explains why the third and fourth decades of the Fifth Republic have seen an enhancement of the place of the constitution itself within political life. The constitution can be changed, though not lightly or easily. It can no longer be ignored or set aside. Another major factor in emphasising the fundamental role of the constitution is the experience of *cohabitation*, to which the next section turns.

EXHIBIT 2.7

**Type and number of decisions of the
Constitutional Council to 1 January 1995**

- **Elections**

Type of election	Number of decisions	Results annulled
National Assembly (including by-elections)	1 703[1]	44
Senate (including by elections)	126	1
Presidential elections	56	
Referendums	14	

	Number of decisions
• **Status of members of Parliament**	13
• **Constitutionality of a treaty**	5
• **Obligatory consideration**	132

	Number of decisions	
Of which Parliament's standing orders	52	
Organic laws	80[2]	
• **Constitutionality of laws**		222[2]
Of which before 1974 reform	9	
after 1974 reform	213	
• **Division between legislative and regulatory areas**		183
Of which under Article 41	11[3]	
under Article 37	172	

Notes:
1 Of which 648 out of the 887 in 1993 related to the new legislation regulating electoral expenditure.
2 113 of these 302 (80 + 222) decisions found the text submitted not in conformity with the constitution.
3 In four of these 11 decisions the Council declared itself not competent.

Source: Compiled from figures provided in Maus (1995, *passim*).

'Cohabitation'

The authors of the constitution did not think in terms of a presidential majority. Their expectation of the working of the constitution, extrapolated from previous experience, seems to have involved governments formed from relatively unstable coalitions, held together by the institutional glue of reformed parliamentary procedure and strengthened executive powers, protected by a Constitutional Council and supervised benignly by a President whose role was to protect the country from the damage that instability might otherwise cause. From the start the evolution of the regime belied this image; the institution of direct election affirmed the President's legitimacy, and allowed successive presidents, for as long as they could command a majority of the votes within Parliament on the basis of the political majority revealed by general elections, to develop the presidential role. But the evolution of the regime did not rapidly provide an answer to the question of how the system would work in the absence of a majority. For 28 years it seemed as if the French electors had accepted and acted upon what might be called 'the logic of presidentialism'. Parliamentary elections as they fell due at the expiry of normal five year terms in 1967, 1973 and 1978 returned majorities which supported the President in office. In 1962 and 1968 the election results reaffirmed support for the President. In 1981 a newly elected President caused the electorate to confirm their choice, and a majority supporting him was returned. But there was nothing inevitable about this process, as presidents at the time of general elections more or less explicitly pointed out.

Four possibilities are open to presidents who find themselves faced with a general election that returns their political opponents. First, they might ask the country to think again, by a rapid dissolution and a second general election. The risks in such a course, which might look like contempt for the judgement of the electorate, would obviously be high. Secondly, some commentators (Quermonne, 1980, p. 581) took the view that a disavowal by the electorate of the parliamentary majority that had been supporting the President would amount to a disavowal of the President himself, who ought therefore to resign and thereby bring about a new presidential election which might bring the two institutions into line again. This was not the view of either President Giscard d'Estaing, who faced the possibility (which did not in fact materialise) of a defeat for his ruling coalition in 1978, or of President Mitterrand at the time of the defeat of Socialist governments in 1986 and 1993. Both chose to indicate that they would continue in office. Nevertheless in 1978 President Giscard d'Estaing warned the electorate that they could not expect that he would be able to protect them from the consequences of the choices that they might make. A government based on their electoral decisions would have a policy which it would be in a position to apply. In 1986 President Mitterrand did not attempt to impose some compromise government that he might dominate and which just might have maintained its position in Parliament. He adopted instead the fourth of the possible strategies and called on Jacques Chirac, the leader of the party which had the largest number of seats in the National Assembly, to form a government. He did so again in 1993, on that occasion appointing, not Chirac himself, but Chirac's nominee, Edouard Balladur. He thus made it clear that he was respecting the electorate's choice although he also stated that his choice of Balladur was a personal one, reflecting his appreciation of Balladur's qualities. In both cases he was insistent that he retained and had exercised the President's right to make a choice.

The political history of the period since 1981 has encompassed

- *alternance*: the replacement in 1981 of a government of the right wing political orientation which had up to then characterised all governments since 1958 with a left-wing government;
- the first two year period of *cohabitation*, from 1986 to 1988;
- the re-election of President Mitterrand in 1988
- the subsequent general election which produced a minority Socialist government;
- a return to *cohabitation* in 1993;
- and in 1995 the victory of Chirac, who retained the Parliament elected in 1993 in which he enjoyed a majority but with a new prime minister and ministerial team.

In constitutional terms the effects of this history have been as follows.

- To force President, government and parliamentarians to fall back upon the actual provisions of the constitution and to explore and exploit more fully the possibilities it offers; the consequence has been a long-term strengthening of the constitution within the regime.
- To demonstrate the extent to which the constitution provided an accepted and unchallenged framework for the institutions of government in France; major shifts in political orientation and in the balance of power within this framework were possible without the constitution itself being contested.
- To demonstrate the flexibility of the constitutional framework, which has proved able yet again to accommodate changing circumstances.

Even during the periods of *cohabitation* the President remained a key figure in French political life. The importance of the prospect of the impending presidential elections within much political life in 1986–8 and 1993–5 demonstrated the extent to which 'normality' was defined in presidential terms.

Part II

The Governmental System

3

The Presidency

The role of the President continues to be central to both political and governmental life in France. The Fifth Republic differs from its predecessors in 'the emergence of the presidency as the major focus of political decision-making in France' (Wright, 1989, p. 336). An examination of the power, changing practices and limitations of the presidency therefore forms an essential starting point for an understanding of the mechanisms of politics in France. This chapter is concerned with the nature of the presidency, the resources at the President's disposal, the ways in which presidents have operated, and the constraints upon their freedom of action.

The Nature of the Presidency

As President, Charles de Gaulle permanently moulded the nature of the presidency (see Exhibit 3.1). He created a particular image for the post, and set expectations and approaches which his successors have adopted – and adapted. His charisma, his appearance and the physical impression he made, his status as in some senses the double saviour of France, and the very personal and strong notions of the role of the President which he conveyed inevitably proved to be amongst the major factors fashioning the development of the office.

In considering the nature of the presidency, two factors seem important; first, the President's role is legitimised by election through direct suffrage. Incumbency in the office is the outcome of choice by French voters. Secondly, the relationship of the President to the political life of France, as expressed through political parties, is a complex and ambiguous one.

EXHIBIT 3.1

The presidents of the Fifth Republic

January 1959 – December 1965	Charles de Gaulle
December 1965 – April 1969	Charles de Gaulle
(interim – acting President	Alain Poher)
June 1969 – April 1974	Georges Pompidou
(interim – acting President	Alain Poher)
May 1974 – May 1981	Valéry Giscard d'Estaing
May 1981 – May 1988	François Mitterrand
May 1988 – May 1995	François Mitterrand
May 1995	Jacques Chirac

De Gaulle's actions, as President, were, as we have seen, initially legitimised by the high level of popular support for the constitution which he recommended, as demonstrated by the results of the referendum of September 1958 and the parliamentary elections of November 1958. Thereafter, the paramount need for the achievement of a settlement in Algeria fulfilled much the same purpose, so that the outcome of the January 1961 referendum on self-determination for Algeria was again clearly a renewal of de Gaulle's mandate which allowed him a very free hand. With the settlement in Algeria in the Spring of 1962 that source of legitimacy disappeared, and the introduction of presidential election by direct suffrage was linked to the need to find a new way for the President to retain a mandate for the degree of freedom of action which he had come to enjoy. The 1962 constitutional amendment has undoubtedly been a major support for the continued pre-eminence of the President.

One of the most enduring aspects of de Gaulle's legacy which has so shaped the nature of the presidency has, however, been the relationship of the President to the party political life of the country. In a country where party political differences have all too often been the product of deep and bitter ideological conflict which has frequently found expression in the rejection of the entire political and constitutional settlement, rather than simply in disagreement about programmes of government, de Gaulle's rejection of the politics of party could seem plausible and welcome. The discrediting of the Fourth Republic, which de Gaulle had from the start condemned as too much under the influence of the political parties, strengthened acceptance of this attitude. De Gaulle himself, although greatly assisted throughout his term of office by the presence in parliament of a majority focused around members pledged to support him, did not accept that he was in any way beholden to a party. He resolutely refused to allow his name to be formally attached to the party that grew up around him, although the adjective Gaullist was from the start consistently applied to it. No party political programme could, in this view, ever reflect the interests of more than a particular fraction of the French people; only a President who is genuinely above party politics can care for the common interests of all.

The electoral system for the presidency supports this approach. Candidates for election to the presidency must be nominated by 500 sponsors, who must themselves hold electoral office and be drawn from at least 30 different *départements* or overseas territories, with no more than 50 coming from any single *département*. The intention is that the presidential candidates should neither necessarily depend upon organised party support nor be the candidates of irresponsible groups or strictly local interests. Moreover, since the final run-off is between two candidates, both have every interest in attracting as wide as possible a range of voters from a variety of party allegiances.

Whilst profound distrust of party politics was particularly a characteristic of de Gaulle, all his successors have at one and the same time enjoyed, or sought to establish, a sound party base whilst equally seeking to distance themselves from too close an identification with that base. President Pompidou's base was within the Gaullist party; as Prime Minister he had been careful to nurture and oversee it, taking a personal interest in the selection of candidates for the 1967 general elections, for instance, and playing a major role in placing it on a sound organisational footing. President Giscard d'Estaing's party basis was in a much smaller grouping, the Independent Republicans, the junior partner in the Gaullist governmental coalition. His own image and personality, and the support of a number of Gaullists, who preferred him to the Gaullist candidate, were sufficient to propel him into the second ballot and victory, albeit a narrow one, over François Mitterrand in 1974. He felt the need for a broader basis for political support, and the result (see Chapter 8) was the foundation of the UDF. He did not, however, campaign for re-election on the strength of a party programme or even overt party organisation. When he finally announced that he would be a candidate for re-election in 1981 'Committees for the re-election of President Giscard d'Estaing' sprang 'spontaneously' into life.

Both François Mitterrand and Jacques Chirac had much more blatantly party political careers than the first three presidents of the

Fifth Republic. Mitterrand had shaped the fortunes of the Socialist Party as its First Secretary for a decade before his election in 1981, although he found it prudent to resign from that position just before announcing his candidacy. Chirac created the RPR in 1976 by a profound remodelling of the Gaullist party and was its effective leader thereafter whatever the formal office he held within it. Voters could expect that their programmes would be broadly consonant with the stance of the parties which they had led for so long and that their victory would be likely to result in a government of that complexion. However, their programmes for their election campaigns were in no sense party manifestos, as their titles – Mitterrand's *Letter to all the French People* in 1988 and Chirac's *France for Everyone* in 1995 – were at pains to suggest.

To those accustomed to different styles of political competition the insistence that people who are fundamentally politicians should, as President, become in some sense apolitical may seem disingenuous, even hypocritical. This insistence, however, reflects something of the curious balance which the President continues to maintain between a role as head of state and a role as head of government.

The Resources of the Presidency

The way in which successive presidents have interpreted and carried out that role has highlighted the strengths and resources upon which they can draw. Five aspects of these seem particularly important: the President's own personality and personal approach; the formal powers he can deploy; the political relationships which he enjoys and the way in which he cultivates them; his use of, and relationship to, the mass media; and the nature and role of his personal staff.

Personality and Personal Approach

De Gaulle, as we have seen, was no dictator, and the fears of those who saw him as some kind of latter-day Mussolini were evidently misplaced. He was nevertheless an austere and aloof man, regarded by many as colossally arrogant. He can be protected from that charge only by the observation that he was never self-seeking; his claims for himself, and they were always far-reaching, were based on an unshakeable conviction, which he managed, when it mattered, to impose upon others, that he represented and spoke for the true interests of France. He was constrained by the values he thought truly worthy of France – republicanism and democracy, for example – but was deeply distrustful of anything that seemed like special pleading, whether for capitalism, whose representatives had, in his view, so singularly failed France in the 1930s and 1940s, or for the forces of class conflict which could only shatter a country that he regarded as special and indivisible. He was certainly constrained neither by personal loyalties or obligations, nor by constitutional niceties.

By choosing to occupy the presidency de Gaulle brought to the office a degree of status and prestige greater than any which previous incumbents during the Third and Fourth Republics had succeeded in bestowing upon it. It is tempting to conclude that he designed the office specifically for himself, and there is no doubt that the constitutional expression of its formal powers reflects some of his particular concerns. However, de Gaulle's effect upon the office was rather like that of an awkwardly-shaped foot upon a tight fitting shoe; stretching, cracking and reshaping.

President Pompidou's term of office as prime minister, from 1962 to 1968, established his credentials as a potential President. Educated at an elite academic institution, the Ecole Normale Supérieure, he was recruited from his teaching post into de Gaulle's private office in 1945, and when de Gaulle left office was rewarded with a post in the Council of State. From there he entered Rothschild's bank. Throughout the period of the Fourth Republic he remained in close contact with de Gaulle who appointed him as the head of his personal staff when he was himself prime minister between May and December 1958. In 1962 de Gaulle appointed him as prime minister, despite his minimal experience of public life. He remained as prime minister until his dismissal in 1968, and was elected President after de Gaulle's resignation the following year. During his term of office he had established himself as a very astute and effective politician, a powerful organiser and, especially in the confusion of the events of May 1968, a determined government leader. Until his long-drawn-out fatal illness he brought these same qualities to the presidency.

President Giscard d'Estaing's carefully cultivated image, at the time of his election in 1974, was one of youthfulness, dynamism, change and modernisation; change, however, as his election slogan proclaimed, without risks. His attempts at proving himself to be at home with people of all stations of life – invitations to dinner with 'ordinary' families – were never quite convincing, for he had emerged from the technocratic and political elite, passing through two of the top educational establishments (the Ecole Polytechnique and the Ecole Nationale d'Administration) into a senior civil service post followed by election, in 1956 at the age of 29, to Parliament for his grandfather's former seat. Valéry Giscard d'Estaing brought a technocratic confidence and experience in one of the most powerful ministerial posts – that of minister of finance – to the presidency, and throughout his term of office the extent of his personal involvement in all aspects of governmental and political life was very clear.

President Mitterrand succeeded in turning what might have been a handicap into an advantage. He was associated with the discredited Fourth Republic – he had been a member of Parliament and eleven times a minister – and twice an unsuccessful presidential candidate. Yet his 1981 electoral campaign managed to present what might have been perceived as a career of failure as one of slowly advancing yet irresistible achievement. *La force tranquille* – the quiet strength – was his slogan. A complex, perceptive, calculating and clever politician, it was he who was obliged, between 1986 and 1988, to find a way to accommodate the presidential office to a parliamentary majority and government of a sharply different political persuasion. He did so with well-judged astuteness and his behaviour during the period of *cohabitation* undoubtedly contributed to his re-election for a second term in 1988.

Astuteness, however, grew, during Mitterrand's second term of office, to look more like deviousness, and cleverness seemed mere machination. Some of his gambles failed to pay off. The Maastricht referendum result was closely balanced, and in no sense a vote of confidence in his government, and his apparent support for populist centre–left politician Bernard Tapie turned out to be the endorsement not of a successful and vote-winning politician but of a cheating bankrupt. The Socialist candidate for the battle to succeed him in 1995 was not Emmanuelli, whose cause he had favoured, but Jospin. The party itself was at a low ebb, almost as fragile and improbable a basis for a bid a power as it had been when he took it over in 1971. Scandal and tragedy did not spare him. The closing years of his period of office encompassed the suicide of two close associates, one of them former Prime Minister Pierre Bérégovoy; the revelation of the right-wing activities of his youth and suspicion over some of his continued loyalties; allegations of financial improprieties by others close to him; and the discovery that he had housed his mistress and their daughter in official apartments. He became increasingly physically frail as his terminal illness (cancer of the prostate) gripped him, although he confronted it with openness and dignity, and survived, against the expectations of many, to the end of his mandate and beyond. It has, perhaps justly, been said of President Mitterrand that he 'had all the conditions for greatness except greatness itself'.[1] However, his mark on the presidency, not only as a consequence of longevity in office but also of his choices and personal style, was as profound as that of de Gaulle. It was not the least of the paradoxes of this complex man that, having opposed the Fifth Republic's constitution, he presided over a period where the role of that constitution in the working of the presidency and in political life was accentuated.

Jacques Chirac thus took over a presidency that had changed in shape and emphasis. He had fought for it since 1981, like Mitterrand succeeding at his third attempt. Despite his depth of political experience, as the first, and until he resigned after his election as President, the only Mayor of Paris since the office was restored by the reforms introduced in 1977, and through two periods as prime minister, separated by a decade, his early days at the Elysée were troubled. His campaign had been tough, vigorous, political and unashamedly populist, despite his tendency to appear stiff and blustering on television. He had argued for social inclusion, for a combination of low taxes and a flexible labour market, and above all for a rapid decrease in unemployment. After several months his popularity in the opinion polls had fallen drastically. Taxes had risen, unemployment was only creeping down, the new government was troubled with dissent, which had resulted in the resignation of the minister of finance, and was already tainted by scandal inherited from the municipal administration in Paris from which many of the ministers and presidential staff had come. The old image of impetuousness and hotheadedness had not been lessened by his decision, in the face of massive international protest, to resume nuclear testing in the Pacific and by his abrasive and intransigent approach to his relationship with the German Chancellor Helmut Kohl. Chirac used his prime ministership in 1986–8 as the launchpad for his unsuccessful attempt on the presidency in 1988, and eschewed the office of prime minister in 1993 in the hope that his bid for the presidency would be enhanced by distance from the pitfalls of power. In the tradition of Gaullism he regards the presidency as the appropriate setting for a strong leader. He brings to it undoubted energy and strength. His sense of direction is less certain.

The President is the holder of a very exposed and public office; his experience, his astuteness, his ability to choose and present a style of behaviour (for example, the unpopularity of Giscard d'Estaing's increasingly 'monarchical' presidential style certainly contributed towards his 1981 defeat), his own strengths of personality, are all important resources that he must deploy in interpreting and fulfilling the role of President.

Formal Powers

The starting-point for the development of the presidential role is the formal powers which the constitution gives the President (see Exhibit 3.2). These can be considered under two heads: there are the traditional powers inherent in the President's role as head of state, and in addition the new powers that differentiate the constitution of the Fifth Republic from its predecessors. Following Jean Massot (1987, pp. 93ff) the traditional powers may be grouped into four categories: those in the judicial, in the legislative and in the diplomatic spheres, and those related to appointments in the public and military services. Even in these areas the constitution of 1958 tended to extend the scope of presidential action compared with the previous system.

In the judicial sphere the President retains the power, granted to all heads of the French state since 1802, to grant pardons (Article 17). Articles 64 and 65 of the constitution specify moreover that the President guarantees judicial independence, and presides over the body which regulates judicial behaviour, the Conseil National de la Magistrature.

In the legislative sphere the President is, like his predecessors, not allowed to attend parliamentary sessions even for purely formal purposes. President Mitterrand, with his very lengthy experience of life as a member of the National Assembly, apparently regretted being unable to visit Parliament even as a guest. He remarked, in a speech in 1990, that he felt he was missing something when he saw serious debate going on in Parliament.[2] He can, however, send a written message to Parliament. He retains the head of state's duty to promulgate laws within a fortnight once they have been passed, but he also retains a right, which has figured in French constitutions since 1848, to demand a further reading of a bill. This occurs only very rarely, but in 1985, for example, President Mitterrand referred back a clause in a bill relating to New Caledonia. Presidential decrees

EXHIBIT 3.2

Presidential powers in the Constitution of the Fifth Republic

Title Two Article 5 The President of the Republic shall see that the Constitution is respected. He shall ensure, by his arbitration, the regular functioning of the public authorities as well as the continuity of the State.

He shall be the guarantor of national independence, of the integrity of the territory, and of respect for Community agreements and for treaties.

Article 8 The President of the Republic shall appoint the Premier. He shall terminate the functions of the Premier when the latter presents the resignation of the Government.

On the proposal of the Premier he shall appoint the other members of the Government and shall terminate their functions.

Article 9 The President of the Republic shall preside over the Council of Ministers.

Article 10 The President of the Republic shall promulgate laws . . . he may ask Parliament for a reconsideration of the law or of certain of its articles. This reconsideration cannot be refused.

Article 11 The President of the Republic, on the proposal of the Government . . . or on joint motion of the two Assemblies . . . may submit to a referendum any Bill dealing with the organisation of the public authorities, entailing approval of a Community agreement or providing for authorisation to ratify a treaty which, without being contrary to the constitution, might affect the functions of the institutions . . .

Article 12 The President of the Republic may, after consultation with the Premier and the Presidents of the Assemblies, declare the dissolution of the National Assembly . . .

Article 13 The President of the Republic shall sign the ordinances and decrees decided upon in the Council of Ministers. He shall make appointments to the civil and military posts of the State . . .

Article 14 The President of the Republic shall accredit Ambassadors and Envoys Extraordinary to foreign powers. Foreign Ambassadors and Envoys Extraordinary shall be accredited to him.

Article 15 The President of the Republic shall be commander of the armed forces . . .

Article 16 When the institutions of the Republic, the independence of the nation, the integrity of its territory or the fulfilment of its international commitments are threatened in a grave and immediate manner, and the regular functioning of the constitutional public authorities is interrupted, the President of the Republic shall take the measures required by these circumstances, after official consultation with the Premier, the Presidents of the Assemblies as well as with the Constitutional Council . . .

Article 17 The President of the Republic shall have the right of pardon.

Article 18 The President of the Republic shall communicate with the two Assemblies of Parliament by means of messages which he shall cause to be read and which shall not be the occasion for any debate . . .

Article 19 The acts of the President of the Republic other than those provided for in Articles 8 (1), 11, 12, 16, 18, 54*, 56* and 61* shall be countersigned by the Premier and, should circumstances so require, by the appropriate ministers.

Note:

* These articles relate to appointment to the Constitutional Council and the referral of texts to it.

open and close special sessions of parliament, and the President has, and uses, the right to dissolve Parliament, though not within a year of a previous dissolution.

In foreign relations the President fulfils the traditional function, for a Head of State, of receiving the credentials of foreign ambassadors, and accrediting and recalling French ambassadors abroad (Article 14). Article 52 of the constitution retains phrases used in previous constitutions to provide that the President ratifies international treaties, and the 1958 constitution also specifies that he negotiates them. To these traditional concepts the Fifth Republic added the strength of the formula found in Article 5, which insists that the President is the guarantor of national independence, of territorial integrity and of the observance of treaties and agreements.

The President has the right to authorise the appointment of large numbers of senior officials; Jean Massot (1987) estimates that he signs some 5000 appointments or promotions a year. The procedure is largely formal and automatic, and the most senior appointments require consultation within the Council of Ministers. This power of appointment extends to the armed services. He is chief of the armed services (Article 15), and presides over the two most senior commit-tees concerned respectively with the study of defence problems and the execution of defence policy (Quermonne, 1980, p. 188).

In addition to these powers, which were largely those fulfilled, if essentially in ways which did not constitute the exercise of any real power, by the presidents of the Third and Fourth Republics, the 1958 constitution conferred important new powers upon the President.

First, the constitution specifies that the President is responsible *par son arbitrage* – through his arbitration – for the proper functioning of the public authorities and the continuity of the state. This concept in itself extends the role of the President beyond that of his predecessors.

The role of the President as the guarantor of the state is emphasised in Article 16 which enables him, after consultation with the Prime Minister and the presidents of the Senate, the National Assembly and the Constitutional Council (though he is not obliged to follow the advice he receives), to take the measures required by the circum-stances if there is a serious threat to the institutions of the Republic, the independence of the state, the integrity of its territory or the fulfilment of its international obligations. The President himself, unchecked, may thus decide when such a threat exists and what is to be done. These 'emergency' powers were certainly inspired by de Gaulle's conviction that, had President Lebrun possessed them in

1940 he would have been better able to resist capitulating to the enemy. Parliament automatically reassembles while these powers are in operation, and cannot be dissolved during that time. The powers are potentially immense. They have in fact been used once, between April and September 1961 at the time of an attempted military take-over in Algeria, then still a French colony. Whilst few disputed the need for their use, more controversy was aroused by the length of time they were in operation, which was far longer than the duration of any threat from Algeria.

These draconian, if most exceptional, powers are the clearest departure from the previous pattern. However, the President has other new powers, again linked to the notion of his overall respon-sibility for the functioning of the state. He appoints three members of the Constitutional Council, and may submit proposed legislation or a treaty to the Council for a ruling as to its constitutionality. He may grant or refuse a request that a referendum be held made by either the government or the two houses of Parliament. These powers constitute the formal basis for his authority. They are an important resource, but the nature of his political relationships also contributes to the definition of the role that the president will play at any particular time.

Political Relationships

The political relationships of the President are crucial resources which have enabled him to maintain his role; as the balance of these relationships has changed from time to time, so have some aspects of the President's role. In order to implement a policy programme, the President requires an electoral majority to vote him into office and, potentially, renew his mandate after seven years, a prime minister and government – as Pompidou, then prime minister, told the National Assembly in 1964,[3] 'In the first place, in order to do anything, the President of the Republic needs a government' – and a Parliament that will vote through the legislative measures required.

None of these three resources is unproblematic. The first requires the careful balance, discussed above, between building a sound basis of political support, possibly on the foundation of an organised political party, and avoiding appearing to be so partisan that the President's status 'above politics' is compromised. The role of the prime minister is further discussed in Chapter 4. The key features of the President's relationship to the prime minister are that he has the formal right of appointment (Article 8), and prime ministers have in practice also been dismissed by the President. He also appoints the members of the government on the prime minister's advice.

The President also chairs the weekly meetings of the Council of Ministers (Article 9), and consequently signs such regulations and appointments as have, under Article 13 for example, to be discussed by the Council of Ministers. He is also responsible for other discussions within the Council of Ministers required by the constitution, on bills to be presented to Parliament for instance (Article 39). The President's chairmanship of the Council of Ministers has given him a source of personal political scope which has varied. That it has been perceived as important is evident from the unwillingness of presidents to allow others to deputise for them in the chair. It certainly forces a degree of co-operation between President and prime minister. Throughout much of the Fifth Republic it has been one of the most important ways in which the President has controlled overall governmental policies. No major act which the government plans can avoid the attention, indeed the potential veto, of the president. Votes are not taken, and although on important matters the President might seek the views of all the ministers in turn,[4] his decision is final. When the *cohabitation* governments were implementing a programme to which the President did not subscribe, the President was forced into a more formal role. He did not seek, on policy implementation questions, to impede measures upon which the government had previously decided; equally he did not hesitate to make his doubts about them public (see Massot, 1987, p. 288).

Governmental policy, whether inspired by the President or not, if it requires legislation, has to be voted through Parliament. For much of the Fifth Republic the presence of majorities that would vote the necessary legislation has been a major presidential resource. As we have seen, in the early years of the Fifth Republic, the Algerian War served as an effective substitute for a majority; as long as de Gaulle was desperately needed, his government's policies would be accepted, and the legislation voted through at this period included some major measures, for example on agricultural re-structuring and on education, as well as introducing a number of minor but much needed reforms (a measure aimed at reducing alcoholism, for example) which had long been blocked by the power of vested interests within the Fourth Republic. The general election of 1962 assured a solid majority coalition in support of the President, which lasted broadly until 1981. President Giscard d'Estaing, as a member of a minority party within the coalition found, however, that he could not automatically rely upon unconditional support. Some of his social reform measures – the divorce and abortion law reform bills – were passed only with the support of members of the opposition parties in the National Assembly. After his election in June 1981 President Mitterrand dissolved the National Assembly to which a Gaullist/Giscardian majority had been elected in 1978, and an overall majority of Socialists was returned in the subsequent general election.

Many commentators during that period argued that the voters had recognised what was held to be the inescapable 'logic' of the Fifth Republic. The combination of formal powers and customary practice enshrined within the balance of the institutions ensured the primacy of the President, so it was argued, and the exercise of this primacy equally required that he should be provided with the necessary parliamentary majority. The voters, so it was said, had recognised this, and duly obliged with the necessary choices at the general election.

That this logic was by no means inexorable was demonstrated at the two subsequent general elections. In the 1986 general election a majority opposed to the President was returned, and when in 1988 the President was re-elected, and again promptly dissolved parliament, the voters' choices resulted in a far from clear-cut answer and a government that could not automatically command a parliamentary majority, although Mitterrand had won the Presidential election by a larger margin than in 1981. The crushing defeat of the Left in the 1993 general election presaged the result of the presidential election in 1995. Chirac's victory aligned the political orientation of the presidency and the National Assembly, so no dissolution ensued.

The President and the Media

The early years of the Fifth Republic saw the great expansion of two major means of communication. Television spread relatively late in France. The number of sets installed tripled in the first five years of the Fifth Republic, although still only reaching a quarter of the number in the United Kingdom, and tripled again by 1970 (Ministère de la Culture et de la Communication, 1980, p. 283). At much the same time the exploitation of the transistor meant that small, cheaper, portable radios were also available. The power of these new methods of communication was never more forcefully demonstrated than during the so-called 'battle of the transistors'. In April 1961 a group of army colonels backed by a number of retired generals attempted to organise an armed take-over in Algiers. An important factor in the failure of the attempt was the unwillingness of conscript soldiers to obey officers who supported the take-over, an unwillingness strengthened by the fact that they could and did listen to de Gaulle's personal broadcast appeal against the conspirators.[5]

The ability to use the media as means of direct communication between himself and the citizens has been an important support to successive presidents (see Exhibit 3.3). De Gaulle made use of three types of communication: on grave and important occasions, such as the Algerian putsch noted above, or during the student uprising and general strike of 1968, he would give a direct broadcast address. The tone was invariably solemn and formal, the style designed to express the President's position as the spokesman for all French people.[6] Televised press conferences, dramatic, carefully staged and prepared, took place at regular intervals. Thirdly, presidential travels throughout France – and all the presidents have made frequent 'royal progresses' through *départements* or regions – provide occasions for speeches to large audiences that might contain important policy announcements or political statements.[7]

De Gaulle's successors have continued to use television to address the nation, sometimes, as in the case of Mitterrand during the 1991 Gulf War, with considerable success.[8] Presidents have also continued to hold press conferences, if at a less steady rhythm. A full-blown presidential press conference is a major event, which no doubt explains why President Mitterrand did not hold any during the periods of *cohabitation* (see Exhibit 3.3). It can be argued (Laughland, 1994, p.91) that this represents a decline in the accountability and accessibility of the President. However, styles of broadcasting have evolved since the 1960s, and the formal, stage-managed press conference can look anachronistic. Since the 1970s presidents have made rather more relaxed and informal television appearances, both as participants in regular programmes, such as *L'Heure de Vérité* or the literary programme *Apostrophes*, and through individual interviews. President Mitterrand's televised instant reactions to the August 1991 attempted coup in the Soviet Union failed correctly to anticipate the course of events and constituted a political gaffe which he then sought to remedy by holding a more authoritative press conference a couple of weeks later. In contrast he was generally held to have

---

EXHIBIT 3.3

Presidential press conferences

		Number of conferences
President de Gaulle	1959–69	17
President Pompidou	1969–74	9
President Giscard d'Estaing	1974–81	9
President Mitterrand	1981–91	6

Notable moments of presidential press conferences

May 1962 De Gaulle derided the process of European integration as leading to integrated double dutch (*volapük intégré*)

January 1963 De Gaulle announced veto on UK membership of the European Community

January 1964 De Gaulle described the distribution of power between President and Prime Minister and denied there was a dyarchy

February 1965 De Gaulle spoke of his vision of a Europe from the Atlantic to the Urals

September 1965 De Gaulle said he refused to be a President confined to opening flower shows (*inaugurer des chrysanthèmes*)

March 1972 Pompidou announced a referendum on the enlargement of the European Community

May 1975 Giscard d'Estaing defined his vision of an advanced liberal society

April 1976 Giscard d'Estaing announced that he would not resign even if the Left won the 1978 general election

September 1981 Mitterrand explained that the institutions of the Fifth Republic suited him well

November 1985 With a general election due in 1986, Mitterrand said that France's best interests would be served by pursuing the policy undertaken since 1981

September 1991 Mitterrand discussed the future of Europe and expressed his confidence in Mme Cresson

Source: Adapted from André Passeron (*Le Monde*, 11 septembre 1991).

---

outperformed his rivals in the marathon television programme in support of the 'yes' vote staged at the Sorbonne in the run-up to the Maastricht referendum in 1992, where he answered questions, held a discussion with German Chancellor Helmut Kohl and debated with Philippe Séguin, one of the leaders of the 'no' campaign.

De Gaulle always refused individual press interviews; all his successors have granted such interviews. In addition Giscard d'Estaing published a book, *Démocratie Française* (1976) during his presidency.

President Mitterrand had been a prolific author before his election, but not since.

The President's relationship with the media, which is such a potentially powerful means for him to present his personality, approach and priorities, is managed in two ways. First, the French government enjoyed, until the early 1980s, a very close control over the broadcast media; both radio and television were in the hands of people appointed by the government, and overseen through a Ministry of Information. It was in the field of television that some of the most rapid movement of officials occurred after Mitterrand's 1981 election. Although steps have since been taken to detach broadcasting somewhat from direct governmental influence, connections remain close. Secondly, the presidential office has a presidential spokesperson and a press officer, who keep in touch with journalists, writers and broadcasters.

The Presidential Staff: The Elysée is not the White House[9]

Amongst the most important resources upon which the role and position of the President depend is the presidential staff. The President's official residence is the Elysée Palace. The presidential staff is not a large and administrative department. Many of the 750 or so people who work at the Elysée effectively constitute a household rather than a staff, and are concerned with maintaining the dignity and representational functions of the presidency like the household of any other head of state. They do not necessarily change when the presidency changes hands. There is, however, a small staff who fulfil political and executive, rather than 'domestic' duties. De Gaulle never had more than 33 civilian and thirteen military staff, Pompidou had a maximum of 40 civilians and six military staff, and Giscard d'Estaing's staff, at its largest in 1981 consisted of 24 civilians and seven military members. Mitterrand's staff grew in the course of his time in office, rising from nearly 30 to just under 40 civilians and seven military members. Under Chirac the number declined again, with an initial team of eighteen civilians. Both Mitterrand and Chirac had one of their children on their staff: Mitterrand's son Jean-Christophe was his advisor on African affairs, and Chirac's daughter Claude a *Conseiller* on communications.

Under de Gaulle this staff was divided into four sections: the private office (*cabinet*), the military staff, the secretariat general of the presidency and the secretariat for African and Madagascan affairs.[10] A *cabinet* and a military staff have traditionally formed part of the presidential household. The number of staff in the *cabinet* has varied over time, but has never risen to more than ten. The private office nowadays, as always, is responsible for the President's day-to-day activities – his diary and engagements, his meetings and travels and his personal security. A separate section of the office deals with the daily flood of correspondence from a multitude of private citizens who write in with grievances, requests and suggestions.

Under de Gaulle and Pompidou the role of the military staff was largely confined to assistance with the inevitable military aspect of the representational duties of a Head of State and to liaison between the Elysée and the other institutions concerned with defence. Under Presidents Giscard d'Estaing and Mitterrand the head of the military staff gained a much higher profile. During the Gulf War in the winter of 1991 Mitterrand relied heavily on his military staff to assist him in taking decisions relating to the conduct of the war, during which he 'fully assumed his responsibilities as Commander in Chief'.[11]

De Gaulle made a major innovation by establishing a section of the presidential staff which, in the light of the new role of the Fifth Republic's President, would maintain the President's communication with the state. That section is the general secretariat of the presidency.[12] In general a system which assigns a staff member (*conseiller*) to each large area of activity has persisted since it has proved efficient and limited conflict between staff members (Debbasch *et al.*, 1985, p. 290). Conflicts have not, however, been entirely eliminated, and the system has been diluted and complicated by a proliferation of extra-hierarchical positions. Examples of conflict include the relationship between Jobert, Pompidou's secretary-general and Juillet, his special advisor – Juillet retired indignantly to his sheep-raising activities in central France for months at a time when he felt his voice was not carrying enough weight. Jacques Attali, from his position as special adviser to President Mitterrand, worked with a small group of the staff, who were technically attached to the *cabinet* in more or less official capacities. As a result in the early years of the Mitterrand presidency relationships between the secretary-general and Attali became very poor.[13]

The main functions of the presidential staff, in addition to the day to day running of the President's life, are fourfold. First, the staff ensure that the President is very fully informed of developments in all areas. They do this partly by maintaining a very wide range of contacts within and outside the the administration, partly by attendance as observers at governmental meetings which prepare policy and its implementation, and partly by close liaison with other parts of the administration. Secondly, the staff provide the President with briefings and drafts for his speeches, interviews and other public utterances. Thirdly, the staff provide briefing and advice on all the matters which come before the Council of Ministers, including appointments to senior posts. Fourthly, the staff monitor the progress of policy proposals as the details are formulated and implementation worked out. In these cases the main role of the Elysée staff member is to warn the President if anything is going awry.[14]

The secretary-general of the Elysée plays a key role in all these functions. He[15] is the chief point of contact for the staff of the Prime Minister and of other ministerial private offices. He is the channel through whom advice and information, warnings and suggestions reach the President. He is responsible for the smooth running of the office and often for the choice of those who will work within it. It is vital for the secretary-general to find a concept of his role and a way of managing his relationship with the President that both will find comfortable and congenial. The secretary-general has never been the President's sole adviser, indeed often not even his most important confidante, but in terms of the functioning of the governmental machine in France his role is a central one.

President Pompidou introduced another major element into the structure, by appointing Pierre Juillet to a post outside the hierarchy. Juillet was appointed as *chargé de mission auprès du Président de la République*, a post which gave him a particular status as the President's personal adviser. Pompidou's successors have also each included amongst their staff personal advisors outside the hierarchy. Under de Gaulle only one person came close to fulfilling such a role – Jacques Foccart, a shadowy, somewhat sinister figure, whose connections within the Gaullist Party, and within the French security services ran deep, in addition to his official responsibilities for African and Madagascan affairs. One or two of President Giscard d'Estaing's staff also fulfilled the role of personal political advisers and confidantes. President Mitterrand retained the notion of appointing personal advisors outside the hierarchy, and indeed widened the scope of such appointments. From 1981 until he took up the post of Director of the Bank for European Reconstruction and Development in April 1991 Jacques Attali, civil servant, writer, and member of the Socialist Party's executive committee, was *conseiller spécial auprès du*

Président, occupying as such, both literally and figuratively, a key position in the operations of the Elysée. In addition since 1982 two or three staff members have held the title *conseiller auprès du Président*. This has provided a separate structure for specific functions; for African affairs, for example, for the position was given to Guy Penne from 1982, and subsequently to Jean-Christophe Mitterrand.

It is the presence within the general secretariat of officials concerned, from the President's point of view, with the sectors of governmental activity combined with the presence of advisers whose influence has been perceived as far-reaching, that has encouraged the view that in a certain sense the 'real' government was to be found within the Elysée palace. It is certainly true that the existence of such a staff enables the President to keep a very close eye on governmental projects and initiatives. When ministers are conscious of loyalty to the President the presidential staff have access to key documents and meetings, and can ensure that the general orientation of government policy initiatives is in line with the President's wishes. Where the President wishes to intervene directly his staff constitute the mechanism that enables his intervention to be effective. In some cases indeed, the presidential office may pursue a policy initiative to the exclusion of the ministry concerned, especially where there may be some opposition from that ministry.

The effectiveness of the presidential staff crucially depends upon the other factors which determine the President's relationships with the government. During the periods of *cohabitation* their effectiveness in executive terms was limited. In the first period they were excluded from close contact with the ministries – indeed ministerial staff were instructed by the prime minister to refuse telephone calls from the Elysée, since all contact was to be routed through the prime minister's office. Relationships were better in the second period, but the Elysée's effectiveness was still limited. The staff are influential; they are very competent and immensely hard-working; they are always there, and often closest to the President. In so far as they are not merely influential but powerful, their power is an exact emanation of the President's own position. The President and his staff are at their strongest within the governmental machine when they are successful in uniting all those concerned, especially the Prime Minister and the ministries, around the President's overall political line, approach and style. It is upon his political position and success that the staff rely to convert potential into actual power.

Limitations and Constraints

'The most powerful leader of the Western World', 'An elected monarch' – journalists have used phrases like these to describe the French President. As we have seen, his position as both head of state and, for much of the Fifth Republic, in certain senses head of the government as well, combined with the absence of some of the formal checks and balances which apply to the other prominent leader with similar assessments, the President of the United States, support such characterisations. Nevertheless the President does act within a complex framework of checks and balances. De Gaulle's dominant personality overrode many of them, but changing personalities and changing political circumstance mean that as the regime has matured, the nature of the balance which does exist within it has become clearer. This section examines the checks and constraints which shape and limit the President's ability to develop and impose his policies.

Countersignature

Article 19 of the Constitution specifies that with certain listed exceptions, presidential decisions must be countersigned by the prime minister. The exceptions relate to the appointment of the prime minister, the referendum procedure, the dissolution of Parliament, the assumption of special powers, the transmission of presidential messages to parliament, the nomination of members of the supreme council for the judiciary and the President's relationship with the Constitutional Council. These decisions which the President undertakes on his responsibilty alone are clearly those that de Gaulle, for example, regarded as crucial to the ultimate exercise of power within the state. Nevertheless, apart from the assumption of emergency powers, many of them are also enjoyed by heads of state eleswhere with much more limited roles than that of the President of France, and it is the involvement of the President with a much wider range of decision-making that constitutes the specificity of French presidentialism. The exercise of all the President's other constitutional powers requires the countersignature of the prime minister and any other ministers involved in the application of the decision.

Countersignature in France is a procedural device which fulfils two functions. First, it is conventionally normal, within regimes where the offices of head of state and head of government are formally separated, for the head of state to act in almost all matters on the advice of the government, since only the government can answer for any actions before Parliament. The requirement for countersignature maintains this convention within the French system. Secondly, the provision that governmental or presidential acts must be counter-signed by all the ministers concerned is a formal process which provides for a measure of collective responsibility for policy and its implementation. Under *cohabitation* the impact of countersignature was to reverse the normal direction of relationship at the centre. The initiative now rested with the prime minister, although the President's right of countersignature provided him with some scope for negotiation (Charlot, 1994, p. 195). As with so many other constitutional provisions, the rules can compel behaviour only in the most formal and general ways: but behind the formal procedures is the expectation that they will both reflect and shape much more detailed behaviour.

Constitutionality and Legality

The constitution, as we have seen, gives the President very wide powers, that may, in periods of crisis and emergency, be virtually dictatorial. However, these powers can be exercised only within the framework of the constitution, and there are two bodies in particular which supervise the constitutionality and legality of the President's actions. They are the Council of State (*Counseil d'Etat*) and the Constitutional Council. The necessity of having regard to the views of these bodies constitutes a constraint on the President's ability to use his position and powers in an unfettered way. The outlook and attitude of these bodies has shifted during the period of the Fifth Republic, and their importance has grown. No French President, even with a government and a parliamentary majority behind him, enjoys the same ability to get his own way as the British doctrine of the absolute sovereignty of parliament confers upon a British Prime Minister with a sizeable parliamentary majority.

With the growing maturity of the Fifth Republic and the development of varying ways in which the government's actions can be challenged, the role of the Council of State (see also Chapter 5 below) has become less prominent. However, since the end of the Second World War the Council has developed a doctrine which insists upon the respect of certain fundamental principles, and it has used these to test the validity, especially, of governmental regulations. This practice certainly constitutes a constraint upon the freedom of action of the state. In the early years of the Fifth Republic, when there was very little challenge to the political supremacy of de Gaulle, the Council of State constituted, it has sometimes been argued, one of the few places where a genuine and principled opposition was expressed.

Two episodes illustrate the stand of the Council; first, in 1962 the Council advised de Gaulle that the procedure he proposed to use for the amendment of the Constitution was itself unconstitutional. The government did not in fact pay any heed to this advice, which was given confidentially, but knowledge of it leaked out. Earlier, in 1961, the Council had acted more rapidly and decisively to curb governmental excesses in the *Canal* case (see Exhibit 3.4).

EXHIBIT 3.4

The *Canal* case

In April 1962 General de Gaulle put to a referendum, as the constitution provided, a bill that incorporated the peace agreement reached with the Algerian liberation movement. The bill included provisions allowing the President to make decrees relating to Algerian matters. Using these powers de Gaulle set up, by decree, a Military Court of Justice to judge cases related to the Algerian war and the associated terrorism. No appeal was allowed against the Court's decisions.

André Canal was an active member of the terrorist OAS (*Organisation de l'armée secrète*) which fought against the French Government's policy towards Algeria. He was responsible for a number of bombings. In the Summer of 1962 he was arrested and charged with a bomb attack in which a young child had been injured. On 17 October the Military Court of Justice condemned him to death. He asked for a ruling from the Council of State, which, acting very speedily, since it was supposed that Canal's execution was imminent, on 19 October declared that the decree which had set up the Military Court of Justice was contrary to the general principles of the law, since it allowed for no appeal. It therefore annulled the decree instituting the Court.

De Gaulle was furious. A Committee was set up to 'consider the problems posed by the operation and activities of the Conseil d'Etat'.

In January 1963 the government passed a law through Parliament, giving the force of statute law retrospectively to the decree setting up the Military Court of Justice. However, the law replaced the Military Court of Justice with a State Security Court which contained civilian magistrates, and from which appeal was possible to the Court of Appeal. To that extent the Conseil d'Etat's point of view was vindicated.

Canal's sentence was commuted to life imprisonment, and he was subsequently amnestied as part of the general amnesty for those convicted of crimes related to the Algerian war.

Since the 1960s the Council of State has not found itself faced with such very highly charged cases although its advice may still be sought in difficult circumstances. In 1993, faced with a conflict between its international obligations undertaken in the Schengen agreement and the Constitutional Council's negative ruling on the constitutionality of a bill to implement them, the government asked the Council of State for advice before proceeding to amend the constitution. The Council of State remains crucial in regulating the day to day grievances of the citizen in his or her dealings with the state. However, the Constitutional Council, which initially played a somewhat modest role, has more recently emerged as an important source of limitation and constraint upon the actions of the government. If the impact of the Constitutional Council upon the President's abilities to implement his policy was, during the first fifteen years of the Fifth Republic, minimal, the Council subsequently demonstrated that its potential powers could not be ignored, (see above pp. 54–60). No President, even when he enjoys the support of the governing majority at both national and local levels, can exercise power without keeping a wary eye upon the constitutional framework as the Constitutional Council has defined and applied it. The real importance of the role and activities of the Constitutional Council serves to emphasise the point that the President is a 'constitutional monarch', and the constraints as well as the opportunities which the constitution provides have become steadily more apparent during the lifetime of the Fifth Republic.

The Political Environment

The President is not directly answerable to Parliament, and there is no formal political institution within which his record can be constantly challenged. Moreover, a President's lengthy (seven-year) term of office could potentially provide a considerable degree of insulation from the operation of political and electoral pressures. Nevertheless, the seven-yearly election campaigns cannot be completely forgotten by a President who may seek re-election. Moreover, other election results act as indicators of the standing and legitimacy of the president. Electoral campaigns in France – municipal, *départemental*, regional, national, European – punctuate political life with sometimes bewildering frequency, though seldom in quite such close order as in 1988–9, when presidential, general, local and European elections, and a referendum all occurred within the space of just over a year.

Presidents may wish to be above politics, but the electorate will judge their political performance, as de Gaulle was forced to recognise when, to his chagrin and surprise, he found himself forced into a second round in the 1965 presidential election. Presidents have sought to ensure that the results of parliamentary elections give them a majority within parliament with which they could work to achieve their programmes (Massot, 1987, pp. 204ff). In 1967 and 1968 de Gaulle made it clear that he did not wish to be faced with a Parliament which could prevent him fulfilling his policies, whilst his successors, before each general election, tried to encourage what they thought would be the 'right choice' for the electors. It is perhaps salutary for presidents to ponder the fact that apart from the special circumstances of the Algerian conflict and the events of 1968, all those general elections which have fallen part-way through a presidential term of office (1967, 1973, 1978, 1986, 1993) have seen a fall in the number of seats held by the President's own party. Despite constitutional status and longevity in office, the French President is subject to democratic and electoral constraints.

Public Opinion

Apart from the seven-yearly presidential contests, however, the electoral battles do not impinge directly upon the President. His standing in public opinion polls is an even more indirect and informal means by which public pressure may act as a constraint. Nevertheless, public opinion polling in France is highly organised, well publicised and taken very seriously. The institutes which carry out the polling are advised or directed by leading academic political scientists. Many of the political opinion polls are concerned with the standing of political leaders, and with the popularity of the political parties. One key question, however, relates to the views expressed by those polled of the President, and it is possible to trace the evolution of opinions over the whole period of the Fifth Republic. In 1980, for the first time, a higher percentage of those questioned said that they were unhappy with the President than satisfied with him, a shift in opinion that presaged President Giscard d'Estaing's defeat at the polls in 1981. President Mitterrand's fortunes have been more mercurial (see Portelli, 1987, pp. 330–3). A period when the majority of those polled expressed dissatisfaction with him as President preceded the victory of the right in the 1986 parliamentary elections, but very shortly after that the trend was reversed and the period of *cohabitation* saw a marked improvement in his image, which was followed by his re-election in 1988. His standing in the polls slumped again in 1991, reaching the lowest ever for a French President at the end of that year.

In 1995 President Chirac gained the unenviable record for the shortest post-election honeymoon (see Figure 3.1). The proportion of those polled who expressed satisfaction with him dropped by over 20 percentage points, from 59 to 33 per cent, in the space of three months. Great expectations had been aroused by his campaign, which had promised lower taxes, no constraints on wages and job creation; disappointment when increases in taxation, a very small fall in unemployment and a freeze on public sector pay ensued was correspondingly greater. Matters were not improved by proposals to reform the much cherished, but highly expensive, social security system (see Figure 3.1 and Exhibit 3.5). While a seven-year term of office may seem to provide scope to ignore initially poor ratings, the President could not afford to forget that parliamentary elections were due in 1988.

FIGURE 3.1
Approval ratings of presidents in their first semester

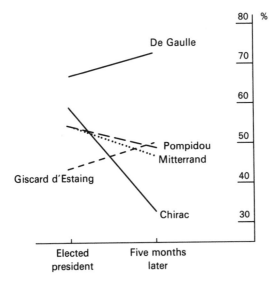

Source: © *The Economist*, London, 30 September 1995.

EXHIBIT 3.5

1995 – discontent and protest

The late autumn of 1995 witnessed an outbreak of social and political discontent and unrest that proved longer lasting and more disruptive than any since 1968. A number of political and public policy issues came together in strikes, demonstrations and protest. The context included the following problems.

- The aftermath of the presidential election of May 1995 (see Figure 3.1). Jacques Chirac's programme had appeared to promise a combination of tax cuts – 'It is possible to cut taxes. . . . Compulsory contributions must be reduced' (Chirac, 1995, p. 19) – and reduced unemployment – 'I cannot accept so many young people, so many executives, unemployed. I am not resigned to the inevitability of long-term unemployment. . . . We must act differently' (Chirac, 1995, p. 11). But between spring and autumn unemployment began to increase, industrial production and sales dropped, the economy scarcely grew.

- Public expenditure levels. Although the minimum wage was increased by four per cent, the Juppé government, in its September budget, raised taxes in an attempt to keep France on course to meet the Maastricht Treaty condition for participation in a European single currency from 1999 of a budget deficit of no more than 3 per cent. A freeze on civil service pay was announced, affecting some five million employees but no other major spending cuts. The money markets lost confidence in the franc after the September budget, and raised interest rates followed.

- Deficits in the social security system. The complex system is composed of a combination of insurance based funds, managed (some critics would say mismanaged) by joint bodies including representatives of employers and unions, and government contributions. It provides generously for pensions and health care and for unemployment benefit.

- Privatisation proposals which included the state-owned telecommunications enterprise, France Telecom. This, combined with requirements imposed by the competition policy of the European Community for greater competitivity, threatened the jobs and working conditions of the employees.

- Conditions in French universities. These were facing continued growth in student numbers, fuelled by success in moving towards meeting government targets of increasing the proportion of the age cohort with the baccalauréat which is the automatic qualification for university entrance, and youth unemployment, which reduces alternative outlets. The universities were crowded, underequipped, poorly housed and indebted.

- A re-emergent terrorist threat. This surfaced in France in the autumn of 1995. There were bomb attacks on the Paris Metro, probably linked to the highly unstable political situation in Algeria. A police clampdown followed.

In October and November 1995 a wave of demonstrations and protest occurred. Students, especially at some of the new smaller universities, demonstrated for better conditions. Talks between the students and the minister of education failed to produce a reasonably speedy settlement. Simultaneously, heavy handed police methods against those who might be Islamic fundamentalist terrorists or sympathisers were producing hostility and violence in the housing estates and suburbs where many of those of North African origin live. When, in October, the police shot dead a young man suspected of involvement with the bombings, riots ensued in the suburb of Lyons from which he came. Civil servants and public sector workers mounted very large marches and demonstrations against their pay freeze. Proposals to reform the social security budget, including an attempt to reduce patients' open access to specialists within the health service, and to extend the qualifying period for receipt of a full pension, met with fierce protests. Public sector employees, including those from France Telecom, and from the railways, where spending cuts threatened reduced state subsidy and hence service and job cuts were at the forefront of the protests. A transport strike stopped rail services, buses and the Metro. Power station workers reduced energy output. By early December nationwide strikes or days of protest were being called by teachers, lorry drivers, postal workers, airline staff, tax officials and even doctors.

The events provided a graphic insight into many of the issues, difficulties and paradoxes of French politics. The government appeared tightly constrained between their European policy, which involved the meeting of the Maastricht single currency convergence criteria and the maintenance of the linkage of the franc to the Deutschmark, and its domestic consequences. The opening up and liberalisation of sectors, from telecommunications to banking, that had previously been much protected by the state, as a consequence of European liberalisation and globalisation caused painful adaptations without a powerful ideological rhetoric to legitimise them. France is no more immune than the rest of Western Europe from the difficulties posed by rising social expectations, and increased costs in medical services and pensions, for example, in a period of recession and global competition. The issues surrounding the repercussions in France of difficulties and conflicts in Algeria were again thrown into sharp focus.

The government appeared incompetent, and the President, who left France for a Francophone summit in Africa in the middle of the crisis, inconsistent and inconstant (see Figure 3.1). But there was great division, both within the governing coalition and in the Socialist Party. Public opinion vacillated. The trade union confederations were by no means solidly united behind the protests, and in any case represent only a small minority of workers, although they are more strongly present in the public sector, which was at the forefront of the protests. The student leadership was inchoate, with no settled programme of demands.

Public opinion polls are seriously conducted and taken seriously, as is evident from the prohibition of the publication of political polls in the week preceding an election, lest voters should be influenced in their choices by the intentions of others. The President's staff includes a staff member with a specific responsibility for interpreting the polls, and indeed commissioning opinion surveys specifically for the President. Opinion polls can, however, at best indicate rather broad trends.

The constitution has provided one mechanism by which the President can seek the opinion of the citizens very directly on a particular question: the referendum (see Exhibit 3.6). Initially confined, under Article 11 of the constitution, to questions about the organisation of public institutions or the ratification of treaties which would affect the operation of public institutions, the right to hold a referendum was, by the constitutional amendment of July 1995, extended to questions concerning economic and social policy and the services which implement these (see below, p. 46). De Gaulle treated referendums primarily as a plebiscitary confirmation of his own standing. In 1958 the referendum which approved the new constitution was essentially a vote of confidence in de Gaulle – discussion of the details of the constitution took a very minor place. The two referendums on Algeria, one, in January 1961, to approve the principle of self-determination, and the second, in April 1962, to accept the Evian agreement which ended the conflict, also clearly demonstrated the electorate's willingness to accept whatever would lead to peace in Algeria and their confidence in de Gaulle's powers to bring it about.

In 1962 a referendum was used to push through the amendment to the constitution that instituted direct elections to the presidency. The reform proposed was controversial, since it could be interpreted as setting the seal on a presidential interpretation of the constitution and a balance of institutions which some of the political parties and groupings, especially those on the Left, were very unwilling to accept. This referendum was also a plebiscite – a vote of confidence in de Gaulle that would legitimise his continuation in power although the immediate crisis he had been brought in to solve had ended. In a broadcast he said as much – if there were only a feeble or doubtful majority in favour of his proposals he would resign. In 1962 the French electorate was not prepared to take that risk.

By 1969 the situation was different. Faced with the enormous challenge to regime, government and his personal standing represented by the student uprising and the general strike of May 1968 de Gaulle's first instinct was again to reconfirm his legitimacy by a referendum. He was dissuaded from this and instead dissolved Parliament and called a general election. A landslide victory for the Right resulted, but the following year de Gaulle again called a referendum (see Exhibit 3.6). His motives were undoubtedly complex. The issue on which the voters were invited to decide was the reform of the upper chamber of Parliament – the Senate. This was linked to a reform of local government that would have given a greater emphasis to regional structures. That de Gaulle attached great importance to these reforms was evident. However, it is probable that de Gaulle wanted in effect to use the referendum to force his own parliamentary majority into adopting policies that they did not want.[16] France had changed since the early 1960s; political life without de Gaulle was no longer unthinkable. Unpopular proposals could not be carried on the strength of the plebiscitary element of the referendum. The proposals were defeated and de Gaulle resigned.

Since 1969 there have been three referendums: in 1972 on the enlargement of the EEC, in 1988 over the future of New Caledonia and in 1992 on the ratification of the Maastricht Treaty of European Union. In 1972 the referendum served clear political purposes. There was little risk of the President being defeated, and their attachment to the ideals of European integration would ensure that the parties of the Centre would align themselves clearly with the Gaullists. On the other hand it was an embarrassment to the Left, for it divided the Socialist Party and placed the Communists, who were clearly opposed to EEC enlargement, in conflict with at least part of the Socialist Party. Pompidou had not made the outcome a resigning issue, and indeed 68 per cent of those who voted (comprising, however, only 36 per cent of the electorate) supported him. But the high rate of abstentions was much commented upon, and the President could not draw from this result an overwhelming confirmation of his position. Thereafter, until the 1980s, presidents preferred to rely upon the normal calendar of elections and the representative institutions rather than direct approaches to the population to confirm and legitimise their policies.

EXHIBIT 3.6

Referendums in the Fifth Republic

	Subject	Result
September 1958	Proposed constitution	Approved
January 1961	Self-determination for Algeria	Approved
April 1962	Independence for Algeria	Approved
October 1962	Constitutional amendment: direct election of the President	Approved
April 1969	Reform of the Senate and creation of regions	Rejected
April 1972	Enlargement of the European Community	Approved
November 1988	Future of New Caledonia	Approved
September 1992	Ratification of the Maastricht Treaty of European Union	Approved

---

In 1984 President Mitterrand found his legitimacy severely challenged by two events: the rather poor showing of the Left in the direct elections to the European Parliament, and the very large demonstrations against his government's educational reform bill, which eventually resulted in its withdrawal. The opposition, seeking to benefit from the resistance to the bill despite the Left's parliamentary majority, called for a referendum on the issue. This the majority would not concede. Nor did the President concede a dissolution, but instead suggested a referendum on an issue – the revision of Article 11 of the constitution to widen the issues on which the President can directly call a referendum to include laws related to civil liberties – on which he was virtually certain to gain a majority. Suspecting a strengthening of presidential legitimacy which an endorsement by referendum of any policy of his would ensure, the politically hostile Senate refused to support the idea and it was abandoned. Proposals to hold a referendum had become a weapon in a rhetorical battle over legitimacy, and the result was stalemate.

In 1988 the referendum over New Caledonia took its inspiration from the Algerian referenda of the early years of the Fifth Republic, and was intended both to endorse the position of the minority Socialist government under Prime Minister Rocard, and to endow the careful solution of the problem of the future of New Caledonia at which he had arrived with sufficient backing to ensure that it would be stable and entrenched. In these fairly limited objectives it seemed to succeed.

In marked contrast the 1992 referendum on the ratification of the Maastricht Treaty amplified the political difficulties of both government and opposition. It opened up political cleavages in ways which had effects well beyond the scope of the referendum. It is probable that at least some of these effects were intended: it is equally probable that many of them were not. The constitutional amendments required to permit the application of the terms of the Treaty had passed with little difficulty, and the Treaty could have been ratified by a parliamentary vote. Mitterrand took the decision to utilise the alternative method of ratification allowed for in the constitution and put the Treaty to referendum. This decision was taken in the context of opinion polls showing a comfortable majority of French people in favour of greater European integration, combined with evident disarray amongst the parties of the opposition on the issue, revealed by the constitutional amendment procedure. Public support for the Treaty declined rapidly during the campaign, and voters conspicuously failed to follow the advice of the party leaders. The leaders of the opposition parties (the RPR and the UDF) eventually, and warily, ensured that their parties officially made common cause in favour of a 'yes' vote, but prominent politicians from those parties campaigned vigorously for a 'no' vote. Mitterrand was himself obliged to play a notable part in the campaign, but did not receive the endorsement of his position – and by extension of his flagging government – which had no doubt been intended. The result was approval by a bare majority (51 per cent) but the political repercussions were felt in the parliamentary, European and presidential elections of subsequent years (see Chapter 9).

These difficulties and their impact illuminate some of the reasons why the development of presidential government has come less and less to rely upon a direct dialogue between President and people through the plebiscitary mechanism of a referendum. For much of the Fifth Republic representative democracy and its expression through political parties has proved more stable and acceptable. President Chirac's extension of the possibilities for the use of the referendum is thus the more surprising. It harks back, first, to the unsuccessful call by the then opposition for a referendum on schools policy in 1984.

That policy issue returned to the centre of political debate under the Balladur government in 1993, and from then on Chirac had campaigned on the promise of a referendum which he suggested would allow progress in areas where parliamentary processes had resulted in deadlock. It also revives a quite specifically Gaullist theme, reverting to a more presidential view of the constitution, within which an alliance of President and voters could potentially outweigh a Parliament which has, over the last two decades, steadily been increasing its importance (see Chapter 7). But a referendum is always a gamble, and presidents have to work within the political complexities that may ensue.

Presidential Practice

Within the framework of the resources and constraints described above presidential practice has been shaped by the individual priorities and perceptions of the presidents, and by the political situations of the moment. It has throughout been characterised by two major features – a high degree of autonomy on the part of the President, and equally a high degree of flexibility in the way in which the demands and opportunities of the office have been characterised.

The President has never been seen as part of a team. Nor has he been encompassed by any notion of collective responsibility. When the President has been effectively the head of a governmental majority, a great deal of government business has been conducted either directly by the President, or by the President in conjunction with an individual minister.

In certain spheres where this presidential autonomy has been particularly marked it has sometimes been argued that the combination of constitutional powers and traditional expectations gave the President a particular sphere in which he could and should act quite alone: foreign affairs, relations with Francophone Africa and defence can be seen as major components of this *domaine réservé* – protected area. The exigencies of the period meant that in the early years of de Gaulle's presidency these areas were particularly high amongst his priorities. De Gaulle, however, later denied that he had entertained any notion of a protected area.[17]

Presidents have always intervened in the large programmes of governmental policy. President Pompidou, for example, defined and sustained the industrial policy that furthered the development of large companies and the identification of 'national champions'. It is said that he summoned the head of the large electrical firm Jeumont Schneider and told him that the head of another large electrical firm wished to merge his company with Jeumont Schneider. Pompidou said he would like to see negotiations to this effect take place so that France would have one truly giant enterprise in that area. The industrialist was shocked (Suleiman, 1978, p. 262). It was President Giscard d'Estaing's personal impetus that produced the abortion and divorce reforms of the mid-1970s. All the presidents have had a particular interest in the embellishment and cultural development of Paris, and the nature of large scale projects there has been largely due to direct presidential decisions. President Pompidou set the construction of the Pompidou Centre under way. President Giscard d'Estaing initiated the conversion of the Gare d'Orsay from redundant railway station to stunning museum. President Mitterrand insisted upon the removal of the Ministry of Finance from the Louvre buildings, the extension of the museum and the construction of the great glass entrance pyramid in the courtyard, and the building of the Opera House at the Bastille as well as the highly controversial and expensive national library (Collard, 1992).

If the buildings presidents commission constitute particularly visible and evident reminders of the scope of presidential action, they should be seen as symbols for a much broader scope of activity which goes well beyond merely setting the general orientation of policy. It should not be forgotten that Presidents Chirac, Mitterrand, Giscard d'Estaing and Pompidou had all had considerable experience as ministers, and in the case of these last two this experience was recent and extensive. Both Pompidou and Chirac had been prime ministers. Presidents have intervened decisively in economic, industrial, social and cultural policies, and have always been willing to step in when a matter has been either highly contentious, or particularly close to their personal concerns – the withdrawal by President Mitterrand of the Savary education bill in 1984, and President Pompidou's intervention to protect the place of Latin in the school curriculum are examples of interventions of this kind in an area which has not on the whole attracted much presidential attention.

In undertaking such intervention the President is able to exploit various resources. His chairmanship of the Council of Ministers means that he is fully aware of the future agenda of the government. The participation of staff members in a large number of governmental meetings, at ministerial and official level, means that, except during *cohabitation*, he is likely to be fully briefed on proposed developments. Moreover the President himself may hold meetings with small groups of ministers to discuss a particular issue – the so-called *conseils restreints* – and all presidents have held regular meetings, normally at least once a week, with the prime minister. Even if the President's active intervention in the day to day conduct of the government hardly accorded with the intention of the constitutional definitions of the prime minister's role, because the government and the parliamentary majority acquiesced in the situation there was, between 1958 and 1986, no constitutional, institutional or political way of distinguishing between governmental and presidential decisions (Luchaire *et al.*, 1989, p. 143).

There have been circumstances in which the President's autonomy has been greatly reduced. Presidential practice has responded to these with the flexibility which has proved to be its other leading characteristic. If the period when President Giscard d'Estaing issued presidential directives to the government, in the form of biannual open letters setting out the government's programme of work for the next half-year, marked a particularly high point of presidential pre-eminence, the period of *cohabitation* required a rather different type of presidentialism.

The first major step which indicated a new form of presidentialism was Mitterrand's decision to ask the leader of the party which had gained the highest number of seats in the 1986 election, Jacques Chirac, to form a government. Whilst it became clear that the President did retain an ability effectively to veto the appointment by the new prime minister of certain individuals to certain governmental posts, the recognition by the President of a democratic imperative, and the renunciation of any attempt to continue presidential pre-eminence, through a minority government, for example, marked a clear evolution. The President's strategy in this period and again in 1993–5, was to retain his status in those areas with which the President had traditionally been closely associated. Hence he continued to attend meetings of the heads of government of the seven major economic powers (G7), for instance in Tokyo soon after the election, and of the European Council. Some confusion in protocol resulted, from which the prime minister emerged the loser. Balladur heeded the lesson and refrained from accompanying Mitterrand to the G7 meeting in July 1993 (Mény, 1993, p. 102). In foreign relations and in matters of defence, where it clearly remained the

President whose finger would ultimately be 'on the button', he was not prepared to relinquish his standing. Equally, the major construction and cultural projects associated with the presidency – the pyramid of the Louvre and the Opera at the Bastille – went forward, if not without controversy.

On day-to-day matters, however, the President carefully dissociated himself from the actions of the government. Mitterrand took various opportunities to express an implied, if fairly direct, criticism of the government's actions, without formally overstepping the strict constitutional proprieties. Thus in July 1986 he refused to sign the governmental decrees launching a programme of privatisation and economic liberalisation. He did so again in October and in December 1986, on measures relating to electoral boundaries and to flexible working hours. In all three cases the effect was to oblige the government to take the issues back to parliament as specific laws, and once they had, not without some trouble, been duly passed there, the President had no option but to promulgate the laws. Equally he refused to allow discussion of a change in the status of the nationalised Renault car company to be discussed in a special session of Parliament called for early 1988 specifically to consider a new law on the financing of political parties. Similarly, he prevented a bill on subsidies for church schools from coming before a special session in 1993. In all these instances the President was careful to obstruct the government only in ways which the constitution legitimised: he depended upon legal exactitude to reinforce his personal stance.

President Mitterrand did, however, take other opportunities to criticise the government, either in speeches where he took pains to defend past achievements, or through actions such as his reception at the presidential palace of a deputation of striking railwaymen in the winter of 1987. For Mitterrand personally the strategy worked. His popularity in the opinion polls rose sharply and stayed high: in 1988 he was re-elected, by an increased majority. Public opinion about *cohabitation* had fluctuated but Mitterrand's popularity had remained generally higher under *cohabitation* than during the period before 1986 (see Figure 3.2). Patience, a degree of detachment and immense political astuteness enabled him to emerge as the winner from the period.

Mitterrand's re-election and the return of a Socialist government in 1988, though not of an overall Socialist majority in the National Assembly, did not immediately much alter the President's stance. His electoral programme – the *Letter to All the French People* – was

FIGURE 3.2
Public confidence in President Mitterrand, June of each year
(positive opinions in percentages)

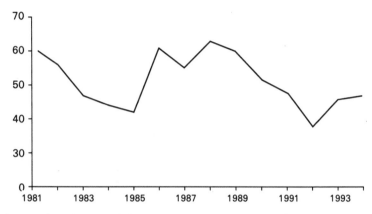

Source: Compiled from BVA/*Paris Match* polls.

extremely vague as a policy programme, although under Prime Minister Rocard such policy proposals as it did contain were implemented (see Elgie, 1991, p. 18). The popularity of the prime minister equalled or exceeded that of the President for a good part of 1989 and early 1990. It seemed that a balance of power much closer to that envisaged by some of the authors of the constitution was emerging, and not only under *cohabitation*. At least under Mitterrand any return to the dominance of presidential policy direction such as had characterised the period of Giscard d'Estaing seemed improbable and it was possible to speculate that a new style had been set.

However, the second half of 1990 and the beginning of 1991 was marked by the Gulf crisis and war. The predominant position of the President in foreign and defence affairs meant that Mitterrand took the leading role in France in the conduct of the war, having conducted a very high profile international diplomatic effort to try to avert its outbreak. Moreover the impact on France of recession and rising unemployment, which had reached over 2.8 million by the end of the year was important. President Mitterrand's replacement of Michel Rocard as prime minister by Mme Edith Cresson who, unlike Rocard, was known to be politically close to the President, seemed to mark a return to a more active political role by the President, concerned by the falling ratings of the Socialist Party in the opinion polls and the (accurate) predictions of disaster for the Socialists in the local elections in the Spring of 1992 and the general election of 1993.

This period served as a reminder that when international events play a major role on the political scene – for the Gulf War was followed by the civil war in Yugoslavia and by the conclusion and ratification of the Maastricht Treaty – the President cannot take a back seat. It also served as a cautionary tale. Despite his initiative in changing the government, and also in suggesting measures of constitutional reform within a couple of months of the appointment of Mme Cresson, public approval not only of the government but also of the President plummeted. Edith Cresson was hastily replaced by Pierre Bérégovoy, but nothing could avert the rout of the Socialists in 1993.

Between 1986 and 1988 the relationship between President and government was sharpened by the expectation that both President Mitterrand and Prime Minister Chirac would be – as indeed they were – candidates in the presidential elections of 1988, and by the continued presence of a substantial Socialist presence in Parliament. In 1993 Mitterrand was not expected to be a candidate in 1995 and nor, at first, was Balladur. Balladur's stately personality, compared to Chirac's combative approach, as well as Mitterrand's encroaching illness, may also have contributed to the impression that *cohabitation* was becoming a calmer, more normal, aspect of French politics. The advent and presidential style of Jacques Chirac, supported by a large majority in the National Assembly, and choosing a prime minister, Alain Juppé, who had long been a colleague, both in the Gaullist Party and as deputy mayor in Paris, proved, as in 1988, that periods of *cohabitation* are interludes which may inflect and shape the evolution of presidential practice, but do not fundamentally alter it.

Presidential practice undoubtedly evolved and changed throughout the 1980s. De Gaulle was able to exploit his dominance to stamp his own interpretation indelibly upon the presidency. But it was the political conditions of the time that made this possible. After 1981 the possibility of real changes in the tenure of power at the centre became a feature to be reckoned with in French political life, and the constraints and limits upon governmental and presidential practice assumed a greater political importance. President Mitterrand's approach to the exercise of presidential power responded to the conditions in which he found himself. Even before the 1986 elections some observers detected the emergence of a less interventionist and more aloof presidency. Similarly, the development of a more parliamentary application of the constitution has been a longer-term process spanning the periods of *cohabitation*. In some senses *cohabitation* merely made the underlying changes in some of the assumptions upon which behaviour was based more obvious and explicit.

The style of the exercise of presidential power has certainly changed, though it is likely that future presidents will find that it still offers a great deal of scope for flexible, if politically hazardous, interpretation. Over the past decade the checks and balances inherent in the system that was created in 1958 have become more prominent. It seems likely that future presidents will have to reckon not only with the opportunities and extent of presidential power, but also with its limitations and boundaries.

4

The Governmental Machine

The constitution of France provides a distinct role for the government, and specifies that the prime minister is the head of that government. Even throughout the periods when the President has dominated politics and policy the government has had a major role in the formation and execution of policy in many areas. This chapter examines the structure and working of that machinery from the political viewpoint; Chapter 5 looks at the workings of government from an administrative angle. This chapter is concerned with the nature and role of the prime minister and the ministers of the government; with the French 'machinery of government' – that is, the structure and functions of the various ministries and departments; and with the mechanisms for co-ordination between them.

The Prime Minister: Position and Power

The Scope of Prime Ministerial Power

The office of prime minister in France might at first sight appear to have been one of the casualties of the Fifth Republic. In 1964, speaking in a debate in the National Assembly, François Mitterrand, then an opposition member attacking the balance of the institutions of the Fifth Republic, said to the prime minister, 'You are, I recognise, a victim of the system imposed on you.'[1] Under the Fourth Republic the prime minister, then known as the President of the Council of Ministers, however brief his incumbency, was the pre-eminent political figure. The President of the Republic seemed to have a more shadowy and ceremonial role and the ministers owed their offices to prime ministerial choice. Under the Fifth Republic de Gaulle's choice of the presidency as his role marked it out from the start as a major focus of political power. The government at that time seemed to be 'his' government, and to some observers the prime minister seemed little more than a chief of staff, dealing with the humdrum domestic details whilst the President concerned himself with the major affairs of the nation. De Gaulle himself disliked the use of the term '*chef du gouvernement*' to designate the prime minister who was rather to regard himself or herself, as the appellation under the new constitution suggested, as the first amongst the ministers.

This perception of diminished power for the prime minister is, however, in many ways misleading. The prime ministers of the Fourth Republic operated within multiple constraints. The first was the necessity of putting – and holding – together a coalition government. The opportunities then available to Parliament to hamper the enactment of policies or to propose alternative courses of action made the taking of determined initiatives a hazardous business. In the end the legitimacy of the government was so weakened that the prime minister's wishes could be openly flouted, for example by the army. With very few exceptions – most notably Pierre Mendès France – the Fourth Republic's prime ministers were largely forced to exercise their role chiefly as brokers and mediators between conflicting interests, rather than as possessors of power and legitimacy. They might well encounter a greater length of tenure in office and claim to position amongst their ministers than they themselves enjoyed. The brevity of so many prime ministers' periods in office between 1946 and 1958 emphasises the limitations within which they acted.

The prime ministers of the Fifth Republic in fact reaped the benefit of the changes which resulted from the rejection of the previous pattern. The limitations on the power of Parliament (see Chapter 7) have freed them from the uncertainties provoked by shifting coalitions. The extension of executive power and the reinforcement of the role of the government have increased the scope and legitimacy of the prime minister as the leader of the government. The development of the party system (see Chapter 8) and the advent of governments based securely upon a dominant party have given some of the Fifth Republic's prime ministers a strong political base and have enhanced the standing of the office. In all these respects prime ministers of the Fifth Republic have been more secure, and more legitimate than their predecessors of the Fourth Republic, and they have enjoyed greater freedom of action and a stronger pre-eminence within the government.

The Prime Minister and the President

It is a particular feature of the French political system, however, that governmental and political power is characterised by a duality at the top (Fournier, 1987, p. 53). The constitution specifically provides for a sharing of power, and in effect forces President and prime minister to co-operate. The functioning of the Cabinet (Council of Ministers), the preparation of legislative texts, senior appointments, and the conduct of certain policy areas cannot proceed, if only because of the requirements of countersignature, unless President and prime minister manage to find methods of working together. In the periods during which the presidential majority which had brought the President into power was broadly the same as the governmental majority resulting from the general election the pre-eminence of the President was evident, and the sharing of power tended to be based largely on practice and convenience, rather than on any strict interpretation of the constitutional texts. The periods of *cohabitation* have proved that such a sharing remains possible, even when based upon the assertion of the legal powers of the two parties and their independent spheres.

Nevertheless, the necessary co-existence between President and prime minister has not always been easy or without tensions. The relationships between Presidents and their successive prime ministers have been marked by a shifting balance of prestige and influence, related both to the political circumstances of the time, and to the personalities and expectations of the incumbents (see Elgie and Machin, 1991, pp. 73–4). Constitutionally President and Prime Minister, once an initial choice has been made, are condemned to live together; the President appoints the prime minister, but has no formal right of dismissal. In practice prime ministers have been dismissed (Debré in 1962, Pompidou in 1968, Chaban-Delmas in 1972, Mauroy in 1984, Rocard in 1991 and Cresson in 1992). Usually it has been clear that the prime minister concerned has agreed from the outset that he would not stay in office if the President required his resignation (Massot, 1987, p. 233).

The relationship, between five presidents and fifteen prime ministers – see Exibit 4.1 – has been characterised by a number of factors.

- First, whenever political and electoral support for the President found its expression in an electoral majority in the country both for him and for a government that would broadly support his policies, the pre-eminence of the President was assured. All the prime ministers who operated under these conditions expressed the view that the confidence of the President was essential to them (Massot, 1987, p. 233).

- Secondly, however, prime ministers cannot dispense with the support of the National Assembly. Pierre Mauroy recognised this in 1982 when he said that without the double approval of the President and the National Assembly, 'which both benefit from the legitimacy conferred by universal suffrage', the prime minister would be unable to continue in office. It was this factor which President Mitterrand acknowledged in 1986, when he chose to ask Jacques Chirac, leader of the largest party in the Assembly, to become the prime minister, rather than seeking a prime minister who might have been politically closer to himself, and have been able to form a minority government, but who would not have represented the electorate's choice.

- Thirdly, prime ministers have been chosen from a variety of backgrounds. There is no single pre-requisite for office. Some have come into power from a clearly political base – Chaban-Delmas had deep roots within the Gaullist party, as did Pierre Mauroy within the Socialist Party, and both were very long-standing mayors of large towns, an office which involves a great deal of political and executive autonomy and management. Debré and Fabius were both close personal associates of the President. Some prime ministers, Pompidou, Couve de Murville, Barre, had never contested a parliamentary seat before they became prime minister, though both Couve de Murville and Barre had previous ministerial experience. More striking is the fact that out of fifteen prime ministers only Barre, Mauroy, Cresson and Bérégovoy had not held a post as a top administrative civil servant at some point in their career, and Barre had been a university professor (which in France is a civil service post) and a Commissioner of the European Communities. Five of the prime ministers (Chirac, Fabius, Rocard, Balladur, Juppé) are graduates of the elite civil service training school, the Ecole Nationale d'Administration, which their predecessor Michel Debré had founded in 1946.

- Fourthly, Elgie (1993, p. 166) classifies the relationships of prime ministers to presidents into three types: subordinate, a category in which he includes all of de Gaulle's prime ministers; rival; and opponent, this latter category covering the prime ministers of *cohabitation*. However, not only does each relationship have its own particular nuances – the opponent relationship between Mitterrand and Chirac was not the same as that between Mitterrand and Balladur – but the relationships may change during the period in office. Even when the President has sought to minimise any challenge to his own political pre-eminence by appointing a prime minister whose administrative qualifications and qualifications and lack of a personal political power base seemed to qualify him for an essentially ' chief of staff' role, that prime minister has increasingly taken on a political role. The two most telling examples of this evolution are Georges Pompidou and Raymond Barre. Both were appointed from essentially non-political backgrounds, and became major political leaders, building up party support, and emerging themselves as presidential candidates – one successful, one unsuccessful. Similarly, the post of prime minister proved the inspiration for Balladur's candidacy in the 1995 presidential elections. Presidents and political colleagues have had to reckon with the fact that the post of prime minister provides a basis and a standing which are an excellent spur and support to presidential ambitions.

EXHIBIT 4.1

The prime ministers of the Fifth Republic

Michel Debré	January 1959 – April 1962
Georges Pompidou	April 1962 – July 1968
Maurice Couve de Murville	July 1968 – June 1969
Jacques Chaban-Delmas	June 1969 – July 1972
Pierre Messmer	July 1972 – May 1974
Jacques Chirac	May 1974 – August 1976
Raymond Barre	August 1976 – May 1981
Pierre Mauroy	May 1981 – July 1984
Laurent Fabius	July 1984 – March 1986
Jacques Chirac	March 1986 – May 1988
Michel Rocard	May 1988 – May 1991
Edith Cresson	May 1991 – April 1992
Pierre Bérégovoy	April 1992 – April 1993
Edouard Balladur	April 1993 – May 1995
Alain Juppé	May 1995 –

The Functions of the Prime Minister

The Prime Minister's Governmental Role

According to General de Gaulle, the role of the Prime Minister was to direct, coordinate and oversee (*orienter, coordonner, suivre*) (Claisse, 1972, p. 170) the actions of the other ministers. For much of the first three decades of the Fifth Republic this direction and control took place within a framework laid down by the President. In 1972 one commentator (Claisse, 1972, p. 171) could note that it was not so much a question of following orders as developing and implementing ideas. During the presidency of Giscard d'Estaing, however, this function seemed more to resemble the carrying out of orders. For instance, at a time when presidentialism was at its height Prime Minister Barre, presenting his political programme to Parliament in 1977, spoke of fulfilling the tasks which the President had set him, and indeed from 1975 until the end of 1980 the President periodically set out, in eight public letters, the programme of work which he expected the government to follow (Massot, 1987, pp. 240–3).

Under the Socialist governments, between 1981 and 1986 and after 1988, whilst the President did decide upon the governmental agenda and priorities in conjunction with the prime minister the exact content of the programme was not made public, and the action lost its presidentialist symbolism. During *cohabitation* it was the prime minister who took the lead in defining the governmental agenda, at the monthly meetings of all the ministers that were held without the President.

The prime minister's powers of direction and coordination are particularly important in a system which does not incorporate a strong notion of the collective responsibility of the government. French ministers come from varied political and career backgrounds; all governments have included ministers from a number of parties; they may be held together by a loyalty to the President or, as under *cohabitation*, to the idea of a government of a particular political conception, but there is no convention in the written constitution nor in constitutional practice that requires them to act in a unified way, and conflicts may be fierce and public, whether over policy issues or political stances. For this reason the prime minister has a key role to play. He or she may try to minimise dissent. Michel Rocard, for example, on his appointment in 1988 announced his intention of ensuring the coherence and propriety of government action by issuing periodic general circulars to all ministers. Amongst the topics subsequently covered by circulars were the government's European policy, and the measures to be taken for the modernisation of the civil service. The prime minister's role goes a very long way beyond exhortation and encouragement, however. The structure of the French governmental machine means that a great deal of policy is coordinated, settled and decided by *arbitrage*, a process of hierarchical decision making which involves the ministers concerned bringing the matter to the prime minister, and setting out their case for his or her decision. This occurs in many policy areas (see Elgie, 1993, p. 153), not only in the most institutionalised of the areas of conflict, that is the preparation of the estimates of public spending, where the prime minister makes the final decisions wherever the Ministry of Finance has been unable to reach agreement with a spending ministry.

The Prime Minister's Administrative Role

The Prime Minister has administrative functions attached to his office, and a number of junior Ministers with special responsibilities form part of his department. The central role and the prestige of the Prime Minister's office have ensured that four types of administrative work are attached to it (Massot, 1979; and Fournier, 1987, p. 152): first, the central role of servicing the collective action of the government is attached to the Prime Minister's office. This role is fulfilled by the General Secretariat of the Government. Although General de Gaulle ensured that the General Secretariat worked with the President in setting the agenda for the weekly cabinet meetings and servicing them, the location of the General Secretariat in his office means that the prime minister cannot be ignored or bypassed in this field. The Mitterrand government in 1981 maintained in office the General Secretary of the Government who had served its Giscardian predecessor. Indeed, it was subsequently acknowledged that the then General Secretary, M Marceau Long, had greatly assisted the incoming government in handling the unprecedented problems of a complete hand-over of power. However, in 1986 Chirac, perhaps distrusting the close association with the President of the incumbent, Jacques Fournier, who had come into the post from the presidential staff, succeeded in having him replaced, a move which has, however, not been repeated by subsequent incoming governments.

Secondly, there are co-ordinating functions which potentially concern almost all government departments; the co-ordination of government policy towards the European Community is one of these, and the body responsible for this – the General Secretariat of the Interministerial Committee for questions of European Economic Cooperation (SGCI) – is attached to the prime minister's office. Until 1988 the Minister for the Civil Service and for Administrative Reform was normally a junior minister under the prime minister.[2] Official printing and publication also come under the prime minister.

Thirdly administrative tasks have been embarked upon, at different periods, which have been deliberately designed to cut across existing administrative boundaries, and ensure rapid and fruitful action. The prime minister, wishing to give a high status and political encouragement to these activities, has attached them to his own office (Fournier, 1987, pp. 157–8).

In most cases this attachment has proved to be a transitional one, even if sometimes of quite lengthy duration, which has led on to more independent ministerial status. The subsequent fate of the administration concerned has depended upon the degree of political status and priority accorded to it at any period. The Economic Planning Commission, founded in 1946, was for a long period attached to the prime minister's office. The interministerial nature of the Commission's responsibilities and the need for it, if it were to be effective at all, to have an institutional position of sufficient status to allow for some balancing of the Ministry of Finance, combined, initially with its political importance as a symbol and motor of post-war reconstruction, and subsequently with the weight of tradition, to explain this continued central attachment for the Plan. It became an independent ministry with a minister of cabinet rank (Michel Rocard) in the early years of the Mitterrand presidency. When Rocard himself became prime minister he took it back into his own department, with a junior minister in charge. After a period of eclipse it is placed in the Juppé government under a cabinet minister for economic development and the Plan.

In contrast to the Economic Planning Commission, the organisation concerned with spatial planning and regional development, the *Délégation à l'aménagement du territoire et à l'action régionale* (DATAR), rose in status in the early 1990s, reflecting perhaps the growing role of local and regional initiatives since the decentralisation reforms of 1983. The promotion of scientific research and care for the environment were also both launched from the prime minister's office. All these bodies experienced attachment for a period to another ministry, sometimes reverting thereafter to the prime minister's office, and became, in early 1990s, the responsibilities of ministers of full cabinet rank.

In general the collection of responsibilities which accrues around the prime minister in this way can be heterogeneous and unwieldy, reflecting as it does the specific political exigencies and the particular priorities of the government of the day. Thus the priority attached to the repression of alcoholism (in the 1950s) and drug addiction (in the 1980s), the promotion of road safety or the problems of urban deprivation (in the 1990s) has in each case resulted in the setting up of a body serviced within the prime minister's office. In each case these responsibilities were transferred to the appropriate sectoral ministry after a few years. The Mission to organise the 1989 celebrations of the bicentenary of 1789 was also, despite the obvious interest of the President, attached to the prime minister's office. Periodic reorganisations result in the removal of some of these bodies from the prime minister's jurisdiction although others remain so clearly in disputed territory between ministries that there is no other home for them.

The fourth administrative activity attached to the prime minister's office is the provision of administrative support for a number of autonomous institutions. The staff of the *médiateur de la république* (ombudsman), of the committee for access to official documents (freedom of information) and the broadcasting authority are for organisational purposes carried on the budget of the prime minister's office.

The Political Role of the Prime Minister

The President of France has developed a style of political leadership that has emphasised detachment from party. In so far as he can formally be held to account for his actions and political programme, it has been, since the abandonment of the use of referendums for this purpose (see Chapter 3) through the seven-yearly presidential elections, and he is accountable directly, and hence in the broadest way, to the citizens at large, and then only if he chooses to stand for re-election. The President does not account to Parliament for his actions: he cannot be invited to attend debates, he does not speak in them, he cannot be questioned by members of Parliament. The prime minister has a crucial political role, whatever his or her relationship with the presidency, though clearly its balance and intensity alters during periods of *cohabitation*.

The political role of the prime minister has three aspects: in relation to the government, for whose political cohesion he or she is largely responsible; in relation to Parliament, where the government must carry its programme and to some degree account for its actions, and in relation to the party or parties that support the government.

In seeking to ensure the political cohesion of the government the prime minister operates under a number of handicaps:

- He or she may not be solely responsible for the composition and nature of his team, whose careers certainly do not depend merely upon his or her decisions. From the presidency of General de Gaulle onwards the President has played a key role in the appointment of ministers, despite the prime minister's formal responsibility. General de Gaulle was in the habit of naming those whom he wished to see in the key posts – defence, foreign affairs, the interior – and ensured the continuation in office from 1959 to the end of his presidency of André Malraux as Minister of Culture. President Pompidou is alleged to have concerned himself individually with every ministerial appointment (Antoni and Antoni, 1976, p. 39) and Françoise Giroud's memoirs document in amusing detail the conflict between President Giscard and Prime Minister Chirac over the status of her appointment in 1974 as minister for women. Even a prime minister hostile to the President proved not to have an entirely free choice of his own governmental team. In March 1986 President Mitterrand strongly and effectively opposed the appointment of certain leading figures to those posts closely linked to the constitutional sphere of presidential action, foreign affairs and defence. Reshuffles may involve compromises. In the governmental reshuffles of 1990, for example, two ministerial departures (including that of Edith Cresson who was appointed prime minister the following year) were attributed to the wishes of the prime minister, two new appointments to the wishes of the President, and one more was alleged to have served the (different) interests of both. As one commentator said, there could be no better demonstration of the need for agreement between President and prime minister.[3]
- He or she does not necessarily, or indeed usually, combine party leadership with the role of prime minister. He or she cannot, therefore, automatically count upon the party loyalty of his governmental team which may include members with powerful

individual political power bases of their own. Pompidou, as prime minister, and Jacques Chirac after him both handled this problem by ensuring that they used their prime ministerial position to ensure their dominance within their party – Jacques Chirac took over as Secretary General of the Gaullist party during his term of office in December 1974. In 1976 he was replaced as prime minister by Raymond Barre who intended to concentrate upon dealing with economic and social problems. His government included leaders of the main coalition groupings, with a senior status, in the hope that they would be able, within the government, to contain and handle inter-party conflict. The experiment was not a happy one, and proved that a prime minister cannot with impunity simply abdicate the political leadership of the parliamentary majority. In 1977 a government reshuffle saw the departure of the party leaders, and Barre began to assert himself as the political leader of the government (Portelli, 1987, pp. 157–9). Even with political leadership from the prime minister the coalition within the government team has to be accommodated and managed. Contrary to some expectations the inclusion of four Communist ministers, who were not, however, chosen from amongst the very top ranks of the Communist Party leadership, in the Mauroy government of June 1981 produced few problems, although the replacement of Mauroy by Laurent Fabius in 1984, and the new approach that this symbolised, caused them to leave the government. In any coalition government however, the problem exists. For example, Elgie's study (1993, p. 20) shows that Chirac's response to the 1986 education bill crisis was hampered by the need to hold his ministerial team together.

- Certain administrative positions give some ministers administrative power-bases that enable them to exercise a considerable degree of autonomy that is not mitigated by a clear concept of collective responsibility. In 1993–5, for instance, Charles Pasqua, the tough right-wing minister of the Interior, operated virtually independently and ensured that he was publicly seen to be doing so. This is particularly true of the minister of finances; in the early 1970s Chaban-Delmas, reflecting on his experiences as prime minister, with Giscard d'Estaing as finance minister, accused the finance ministry of running its own, alternative policy. A little later Jacques Chirac, as prime minister, was alleged to be scarcely on speaking terms with Fourcade, President Giscard d'Estaing's choice as finance minister, while in 1992 Finance Minister Pierre Bérégovoy was said to be 'waging war' on Prime Minister Cresson. In the early 1980s, however, Mauroy as prime minister and Delors as finance minister were united in urging a policy of reduction in public spending and a period of austerity to deal with economic problems, against the views of other members of the government. In the end it was President Mitterrand's decision that confirmed the policy of the prime minister and finance minister.[4]

- Except during *cohabitation* a prime minister has always to reckon with the fact that certain ministers may be in a position to appeal over his or her head directly to the President. Under Mitterrand Jack Lang, the long-serving minister of culture, was considered to be particularly close to the President, as was Charles Hernu, the defence minister who had to resign over the sinking of the *Rainbow Warrior*. Paradoxically it was the independence that he consequently enjoyed that shielded both Mitterrand and Laurent Fabius, who was then prime minister, from greater implication in the scandal. Fabius himself, when prime minister, described in an interview how, as a minister, he had been in the habit of 'short-circuiting' the prime minister; an action which he later regretted, for it undermined the prime minister's authority (Elgie and Machin, 1991, n. 18).

The second aspect of the prime minister's political role is the responsibility for ensuring the passage of government measures through Parliament. Despite the limited powers of the National Assembly (see Chapter 7) this is by no means always straightforward. The French political system does not put a high premium on unwavering obedience to a party line within the parliamentary parties, and prime ministers have regularly needed to resort to various devices to mask or curtail dissent among their own supporters. The difficulties that the Barre government experienced in 1979 in getting its expenditure estimates passed, or the backbench pressures which forced amendments in a carefully calculated Education Bill in 1984 (with the ultimate effect of wrecking the Bill) were examples of the difficulties with which Prime Minsters may have to contend. Rocard, at the head of a minority government after 1988, had to devote a good deal of time and energy to putting together the necessary package of parliamentary support to ensure the passage of each of the measures his government wished to introduce.

Prime Ministers' relationships to parties have fluctuated. Nevertheless, elections are fought on governmental records amongst other factors, and no prime minister has been able to ignore the impact of governmental performance on the electorate at large. Before the 1978 general election Prime Minister Barre, despite his minimal party attachments, presented himself as the leader of the governing coalition in a televised debate with Mitterrand, then the First Secretary of the Socialist Party. Socialist prime ministers since 1981 have had a clear, if not always easy, relationship with the Socialist Party; in choosing Mauroy as his first prime minister, Mitterrand picked a leader who possessed a strong power base within the party and who was trusted by it. He and his successors maintained a steady working relationship with the General Secretary of the party. Chirac in 1986 came into office as the leader of the Gaullist party, and in the expectation that he would be their presidential candidate in 1988. His relationship with party and electorate was thus of crucial importance to him, and he certainly used his role as prime minister in an attempt to maximise his electoral chances, for example in taking credit for the release of French hostages from the Lebanon in the days before the Presidential election in 1988. His lack of success in that election may have encouraged him, in 1993, to concentrate on his role as party leader rather than undertake the leadership of a government in what were undeniably difficult economic circumstances. He chose not to serve as prime minister. His nominee in that post, Edouard Balladur, nevertheless found himself increasingly assuming the role of both governmental and political leader. His public standing was high and he decided to become a candidate in the 1995 presidential election. His ministers were faced with a choice between support for Chirac or for Balladur. The result was a divided party and an increasingly querulous government team.

Ministers

The French government normally consists of between 40 and 50 ministers.[5] The size of the full cabinet has grown during the Fifth Republic. It only once (under Pompidou at the end of May 1968) exceeded 20 ministers before 1981. Under Mauroy there were 30 cabinet ministers, under Rocard 32, and under Cresson 29. Laurent Fabius and Jacques Chirac went back to smaller numbers with 22. The remainder are junior ministers. The Balladur government of

1993 to 1995 contained only 29 ministers and no junior ministers. With 26 cabinet ministers, two delegated ministers and 14 junior ministers, Alain Juppé's first government in 1995 was the largest right-wing government of the Fifth Republic. Revealingly, it lasted less than six months, and was replaced by a much more compact team of sixteen Cabinet ministers, eleven delegated ministers and five junior ministers (see Exhibit 4.2). The honorific title Minister of State (*ministre d'état*) may be given to the most politically important or senior government members as a mark of status and prestige.[6] Ministers without a full department of their own carry the title Delegated Minister (*ministre délégué*), which usually carries full cabinet status. Junior ministers are called Secretary of State (*secretaire d'état*), a nomenclature that contrasts with the British pattern, where the title Secretary of State is held by the cabinet ministers, and a minister of state ranks rather low in the hierarchy of junior ministers. In France ministers, including junior ministers, have a clearly defined array of responsibilities for specific subjects, and whilst most junior ministers are technically attached to the senior minister of the ministry, there is little concept of a ministerial team within a department.[7] The division of responsibilities results from decisions by the prime minister (in consultation with the President) when ministers are appointed, rather than from internal decisions by the senior minister in each ministry. The precise definition of the scope of each minister's responsibilities is set out in a legal document (*décret*). If the structure remains unchanged from one government to another the *décret* can remain unchanged, but in practice the formation of a new or reshuffled government can give rise to disputes about the sharing out of responsibilities. In 1986 the Chirac government came into power on 20 March, but it took a further six weeks before all the appropriate *décrets* had been published.

Over the course of the Fifth Republic there have been a number of modifications and changes in the structure of ministerial responsibilities – the machinery of government. The ministries of foreign affairs, interior, justice, defence, agriculture and war veterans have stayed broadly unaltered throughout the period (Elgie and Machin, 1991, p. 67). In general modifications have resulted from the specific political circumstances of the period rather than from any clear or ideological view about how the government should be shaped. Concern for the rights and conditions of women was one of the features of the social reform aspects of the early years of Giscard d'Estaing's presidency.

The result was the creation of an administration which was placed for the some of the period (initially against the wishes of the prime minister (Giroud, 1977, pp. 60–9)) under a minister, and in the later years under an administrative official. In 1981 these activities, became a fully fledged ministry under a minister (Yvette Roudy). Under Chirac the ministry was abolished. Since 1988 they have been placed successively under a free-standing junior minister and then under the Ministry for Labour, Employment and Vocational Training. Since 1981 there has been a Ministry for European Affairs, sometimes with a full cabinet minister, and normally attached to the Ministry of Foreign Affairs.

One influence on the shape of government may be a prime ministerial 'divide and rule' strategy. This seems to have been the motive in 1978 when Raymond Barre, seeking to reduce the influence of the Ministry of Finance, and to ensure his own overall control over economic policy, split the ministry into two parts – a Ministry of the National Economy and a Ministry of the Budget. This division lasted only until 1981. Under Balladur in the first period of *cohabitation* and Bérégovoy in 1991 the Minister of Finance again brought together a very wide range of financial and economic responsibilities. When these two former finance ministers each in their turn became prime minister they were notably wary of the power they had themselves exercised and ensured a much wider division of tasks between various ministers. Juppé adopted a solution midway between the two extremes but had ousted his first finance minister, Alain Madelin, from the government within four months. Under the Mauroy government after 1981 transport, housing and town planning and the environment were all separate ministries. In 1986 Chirac brought transport, housing and the environment together under a single ministry, with junior ministers for transport and for the environment. Rocard reseparated these responsibilities. Similarly, a large number of areas of social policy were combined by Balladur within one ministry under the popular Simone Weil. Juppé redivided them.

These movements do, of course, affect the representation in the Council of Ministers of specific interests, such as transport. For the staff of each ministry concerned they have relatively little effect. Each minister, including junior ministers, has a great deal of autonomy within his or her own sphere of responsibility, and there is very little sense of collegiality, either within ministries or at central government level.

EXHIBIT 4.2

The French government in November 1995

Prime minister Alain Juppé (RPR)

Ministers

Jacques Toubon (RPR)
  Justice
Charles Millon (UDF–PR)
  Defence
Hervé de Charette (UDF–P&R)
  Foreign Affairs
Jean-Louis Debré (RPR)
  Interior
Roger Romani (RPR)
  Relations with Parliament
Philippe Douste-Blazy (UDF–CDS)
  Culture
Philippe Vasseur (UDF–PR)
  Fisheries, Agriculture
Jean Pierre Raffarin (UDF–PR)
  Small & Medium-sized Businesses,
  Trade

François Bayrou (UDF–CDS)
  Education
Bernard Pons (RPR)
  Infrastructure Transport
Jacques Barrot (UDF–CDS)
  Labour,Social Affairs
Jean Arthuis (UDF–CDS)
  Economy and Finance
Corinne Lepage (formerly GE)
  Environment
Frank Borotra (RPR)
  Industry, Posts, Telecommunications
Jean-Claude Gaudin (UDF–PR)
  Economic Development, Inner Cities
Dominique Perben (RPR)
  Civil Service, Reform of the State,
  Decentralisation

Delegated ministers

Pierre Pasquini (RPR)
  War Veterans (Prime Minister)
Guy Drut (RPR)
  Youth and Sport (Prime Minister)
Jacques Godfrain (RPR)
  Overseas Aid (Foreign Affairs)
Anne-Marie Couderc (RPR)
  Employment (Labour)
Yves Galland (UDF–Rad)
  Finance and External Trade
  (Finance)
Eric Raoult (RPR)
  Integration, fight against exclusion
  (Economic Development)

Jean-Jacques de Peretti (RPR)
  Overseas Territories (Prime
  Minister)
Pierre-André Perissol (RPR)
  Housing (Infrastructure)
Michel Barnier (RPR)
  European Affairs (Foreign Affairs)
Alain Lamassoure (UDF–PR)
  Government Spokesman, Budget
  (Finance)
François Fillon (RPR)
  Information Technology, Posts
  (Industry)

Junior ministers

Xavier Emmanuelli
  Humanitarian Action (Prime
  Minister)
Anne-Marie Idrac (UDF–CDS)
  Transport (Infrastructure)
Hervé Gaymard (RPR)
  Health and Social Security (Labour)

François d'Aubert (AUDF–PR)
  Research (Education)
Margie Sudre (Other Right)
  Francophone Countries (Foreign
  Affairs)

Notes

CDS – Centre des Démocrates
  Sociaux
P&R – Perspective et Réalitiés
RPR – Rassemblement pour la
  république

GE – Génération Ecologie
PR – Parti Républicain
UDF – Union pour la démocratie
  française

The ministers who have constituted the governments of the Fifth Republic (see Table 4.1) have a number of distinctive features:

- A small number of them have not held elected office at national level, though numbers have varied greatly. All who happen to be members of either house of parliament are obliged to renounce their membership on appointment as a minister
- Those who have held national elected office have almost all held locally elected positions as well and some ministers who have fought elections have only done so at local level. Ministers' links with local politics are powerful (see below, p. 171). Leading ministers, including prime ministers, may combine the post with that of mayor, sometimes of a major town. Chirac in Paris, Defferre in Marseilles, Chaban-Delmas followed by Juppé in Bordeaux, and Mauroy in Lille are notable examples, but in the summer of 1995 after the municipal elections no fewer than 22 ministers then serving were also mayors and a further eight members of municipal councils. Moreover, three were presidents of regional councils and six presidents of departmental councils. The law that forbids the holding of multiple offices does not apply to the position of minister, which is not an elected post.
- A high proportion of the ministers have had previous experience of administrative life as officials.
- They have mostly been men. There was only one woman minister between 1958 and 1972; between 1972 and 1974 there were two women ministers, and there were three in the Chirac government of 1974–6, Thereafter the numbers rose slightly – seven women in Barre's government, seven under Mauroy, six under Fabius (Gaxie, 1986). With the return of a government of the Right the number fell again to four. Between 1988 and 1993 there were six or seven women in each government, but in the right-wing government of Edouard Balladur between 1993 and 1995 numbers dropped again. During the 1995 presidential election campaign the candidates were pressed to make commitments about the number of ministerial posts that would be given to women. Jacques Chirac refused and said he would not support constitutional changes imposing quotas for female candidates in elections. However, in the first government of his presidency, under Prime Minister Alain Juppé there were twelve female ministers (28.6 per cent), four of them with cabinet rank. This

TABLE 4.1

Party composition of selected Fifth Republic governments

President	De Gaulle			Pompidou	Giscard d'Estaing		Mitterrand				Chirac
Prime minister	Debré	Pompidou	Pompidou	Chaban-Delmas	Chirac	Barre	Mauroy	Fabius	Chirac	Rocard	Juppé
Political Party	January 1959	April 1962	April 1967	June 1969	June 1974	August 1976	June 1981	July 1984	March 1986	June 1988	May 1995
Gaullists	6	9	21	29	12	9			20		22
Republicans		3	3	7	8	10			7	1	7
Centrists	3[1]	5[2]		3[3]	2	2[4]			7[5]	1	7
Radicals	1	1			6[6]	5			2	1	1
Left Radicals							2	3		3	
Socialists							37	36		25	
Communists							4				
Miscellaneous	7						1[8]	1[9]		3[10]	4[11]
Non-party	10	11	5		8	10[12]		3	6	15	2
Total (including PM)	27	29	29	39	36	36	44	43	42	49	43

Note:

1. Christian Democrats (MRP).
2. Christian Democrats (MRP).
3. Centre for Democracy and Progress.
4. Social Democrat Centre (CDS).
5. CDS.
6. Reformers.
7. Includes five independents.
8. Michel Jobert, ex-Gaullist whose *Mouvement des Démocrates* supported Mitterrand in the presidential election.
9. Huguette Bouchardeau of the *Parti Socialiste Unifié*.
10. Direct members of UDF.
11. Two UDF, one former ecologist, one Other Right.
12. Designated as presidential majority.

Source: Adopted and adapted from Safran (1995) p. 174.

exceptional situation lasted only a few months. In the government reshuffle of early November 1995 eight out of the twelve lost their posts, and of the remaining four only one was of Cabinet rank.

- Despite the arrival in power of the Socialists in 1981 90 per cent of all the ministers of the Fifth Republic have come from positions in the upper ranks of industry, the public services or the professions and 80 per cent of all ministers have a higher education qualification (Gaxie, 1986).

However, the experience of fighting elections has not been an essential pre-requisite for gaining office. 20 per cent of the ministers of the Fifth Republic had not, at the time when they were appointed minister, held any form of elective office, at either local or national level or within the party organisations (Gaxie, 1986, p. 62).

In the first governments of the Fifth Republic a rather high proportion of the members of the government did not hold a parliamentary seat at the time when they were appointed minister; in the Debré government of 1959–62 15 out of the 40 ministers were not members of Parliament. The proportion remained relatively high (an average of 27 per cent) until 1968, but then dropped sharply as would-be ministers and those who already held office sought election, even if it their appointment or re-appointment meant that they had immediately to abandon their seats. Between the mid-1970s and 1993 the proportion of non-parliamentary ministers rose again to around 30 per cent. In some cases such non-parliamentary ministers were chosen because they are prominent within the parties of the governing coalition, but have chosen not to seek election, or been unable, perhaps because their party is small, to secure it – the Communist minister Charles Fiterman, appointed in 1981, was an example of the first sort, the leader of the small Parti Socialiste Unifié, Huguette Bouchardeau, of the second. Sometimes such ministers are leaders of other important organisations – for example the farmers' leader, Michel Debatisse, was appointed a minister under Giscard. Other ministers may have been closely linked to the President without having been involved in electoral politics – Pierre Bérégovoy or Jack Lang, for example. All these ministers had, however, in some way been linked to political life; other ministers have been appointed to posts linked to their previous professional experience. Whilst their political sympathies clearly lie with the government, it is their expertise which explains the appointment. Under President Giscard academics were appointed to the Ministry of Education and of the

Universities, and economists (Barre himself, Fourcade) to economic ministries. Under Mitterrand the first Minister of Industry was the former chairman and managing director of the vehicle manufacturers Renault (Pierre Dreyfus) and in the 1988 Rocard government the Minister of Industry was the former head of the huge glass-makers, St Gobain. The Juppé governments formed in May and December 1995 included a lawyer specialising in environmental law as Minister of the Environment. Such appointments may contribute to an image of competence and professionalism for the government. This 'depoliticisation' and 'legitimation by competence' (Gaxie, 1986, p. 66) seems to be particularly important when politics are in transition (as in 1959) or when political circumstances are difficult. In the minority government of Michel Rocard in 1988 there was a higher proportion of 'non-political' appointments (eight out of 48) than had been the norm for the 1980s.

However, political inexperience amongst ministers may sometimes be a hazard; one of Rocard's ministers – a famous surgeon appointed as minister of health – lasted only a few days in office. Moreover, even if they are not 'professional politicians' at the outset of their ministerial career most rapidly become so, and seek electoral legitimacy, either, like Pompidou and Barre, through general elections, or, like Simone Weil, a magistrate before she became minister of health, in the European elections, or, at the very least, at a local level. It was President Mitterrand's instruction that he expected all his ministers to present themselves to some electoral process that caused a very small town in the Pyrenees to have a government minister as mayor after the 1989 local elections.

A much-remarked characteristic of the governments of the Fifth Republic has been the extent of the connection between ministers and the civil service. There was a popular perception that the coming of the Fifth Republic had blurred the distinction between political functions and administrative functions, and that to an important extent officials were being appointed directly into ministerial posts – a tendency which, it was argued, extended into political life the worrying features of administrative domination already evident in other areas, especially economic and industrial life. The proponents of this view could point to the proportion of ministers who had spent some part of their career as senior government officials. Between 1959 and 1981 just under 40 per cent of all ministers came into the government with a background of this sort; under the Socialists the proportions dropped to 14 per cent but, despite Chirac's attacks on technocracy during his campaign, rose to 20 per cent in the first government of his presidency. Nevertheless, the argument that what was occurring was a take-over by the civil service (*la fonctionnarisation de la politique*) is too simplistic. In France (see Chapter 5) senior positions in the civil service come early to those who are successful within the top educational establishments, and may be seen as a starting point for a variety of careers, including, since there are no restrictions upon the political activities of civil servants in their private capacities, careers in politics, but also careers in industry that may, as in the case of Rocard's industry minister Roger Fauroux, lead into a ministerial post. Nor have civil servants necessarily been appointed directly to ministerial posts. They may have come into political activity in a number of ways; through contact with politicians, for example in their private offices within ministries; through an invitation to be involved in the study of a particular problem; through membership of and activity within a party. For example, Anne-Marie Idrac, appointed junior minister for transport in Juppé's government directly from a senior official post in the ministry was an active member of the CDS. Political activity, including membership of central party committees and the fighting of elections, is not incompatible with civil service status, and indeed the prestige and reputation which senior civil posts bring with them may prove to be a distinct advantage (Gaxie, 1986, p. 78). Thus two former senior officials who enjoyed a rapid ascension through ministerial posts culminating with that of prime minister, Chirac on the Right and Fabius on the Left, both commenced their ministerial careers by fighting parliamentary elections, and Fabius indeed served from 1978 to 1981 as an opposition member of Parliament.

The Pathology of the Ministerial Role: Corruption and Scandal

Ministers are located, in France, at the intersection of politics and administration not only at national, but also, in many cases, at local level. These local connections are very important, since many of the scandals which have arisen around certain leading politicians have been linked to their involvement in local administrations at various levels. But the scandals achieve a wider resonance because of the national prominence of the protagonists. Ministers receive a good deal of social deference. Their offices, and those of their close administrative collaborators, tend to display a style and elegance appropriate to the greatness of the state which they serve and represent. They enjoy considerable autonomy and extensive powers of patronage. They are subject to little critical scrutiny. Parliament's control (see Chapter 7) is not intense. There is little tradition of a campaigning and investigative press, although some newspapers and periodicals (notably *Le Canard Enchaîné* and *Le Monde*) have conducted effective enquiries and published revelations. Private life is protected by fierce privacy laws, so what may be common knowledge in the gossip of *le tout Paris* is well concealed from the general public,[8] which is in any case little interested in some of the peccadillos of the establishment. Television and broadcasting are no longer totally under the government's thumb, but, as Harrison[9] points out, the government ensured it had a friend at the head of the regulatory agency and, despite increasing professionalism, 'interviews with senior politicians remained deferential'.

This is a context in which the line between acceptable and scandalous behaviour may, for some, become very indistinct. Scandal, of various kinds, has long been a feature of French political life. Philip Williams in 1970 (p. 3) said France was 'the classic land of political scandal' (see also Jenkins and Morris, 1993). The 1980s and 1990s have seen a proliferation of political scandals in France, most of them involving ministers. Most of the scandals fall into one of three categories.

- The abuse of power leading to immoral or criminal policy decisions motivated by national, administrative or sometimes political expediency. This category includes the planting of a bomb on the Greenpeace ship *Rainbow Warrior*, which killed a crew member, and the decision that the blood transfusion service should stock and distribute blood which had not been screened for HIV contamination, although the risks were known. Illegal surveillance and telephone tapping have also been undertaken. The *Rainbow Warrior* case led to the resignation of the minister of defence, but to little public indignation. The case of contaminated blood resulted in the imprisonment of the head of the transfusion service and, nine years later and after much press and television drama and associated political debate, the referral of the three ministers (the then junior and the senior ministers of health and the then prime minister, Laurent Fabius) to the Court of Justice of the Republic which is the only body constitutionally capable of impeaching ministers.

- The abuse of patronage or influence in order to raise funds for political parties or purposes. Given the rising cost of political campaigning and electioneering and the difficulties which French political parties have had in ensuring a legal flow of funds to finance their activities, a variety of means have been used to obtain funds. A long-standing and fairly systematised, if clandestine and illegal, method involves the raising of what amounts to a levy on contracts for public works and other services provided to local authorities through false invoices or 'dummy' consultancies. This was the method employed by the Urba group of companies to provide a flow of money into party coffers, and it was the possibility of criminal charges arising out of this that overshadowed Henri Emmanuelli (a former treasurer of the Socialist Party) in the contest with Lionel Jospin for the Socialist nomination as candidate in the run-up to the 1995 presidential election. Other forms of 'kickback' are also said to have been practised. The Luchaire affair in the late 1980s allegedly involved both illegal decisions in relation to the supply of arms to Iran and the subventions to the Socialist Party by the contractors. However, the acquisition of funds by means on the fringes or over the borders of illegality to support political and electoral activity has not been confined to the Socialist Party. All the major political parties have been implicated in such dealings (Leyrit, 1995, p. 57). For example, similar allegations about kickbacks arose in February 1995 against members of the RPR in the Paris region. Allegations of dubious financial dealings related to political activity led to charges against the Mayor of Lyons, Michel Noir, who had challenged Jacques Chirac for the leadership of the RPR before being expelled from the party. During the 1990s new legislation has been introduced to control the sources of finance for political parties and electoral expenditure (see Chapter 9) accompanied by an amnesty law exempting from penalties those who had previously been involved in illegal activities for the benefit of political parties from which they had secured no personal benefit.

- The third major category of scandal has concerned those in which position or influence has been used to acquire direct personal benefit for example through insider trading. A major example of a scandal of this sort was the allegations that profits had been made by those closely associated with President Mitterrand and the then minister of finance, Pierre Bérégovoy, through insider trading associated with the take-over of an American company by the nationalised French company, Pechiney. Allegations of this kind have been linked, not only to Socialists, but also to ministers from governments of the Right. The charges against Alain Carignon, which led to his resignation from Balladur's government and a prison sentence in 1995 included allegations that he had received not only payments to cover his campaign expenses but also personal benefits and gifts worth more than 20 million francs (Leyrit, 1995. p. 65). Perhaps less serious but even more damaging were the allegations that surfaced against Prime Minister Alain Juppé that he had used his position in the municipal administration of Paris to secure very low rents on high quality municipal flats for himself and members of his family and the suggestion that government influence was being used to hamper investigation of the matter.

A number of commentators (Bornstein, 1990, Jenkins and Morris, 1993) have argued that scandals have had only a limited public impact. It is true that there has been little sustained and vocal public outcry. It is also true that Balladur was a credible presidential candidate and Chirac won the presidential election in 1995 despite being, respectively, prime minister and party leader associated with a government which saw three of its members (Longuet, Roussin and Carignon) resign under the cloud of financial scandals within six months in 1994. It is, however, equally true that the Socialist Party was regarded as being tarnished and handicapped by the scandals with which it was associated, including, for example President Mitterrand's support for Bernard Tapie, the flamboyantly populist businessman, politician and football club owner whose business dealings turned out to be distinctly dubious and resulted in bankruptcy. It may be, as Morris and Jenkins suggest, that 'the French public, by endorsing [the] concentration of power [in the presidency], have sacrificed "open government" for things they value more highly – continuity, stability and simplified political choices. Does this imply therefore that scandal has become an acceptable "trade-off" for these other advantages?' (p. 163).

On the other hand the marked disillusion of the electorate with the traditional political parties in the 1990s was certainly linked with repugnance at immoral, criminal or self-seeking behaviour. Some commentators (Mény, 1992, Laughland, 1994) have denounced the corrosive impact of corruption. Some investigating magistrates and journalists have pursued cases with tenacity and vigour. The extent to which the context within which ministers and leading politicians operate offers temptations and opportunities for corrupt practices cannot be ignored. Nor is it clear that politicians can continue to rely on previous levels of public tolerance and indulgence.

The Co-ordination of the Work of the Government

French government ministers enjoy a striking degree of deference within France's political and administrative structures, and, legally, a good deal of autonomy within their own fields. They may be very closely subject to control by the President or the prime minister; they may be engaged in bitter conflict with their colleagues over the scope of their responsibilities or the nature of their policies; but they are not, and do not, on the whole, feel themselves to be, part of a collegial enterprise. The weekly meeting of the Council of Ministers, with its communiqué drafted well in advance (Schifres and Sarazin, 1985) is essentially a ritual rather than an opportunity for major discussions or unanticipated decisions.

Policy co-ordination – Within the Ministries

Within the ministries policy co-ordination is effectively the task of the minister's private office, his *cabinet*. The current shape and role of ministers' *cabinets* in France developed during the nineteenth century and has evolved since. Every minister has attached to him a personal staff with important political and administrative functions. A minister has a free choice of these staff members; in practice, ministers have almost invariably chosen, as the head of this staff *(directeur de cabinet)* a person to whom they are politically and personally close. The composition of the rest of the team may then be left to the *directeur*. Membership of a minister's personal staff will imply sufficient attachment to the minister's political views to ensure a degree of loyalty, but does not require identity of views. Two other qualities are also important: professional competence and knowledge of the workings of the governmental machine.

The size of a *cabinet* may vary. There is a statutory limit on the numbers of the staff, reduced by Alain Juppé, fulfilling one of

Chirac's campaign promises, from ten to five for members of the Council of Ministers and from between three and five for junior ministers to three but this limit is frequently evaded by the attachment to the *cabinet* of 'unofficial' members.

Ministers are allowed a rather small sum of money with which to pay for their *cabinet*. They consequently need to seek official and unofficial members whose salaries can be met from other sources. If the *cabinet* member is a serving official, he or she will be seconded to the *cabinet* with salary costs met by their department of origin. Academics are usually serving officials, and hence covered by this provision. Other bodies, too, may be able and think it worthwhile to meet salary costs for a seconded staff member. This financial constraint is an important reason for the employment in *cabinets* of a large number of serving officials from within the ministries. The need for staff members who are familiar with the working of the governmental machine is the second major reason for the choice of officials. In the 1970s some 80–90 per cent of *cabinet* members were serving civil servants. With the coming of the Socialist government in 1981 this proportion dropped to below 70 per cent, as an increased number of people who had been on the staff of the party or of one of the trade union federations or outsiders such as journalists were appointed. In 1986 when the Chirac government came into office the proportion rose again to around 80 per cent. At the senior level of *directeur de cabinet* the number of 'outsiders' has been very limited indeed – varying from none (under the 1986 Chirac government) to five out of the 84 people who were *directeurs de cabinet* in the period of the Mauroy government between 1981 and 1984.[10]

The organisation of the *cabinet* may vary according to the Minister's personal predilections – some are loosely structured, others more formal and hierarchical. In some cases the minister may have a special adviser (*chargé de mission auprès du ministre*) who stands outside the hierarchy and is actually more powerful and influential than the *directeur de cabinet*.

The *cabinet's* tasks almost invariably fall under four headings; first and most mundanely, the *cabinet* is responsible for looking after the minister – ensuring that he or she has an organised round of appointments, is at the right place at the right time with the right papers. Secondly the *cabinet* has the task of assisting the minister with his or her political life and with the political exposition of his or her policies. This has three facets: relationships with the party and the minister's former constituency; relationships with Parliament – preparation for debates, questions and other business; and relationships with the press and the public. In all these fields the *cabinet* staff take an active role, drafting or preparing for speeches, appearances in the media, press articles and other aspects of the minister's political life. The *cabinet* may draw on the resources of the ministry to assist, but the administrative division will not normally expect to be actively involved in the defence of policy. That is seen to be the *cabinet's* task. Thirdly, the *cabinet* staff are deeply involved in watching over and co-ordinating the work of the ministry. French ministries do not have one single official at their apex – they have no 'permanent head'. Rather they are confederations of functional units (divisions – *directions*) each under a *directeur* or *directeur général*. Usually a group of the ministry's functions is placed under the oversight of one of the *cabinet* staff. That person will keep an eye on all that is being done, ensure that the minister's wishes are being carried out, and transmit the proposals of the ministry through to the minister. Ministers do not necessarily meet their *directeurs* very often; instead they rely upon their personal staff to act as a channel of communication. In these circumstances the role of the *cabinet* in the initiation, formulation and co-ordination of ministerial policy is crucial. In undertaking this role their understanding of the minister's political intentions is very important. 'Fourthly, *cabinets* are centrally involved in interminister-ial co-ordination. The *directeur* or another member of staff represents the ministry at a great many of the interministerial meetings where policy is discussed and the different views of the different ministries are expressed. Members of the *cabinet* staff will maintain relationships with contacts in the other ministries concerned with their policy area so as to ensure that as far as possible the way is smoothed for their policy approach. For this reason it is extremely useful for a minister to ensure the presence in his or her *cabinet* of people from the *grands corps* (see Chapter 5) who will be able to bring into play their particularly close network of contacts.

Cabinets have recently come in for a good deal of criticism, and even some suggestions, in reports on administrative reform, that they should be, if not abolished, at least confined to a narrower, more specifically and overtly political role. This, it is argued, would underline their political advice function, and ensure that the policy functions of the directorates within the ministries were not usurped or bypassed thus improving the quality of policy formulation and decision making. Compared, for example, with their counterparts in the United Kingdom, French ministers tend to have less direct non-hierarchical contact with the officials in their ministries. However, *cabinets* have both policy co-ordination and political exposition roles which, given the nature of the administration (see Chapter 5), could not easily be located elsewhere. The *cabinet* is well described as the flexible gangplank that links the solid and unmoving quay of the administrative structures to the minister who rises and falls upon the more shifting yet dynamic waters of political life.

Policy Co-ordination – Between the Ministries

Some countries have an established and fixed system of committees linking together various ministries to ensure that all government policy is collectively reviewed and co-ordinated whilst it is being formulated at the administrative level. This is not the case in France. Ministers guard their autonomy, and there is no convention of collegiality to enforce such structures. However, there are two mechanisms that substitute for such a convention. First, any legislative text, whether it be a bill presented to Parliament for its approval, or a regulation made under the government's constitutional powers, must bear the signature of all the ministers concerned by the proposal. Secondly, the role of the prime minister in co-ordinating governmental action, discussed above, results in large numbers of meetings between the representatives of different ministries. These meetings are called and serviced by the general secretariat of the government, usually on an ad hoc basis. Sometimes the prime minister may wish to call one to ensure that governmental plans are progressing. In other cases a minister may seek the prime minister's decision to resolve a conflict between ministries. The meetings are usually attended by members of the *cabinets* of the ministers concerned.

The usual outcome of such meetings is a decision taken either directly by the prime minister or on his behalf. There is a very large number of meetings – in one month (June 1985) there were 105 (Fournier, 1987, p. 201) and there may be up to 1500 in the course of a year. This figure varies. For example, having been rising steadily through the 1970s and early 1980s it dropped sharply in the first year of *cohabitation*, probably because meetings were taking place elsewhere and possibly more informally. The president's staff is informed of the meetings as they occur, and of the outcome, and this continued during the periods of *cohabitation*, but during this time members of the President's personal staff attended only those interministerial meetings that were specifically concerned with foreign affairs and defence, rather than being present at almost all interministerial meetings, as had previously been the case (Fournier, 1987, p. 210).

At a higher level of co-ordination there are meetings not between officials but between ministers, which may be called either by the prime minister, or by the President. Such meetings may take the form of permanent committees, but these tend to be rapidly overtaken by events when the subject that has caused them to be set up has lost its immediacy or the meetings become merely formal. As at official level, ad hoc meetings are much more important. These may be more or less formal meetings, of which a record is kept and distributed, or they may be informal, indeed individual, meetings such as those which the prime minister has with each minister in relation to the forthcoming year's expenditure plans. The prime minister plays a much more active, though not necessarily more influential, role than the President and different prime ministers have varied in the use they have made of such meetings; Mauroy, for example, made greater use of formal meetings in which decisions were taken; Fabius held fewer formal meetings and those often at the start of the process of elaborating a policy, but more often met ministers informally.

Much of the tone and style of French public policy decision making is set by the practice of prime ministerial arbitrage – an almost judicial choice between the rights and wrongs of conflicting but strongly argued viewpoints. That such a style is quite typically French and not necessarily shared throughout Western Europe becomes particularly apparent when such decisions have to be taken in new contexts, particularly the more consensual and collegial decision-making structures of the European Commission in Brussels, to which French officials find 'great difficulty' in adapting.[11]

Conclusion

The role and conduct of the government – prime minister and ministers – shapes and conditions large areas of political life within France. However dominant the President, the government machinery is indispensable if political initiatives are to be realised and policy implemented. This machinery has a life and dynamic of its own; the role of the prime minister is crucial, and has, over the period of the Fifth Republic, become more, rather than less, central within public policy. Other ministers, however, may enjoy a good deal of autonomy within their own spheres, and seem at times almost to challenge the pre-eminence of the prime minister. In the complex relationships at the centre of governmental business the personal staffs of President, prime minister and ministers play a key part. They are the links between the world of the politicians, and that of the administration. The civil service in France enjoys a mixed and paradoxical reputation. It is greatly esteemed at the top, especially for its technical competence, yet criticised for pretension, elitism and politicisation, and equally castigated for its cumbersome bureaucracy at lower levels yet admired for what are seen as essential contributions to France's prosperity and well-being. This administration forms the subject of the next chapter.

5

The Administrative System in France

Western democracies have evolved systems which balance political direction and control against the need for effective and efficient management of the administrative functions which complex modern societies require. It is impossible to understand French public and political life without some understanding of the role which the French administration plays within society. This chapter considers first a number of ways in which the French administrative system is distinctive and secondly some of the consequences of this distinctiveness and the explanations that have been offered for these consequences.

The Distinctiveness of French Administration

The French Administrative Tradition

France was unified slowly and strong local customs, including local ways of administering justice and maintaining law and order, persisted. The kings of the seventeenth and eighteenth centuries sought to weld the country together under their unchallenged authority. Their policies, both abroad and at home, required resources – money and manpower – and this meant the development of an administrative structure that would extract and deploy these resources. Moreover, the prosperity of the country had a direct effect upon these resources, and the King and his ministers regarded this as their concern, and took steps to foster certain types of economic activity.

This activity became known as Colbertism, from the name of Louis XIV's minister Colbert, who was particularly active in economic policy.

The coming of the Revolution altered some aspects of this system, but reinforced others. The possibility of discussing and questioning governmental actions, and the possibility of making appointments to official positions on a basis that did not depend on inherited rights or the King's personal whim and favour were both opened up. It took a well over a century for both these principles to become accepted and entrenched. Since the monarch was no longer the source of authority and direction, the idea of the state became important. Just as the King had been seen as holding an overall responsibility for internal peace and order and the smooth working of society, so now the state, which was considered to be the expression of the general will of the whole nation, took over this role. The idea that central government had a good deal of responsibility for the prosperity and economic well-being of the country persisted. The revolutionary concern for equality meant that local variations and customs, and also local resistance to the authority of the central government, were suppressed. Uniformity was imposed, through the exercise of centralising power in the name of revolutionary principles. Of crucial importance to the later development of the administration was the emergence of a body of officials in salaried posts, not purchased offices, by whom this power was exercised.

Napoleon followed the Revolution, and much of the pattern of French administration today can be traced back to the system which he developed (see p. 14, above). For much of the Napoleonic period France was on a war footing. Napoleon needed soldiers and money to fight his wars, and made sure he had an administration which would produce them. This administration was marked by centralisation, by authority and by quasi-military organisation. Napoleon saw the administration as a force which would embody the power and the legitimacy of the state – and hence of the general interest of the nation as a whole – and act as a check and restraint on the narrower, more local and individual pressures and vested interests which were represented through democratic and representative institutions.

After the Second World War some of the aspects of the Napoleonic administration which had become attenuated were strengthened again. Some of the old political forces and some parts of the administration, especially the top administration, had been discredited by defeat and collaboration; but a few high ranking civil servants had distinguished themselves in the Resistance. The mood of the times was for reform and restoration and, in France as elsewhere, for social democratic programmes involving, for example, nationalisation and the establishment of a welfare state, that considerably increased the scope for administrative intervention. The administration of the period was confident and active, clear that the restoration and rebuilding of the French economy and society depended upon them as much as, if not more than, upon the politicians. A comprehensive reform and codification of the legislation governing the structure, terms and conditions of the civil service was undertaken, and recruitment to senior administrative posts transformed by the setting up of a new recruiting and training establishment, the Ecole Nationale d'Administration.

One of de Gaulle's objectives in establishing the Fifth Republic was to strengthen the legitimacy and the standing of the state. His reform of the balance of power between Parliament and government altered the previous balance of power in favour of the executive. Administrative scope increased, both because more matters were left to executive regulation rather than parliamentary legislation, and because the emergence of a stable governmental majority within Parliament facilitated the passage of the legislation that was required. Foreign observers remarked upon the competence and confidence of top level French civil servants. The high standing of the administration, the policy stability implied by the continuation in power of governments from within one political coalition between 1958 and 1981 and the long-term effects of the 1945 reforms upon the esteem and confidence of those who were reaching senior positions all contributed to this image.

At the same time this system was increasingly challenged and contested. To the ordinary citizen it seemed remote, bureaucratic, complicated and uncaring. In the 1950s Pierre Poujade, a small businessman, led a political movement which took much of its force from protests against bureaucracy, especially tax collection (see Exhibit 8.3), and these continued into the 1970s as one of the major complaints of the right-wing groupings of small businessmen and middle class interests. Goscinny and Uderzo, creators of the cartoon character Asterix, caricatured the smooth, elitist products of the top civil service training establishments and portrayed the task of extracting an official document from a government office as akin to one of the labours of Hercules. The movement that led to decentralisation (see Chapter 6) resulted from dissatisfaction with the centralised nature of much of French government. The strength of these criticisms reveals the strength of the administrative tradition.

The Structure of the French Civil Service: Who is a Civil Servant?

In 1945 a general law – the *Statut général de la fonction publique* – laid down the outlines of the terms and conditions of service for civil servants. This law was completely overhauled in 1983–4. The civil service is held to be based on two fundamental principles: that access is equally open to all qualified people on the basis of public competitive examination, and that it is a career service, offering lifetime employment. The law describes, in general terms, the procedures through which a person may acquire the status of a civil servant – a *fonctionnaire*. Once this status has been acquired, it conveys certain legal rights and duties and can be lost only as a result of retirement, voluntary resignation, or serious disciplinary proceedings. Civil servants can, and do, enforce the rights which their status confers on them before the courts. In addition to the rights which civil servants enjoy the law also places them under a number of obligations – to obey their hierarchical superiors, to be moderate in their public statements about what they do (the *obligation de réserve*), and (since the 1983 reforms) to be as informative as possible towards members of the public.

The civil service includes quite a wide range of people with differing tasks and functions. Ministries are organised into central administrative sections and field services (*services déconcentrés*). These field services are groups of officials who are attached to the central ministry and organised by them, but who are stationed throughout France. Customs officers and tax inspectors are attached to the Ministry of Finance, the police of the national police force are attached to the Ministry of the Interior and the *Gendarmerie* to the Ministry of Defence, whilst all teachers in state education, at every level from nursery school to university, are officials of the Ministry of Education. Social security in France, however, is organised through a network of agencies which employ their own staff, so those who deal with claims and benefits are not civil servants. The consequence of these structures, combined with the French notions of the role of the state and the public services, is a relatively high level of staffing, concentrated in the central ministries.

The key role of the state and the central administration is symbolised within each of the 96 *départements* (counties) of France by the presence of a central government official, the Prefect, who is the local representative of the State, with an appropriately impressive uniform and ceremonial functions, but also with the task of overseeing the activities of the central field services within the area (see Chapter 6).

Corps and Grands Corps

In both the central administrations and the field services civil servants are organised into categories defined by the educational qualification required for entry. Each of these categories is made up of a number of different *corps*.

In English the word 'corps' is familiar from its use for the diplomatic corps, and also for certain groups within the armed services. In France the oldest civil service *corps* were originally formed of civilian technical specialists, the bridges and highways engineers (*corps des ponts et chaussées*) founded in 1747 and the mining engineers, whose *corps* dates from 1744. Nowadays all established civil servants are members of a *corps*, that is a group of officials engaged at different levels in the same task or group of tasks, all of whom enjoy the same specific terms and conditions of service, and who may expect to enjoy a career progression within the corps. The largest *corps* is the primary school teachers, a *corps* in Category B, that is to say that the basic entry level requirement is at the level of at least the *baccalauréat* (the school leaving examination taken at age 18) but below full degree level.

Members of a *corps* may start their career with a period of specialised training: thus tax inspectors (a category A *corps* requiring a degree level qualification for entry) start at the national taxation college (*école nationale des impôts*) and magistrates (a category A *corps* attached to the Ministry of Justice) at the national magistrates' training college (*école nationale de la magistrature*).

The *corps* system with its competitive entry examination system, a feature which is held to be essential in ensuring objectively equal chances to all qualified applicants, puts specific hurdles in the path of any career rising from the lowest to the highest position, and in fact very few do so. It also puts clear limits on the extent to which promotion on the basis of performance on the job is possible. Equally, however, especially within the smaller *corps*, close connections and co-operation can develop. This may foster co-ordination, working together, even innovation, though it also fosters defence of common and vested interests and determination not to surrender acquired rights and status.

The most prominent *corps* are the so-called *grands corps* (see Exhibit 5.1). They, with the recruitment and training establishments through which most of their members pass, have a special and distinctive place within the administration and within French social structure. All the *grands corps* were founded over 150 years ago. All are small, cohesive and influential. Although each has specific tasks formally assigned to it, and in some cases other areas of activity to which it has staked a

---

EXHIBIT 5.1

Grands Corps and *Grandes Ecoles*

Corps	Founded	Membership		Recruited through	Entry level
		Total	Active within *corps*		
Mining engineers	1793	835*	520	*Ecole polytechnique,* founded 1794	*Baccalauréat* plus preparatory classes
Bridges and highway engineers	1713/1716	3 600*	2 100		
Prefects	1800	110**		Ecole Nationale d'Administration, founded 1945	University degree or period in service
Diplomatic Corps	1589 (ministry) 1799 (*corps*)	2 628**			
Council of State	1800	292**	196		
Court of Accounts	1807	370**	226		
Finance Inspectorate	1831	227**	72		

Notes:
* December 1995.
** June 1994.

Source: Ministère de la Fonction Publique (1995).

long-standing and by now irrefutable claim, the prestige and status which each enjoys allows its members to benefit, both individually and collectively, from a high degree of autonomy in the organisation of their working life and careers.

There are reckoned to be three, or perhaps five, 'administrative' *grands corps* and two 'technical' *grands corps*. The three leading administrative *grands corps* are all, formally, importantly concerned with controlling and checking the work of other civil servants. Indeed, in general within the French civil service, those who are concerned with checks and controls tend to enjoy a higher status than those whose chief task is the execution of policy. The administrative *corps* are the Council of State, which is the highest court in administrative law cases and also the government's chief legal advisory body (see below), the Court of Accounts, which is the audit authority for public funds, and the Finance Inspectorate, whose formal task is the checking and control of financial procedures in any body which disburses public funds. The prefectoral *corps* and the diplomatic service are also categorised as *grands corps* by some commentators. The technical *grands corps* are the bridges and highway engineers and the mining engineers.

The administrative grands corps are mainly, though not exclusively, recruited through the National Administrative College – the *Ecole Nationale d'Administration* (ENA). This college was set up in 1945 in order to reform and revitalise recruitment to the senior levels of the French civil service. It now numbers amongst its former students two Presidents and five prime ministers. It has from the start admitted men and women, though women constituted only 4.6 per cent of those who attended the ENA in its first 30 years. Since the mid-1970s the proportion of women has risen to around 15 per cent of each entry. The number of places offered each year has varied. In the 1960s the annual intake was around 60 to 70. In the 1970s the intake was expanded, rising from about 130 to around 150 by the mid-1980s. It was cut back sharply in 1986, partly to preserve the ENA's high status and partly to emphasise the government's determination to reduce the scope and role of the state. Between a half and two thirds of its places each year are offered, by competitive entry examination, to people with at least a university degree. Most of the remaining one third to one half of the places (the proportion has been varied over the years) are offered to those who have already served for a certain period within the public service without the formal requirement of any academic qualification, although in practice success in the competitive examination for these places requires academic ability of a level comparable to degree standard, and many successful entrants from within the public service have been at least as well qualified academically as their colleagues from the other 'external' competition. Under the Socialist government of the early 1980s a highly controversial new form of entry was introduced, in an attempt to restimulate one of the original motives for the creation of the ENA, that of 'democratising' the entry. This so-called 'third way' (*troisième voie*) was immediately denounced by the government's opponents as a backdoor way of opening up civil service posts to Communist trade union delegates. Although the Chirac government abolished this after 1986 the need to open up the ENA away from its rather restricted and strongly Paris-based recruitment and environment was acknowledged by all. A modified and much less controversial *troisième voie* was created. Part of the training of each cohort of students now takes place, expensively and inconveniently, in Strasbourg so that its European dimension is more fully developed.

The ENA serves three main purposes; first it conducts the initial recruitment of potential top civil servants; secondly, through its own testing, examining and ranking processes it selects the members of the different *corps* and thus marks out those who are destined for truly high-flying careers, and thirdly it provides an initiation into various aspects of administrative life and a measure of work experience and training.

The technical *grands corps* are recruited through the *Ecole polytechnique*. This recruits all its students from outside the public service, taking in about 300 a year. Its competitive entry examinations require two or three years of preparation in the special classes attached to some secondary schools, at well above the level of the *baccalauréat*. The *Ecole Polytechnique*, founded in 1794, is a military establishment, not opened to women until the early 1970s, and its students always take a prominent place in the military parades of the 14 July, but they are not necessarily destined for military careers. Its curriculum is a broad one, in applied science and engineering science, with some economics and management, though ability in mathematics remains the key to success. As with the ENA, the final ranking of the students is perhaps its most important function. Those achieving the highest places go on to further technical and management training in the college of their particular *corps*, and then into the appropriate ministry.

The *grands corps* are not the only *corps* into which the ENA and the *Ecole Polytechnique* recruit – students from the ENA who do not achieve the *grands corps* go on, amongst other possibilities, to be general administrators (*administrateurs civils*) or judges in the administrative courts. They are, however, particularly prominent. There is no longer automatically a 20 per cent gap between the starting salary of an ENA graduate in the Council of State, the Finance Inspectorate or the Court of Accounts and all the others, but the *grands corps* undoubtedly offer more interesting career prospects. Their small size means that new members quickly build up useful contacts. Senior members of the *corps* attempt to aid the career prospects of their juniors. The reputation which the *grands corps* members enjoy of being the most able of an already highly selected group ensures that interesting offers are made to them. They are able to leave the work of their *corps* on a secondment basis to take up senior policy positions throughout the administration. Certain positions are virtually guaranteed to them. Thus many of the senior posts in the Ministry of Industry are occupied by mining engineers, the bridges and highway engineers are particularly concerned with public works and town planning, whilst members of the Finance Inspectorate are to be found in many senior economic and financial policy posts. At any one time between one-third and one-half of the members of any of the administrative *corps* are likely to be working away from the formal tasks of their *corps*. To these formal tasks they can, however, at any moment return, a 'safety net' which can be of considerable importance in the development of a career.

Civil Service Management

The management of the French civil service presents a number of striking contrasts. In much of the civil service structures are formal and hierarchical. There is an emphasis on rank and a very precise definition of the scope and powers of each official. For example, the signature of letters or contacts with other parts of the administration may be undertaken only at relatively senior levels, so activities pass up and down the hierarchy. Careers in much of the service are predictable, and promotion depends largely upon seniority. The dominant principle of personnel management in the French civil service is the importance of the dignity, regularity and continuity of public service. The notion that management, in the sense of the effective use of personnel and resources, is a task that might be crucial is permeating the civil service only rather slowly under the influence of Anglo-American models.

The rigidity and regulation of the lower levels of the civil service forms a marked contrast to the flexibility and autonomy at the higher levels. At the highest levels hierarchies can be overruled, for example by the device of attaching a young high-flier directly to the head of a section of the ministry to write a report or develop a particular policy. Members of the *grands corps* and other high-fliers can to a certain extent direct their own careers, helped by the assistance and patronage of senior members of their *corps* who will be anxious to 'send the lift back down' to bring up the junior members of their own *corps*, and will seek to ensure that they have positions that reflect well upon the status of the *corps*.

Some very senior French civil servants are able to act with a degree of authority and a public profile that resembles that of some ministers. The reasons that account for this autonomy include French notions that officials serve the state and the general interest rather than being entirely subordinate to a minister; the centuries-old acceptance that officials properly intervene in wide areas of economic and social life; and the legitimacy that civil servants owe to their reputation for technical and academic competence. In such circumstances the balance between politicians and administrators becomes a key factor and the question of the politicisation of the upper levels of the civil service assumes particular importance.

Political–Administrative Relationships

French officials have an obligation to be 'neutral'. This obligation is understood to imply that a civil servant must deal in an even-handed way with all members of the public, regardless of their political or other opinions or actions. For the French the concept of 'neutrality' is applied to the ways that civil servants look outwards towards the public, not to the ways in which they look upwards to their minister. Consequently it has never been thought necessary to restrict the personal political activities of civil servants, beyond the requirement to be discreet about their actual work and avoid direct criticism of their minister.

If ministers cannot depend upon a civil service culture which emphasises subservience to the minister's wishes as a first priority, other methods are needed to ensure that policy congenial to the minister and the government is proposed, prepared and in due course implemented. The *cabinets* discussed in Chapter 4 play an important role, but equally important is the freedom which the civil service law gives to the government to make appointments to senior posts within the civil service from any source. For a certain defined number of top posts the law allows the government to make appointments which take into account the political affiliations of the person appointed. Some 400 posts are affected by this provision, all of them at the most senior levels – prefects, heads of regional educational administration (*recteurs d'académie*), heads of division within the ministries. Many of these posts are not particularly politically prominent or sensitive, and ministers will usually fill them with competent people from within the career, with little attention to their political orientation. Almost all prefects are thus appointed from within the prefectoral *corps*. In the early 1980s the Socialist government appointed three prefects from outside the *corps*, but this is not a precedent which has been followed subsequently.

The government's ability to fill prominent posts with people in whose attachment to their approach ministers can feel a degree of confidence can, at certain times, result in substantial changes. A study by Danièle Lochak[1] has shown that two thirds of the heads of directorates in the Ministry of Education changed in the year following the 1981 change in government; a similar change took place in 1986 and again in 1988. The total number of changes at the heads of central administration directorates within two years after the changes of government in the 1980s was 116 after 1981, 110 after 1986 and 95 after 1988, affecting between 60 and 70 per cent of all such posts. Of the 1988 changes about half seemed to have been undertaken for specifically political motives, nearly half of these in just two ministries: Education and the Interior.

This is possible in part because honourable outlets for those displaced can be found. A number of them move fairly directly into private sector posts but removal from a sensitive post does not necessarily mean departure from the public service. It may be possible for those concerned to take up posts of similar status but less prominence; for members of the *grands corps* a return to their *corps* of origin is a possibility; many senior positions within nationalised industries and public enterprises are filled by former civil servants whose formal position is one of long-term secondment; the new regional authorities have recruited senior staff from the central civil service. Those who replace them almost always come from within the civil service themselves, although there is no formal requirement that they should do so. In the few cases where this has not happened the new appointee has usually had a close professional connection with the post to be filled. Under the Barre government Claude Jouven, with a background in marketing and market research was appointed to head the division concerned with prices and competition in the Ministry of the Economy, and under Mauroy's government a music critic headed the division of the Ministry of Culture concerned with music.

Control of the Administration

The French civil service is subject to four main types of oversight and scrutiny. They are: ministerial and parliamentary oversight, internal administrative oversight, legal oversight, and oversight by the *médiateur de la République* (ombudsman). The minister is legally the hierarchical head of the ministry and consequently has powers to issue circulars and directives laying down the ways in which the ministry, in all its various branches and services, is to operate. Ministerial oversight over these operations is exercised through the minister's *cabinet* and through the minister's ability to appoint his or her own nominees to senior posts. This ensures that the general orientation of the ministry's work is in line with the orientations defined by the government. However, long traditions of administrative autonomy and the absence of a strong political impetus for ministers to exert managerial control of their ministry mean that in practice the minister may intervene relatively rarely in the ongoing activities of many parts of the ministry. Here a major influence is the weight of the traditions and concepts specific to that particular ministry, and the concepts and approaches of the *corps* of officials of which it is made up.

Ministers are not forced by parliament to take a close interest in the individual decisions, and particular activities of the ministry. Equally members of Parliament do not see the resolution of the personal grievances of their constituents as a very major part of their functions. Parliamentary questions (see Chapter 7) are limited in time and scope, and the executive actions of ministries virtually never scrutinised in detail unless a some major public scandal prompts a parliamentary enquiry. The overall policy orientation of each ministry is scrutinised by Parliament when the annual budget (appropriations) for that ministry is voted, but the subsequent execution of the policy is seldom followed up.

Parliamentary oversight over the work of the administration is relatively weak, but there are powerful internal administrative controls. A number of ministries have *corps* of inspectors attached to them; thus a *corps* of inspectors attached to the Ministry of the Interior oversees the activities of the national police force. Amongst other important inspectorates are the inspectors of social affairs, and the general inspectorate of the administration, which is in fact attached to the Ministry of the Interior, which oversees the activities not only of the central ministry but also of the prefectures. The most prestigious of all the inspectorates is the inspectorate of finance. These latter three inspectorates recruit the majority of their members directly from the graduating students of the ENA. Other inspectorates tend to recruit senior officials towards the end of their careers; indeed a post in such a *corps* may be a useful and honourable outlet for a senior official whose previous post is needed for a younger or more politically acceptable successor.

In practice inspections are rare and episodic for any individual part of the administration. However, French financial procedures are generally tightly specified. Expenditure has to be authorised by someone other than the person actually responsible for disbursement, and the Ministry of Finance has one of its officials stationed in each ministry – the *contrôleur financier* – to undertake this. The courts of accounts, at central or regional level, undertake the subsequent audits, and report to the President of the Republic; the officials of the courts of accounts have the status of magistrates and the legal power to fine those found guilty of the improper use of state funds. Such auditing can occasionally reveal major scandals, as when, in 1983 it was revealed that large sums of public money had, in the late 1970s, been transferred supposedly to pay for the development of aeroplanes that would allegedly be able to 'sniff out' underground oil and mineral deposits.[2]

In general internal oversight of the administration has been concerned with ensuring that it operates legally, in accordance with proper procedures. There is as yet little oversight directed towards managerial efficiency or value for money, despite the existence, since 1946, of a central committee on the costs and productivity of the public services. Economic and political pressures for increased attention to such managerial factors are growing, but have not so far penetrated very deeply.

The French legal system includes a system of administrative courts. Ever since the Revolution it has been thought inappropriate for the ordinary civil courts to hear cases which involve complaints against the actions of the state; and it is, therefore, through a system of administrative courts that citizens must seek redress for grievances. Any action by the administration which contravenes general legal principles or which is specifically detrimental to a member of the public can be challenged before these courts, and the legal terms and conditions which govern employment within the public service are also enforceable within these courts. Access to them is relatively cheap and simple, but the courts are very busy, and cases may take a long time – in the early 1980s the average was around two years. Many citizens do pursue their grievances against the administration through these courts, which constitute an important source of protection for the public. Amongst the largest categories of cases which come before the administrative courts are those related to the individual employment conditions of officials, and also those concerned with taxation. Physical planning, and matters affecting the environment, have in recent years given rise to an increasing number of cases (Brown and Garner, 1983, pp. 189–90).

Appeals against the decisions of the administrative courts are heard by the Council of State (*Conseil d'Etat*) in Paris. The Council of State (see also Chapter 2) is a body which can trace its origins back to the royal councils of the pre-revolutionary monarchy. Nowadays it has two main functions: first it is the senior administrative court, acting especially as a court of appeal in administrative law cases. In fulfilling these functions the Council of State operates as a court of law. However, in judging the actions of the state, the Council of State does not technically have the right to question the constitutionality of laws – that right belongs to the Constitutional Council. Secondly, the Council of State is the government's chief legal advisory body. The drafts of laws and of regulations are submitted to it before they are debated in Parliament or issued by the government and the government may also invite it more generally to give its views on legal questions. The government is not obliged to incorporate its amendments into the texts, or to have regard to its views, but they are usually taken seriously.

The independence of the Council's judgements and advice is enhanced by its status as one of the *grands corps*, with the consequent lifetime guarantees of employment and career and in addition the status and independence that comes from tradition, and membership of a small (around 270) and very highly regarded body, where promotion is automatic and dependent only upon seniority. There is a close sense of collegiality – literally an *esprit de corps*. A minority of its members are directly appointed later in their careers, often, but not always, from within other parts of the civil service.

There are, however, many situations where what is at stake is not so much the legality of the administration's activities as its fairness. In 1973 an 'ombudsman' was appointed following Scandinavian precedents. Called the *médiateur de la république*, the person concerned is appointed for a single term of six years (Clark, 1984). Complaints have to reach the *médiateur* through a member of the National Assembly or the Senate, although this rule has at times been quite flexibly interpreted – the *médiateur* sometimes begins to look into a complaint whilst advising the complainant to seek the help of a member of Parliament. If the *médiateur* judges the complaint well-founded he[3] recommends to the administrations concerned the action required to remedy the matter. Although he has no formal legal sanctions to back up his recommendations they have largely been effective. He depends upon the legitimacy of his office and the relationships which have been built up within the different ministries, backed up by the political will of successive governments which have encouraged his work. The *médiateur* has, for example been quite successful in dealing with cases of the type described as 'administrative ping-pong' where members of the public find themselves dealing with two or more different administrative offices each of which is trying to shuffle off responsibility for a particular matter onto the other.

The *médiateur* makes an annual report to the President, which allows him to highlight matters of general concern that have emerged from all the individual cases that he sees. Reports from the *médiateur* were important factors in the introduction, during the late 1970s, of further reforms which have enhanced the ability of members of the public to comprehend and scrutinise official decisions. In 1978 a law specified that individuals had the right to know what information was held about them on computerised records, including official records. Official records may not include information about an individual's social origins or political, philosophical or religious opinions. The application of the law is overseen by the *Commission nationale de l'informatique et des libertés* (CNIL) – the national committee for computerisation and liberties. A similar body, the *Commission d'accès aux documents administratifs* – the committee for access to administrative documents – oversees the application of another law, also dating from 1978, which provides that citizens have a right to see all official documents except those specifically exempt.

Despite a legislative framework that provides a potentially impressive degree of open government, and continuous efforts over the past decade or so to render the administration less forbidding and to assist members of the public in their contacts with it – the provision of better information and reception services for instance – in general the image of the French administration remains one of remoteness, complexity and arcane procedures. The formal mechanisms for controlling the administration are substantial and extensive, but they are not reinforced by powerful political pressures. The opposition is more likely to attack the incumbent government over general policy than over the detailed execution of its programmes, and there is little crusading or investigative journalism. The climate, however, has been changing, even if slowly, partly as a result of decentralisation (see Chapter 6) and partly as a result of the general growth of more 'liberal' ideas, readier to see the citizen not so much as the subject of the state but as the consumer of state services.

The Nature of Policy Making – Image and Reality

The traditions and structures described above are important only in so far as they have real consequences for the shaping of public policy in France. The making and implementation of policies shapes the processes of public life in France and has a major influence on French social and political culture. The final section of this chapter looks at some of the consequences of the nature of the French administration and the debates that have surrounded the analysis of these consequences.

A Technocratic Republic?

The French administration began to recruit specialists to its service before the Revolution. By the middle of the nineteenth century it was already clear, from the discussions of what training should be given to civil servants, for example, that politicians and public expected the servants of the state to be expert and involved in a wide range of practical and technical matters. For some of the top civil servants of the period the *grandes écoles*, such as the Ecole Polytechnique, provided the confidence and expertise which reinforced their involvement. Despite a rhetoric of 'laissez faire' the state came increasingly, at the end of the nineteenth and into the twentieth centuries, to undertake activities in the sphere of economic development, especially the provision of economic infrastructure, and in the central provision of local services, whether education, policing, agricultural advice or public works. The experience of war merely reinforced this trend. The discrediting of some commercial and industrial leaders after the Second World War reinforced the view held by many senior civil servants at that period, especially the younger ones, that the renewal and reconstruction of the French state depended largely upon their efforts. The arena in which they could be active had enlarged with the post-war nationalisations of the major public utilities, as well as about the half the banking and insurance sectors and the Renault car company.

Public opinion has largely supported these claims. The fact that the civil service training schools form the apex of a very competitive education system means that those who succeed in gaining top level posts can easily be perceived as the most able members of society, and hence likely to produce the 'best' solutions. Moreover, problems of public policy and administration have not occupied a large space within French political debate and conflict. Many areas of public policy are thus 'depoliticised' so that civil servants have wide scope for autonomous action. Bruno Jobert has pointed out (Jobert and Muller, 1987; Jobert, 1989) that these themes come together in a 'scientists' consensus' linking the ruling elite, the professionals and public opinion. 'This sacred alliance of science and the state has been the ideological foundation of the concept of public service since the Third Republic. In that positivist age the best solution to the nation's problems seemed to be to let them be treated by scientifically trained professionals with the least possible interference from politicians' (Jobert, 1989). The 'science' and technical competence of French civil servants has legitimised them in the eyes not only of French public opinion, but also of international observers, who have been inclined to ascribe the speed of French modernisation to their efforts, and hold French models of civil service recruitment and training up as examples to be emulated.

The notion that the senior French civil service constituted a 'technocracy' – an autonomous ruling group legitimising its actions by calling upon a coherent 'scientific' doctrine of administration was challenged in the 1960s by Ridley (1966), who argued that there was in fact no shared and coherent doctrine, and in the 1970s by Suleiman (1978) who explored the very general basis of apparently technical competence, and showed how groups of senior civil servants used it rather as a way of reinforcing their own individual or group interests within society and the administration.

French Policy Style

The debate about technocracy is linked to a debate about how policies are made and what the outcome of the policy-making process is. The particular features which combine in any one country to make these processes different there from elsewhere are sometimes described as the national 'policy style'. Observers of French public policy have noted the huge efforts of rebuilding and reconstruction undertaken after the war, the extent of social change in the post-war decades, and the rate of growth in the French economy up to the 1970s. The first two decades of the Fifth Republic saw a new impetus given to major projects and developments: the building of the new airport at Roissy, and of the new suburban rail network in Paris; the high speed train (TGV) network; the vast improvement and modernisation of France's previously very backward telephone system; the huge nuclear power programme which has resulted in the building of over 90 nuclear power stations; the programme of nationalisation that accompanied the arrival in power of the Mitterrand government in 1981 and, in contrast, the privatisations between 1986 and 1988. All these seemed evidence that French policy 'style' was one that could be described as 'heroic'. The state, through the actions of its senior officials, could make large-scale decisions and sustain their implementation. The image is one of a strong and centralised state, capable of making and imposing far-reaching decisions.

The image is certainly not altogether false. These programmes have been successfully implemented. Civil servants were crucial to their launching, sustaining and achievement. Where a political decision has been taken to set a certain priority, and put large resources into it, the control of these resources gives the appropriate part of the administration considerable clout, and may result in a marked degree of success, as in the case of the modernisation of telecommunications or the building of the TGV. But other efforts have failed or been watered down, and many other policy areas are handled in quite different ways. Jack Hayward has talked of a 'dual' policy style in France, and demonstrated, using the case study of the building of the Rhine–Rhône canal, the way in which decisions are hindered and delayed and decisive action may be rendered effectively impossible by a multiplicity of constraints.[4] In these circumstances the evolution of policy can only be slow, incremental, indeed opportunist. Cawson and his colleagues (1990), following a detailed study of policy-making in relation to two key industrial sectors, concluded that in most circumstances and for most of the time the capacity and indeed the willingness of the French administration to formulate and implement a clear and distinctive policy was limited.

Muller (1992) takes the argument further. He notes that many of the major policies of modernisation and construction were based upon the particular vision of groups of civil servants for whom the constraints of the market were only a part of the constraints, including technological and industrial factors, which had to be overcome. The needs of the consumer were thought to be attained by the achievement of the technical objective of the policy. Consequently, the most successful projects – whether the construction of major new public works in Paris, or the TGV, or the Ariane rocket – were achieved where the demand was essentially political, not economic. The TGV is part of a very highly subsidised network which does not pay its way. Not only was this approach a very segmented one, it has, in the 1980s and 1990s, been fundamentally challenged by two new features. They are, first, the increasing importance of European Union policies, which adopt a much more open, market-oriented approach and, secondly, the impact of decentralisation (see Chapter 6) which has increasingly meant the setting of policy agendas at local rather than central levels.

A Shattered Monolith

A major limitation upon the policy formulation and implementation capacity of the French administration is its fragmented nature. Over recent years this has increasingly been recognised, in contrast to earlier emphases, which tended to view the French administration as a vital constituent part of a powerful, monolithic, centralised and coherent state. Observations which focused upon the institutional structures and formal descriptions of the powers and responsibilities of the French administration reinforced this monolithic image. Little traits – the fact that only certain senior officials may be authorised to sign any letters emanating from a ministry, for example – emphasise a rigid hierarchy, as does a certain social and institutional deference shown to senior officials. It is not difficult to assume that the French administration must reflect a combination of the French taste for neat abstract rationality and Napoleonic organisational precision.

During the last 20 years this image has been repeatedly challenged. A number of factors have been identified which produce lack of cohesion, incoherence and conflicts within the administration. They include:

- policy and political disagreements between parts of the administration;
- 'territorial' conflicts within and between ministries;
- the relationship of parts of the administration with their external environment;
- the career patterns of certain administrators.

The policy and political disagreements that produce tensions between ministers (see Chapter 4, above) are reproduced within the ministries. For example, conflicts between the Ministry of Finance and the spending ministries are endemic: 'Finance ministry officials speak with disdain of the planning commission and the industry ministry'.[5] Moreover, not only are all officials, even senior officials, not cast in the same mould, as a study of the ideological and career choices of the graduates of the ENA clearly shows, but they may also change their attitudes as they change posts and functions within the administrative framework. Ezra Suleiman (1974, Ch. IX) argued convincingly that French senior officials take on the approach dictated by the requirements, ethos and tradition of the job they happen to be doing. These changing approaches may well be dictated by the environment of that particular job.

A second powerful factor producing conflict is the definition of the scope of certain activities. In principle, the rational legal framework of administrative responsibilities precludes most such conflict. In practice, boundary disputes do arise. These may result from a whole group of officials attempting to extend their field, as when the bridges and highway engineers moved into town planning, or the telecommunications engineers looked to the extension of information technology and electronic services to extend their range. They may also result from individual disputes between branches of ministries. Sometimes they are based on functions. For example, conflicts between technical administrative considerations and political or electoral considerations in policy formulation and implementation are almost

institutionalised in the often fraught relationships between a ministry's divisions and the minister's *cabinet*. Both these factors are
crucially influenced by administrative relationships with their external environment. In effect the fragmentation and divisions of civil
society are echoed and reflected within the institutions of the state.
For example, Pierre Gremion's highly influential study (1976)
showed that prefects, ostensibly the channel through which the
powerful central state secured the local implementation of policies
(see Chapter 6) were constrained and deeply influenced by local
pressures, and were to an equal degree the means through which local
forces shaped and adapted policy to particular local circumstances.

Dupuy and Thoenig (1985) have argued that policy may be
differentially applied, as administrators seek to pass on its social,
political and indeed financial costs. They cite the example of the local
gendarmerie who will deliberately enforce regulations relating to long
distance lorry freight against vehicles originating outside their own
département (French vehicle number plates make the identification of
such lorries very easy).

Parts of the administration may also be profoundly affected by
their relationship to functional actors and groups (see Chapter 10).
Kevin Morgan[6] comments that French policy towards the telecommunications industry in the 1980s, which at first sight looked as if it
were being directed by the state, owed more to market pressures and
the opportunism of the man who was chairman and managing
director of one large company.

Within the administration, moreover, different groups of officials or
individuals have different personal and career interests. At the very
top the products of the different routes to the top – the graduates of
the Ecole Polytechnique and the ENA, for instance – jealously guard
the particular posts to which they feel they and those who shared
their route to the top are entitled, and try to ward off encroachments
by the rival establishment.

An Interlocking Elite

Such rivalries do not merely occur within strictly official posts. One of
the marked characteristics of the social background to French
government and politics is the closely interlocking nature of the elite
which occupies the senior posts in every branch of activity – politics,
the civil service, public enterprise, the big private companies, the

media. In 1989, of the 50 leading French companies, 21 were headed by former students of the *Ecole polytechnique*, while three further former students were government ministers (Quilès, Stoléru, Renon).[7] This closely linked elite is a relatively small grouping, since it is based effectively on small-scale institutions which largely feed initially into government postings, and it is often underpinned by social contacts, family relationships and marital connections. The debate surrounding the elite has addressed two problems; one is the nature and effects of such a system in its effects on relationships between government and industry, and the other is the nature of the French 'spoils' system' and the extent of the politicisation of the administration.

The *grands corps* system described above, and the 'technocratic' factor come together to influence the career patterns of officials. The result is the phenomenon known as *pantouflage* – putting on one's slippers in the supposedly more comfortable ambience of the commercial or industrial world. The word has been in use since the end of the last century. The competence of government officials in relation to economic and industrial matters is broadly accepted in France. Because senior officials have reached their posts through jumping the highest hurdles in a stiffly competitive educational system; because the necessity for the state to be active in economic affairs has been largely unquestioned; and because experience in high level policy areas is held to provide both a breadth of view and a network of contacts which careers within a firm or company cannot match, former officials, especially from the more relevant ministries, are frequently appointed to senior posts in industrial and commercial concerns, whether public enterprises or private concerns.

This phenomenon contributes to the impression that there may be an almost conspiratorial relationship at the top. Scandals, both those related to policy decisions (the contaminated blood case) and those involving money (Pechiney, Carrefour du Developpement), which have implicated politicians, the officials with whom they collaborate and sometimes businessmen (see Chapter 4) reinforce this view. In practice, whilst the social interconnections that result are undeniable, it can also be argued that the fragmentation within both administration and the competitive world of industry and commerce, combined with clear evidence that approaches and attitudes are importantly influenced by the tasks that senior executives are fulfilling at any particular time, is sufficient to ensure that collusion is kept within reasonable bounds.

The interlocking of the elite extends also across the boundary between politics and administration. During the 1970s a debate emerged (see De Baecque and Quermonne, 1981), around the nature of the political–administrative relationships that were described above, based upon two phenomena; one was the effect upon the administration of a very long period in office by a governing coalition of broadly centre-right views. For many officials this was the political framework within which they had operated for the major part of their careers and to which they were accustomed. Moreover the Fifth Republic under which the governing coalition had been in power provided for a greatly increased degree of executive discretion compared with its predecessor, and much of this discretion was exercised by officials, whose policy-making powers were extensive and whose public profile was high. Secondly, the Fifth Republic had seen a number of central government officials move directly from administrative life to political activity as parliamentary candidates, members of Parliament or ministers, many, but by no means all of them within the governing coalition. In these circumstances it was easy to be fearful that the interconnections were becoming damagingly close and the whole system unhealthily politicised.

This debate has been largely defused by the experience of the 1980s and 1990s, when *alternance* in government became established, and the consequential changeover in appointments to senior posts was on the whole smoothly accomplished. This involved some negotiation between President and prime minister during the periods of *cohabitation*. Especially during the Balladur government one of President Mitterrand's main concerns was that his own close collaborators should be assured of suitable subsequent posts. The French system cannot be described as a 'spoils system', or compared with the effect of changing presidencies in the United States, since it is essentially a matter of rotation within the rather restricted elite of senior officials. It is now clear that the diversity of their political views and administrative competence is sufficient to make this possible.

6

Local Government

Chapter 1 examined the great geographical diversity of France, and drew attention to the way in which the territory of France was brought together over an extended period of time. The creation of a single nation state, with a fairly uniform pattern of administration was quite largely the product of deliberate policy and choice, and has occurred, in historical terms, relatively recently, in the period since the Revolution. The revolutionary ideals entailed an interpretation of liberty and equality which implied a uniform pattern of rights and obligations for all citizens, and hence an end to local diversity in legal and administrative customs. The exigencies of the revolutionary and Napoleonic wars resulted in the emergence of a system which would extract the necessary resources of money and manpower from a broad and diverse territory. The vision of the role of the central state, inherited from Roman law and absolutist views of monarchy, and strengthened by the revolutionary substitution of the state for the monarchy as the central institution with a broad responsibility for the welfare of all the citizens whose general will and interests it embodied, enhanced the image of a highly centralised and controlling central administration. This chapter examines the administrative and political structures which underlie local – as opposed to central – government in France, at all sub-central levels. It will argue that the picture is far more complex than a simple centralised model suggests and that it is changing. Change has been substantial in the decade and a half since 1981 and is likely to continue under the impact of both domestic, and, importantly, international, pressures, especially those deriving from the European Community.

The Units of Local Government

Title Eleven of the constitution specifies *communes* (municipalities), *départements* (counties) including the overseas *départements*, and the overseas territories as the basic units of local government, but allows for the creation by law of other units. This occurred when the law of 2 March 1982 created regions, and the first direct elections to regional councils were held in March 1986. Indeed Article 72 provides that local government units must be administered by elected councils.

France currently has four overseas *départements*, which are regarded as constituting part of metropolitan France and differ from the other *départements* only in that each also forms a region in its own right and therefore has two elected councils; one, the regional council, elected by proportional representation and the other, that of the *département*, elected by territorial divisions (*cantons*). Three of these *départements* are in the Caribbean – Guadeloupe, Martinique and French Guyana – and one – Réunion – is in the Indian ocean. The small archipelago of St Pierre et Miquelon off the Canadian coast, and the island of Mayotte in the Comoros islands near Madagascar in the Indian ocean have a special regime. France currently retains three overseas territories, all in the Pacific – Wallis and Futuna, French Polynesia (including Tahiti and the Mururoa atoll used for nuclear testing) and New Caledonia.

The Commune

The basic unit of local organisation in France is the *commune*. All *communes* have the same structures, and the same legal status and powers, although there is no uniformity in size between them, since they may consist of anything from a small hamlet or village to a very large town. In metropolitan France, with a land area of some 213 000 square miles and a population of about 57 million, there are some 36 750 *communes*. 22 000 of them have fewer than 500 inhabitants and a further 10 000 have between 500 and 2000 inhabitants, but only a quarter of the population lives in these small *communes*. Half the population lives in the 2 per cent of *communes* with over 10 000 inhabitants and 36 *communes* are cities of over 100 000 people. Paris, with two million inhabitants, is simultaneously a commune and a *département*.

Central government attempts to reduce the number of *communes* by encouraging and facilitating mergers have proved largely ineffective. Far-reaching reforms proposed in the mid-1970s (in the Guichard report) have never been implemented, and later reforms of local government have not greatly impinged upon the *communes'* political structures or statutory powers. Local loyalties and attachments to traditional boundaries (the *communes* are based upon pre-revolutionary parishes) have thwarted and daunted tidy-minded reformers. The financial and administrative resources of many *communes* are too small to allow them to operate effectively, while modern urban and suburban development has not respected centuries-old boundaries; consequently various devices have been used to overcome fragmentation, principally the organisation of consortia of communes for one or more specific purposes (see Exhibit 6.1) and the creation of associations and clubs (Mény, 1993, p. 125).[1] *Communes* may, depending upon their size and resources, act in a wide number of areas. These can broadly be characterised as: the maintenance of public health and safety; the development of local infrastructure and the furtherance of local economic development; the provision and maintenance of buildings for nursery and primary schools; the provision of certain cultural facilities.

Traditionally it was upon the leader of the *commune*, the mayor (see Exhibit 6.2) that responsibility for public order and safety within the *commune* fell. French terminology refers to such matters as policing responsibilities, but draws a distinction between administrative policing, which is concerned with public safety, order, health and hygiene, and judicial policing, which is concerned with the maintenance of good order through the suppression of crime. The mayor has powers in relation to public morality and order, for example over whether films that may be judged offensive can be shown in a local cinema, or over the holding of a demonstration or a procession. Mayors may also take measures in relation to the prevention of pollution, whether through noise or other nuisances. Communal responsibilities for matters such as public car parking, refuse collection, water supply and sewage disposal derive from these powers, as does the oversight or provision of the services of undertakers and of slaughterhouses. In the interests of the maintenance of good order some communes maintain a police force; such forces are usually small and their powers limited. In rural communes there may be a *garde champêtre* with a special concern for enforcing regulations relating to the countryside, for example concerning hunting.

EXHIBIT 6.1

Extent of co-operation between *communes*

	Number of consortia as at 1 December 1994
Urban communities	9
Commune communities	75
Districts	322
Consortia	18 058
of which	
single-purpose consortia	14 446
multi-purpose consortia	2 094
Others	15

Principal purposes of consortia (1 September 1991)

Purpose	Number of consortia		
	Single-purpose	*Multi-purpose*	*District*
Provision of water	3 375	455	62
Sewage	794	607	84
Provision of energy	1 400	117	13
Highways	355	1 006	69
School transport	813	379	26
Provision of schools and related facilities	1 807	483	57
Other purposes	6 052		
Total	14 596	3 047	311

Communes also have powers over town and country planning and some infrastructure development. All *communes* may draw up a communal plan designating the land use within their area (POS, *plan d'occupation des sols*). Since 1983 communes have had complete responsibility for the drawing up and approval of these documents; once the plan has been settled the granting of planning permission for new or altered buildings within those communes which have a POS becomes a largely legal and formal matter for the mayor who must simply ascertain that the proposed construction accords with the plan. *Communes* also have some responsibility for infrastructure, especially for the construction and maintenance of local roads and paths, for drainage and water supply, and for street lighting. They may provide public transport. They may, with the assistance of state funds, and often in partnership with developers, become involved in the development or restoration of their areas. They do not directly build or administer low cost housing, but they may set up or participate in the organisations that do build such housing (*habitations à loyer modéré*). They are not allowed to engage directly in industrial or commercial activities, but they may seek to attract investment and employment, for example through subsidies, the encouragement of tourism, and the creation of attractive conditions for life and work. The efforts of the town of Montpellier to promote itself as a location for high-tech industry and major research activities are an example of municipal activity of this kind.

EXHIBIT 6.2

Mayors

Who is a Mayor?

Occupation	Percentage of all mayors			
	1971	1977	1983	1989
Farmers, agricultural professions	45.3	39.5	36.5	28.5
Industry and commerce	14.7	12.7	11.7	9.8
Engineers and private sector managers	10.4	12.5	13.7	14.6
Professions	5.8	5.5	5.4	5.2
Education	4.6	6.8	7.6	8.9
Civil service	2.9	3.2	3.3	3.9
Public sector managers	1.3	1.5	1.3	1.7
Independent means or retired	14.5	18.3	20.2	27.4

Source: Compiled from *Cahiers Français*, 239, pp. 61–2 and *Pouvoirs*, 60, p. 78

How much time do they spend on their tasks as mayor (as a percentage of a sample poll taken in 1987)?

Days a week	Mayors of communes with a population of		
	Fewer than 2000	2000–5000	More than 5000
Not more than one	11	3	0
Between one and three	61	29	15
Four or more	36	66	83
No reply	2	2	2

n = 500

Communes have long had the responsibility for the buildings, upkeep and equipping of schools, and the 1982 laws reaffirmed this role in relation to primary schools. This responsibility is closely connected with the other cultural activities which *communes* may undertake – the provision of cultural centres, including facilities for young people or for the elderly, museums, theatres, public libraries (much less developed in France than in Britain, however). Such activities are largely confined to medium to large-size towns, and are much less common amongst small and rural *communes*; the central government, chiefly through the Ministry of Culture, is often heavily involved with subsidies and general oversight. French plans for the development of cable networks and cable TV were based upon the notion of a partnership with the municipal authorities. In the event the costs and complexities have proved to be a deterrent, and municipal activity in this field is developing very slowly.

The powers and responsibilities of the *commune* may, in the case of large *communes*, provide scope for an important and effective municipal policy. Much depends, however, upon the relationships of the *commune* to other levels of government and to partners in the parapublic and private sector. The *commune* is not simply an implementor of central policy nor, since 1982, is its activity strictly subject to prior approval by central authorities; but limitations of both finance and expertise constrain the autonomy of most *communes* except the largest and wealthiest.

The Département

France was divided into *départements* early in 1790 as one of the means by which a revolutionary equality of all citizens (or rather, all male citizens) before a uniform law could supplant a variable and sometimes arbitrary patchwork of customary and feudal rights and customs (see Map 6.1). The boundaries of the *départements* have remained relatively unchanged over the last 200 years. Their names were largely taken from geographical features, often the principal river of the territory; nowadays they also have a number, in roughly alphabetical order, familiar to many since it identifies the *département* of origin on the number plate of all French motor vehicles. There were originally 89, and later 90 *départements*; the growth of population around Paris resulted in the creation of five new *départements* in the Paris region in 1966, and in 1975 Corsica was divided into two, so there are now 96 *départements* in metropolitan France.[2] Each of the

MAP 6.1
France by *départements*

original *départements* was, it is said, so devised that no part of the *département* territory was further than a single day's ride away from the principal town, and certainly they are fairly uniform in geographical area, though, partly in consequence, not at all uniform in population. The Lozère has 74 000 inhabitants, the Nord 2.5 million.

Essentially *départements* were administrative divisions devised from the centre for central purposes. Only in 1871 were *départements* recognised as units of local democracy, when an elected council replaced what had previously been an appointed advisory council. The decentralisation laws of 1982 increased the autonomy of this council; but they also enhanced the status of the communal mayors, and introduced a new tier of local government, the region, with its own responsibilities and resources. The consequence is that the formal scope for action by the *département* remains quite limited. Nevertheless since the early 1980s *départements* have often been ready to take the initiative in formulating policies to tackle local problems. This is however, still heavily dependent upon their relationships with other authorities. The *département* is also still an important territorial unit for the organisation of central government activities.

The *conseil général*, the elected assembly of the *département* under its *président* (chairperson) is responsible for social work, including work with the disabled, the provision of children's homes and homes for the elderly. The *département* is also responsible for preventive medicine, such as screening for various types of disease and the provision of vaccination and child health clinics.

The construction and maintenance of most roads and bridges and of the smaller commercial and fishing ports forms part of the responsibilities of the *département* as, since 1982, does the building, maintenance and equipping of the *collèges*, which are the schools for the eleven to sixteen age group. The provision and payment of teachers is a matter for the central Ministry of Education. The running of school bus services, except within the limits of a single *commune*'s transport area, is also now the task of the *département*. *Départements* may also, like *communes*, provide for or subsidise museums, art galleries and other local cultural activities or associations.

The Region

During the 1950s it became clear that infrastructure development and economic restructuring might more effectively be planned at an intermediate level between the central government and the *département*. This was not a totally new idea; an initial attempt to create administrative structures at regional level had occurred under the Vichy government but, probably because of the Vichy associations, had been discontinued shortly after the end of the war. In the 1950s much of the impetus came from the economic Planning Commissariat who devised the grouping of *départements* which persists today, apart from the separation of Corsica from the Provence–Alpers–Côte d'Azur region, so that there are now 22 regions.

In 1964 regional administrative institutions were set up, largely concerned with providing for advice and guidance on economic development in the region for the benefit of central government. For this purpose a regional advisory committee (*Commission du développement economique régional* – CODER) was set up consisting of nominated members. In 1969 President de Gaulle proposed a reform which would have created elected regional councils, and put it as part of a package of reforms to the referendum in 1969 which was, however, primarily a test of the nation's confidence in his continued presidency. After the rejection of the reforms and de Gaulle's resignation a further, but more tentative, reform was introduced for all the regions, except the Ile de France around Paris in 1972. The Ile de France was restructured by a 1976 law. The 1972 law established a regional council consisting of the members of the National Assembly and senators for the region together with members nominated from amongst their membership by the councils of the *départements* and some of the communes. However, the council had largely advisory functions, and a small budget which could be used for the conduct of studies or for contributions to infrastructural developments. It was only in 1982 with the Mitterrand government's decentralisation laws that the region became a fully developed level of local government. That law provided for directly elected regional councils, and the first direct elections were held alongside the general election in March 1986.

The regions had, until 1982, no strictly executive functions at all, since they were concerned largely with planning advice, and their financial activities were confined to capital investment, largely through subsidies and joint projects. The 1982 laws specifically gave the regions executive powers, both by making the *président* (chairperson) of the council its chief executive, and by extending the scope of regional activities and allowing for the financing not only of investment but also of running costs.

As a result of their background the powers of the regions are largely related to economic development. Regional resources are not large, although the size of their staff multiplied by six in the five years after 1981. Their budgets quadrupled between 1982 and 1988 and continued to grow, if at a lesser rate, thereafter. Since their operating costs are low, and they are not heavily committed to ongoing programme expenditure, they can spend substantial amounts in high profile investment and subsidies, and by concluding regional development planning contracts with the state (see below) can match their own resources with state funds. They can also in some cases attract European Community funds, and they may borrow.

In 1982 it was envisaged that the regions would be increasingly responsible for economic planning. However, national planning became a marginalised process, inevitably subject to the changing fortunes of the international economic context and of internal political priorities. Moreover, there was some ambiguity in the objectives, as between the regional realisation of a national plan, and local planning at a genuinely regional level. Nevertheless, planning contracts were agreed in 1984, and again in 1989 and 1994. For the period of the Eleventh National Plan the central government's contribution amounted to 67 billion francs (Scargill, 1995, p. 22). Their usefulness derives from their specification of the division, as between the central government and the region, of financial responsibilities for a number of agreed programmes, for example in support of training, of agricultural productivity, of urban rehabilitation or of infrastructural investment such as motorways and dams. Grandiose regional economic development initiatives have not been possible and the regions have concentrated upon underpinning areas of major importance to them, such as, for the Nord–Pas de Calais region, the Channel ferry ports.[3]

Amongst the new possibilities opened up by the 1982 laws was an increased participation by the region in research and technology policy, by means, for example, of research contracts with public or private bodies. Regions are responsible for the maintenance and equipping of the *lycées* (high schools) in their area, and for some training, apprenticeship schemes and adult education. They have been notably active in this area, building 220 *lycées* between 1986 and 1992, compared with 60 built by the state in the preceding five years. They have subsidised university development and are attempting to take on a wider role in relation to vocational training and employment.

The growing prominence of the regions in the political debate at the European Union level has also assisted the very rapid development of the political status and identity of the regions. They have taken their place in the European Union Committee of the Regions and sought to find partners and allies amongst regions in other member states. All the French regions maintain offices in Brussels, though in two cases they are shared with allies from elsewhere: Picardie shares an office with the British county of Essex and Poitou–Charentes and Centre are represented along with the Spanish region Castile-Leon (Hooghe and Keating, 1994).

The Electoral and Administrative Structures of Local Government

Both the *département* and the region began as purely administrative territorial divisions, created to answer the needs of the central government. The *commune* has a longer history of existence as a unit of representative local government, but all three levels of government continue to be involved in a complex intertwining of local government and administration, and the local execution of central government functions. *Communes* are governed by an elected council (see Exhibit 6.3). The smallest councils, for *communes* with less than 100 inhabitants, have nine members, and the number of members rises in proportion to the population so that those *communes* with more than 300 000 inhabitants have 69 member councils, apart from Lyons with 73, Marseilles with 101 and Paris which has 163 seats on its council. Elections are held every six years.

In small *communes* of under 3500 inhabitants councillors are elected by a majority vote system. The voter has as many votes as there are seats on the council. In *communes* of over 3500 inhabitants, candidates are obliged to group themselves into lists, each with as many candidates as there are vacancies, but voters may strike out a name on a list and replace it with a name from another list. In these *communes* there are two rounds of voting; candidates who obtain 50 per cent or more of the votes cast are elected at the first round, the remaining vacancies are filled by those candidates who achieve the highest scores in the second round. For *communes* with over 3500 inhabitants (except Paris, Lyons and Marseilles), a new electoral system was introduced in 1982. Candidates group themselves into lists of as many candidates as there are seats. Electors have one vote,

EXHIBIT 6.3

National and local electoral systems in France

Election	System	Electoral District
Presidential	Two-ballot 'first past the post'	Whole country
National Assembly	Two-ballot 'first past the post'	Single member constituencies
European Parliament	Proportional by list	Whole country
Regional Councils	Proportional by list	*Département*
Département Council (*Conseil Général*)	Two-ballot 'first past the post'	Subdivision of *département* (*canton*)
Town Council (*Conseil Municipal*)	1. Less than 3500 inhabitants: two-ballot 'winner takes all' list system 2. Over 3500 inhabitants: two-ballot list system: 50% to winner, 50% proportionately	*Commune* (except for Paris, Lyons, Marseilles)
Senate	Indirect: election by electoral college	*Département*

Source: Documentation Française (1991, p. 70).

which they cast for one of the lists. If any one of the lists obtains over 50 per cent of the vote in the first round, they are awarded half the seats and their share of the other half which are distributed in proportion to the votes cast amongst all those lists which have achieved at least 5 per cent of the votes. If no list has obtained over 50 per cent, then a second round is held between all the lists which have obtained at least 10 per cent of the votes. The list which obtains the highest number of votes at that stage is the one which takes half the seats, and the other half are divided proportionately between all those lists which have gained at least 5 per cent in the second round. The composition of the lists may be modified by the amalgamation of two lists, but no candidates may stand who were not already candidates in the first round on lists which gained at least 5 per cent of the vote. Nor may candidates who figured on the same list in the first round divide themselves amongst several lists in the second round.

One effect of this electoral system is to prevent the emergence of a 'hung council'; one single list is necessarily assured of a comfortable majority composed of its 50 per cent plus its proportionate share of the other half of the seats. A further effect of these provisions is the encouragement of alliances between parties, so that the first round can to a certain extent act as a 'primary' election, a subsequent merger of lists being shaped by the first round results.

Paris, Lyons and Marseilles are all subdivided into *arrondissements*, 20 in Paris, 16 in Marseilles and 9 in Lyons. Each *arrondissement* has its own council and mayor; one-third of the members of the *arrondissement* council are also members of the municipal council. The two councils are elected simultaneously, and the lists of candidates contain as many names as there are seats on the *arrondissement* council. The electoral system is that applied to *communes* of over 3500 inhabitants.

The mayor is elected from amongst its members by the council of the *commune*. In *communes* of over 3500 inhabitants it is invariably the leader of the majority list who becomes mayor, so that the voters can be said to have some voice in the choice and electoral battles may be quite closely linked to the personality of the potential mayors. Mayors are both the leaders and the chief executives of their *communes*; they combine representational duties on behalf of their *commune* with political and administrative activities on behalf of the council, and with a number of functions on behalf of the state. A French mayor is regarded as being both an elected representative and an official of the state. In consequence mayors are not accountable to their councils; they cannot be dismissed by them. The powers combined by a mayor are considerable: where national political groupings play a large part in local political life the mayor is the main local political leader; the mayor is also the chief executive of the council's decisions. The enlarged executive powers of the council since the 1982 reforms have reinforced the mayor's position in this role. In addition, the mayor exercises some of the prerogative powers of the state, especially in relation to the maintenance of law and order and the prevention of nuisances, so that by-laws on these matters may be made by mayoral decree. The mayor also acts for the state in the registration of births and deaths, and of marriages.

The position of the mayor has always been an interesting and complex one in relation to central politics and the central govern-ment. In many small *communes* the mayor will be a leading local figure, often with purely local connections, but sometimes a local person who has achieved a position in the central administration or national politics. A person who understands the operation of the machinery of national power may, it is often felt, be in an advantageous position to forward the interests of the local *commune*, even if many of the day to day duties of the position have to be carried out by a locally-based deputy. It has been normal practice for many national political figures to be mayor of their local town, and for those who are mayors of large and important towns these positions can constitute a substantial power base. It was, for example, such a power base that facilitated an unsuccessful challenge to Chirac's leadership of the RPR by a number of Gaullist *notables* in 1990. A number of such mayors have held office for very long periods indeed, including the Gaullist Jacques Chaban-Delmas (prime minister during 1969–73) Mayor of Bordeaux from 1945 to 1995 when he was replaced as Mayor by the serving prime minister, Alain Juppé, and Gaston Defferre, Socialist Minister from 1981 to 1986, Mayor of Marseilles from 1953 until his death in 1986. The post of mayor may also be a launching pad to a national political career, as it was for Hubert Dubedout, who became mayor of Grenoble in 1965, elected as the leader of a non-party campaign to develop and modernise the town's infrastructure. He subsequently joined the Socialist party, and in the 1983 elections he was defeated by a young Gaullist opponent, Alain Carignon, who went on to achieve ministerial office in Chirac's 1986–8 government and again in 1993, only to be imprisoned in 1994 for corruption in his management of Grenoble. In 1995 Grenoble elected a Socialist mayor. The mayor may thus be at the centre of an important network of political and municipal patronage and power.

In their capacity as officials of the state mayors are subject to the oversight of the State's local representative, the prefect, and ultimately of the Ministry of the Interior, whose advice and directives are conveyed to the mayors through a multiplicity of circulars and instructions. Relationships with the local mayors continue to be a major preoccupation of the prefect in each *département*. Whatever the formal, institutional pattern of responsibility, the fact that a mayor is simultaneously representative and official blurs the picture; in *communes* of over 3500 inhabitants the mayor enjoys the legitimacy deriving from the voters' direct say in the election: the voters know, when they choose a list, who will be the mayor. In the smaller rural *communes* the mayor enjoys local status and support in dealings with what may be seen as outside forces. Where the mayor is a major political figure, then relationships with central government bodies, and particularly the prefect, have always been very delicately balanced.

Half the members of the *conseil général* of the *département* are elected every three years; each member thus serves a six year term. One member is elected for each *canton* (ward) of the *département*, by a two-round system similar to that used for parliamentary constituencies (see Exhibit 6.3). This electoral system has been in place since the 1870s. The *conseiller général* for any canton has very frequently been the mayor of one of the *communes*. Since the *département* was, until 1983, largely an administrative body rather than an entity of genuine local government, the *conseil général's* role was essentially that of providing a forum for the concerns of the *communes*.

The prefect who, until the 1983 reforms, played the key role in the administrative life of the *département* continues to occupy a prominent and central place. He (only three out of 115 prefects were female in 1992) is the representative of the government in the *département*, and as such takes formal precedence. He plays a major representational role on official occasions, in uniform, and is provided with housing, expenses and an official car to enable him to do so. He is appointed by the President by a decision taken in the Council of Ministers. When Napoleon instituted the prefectoral system, the main task of the prefect in each *département* was to ensure law and order and loyalty to the government, to see that central government decisions were uniformly applied throughout the country, and to keep a steady flow of both taxation and conscripts to support the war effort. The prefect remains responsible for law and order, and for taking whatever measures are required to deal with emergencies and disasters. The prefect is also formally responsible for the oversight of all the services of the central government which operate within the *département*. The prefecture is located in the administrative centre of the *département*, usually the main town, though in some cases other towns have become larger and more important than the one designated nearly two centuries ago as the seat of the prefecture. The *département* is divided into *arrondissements*, each with a sub-prefect located in the principal town of the area. The structure was conceived of as a neat and rational one, which ensured that laws and instructions could rapidly be transmitted, via prefect and sub-prefect, to the mayors, and that they would be smoothly and uniformly executed;[4] nor was the flow purely one way. The prefects were called upon to report regularly to Paris upon the conditions, events and state of opinion within their *département*.

In practice matters were never quite so simple. First, although the prefect was the representative of the state within his *département*, he was also, very frequently, in effect the ambassador of his *département* to the central government. Prefects required the co-operation of mayors and other local leaders if the *département* was to run smoothly, and would endeavour to ensure consensus and compromise solutions to avoid dispute and conflict.

Secondly, the administrative role of the prefect was greatly complicated by the development of bureaucratic structures. From the beginning the services of the Ministries of War, Justice, Finances and Education were placed outside prefectoral control, but other pre-existing bodies, such as the bridge and highway engineers, were brought under the prefect's control. Over the succeeding two centuries the central administration has become more complex, the number of individual ministries has grown, and the task of the prefect has in practice become much more one of co-ordination than of direction and control. As communications have improved, and especially since 1945, much more business has been carried out informally and directly between local services and their parent ministry, and the prefect may be involved, if at all, only in the formal processes. On several occasions since 1945 – in 1953, 1964 and 1970 – attempts were made to reassert the primacy of the prefect, without marked success.

Thirdly, the prefect, as representative of the state, has also, almost from the beginning, been seen as the representative of the government, and hence directly implicated in the political stance of the government of the day. The duties of the prefects from the beginning included the requirement to try to keep local leaders, and local society, loyal to the regime, and in the circumstances of nineteenth and much of twentieth century France where regime and government were inseparable, this involved a highly political role. This undoubtedly at some periods meant that prefects could, and did, use their positions to try to influence elections in favour of the government in place. The development of organised, disciplined, mass-based political parties has diminished the possibility of such influence, but the prefect is still regarded as a highly political official (Schmidt, 1991, p. 385).

Whilst the vast majority of prefects come from within the prefectoral corps, and have gained experience as sub-prefects, or are at least senior officials from elsewhere in the administration, any person may be appointed to a post as a prefect, and this has very occasionally been done. A consequence of this very politicised image is that changes in political circumstances can be accompanied by a *valse préfectorale* – a prefectoral waltz – quite large numbers of prefects are moved from one *département* to another, or find posts elsewhere in the administration or indeed outside it. In 1967, there were 41 changes, in 1981 53, between 1986 and 1988 74 and between 1988 and 1989 a further 49.

The decentralisation reforms of 1982–3 had an impact upon the role and position of the prefect. Indeed, the intention to depart from what seemed a highly centralised model of local administration was signalled by the attempt to abolish the title 'prefect' and replace the prefects with *commissaires de la république* – Commissioners of the Republic. In practice the prefects hyphenated the two designations in a clumsy double title, and the Chirac government of 1986–8 legally reverted to the old nomenclature.

It might be argued that the changes in the prefect's role were similarly illusory. Nevertheless, the decentralisation legislation marked a real change, the full consequences of which have developed slowly. The most important changes were that the councils of both *communes* and *départements* were given powers to determine their own budgets, rather than agree to a budget set by the prefect, and the chairperson (*président*) of the council was given a role as the council's chief executive. This meant the transfer of resources from central government ministries to the local authorities, and also the transfer of staff from the prefecture and other local offices of the central government to the service of the council. Large parts of the social work services (the *direction départementale des affaires sanitaires et sociales*) and some parts of the public works services (the *direction départementale de l'equipement*) as well as of the agricultural and forestry services have been transferred to the *conseil général*.

The prefecture continues to undertake a good number of administrative tasks on behalf of central government, such as the issuing of identity cards and passports, and its staff continue to assist the prefect in his remaining functions. Nor has the prefect's function in relation to the oversight of the local authorities changed quite so much as might have been expected. Before the decentralisation legislation the prefect's legal powers to draw up and then put into effect the local budget were inevitably matters for consultation and negotiation with the local council members, and the prefect's power to veto decisions on grounds either of illegality or inadvisability was seldom exercised. In many respects the decentralisation legislation legalised what had long been informal practice, at least for the *départements* and the larger urban *communes*. The smaller rural *communes* still tend to look to the prefect for guidance and reassurance. Since the new legislation neither budgetary nor policy decisions within the councils' areas of responsibility require prior approval by the prefect, but financial actions (except for those of *communes* of fewer than 2000 inhabitants, where the Ministry of Finance checks the accounts) are scrutinised by the local *Chambre régionale des comptes*, an independent audit body attached to the central audit institution, the *Cour des Comptes*. Prefects may draw the attention of the *Chambre régionale des comptes* to cases where local budgets are not being properly formulated or administered. This is no mere formality and has resulted in some important revelations of dubious practice and corruption (Mény, 1992, pp. 273–6). Equally, policy decisions may be referred by the prefect to the local *tribunal administratif* – administrative court – though only on grounds of illegality, not on the merits of a decision.

It was not until 1986 that the regions became a full tier of local government. In that year the elections for the regional council, provided for in the 1982 decentralisation laws, took place. Regional councils are elected for a fixed six year term. Although in 1986 the elections were timed to coincide with the general election, this is unlikely to happen frequently, for the national assembly's term is five years, and the presidency's seven. The regions had already begun to take over the executive responsibilities assigned to them under the 1982 laws, but under a council consisting of all the local members of parliament and senators, plus delegates from the *commune* and *département* councils. The system used for direct elections in 1986 was a proportional representation system, with each *département* forming a multi-member constituency. Each voter has one vote, which is cast for a list of as many candidates as there are seats in the *département*. Seats are distributed between the lists in proportion to the distribution of the votes; the appropriate number of members is taken from each list, starting from the top.

Given the functions of the region, described above, the administrative services attached to the region, including those transferred from the central government, are relatively small, though rapidly expanding. The chairperson (*président*) of the regional council is its chief executive; the post has been seen as a politically important and influential one, and leading politicians from the party or group holding the majority of the seats in the regional council have been elected. In certain regions the election of the *président* proved to be of considerable political significance, for example in the Provence–Alpes–Côte d'Azur region in 1986, and in Aquitaine in 1988 where the moderate right regional presidents entered into agreements with the National Front. In 1992 the National Front focused upon winning control of the Provence–Alpes–Côte d'Azur region and failed. Also in 1992 two government ministers were elected to regional presidencies, possibly on the votes of National Front councillors. One, J.-P. Soisson, resigned his government post. The other, J.-M. Rausch, gave up his presidency. The first Juppé government contained three regional presidents and the second one, four. Regional politics are steadily acquiring a higher profile.

The Staffing of Local Authorities

Until 1982 a large number of activities which were essentially local in their impact were carried out by central government officials, attached to central ministries. They might act directly, under central government powers, frequently co-ordinated by the prefect, or they might undertake activities as contractors for the local authorities. *Communes*, especially the large ones, often had a good number of employees, but the non-executive roles of both the *département* and the region meant that they employed virtually no staff at all. The transfer of responsibilities, and the widening of the executive scope of all levels of local government meant that the number of local employees rose although those of the *communes* still constitute three-quarters of the total (see Table 6.1). The Socialist government recognised this as a consequence of decentralisation. Moreover, the Socialist party had traditionally found a high level of support amongst those who were employed in local government, and therefore brought them within

TABLE 6.1

**Local government staff on 1 January 1990
(full-time equivalent numbers)**

Type of authority	Number
Region	4 490
Département	142 264
Commune	776 752
Intercommunal Consortia	63 207
Housing Associations (HLM)	49 300
Other	52 263
Total	1 088 276

Source: Ministry of the Interior.

the scope of the reforms in terms and conditions of service that it was introducing for central officials. The law now constitutes local government employees as a specific category of public servant, but recognises the rights of the local authorities to determine their personnel needs. The notion of the local public service as a career service is protected by the establishment of bodies at national level, for senior officials, and at the level of the *département* for others, which undertake recruitment, organise training, and will take responsibility for any official who has become redundant until a job can be found elsewhere.

Continuity and Change: Patterns of Local–Central Relationships

In the 200 years since the Revolution some of the patterns of relationships between central and local bodies became deeply embedded in the pattern of French administrative and political life. The decentralisation reforms of the 1980s were a determined effort to shake up and change some of these entrenched habits. The changes may have been more modest than the rhetoric which surrounded them, but there have been important shifts in power. Any evaluation should not neglect a number of major factors. First, despite the origins of local government units as administrative rather than political bodies and, until recently, the very limited scope for genuine local government, the pattern was always complex. The neat organisational plan of the centralised state was balanced by the strength of local identity and local interests, with whom the agents of the central state were compelled to work.

Secondly, this balance was, and still is, assisted by the operation of the system of *cumul des mandats* – the holding of multiple electoral offices (see Chapter 7, p. 191). Whilst multiple accumulation of offices is no longer possible, the practice of combining two elected offices is likely to continue. The consequence is that local politics tend to be very important to national politicians. They are often the means through which a local power-base and local legitimacy is secured within a constituency or local area. Equally, politicians regard the combination of local and national office as an important means for ensuring that their local area has an effective advocate with central officials, ministers and their advisors.

Thirdly, the complexity of the balance has not diminished. However apparently neat and rational the division of responsibilities between the four levels of government – commune, *département*, region, centre, – the boundaries are not straightforward. Local politicians seek to take the credit for tackling problems which are locally important, and the *cumul* encourages this. But they do not want to carry the can where the problems are intractable: 'responsibility for the care of the elderly stops where medical policy begins, that for the prevention of delinquency where anti-drugs policy starts, responsibility for poor housing stops with the homeless. There would be a long list of areas which the state has been left with because they are difficult and there is little desire on the part of local elected councillors to be held responsible for the outcomes.'[5] Equally, the prefects have reacted flexibly to the changes, laying an increased stress upon their role as co-ordinators and monitors of the implementation of policy, rather than executives. They have thereby retained a good deal of influence. This influence has been reinforced by some new measures, such as those for implementing the safety net income support measures (*Revenu minimum d'insertion*) and the provisions for housing the homeless introduced by the Rocard government, which provided for responsibility to be shared between the prefect and the president of the *conseil général*.

Fourthly, the nature of the French legal framework and of French administrative practice allows, within an apparently highly centralised system, for a considerable degree of local flexibility in the implementation of the law. Most French laws as passed by Parliament set out a broad framework for action. Their implementation requires a number of detailed *décrets d'application* which are promulgated by the minister concerned without further parliamentary discussion, and may be accompanied by official circulars, addressed to the prefect or the mayor. In ensuring the law is obeyed prefects and mayors may, and frequently do, take account of local conditions; if the enforcement of the law is challenged, the courts will be concerned to see that the intentions of the policy embodied in the legislation are being achieved. An example of the application of this discretion is in the general field of control of agricultural pollution; those concerned with implementation at local level will try to assist farmers to meet the national norms in ways that are appropriate to local conditions; but equally higher standards than the national level may be set locally, for example in North Brittany, where local shellfish production may be harmed by water pollution from intensive animal rearing.

Fifthly, the effect of the decentralisation has been to reinforce the powers of the local political elites. An important impetus in the movement for the decentralisation reforms was the desire of local political leaders, especially mayors, to enlarge their scope for action without depending upon the cumbersome and often slow processes of obtaining authorisation from central government bodies. Local leaders have undoubtedly been the main beneficiaries of the reforms. As a number of commentators have pointed out (Terrazzoni, 1987; Rondin, 1985), decentralisation, despite the rhetoric in which it was clothed, has not greatly increased the ordinary citizen's democratic role. The reforms, especially the limitation of the *cumul des mandats*, have, however, opened up participation in local politics to a rather wider circle of active participants, tending to reinforce thereby the role of political party organisation (Schmidt, 1991, pp. 267–77).

Sixthly, although local authorities now have a greater control over their own budgets, subject always to the ability of the prefect to refer to the local audit body any expenditure alleged to be improper, the extent of the central government's role in providing or authorising the resources required to finance local expenditure is obviously crucial to the balance between central and local power. Local authorities levy certain taxes, of which they determine the level; they are taxes on rents, on houses and land, and on businesses (see Exhibit 6.4). In addition, the revenue from certain taxes of which the central government fixes the level, notably vehicle licensing and land registration taxes, is transferred directly to the *départements*, whilst the region receives the sum raised from vehicle registrations. The local authorities may also levy fees for certain services. The transfer of responsibilities from the central government to the local authorities that was instigated by the decentralisation reforms was accompanied by the transfer of resources, some in the form of additional subventions, and some in the form of the product of certain taxes. The resulting system was probably even more complicated than the one which had preceded it, and still leaves problems with the rectification of inequities between different areas, and with control over the potentially inflationary tendencies of expanding local expenditure. On the whole, however, local government in France has not suffered financially, even when central government has been adopting a restrictive financial policy.

EXHIBIT 6.4

Local government expenditure

Decentralisation resulted in a transfer of resources to the various levels of local government:

Total resources, in million francs

Before decentralisation (1982)	After decentralisation (1986)
373.8	541.7

In 1993 total local public expenditure amounted to some 10 per cent of French gross national product.

Expenditure by the regions has risen. Regional resources in 1993 amounted to 60.7 billion francs.

Annual rate of increase in expenditure by regions (%)

	1980	1982	1983	1984	1985	1986	1987	1988	1989	1990	1991	1992
Increase	−4	16	43	24	20	27	17	17	14	12	17	7

Average annual rate of increase of expenditure of other levels of local government, 1980–92: five per cent.

Average local government expenditure per inhabitant 1992 (in francs)

Level	Commune	Département	Region
Amount	6 600	3 400	960

Sources: *Cahiers français*, 239, 1989; Guy Gilbert, 'The Resources of the French Regions in Retrospect', in Loughlin and Mazey (1995).

One reason for the relatively sheltered position which local government has enjoyed in France in the 1980s and the 1990s was the fact that the Socialist governments of 1981 and 1988 did not wish to see the *grande affaire* of decentralisation undermined by local dissatisfaction. An even more important reason is the strength of the defences which local affairs can mobilise against the centre. In France it can be argued that what is still formally a centralised system has in fact been required by the considerable strength of local interests and influence. The prefectoral system ensures that the government hears the voice of local concerns, while the large size and geographical omnipresence of

the *services déconcentrés* gives a substantial part of the central administration a stake in developments affecting those local bodies which
are their neighbours and clients. Moreover, the very late development of national, organised, mass political parties in France has
tended to privilege local roots for politicians, often above political
allegiance, and the *cumul des mandats*, even if now limited, has
entrenched habits of political behaviour which ensure that local
voices can be politically strong.

Finally, the European Community has added a further element to
the complex pattern. As European action and legislation extends to
new fields, and in the wake of the increased consciousness of the
European dimension engendered by the programme to complete the
Single Market by the end of 1992, some of the paradoxes of the
European dimension are becoming obvious. The European Community acts through the national governments of member states. It is the
national governments who are signatories to the treaty, and who
carry the responsibility of seeing that community policies are implemented and enforced. In so far as local authorities are in fact the
bodies to whom the task of implementation actually falls, the central
government is answerable for their actions to the European Court.
Thus the European dimension may work to reinforce the oversight of
the central authorities over the local authorities. Equally, however,
the local authorities find in the policies or the subventions of the
European Community a source of power and resources which
reinforces their position. For example, in the mid-1980s the EC
adopted a programme designed to cushion the impact on the
mediterranean areas of the previous member states of the accession
to the European Community of Spain and Portugal. In France the
regional authorities of one of the regions concerned, Languedoc–
Roussillon, and some central government officials, influenced by the
powerful regional farmers' lobby, felt that subventions from this
programme should be used to aid agriculture. Other central government officials, and the large *commune* of Montpellier, wished to see the
money used to develop the high-technology industrial base of the
area. Although the EC funding was specifically of a regional nature,
the local authorities in Montpellier were able to ensure that it was
their views, and not those of the region, that prevailed, and even to
ensure EC financing for a local project – the construction of an opera
house/convention hall – that the region had specifically refused to
support financially. The European Community was thus invoked to
arbitrate between different levels of local government.

Conclusion

The decentralisation reforms, including the creation of directly elected councils at regional level, have certainly altered the pattern of local government in France. Many of these alterations have been effectively the continuation or enhancement of previous trends. Problems remain. There are still very many – probably far too many – local government entities. There are now three sub-central tiers of government. Rivalries, conflicts of responsibility, for example in training or in social services, and complexity are the consequence. The financing of local government activity is very complicated. Local political bosses, sometimes of astonishing political longevity, with a hold on party organisation, and a foot in both national and local politics, can build formidable clientilist political machines. Amongst the effects of decentralisation has, however, been an increase in local political pluralism and some increase in the sensitivity of local government to local needs (Schmidt, 1991, pp. 390–1).

Local and central affairs in France remain very closely linked, through a complex administrative network, and through overlapping political elites at national and local level. The development of interconnections and integration in ways that do not take account of national boundaries, as well as increasing insistence by local populations on having a say in the development of the area in which they live, prompted, for example, by ecological and environmental concerns, are both likely to contribute to the shaping of the patterns of relationship. Some local authorities may well be growing in confidence and initiative, but the variety, and the fragmentation of the basic level of local government is also an important factor of weakness, and will long ensure a major role for the central government.

Part III

Democratic Politics in France

7

Parliament

Since the onset of the French Revolution, which was marked, in 1789, by the calling together of the Estates General, every government in France has recognised that it requires support from a representative body that embodies and visibly expresses the consent of a large proportion of the population. With the entrenchment of republicanism by the end of the nineteenth century, the principle, now embodied within the constitution, that national sovereignty belongs to the whole people, who exercise it through their elected representatives, was firmly established, although it was not until 1944, after a long history of struggle and debate, that women were recognised as fully forming part of the sovereign people and given the vote.

The Parliament of the Fifth Republic is deeply rooted in the principle of universal suffrage. The introduction in 1962 of direct election to the presidency (see Chapters 2 and 3), combined with the presence in the National Assembly of a presidential majority (see Chapters 8 and 9) had the effect for a while of concentrating political power and activity outside Parliament, if within an institution that could also claim to be supported by the sovereign people. During the 1980s, however, the strength of the rationalised and constrained parliamentary system with which the authors of the 1958 constitution wished to replace the irresponsible and unstable patterns of the Fourth Republic became rather more evident. Both the Left and the Right have discovered the mechanisms which the constitution makes available to them. Parliament's chief function remains the legitimation, through the legislative process, of the programme of a government. In this role the Parliament of the Fifth Republic has been markedly more effective than its predecessor. Another main function of parliaments is 'to make the government behave' (Frears,

1990, p. 33). The French Parliament has in general not performed this function very effectively. This chapter describes the structures and mechanisms of Parliament and considers its functions and the role it plays.

The Structure of Parliament

The National Assembly: Voters and Elections

The French Parliament consists of two houses, or chambers. The 'lower' house, the National Assembly, has 577 members, sometimes called 'deputies'. The French word is *député* which might better be translated as 'delegate'.

The right to vote for members of Parliament is enjoyed by men and women over the age of eighteen. The voting age was lowered from 21 to eighteen in 1974, by a law passed soon after Valéry Giscard d'Estaing won the presidency. Voters must be of French nationality and must not have been legally deprived of their right to vote. Such a deprivation, usually for a certain specified number of years, can form part of the penalty for certain criminal offences.[1] Electors must also appear on the electoral register, which is revised each year.

Members of the National Assembly must be over the age of twenty-three and be French citizens. Most of them acquire their seats at general elections. A general election must be held at least once every five years: in 1967, 1973, 1978, 1986 and 1993 general elections occurred because the sitting Assembly had been in place for five years. General elections also happen after the dissolution of the National Assembly by the President. The general elections of 1962, 1968, 1981 and 1988 followed a presidential dissolution.

Some members of the National Assembly come into parliament at times other than a general election. Members die – ten did so during the parliamentary session which lasted from the March 1986 election to May 1988 – or resign, perhaps because they wish to take up functions which are legally incompatible with a position as a member of Parliament. Posts as government ministers fall into this category, so, for example, 24 people who had been elected to the National Assembly by the 1993 general election resigned before that Assembly even met to take up ministerial posts as the new government was formed. During the 1986–8 Parliament, which was elected by a list system of proportional representation, such vacancies were filled by the return to Parliament of the first unsuccessful candidate from the same party list as the outgoing member. For all the other parliaments since 1958 all candidates at an election have had to nominate, alongside themselves, a *suppléant* – a person to replace them should they be unable to continue as a member. By-elections occur only when the replacement as well as the original member dies or resigns, and are hence relatively unusual. In 1989 when former President Giscard d'Estaing gave up his seat in the National Assembly and a by-election occurred it was his regular replacement, M. Wolf, who was elected in his place.

Election campaigns, which last officially for the three week period between the nomination of the candidates and polling day, are subject to strict official controls, regulating matters such as the siting of posters, and the diffusion of electoral tracts.[2] Candidates pay for the provision of voting slips in their names and their official posters and election addresses, but these costs, up to a limit of 50 per cent of permitted electoral expenditure, are refunded to all candidates who receive over 5 per cent of the votes. A candidate's total expenditure is limited, by a law passed in 1988, to 250 000 francs plus one franc for each inhabitant of the constituency. Unofficial teams of nocturnal bill posters are equally a feature of French elections, and the art of finding the humorous or pointed riposte with which to embellish opponents' posters is highly developed. The exact time allowed for each candidate or party by the broadcast media is carefully measured; even studio debates may be timed by a stop-watch. In an attempt to prevent last minute pressure and unfair influence, all such campaigning has to cease the day before polling day, and the publication of political opinion polls is not permitted in the previous week. Party political commercials on television are banned during the campaign and the three months preceding it, as are all forms of political advertising.

The act of voting requires voters to place a slip of paper containing the name of the chosen candidate in an envelope and post this into the ballot box. Under proportional representation the slip of paper shows the party list. Empty envelopes, or those containing more than one slip are counted as void or spoilt votes.

Most general elections since 1958 have been conducted under the constituency-based two-ballot system. One member is returned by each territorial constituency (see Exhibit 8.2, p. 220). To be elected at the first ballot a candidate requires over 50 per cent of all the valid votes cast. In the 1988 general election this occurred in 72 out of

555 seats in metropolitan France.[3] Otherwise all those candidates who have been voted for by more than 12.5 per cent of the registered electors and who do not stand down go on to a second ballot a week later. The first ballot has come to be regarded as a kind of 'primary' election between parties of broadly similar political orientation, who may agree that a less well placed candidate should stand down in favour of the better placed candidate. In 1993 as in 1978 and in 1981, such *désistement* occurred between Socialists and Communists and between Gaullists and Giscardians in those constitutencies (some 80 of them) where there were candidates from both parties. At the second ballot the candidate with most votes (a simple plurality of votes) wins.

In 1986 a proportional representation system was used, treating each *département* as a multi-member constituency.[4] Voters were required to cast their vote for a list. Candidates were taken in the order in which they appeared on the lists, so voters had no possibility of expressing preferences as between candidates on the same list.

The introduction for the 1986 election of this proportional representation system was an astute, if cynical, manoeuvre. It was largely prompted by short-term party political considerations, even if arguments related to the greater 'fairness' of proportional representation systems, in allowing for representation of all shades of opinion, could be adduced in its support, as could the fact that elections for the Parliament of the European Community in both 1979 and 1984 had used a (somewhat different) proportional representation system. The use of the proportional representation system in 1986 seems to have prevented what President Mitterrand otherwise feared – a landslide defeat for the Left in general and the Socialist Party in particular, if at the expense of letting in 35 members from the extreme-right National Front. The 1986 election installed a right-wing government in power which restored the previous system, redrawing the constituency boundaries in a law drafted within the Ministry of the Interior in consultation with a committee of six 'wise men' and the Council of State and imposed on Parliament as an issue of confidence. In 1988 the National Front retained only one seat and the overall result was a hung Parliament and a minority Socialist government. Despite an attempt by President Mitterrand to revive the issue in 1991 and the landslide victory of the Right in 1993, proportional representation is no longer on the political agenda.

The confirmation of the validity of elections, and hence the determination of the National Assembly's membership is not its own responsibility. A number of cases during the 1950s gave rise to decisions about membership of the Fourth Republic's National Assembly which were widely felt to have been based on highly political motives; this caused some scandal (Williams, 1972, p. 120), and the authors of the Fifth Republic's constitution removed such powers from the National Assembly and gave them to the Constitutional Council, which adjudicates in cases where the election results are disputed or electoral fraud or malpractice alleged.

The Senate

The Senate is the second chamber of the French Parliament. It represents the elected local authorities since each electoral constituency consists of one *département* in which the senators are elected by an electoral college comprising the members of parliament, the members of the *département's* council, and mayors and town councillors. The Senate's full complement is now 321 members[5] who must be over the age of 35, each of whom serves for a nine-year term. The Senate cannot be dissolved. One third of the membership is replaced every three years. The members represent *départements* (including the overseas territories and *départements*) which are divided into three groups, all the members from one of the groups being replaced at each renewal. Twelve senators represent French citizens resident abroad. The method of election of senators gives a national political significance to the results of local elections, since the political complexion of local councils determines that of the Senate. This meant, for example, that the Senate of the first decade of the Fifth Republic reflected the results of local elections under the Fourth Republic, and with a high proportion of rather conservative independent members, was much less supportive of de Gaulle than the National Assembly. Socialist representation in the Senate increased in the early 1980s, following the left-wing gains in the local elections of 1977, and a similar effect occurred in 1995, when Senate elections in September followed municipal elections in June. In the late 1980s the representation of the Right increased following their gains in the local elections of the early 1980s. The process of political change in the Senate is slow, however, given the nine-year term of each senator and the Left have never commanded a majority there. Equally, although the National Front had gained the councils of three large towns (Toulon, Orange and Marignane) in 1995 the party was not represented in the Senate even after the September elections.

Since laws must be passed in identical terms by both houses (see p. 196, below) the Senate can and does influence legislation, often acting to amend and improve bills in technical ways. The Senate's relationship with de Gaulle was poor, largely because of the opposition of its members to the 1962 constitutional amendment. It survived the 1969 referendum which proposed its reform. The outcome of the 1981 election again resulted in a political division beween the majorities in the two houses and the Senate constituted a source of difficulty for the Mitterrand government. Its opposition to the nationalisation programme, the press reform bill and the laws reforming industrial relations slowed the legislative process. The Senate is also an element in the complex pattern of relationships which counterbalances the power of the central state by ensuring that local interests are well represented at the centre. Its method of election ensures that its members have to be sensitive to the views of local councillors. After the 1995 municipal elections over a third of its membership – 131 out of 312 senators – held office as mayor of a *commune*. They included one who was the mayor of a *commune* of 66 inhabitants, as well as the mayor of Marseilles. The Senate has largely been unable to block governmental legislation completely. It does, however, have the crucial ability to block the normal procedures for constitutional amendment, a power it has used.

The Members of Parliament: Characteristics and Conditions

The professional background of members of Parliament has varied according to the party balance within Parliament (see Table 7.1). Thus the advent of a majority of the Left in 1981 resulted in an increase in the numbers of *députés* who had formerly been teachers and officials; out of 285 Socialist *députés* 150 were former teachers. The Socialist Party has traditionally drawn a good deal of its activist membership from these two groups. This increase occurred at the expense of those who had formerly been members of the professions (lawyers or doctors, for example) or businessmen. The proportion of *députés* with backgrounds as junior employees or workers is low – 20 out of 491 in 1978, 23 out of 491 in 1981, 16 out of 577 in 1988.

The number of women members of Parliament in France has never been high. It was highest in 1945 just after women had gained the vote. In recent years the proportion of women members has been between 5 and 6 per cent.[6]

TABLE 7.1

**Representation of selected occupations in the National Assembly
(per cent)**

Occupation	1978	1981	1986	1988	1993
Education	19.7	32.7	25	28	13
Civil service	19.7	23	22	17.5	12.4
Farmers	3.4	2.2	2.3	2.4	3.6
Industrialists/senior management	7.5	4.2	11	5.2	10.7
Professional politicians				4.7	5.0
Employees and workers	4.0	5.6	2.0	2.7	3.3

Sources: 1978 to 1988 figures from Dreyfus and D'Arcy (1993, p. 85). 1993 figures from *Le Monde*, 1 April 1993 and *Pouvoirs*, 66 (1993). Categorisation is not necessarily identical.

A feature of the French Parliament is the number of members who have formerly been civil servants. Officials may claim 'secondment' from the civil service during their period as *députés* and consequently have a particularly secure fall-back should electoral defeat occur. For senior civil servants the contacts with politicians and political life that they have encountered during their official activities can assist the launch of a political career.

French members of Parliament enjoy salaries calculated as the median of those paid to the highest grade of officials. The Communist Party has always insisted that its members of Parliament should hand over this salary to the party. Its *députés* are then remunerated at the average rate for a skilled worker, and the surplus provides an important source of general party funds.

Another striking feature of the members of Parliament is the extent to which they may combine elective offices (*cumul des mandats*) (see Chapter 6). In 1981 82 per cent of the *députés* held one or more elective offices at local level. Indeed 'mayors of major cities have a sort of natural call to be members of parliament' (Masclet, 1982, p. 110) and in 1990 all but of the mayors of cities of over 80 000 inhabitants had been elected to a parliamentary seat. Altogether nearly half the *députés* in the parliaments elected in 1978, 1981, 1986 and 1988 were mayors (Knapp, 1991, p. 19). During the 1970s and 1980s concern about this practice of accumulation of offices grew. After the 1981 Socialist victory resulted in a broad programme for decentralisation which involved increased areas of responsibility for elected councils at the level of the *département* and the introduction of a new tier of elected local government at regional level, this concern became increasingly pressing. Debate focused on the likelihood that where several offices were combined some of them, at least, would not be properly fulfilled. There was also some feeling that decentralisation ought to mean a broadening of political participation and not simply the creation of further offices for those who already constituted a political elite. In addition there was some questioning of the propriety of allowing an individual to retain the salaries that went with a position as mayor or chairman of a regional or *département* council.[7] A law of 30 December 1985 permits the holding in future of only two major elective offices at any one time. After the elections of 1988 the 577 members of the National Assembly between them held 812 local positions, and to comply with the law needed to 'lose' 141 of them. Faced with choices the *députés* almost all preferred to abandon posts at the level of region and *département*. None resigned as a mayor (Knapp, 1991, p. 35). In an interesting exception to this pattern in October 1989 former President Giscard d'Estaing preferred to retain his seat in the regional council of the Auvergne and the European Parliament, and give up his seat in the National Assembly.[8]

Partly as a result of the close linkage between local and central political life symbolised by the practice of the *cumul des mandats* the task of a *député* is conceived as having particularly strong local connections. Members of Parliament are not a major means through which citizens plead their individual cases against the actions of the ministers and ministries – other channels are used for the redress of grievances of that sort. *Députés* are, however, perceived (somewhat erroneously) as able to procure individual favours for their constituents. They certainly are powerful pleaders for the broader interests of their constituency, and do develop strongly clientilistic relationships with the mayors and other leaders in their constituencies. In a centralised system, where much local development and activity is still subject to control and authorisation by central government, and investment and economic development may be heavily influenced by central bodies, a *député* has an important role in trying to push forward his constituency's case within central government. It has moreover been powerfully argued that the slowness and caution with which reforms of local government in France have been approached, and the absence, even in a period of economic recession, of attempts radically to restructure local government structures or expenditures, result from the strength of the links between local and central political levels, and the importance of central politicians' bases within their local areas.[9]

The Organisation of Parliamentary Work

As part of the parliamentary reform embodied within the constitutional settlement of 1958 and intended to tip the balance of the institutions away from Parliament towards the executive, the constitution of the Fifth Republic contains detailed provisions for the organisation of Parliamentary work. These provisions contributed to the partial eclipse of Parliament during the first three decades of the regime. They were only one, and perhaps not the most important, amongst several factors which contributed at that period to Parliament's lack of prominence (see below). However, changes in the context in which Parliament operates, both political (the coming of *cohabitation*, for example) and institutional (the changing nature of the European Union and an increased role for the National Assembly in relation to European Union legislation) have led to changes in its habits and operation. The extent of these changes was marked and symbolised by the constitutional amendment of 1995, which altered the length of the parliamentary session.

In 1958 the constitution had limited the duration of Parliamentary sessions in order, at least in part, to curb Parliament's appetite for business and limit its capacity to hinder and hamper the government. Moreover, the restriction of the matters about which it is permitted to legislate was expected to mean that it would need less time for its business. The Constitution therefore specified the periods during which Parliament may meet: normal sessions for not more than 80 days following 2 October and for not more than 90 days following 2 April every year. In addition special sessions may be called at the request either of the government or of a majority of members of the National Assembly. Particular items of business which have to be specified in advance must constitute the agenda for such special sessions. Such special sessions require presidential approval, and in 1960 De Gaulle refused, on the grounds that the parliamentarians were yielding unnecessarily to noisy demands from a pressure group with particular interests – the farmers. Mitterrand refused to allow consideration of a law to alter the status of the nationalised car manufacturers Renault in 1987 and of a law to change the arrangements for subsidies for private schools in 1993. Genuine emergency sessions occurred only very rarely. The half-day session in late August 1990 called to discuss the Iraqi invasion of Kuwait was the first session since 1959 to have been summoned in response to an international crisis (Maus, 1991, p. 68). However, the fact that between

1974 and 1994 special sessions were called every year but one (1977), if for varying lengths of time – nine days in 1987, following 25 in 1986, a year in which the government had changed, but only two in 1989 – suggested that the legislative requirements of a complex modern state have proved to be more considerable than the authors of the constitution assumed. Indeed the brevity of parliamentary sessions produced unedifying spectacles such as the final passage, at the end of December 1987, of sixteen laws and seven ratifications of foreign agreements within 48 hours.

The constitutional amendment of 1995 changed these provisions. Parliament now meets on not more than 120 days (with the possibility of additional days on the decision of either the prime minister or a majority of members) in a single session lasting from the first working day in October to the final working day in June. The President has thereby lost powers to veto additional days. In addition to accommodating the increasing pressures of both domestic and European Union business this reform was also the logical next step in a process championed by Philippe Séguin, who had presided over the National Assembly since 1993. He had been particularly active in seeking to increase the profile of parliamentary activity, and had in the Autumn of 1993 ensured the passage of a law which allowed for the reception in Parliament of distinguished foreign visitors, for the continuous televising of parliamentary sessions on a Paris cable television network, and for the regrouping of business on three days a week. It was hoped that this would allow members to organise their time more rationally between their parliamentary and local responsibilities and reduce absenteeism. The long single session would mean that Parliament would no longer be absent from public sight for extended periods.

Philippe Séguin has proved to be a notably active *président* (chairman) of the National Assembly. Both Houses of Parliament are presided over by a *président* elected at the start of each new Parliament. The role of this *président*, especially in the National Assembly, has a clear political status, and election to it may be quite hotly contested. It usually goes to a senior political figure from amongst the governing coalition. For example, former Prime Minister Laurent Fabius took over as *président* in 1988, while in 1993 the election of Séguin, who had led the 'No' campaign in the Maastricht referendum, against his party's official line, 'was the pay-off for [general election] campaign loyalty; it was also a convenient way for Chirac to reward an important figure without the embarrassment of having to have him in the government' (Hanley, 1993, p. 425).

The timetable of parliamentary business is effectively drawn up by the government, another measure introduced by the 1958 constitution to curb the excesses of the Fourth Republic. The government has the right to insist that discussion of its bills, and of any private members' bills which it accepts, takes priority except on one day a month when, under the 1995 constitutional amendment, the members of the house may decide the agenda. This may provide more scope for backbenchers to insist on debating particular topics, but in the absence of any concept of 'official' opposition to which time would be allocated does little to extend the scope for the 'opposition' to initiate debates on particular issues other than by moving a motion of censure on the government (see p. 204, below).

The right to speak in the Senate and the National Assembly is not confined solely to their respective members, since ministers, who are not members of Parliament and consequently have no vote, may be present for debates and questions and speak.

Parliamentary questions are provided for, but only the author of the question and the minister concerned may speak. Written questions may also be tabled. The procedure for questions is rigid. The practice of holding debates round questions, not uncommon in the first two decades of the Fifth Republic, has disappeared since 1975. After an initial attempt to launch a more vigorous question time in 1970, 'questions to the government' were launched in 1974. These questions are taken at the beginning of the Wednesday afternoon sitting. The time allowed is divided up very precisely between the political groups in the Parliament and during that time they may put to ministers questions of which only an hour's notice need have been given. These questions are concerned with immediate issues and problems and, despite both their being televised and the insistence of successive *présidents* that both questioners and ministers should not simply read from their notes, do not normally provide a forum for highly-charged political debate and conflict. Further attempts to enliven procedures and enhance parliamentary scrutiny of government activity have had a limited impact. The autumn debates on proposals for government expenditure have been given a more question-and-answer format but the 1993 Parliament did not continue the practice, introduced in 1989, of further questions to ministers on Thursday afternoons in the spring session.

The laws which Parliament passes originate either as government bills (*projets de loi*) or as private members' bills (*propositions de loi*). Bills are immediately sent for examination to a committee. The constitution (Article 43) limits the number of permanent committees to six in each house (see Exhibit 7.1). It is within these committees that the bulk of the detailed examination of the bills and proposed amendments occurs. The committee hears the minister concerned, if the bill is a governmental one, but may also undertake other enquiries and investigations. A report is produced which is presented to the plenary sessions of the National Assembly, indicating the text and the amendments which the committee supports. Following the completion of the committee's report the bill, when it appears on the agenda, comes before a plenary session of the National Assembly, where it will normally be discussed article by article and may be amended. A final vote confirms the adoption or rejection of the final version of the whole law. The law is then passed to the other house, where a similar procedure ensues.

The result of the discussions in the other house may be some divergence from the text originally approved where it was first discussed. In this case the text returns to the original house for a vote on the amended version. If an agreement is still not reached a procedure known as the 'shuttle' (*navette*) occurs. The text may be passed back and forth until agreement is reached. However, the government may interrupt this process and set up a joint committee of members of the two houses to attempt to arrive at an agreed text.

EXHIBIT 7.1

The committees of Parliament

The National Assembly committees	The Senate committees
Cultural, family and social affairs	Cultural affairs
Foreign affairs	Foreign affairs, defence and the armed forces
National defence and the armed forces	Economic affairs and the plan
Finances, the economy and the plan	Social affairs
Constitutional laws, legislation and general administration	Finances
Production and trade	Constitutional laws, legislation, voting rights, regulation and general administration

Where this proves impossible, or where the two houses still refuse to approve an agreed text, the constitution provides that the National Assembly shall have the last word.

In 1993 and 1994 between 30 and 40 per cent of the laws voted by the National Assembly, other than those which ratified international agreements, were referred to a joint committee. However, agreement between the two houses was reached on all but one of the texts. This contrasted with the experience of the Socialist governments of 1988 to 1993, when nearly half of all disputed texts (79 out of 163) were finally adopted without the Senate's consent.

The Functions of Parliament: Opportunities and Constraints

Parliaments in liberal democracies usually fulfil a number of functions: they enact legislation; they may act as an arena for political debate; they may provide the government with the formal expressions of support it needs to maintain its legitimacy; they may constitute a forum for the exchange of information, serving both to educate their members, and through them the voters in the policies, needs and constraints of government, and to act as channels for the expression of the grievances of the citizen; they may control and supervise the work of the administration; they may be the place where political apprenticeships are served, providing a reservoir of potential ministerial office holders.

Legislation

The French Parliament enacts legislation. However, unlike some parliaments, its ability to do so is not absolute. Parliamentary sovereignty is limited by the constitution. First, the 1958 constitution specifies the areas in which Parliament may make law (see Exhibit 7.2). These areas cover the fundamental aspects of the organisation of society, so that, for example, nothing can be made a criminal offence except by a parliamentary law. However, many aspects of the detailed application of these principles are dealt with by governmental regulation, which is not directly subject to parliamentary control. Secondly, the laws which Parliament passes have to conform to the principles set out in the constitution. It is the Constitutional Council (see Chapter 3) which has the responsibility both for determining whether Parliament is acting outside its sphere of

EXHIBIT 7.2

The Powers of Parliament

Article 34 of the Constitution.

Laws shall be voted by Parliament.

Laws determine the rules concerning:

- civil rights and the fundamental guarantees granted to the citizens for the exercise of their public liberties; the obligations imposed by national defence upon the persons and property of citizens;
- the nationality, status and legal capacity of persons, marriage contracts, inheritance and gifts;
- the determination of crimes and misdemeanours as well as the penalties imposed therefor; criminal procedure, amnesty, the creation of new juridical systems and the status of the judiciary;
- the basis, the rate and the methods of collecting taxes of all types; the issue of currency.

Laws shall likewise determine the regulations concerning:

- the electoral system of the parliamentary Assemblies and local assemblies;
- the establishment of categories of public institutions;
- the fundamental guarantees granted to civil and military personnel employed by the state;
- the nationalisation of enterprises and the transfer of the property of enterprises from the public to the private sectors.

Laws shall determine the fundamental principles of:

- the general organisation of national defence;
- the free administration of local communities, their powers and their resources;
- education;
- property rights and civil and commercial obligations;
- legislation pertaining to employment, unions and social security.

The financial laws shall determine the financial resources and obligations of the state, under the conditions and with the reservations to be provided for in a organic law.
Laws pertaining to national planning shall determine the objectives of the economic and social action of the state.
The provisions of the present article may be detailed and supplemented by an organic law.

competence, and for ensuring that constitutional principles are respected. The President, the prime minister, the Presidents of the Senate and the National Assembly, or at least 60 members of the Senate or at least 60 members of the National Assembly may ask the Constitutional Council to examine the constitutionality of a proposed law after it has been voted but before it is officially promulgated.

The legislative action of Parliament is not only constrained by constitutional provisions. It is also largely determined by the government. Indeed, governments tend to judge whether Parliament is 'working well' by the efficiency with which the government's policy objectives are translated into legislative measures.[10] In this they are assisted by two types of resources, procedural and political. In 1958 the authors of the constitution were particularly concerned that governments must be enabled to get their laws through. They envisaged the possible prolongation of the shifting and unstable coalitions of the Fourth Republic, and wanted to give governments better possibilities of insisting, procedurally, upon the passage of their legislation. For this reason government bills take priority in the drawing up of the parliamentary agenda. The restriction of the number of committees was intended to ensure that they would be large and general, and to limit the possibility that specialised committees might act virtually as alternative ministers, subject to lobbying by interested parties and able to produce laws which differed fundamentally from those initially submitted to them. More important is the provision of Article 44 of the constitution which enables the government to insist that a draft law, or any part of it, should be taken as a whole along with such amendments as the government chooses to accept. This procedure, known as the 'block vote' (*vote bloqué*) acts as a 'guillotine' to cut short plenary discussion, and may also serve to prevent dissent within the majority coalition from being expressed – the text has to be accepted or rejected in its entirety.

This procedure was used quite frequently, up to 21 times a year, in the first decade of the Fifth Republic, but since 1970 the number of such votes has gone into double figures in only four years, and has only once exceeded 13. This was in 1986 when 69 out of the 80 occasions on which the procedure was invoked related to one bill, on the ownership of the press.

A second important procedural device is the provision of paragraph 3 of Article 49 of the constitution whereby a government may declare a particular text an issue of confidence (see Exhibit 7.3). The text will automatically be regarded as being approved unless a motion of censure is tabled and voted. In 1979 President Giscard d'Estaing's Prime Minister, Raymond Barre, used this procedure to ensure the passage of his budget and even the Socialists who had been highly critical of the procedure had recourse to it eleven times between 1981 and 1986, despite their absolute majority. Since then, in the context of *cohabitation* and a hung parliament after 1988 the use of this method to force legislation through has become a great deal more common (see Exhibit 7.3). In 1986, the first year of Chirac's *cohabitation* government, the device was used seven times, and on six of these occasions a motion of censure was actually tabled, but lost. Between 1988 and 1993 the Socialist governments of Prime Ministers Rocard, Cresson and Bérégovoy, facing a hung parliament and thus rather closer to the situation which the authors of the constitution had originally envisaged, used the provision a total of 39 times, in order to gain approval of nineteen different laws.[11] The procedure is not without its risks. In November 1990 the Rocard government survived a censure motion tabled against a law increasing social security contributions by a margin of only five votes.

A third constitutional provision allows the government to attempt to avoid altogether detailed discussion of potentially contentious matters that have to be regulated by law. This is the possibility of obtaining from Parliament delegated authority to legislate by regulation for a certain period in a certain field. Called a *loi d'habilitation*, the device has been used to avoid the emergence in public debate of divisions of opinion amongst the majority. It may also be used to speed up legislation. Such a law gave Pompidou's government, under President de Gaulle, powers to reform the social security system in 1967. The use of the procedure became more controversial during the period of *cohabitation*. President Mitterrand twice refused to sign the regulations which the government had drawn up under such a law. On the first occasion it was to mark his disagreement with the privatisation programme. On the second occasion the *loi d'habilitation* concerned the new constituencies proposed under the return to the two-ballot system. Parliament ought, the President said, to have its say on its own membership. In both cases the government very hastily put the proposed legislation directly to Parliament as a normal law, and in the circumstances was able to carry its majority with it. The laws were duly promulgated. Between 1986 and 1995 the procedure was used on three occasions, each time for laws concerning France's overseas territories.

EXHIBIT 7.3

Use of Article 49, paragraph 3
(Bill declared by government to be an issue of confidence)

Governments	Total	Censure motion tabled	No censure tabled
Debré 1959–62	4	4	0
Pompidou 1962	3	1	2
Pompidou 1962–67	0	0	0
Pompidou 1967–8	3	3	0
Couve de Murville/ Chaban-Delmas/ Messmer/Chirac 1968-76	0	0	0
Barre 1976–81	8	7	1
Mauroy/Fabius 1981–6	11	7	4
Chirac 1986–8	8	7	1
Rocard 1988–91	28	5	23
Cresson 1991	8	2	6
Bérégovoy 1991–3	3	1	2
Balladur 1993–5	1	1	0

Source: Elgie and Maor (1992); Maus (1995, pp. 175–8).

Secondly, the government does, of course, have political resources to assist it with the passage of its business through Parliament. Until 1986 all presidents were supported by a presidential majority within Parliament. Even during periods when party discipline was not well established, as was the case between 1958 and 1962, or when the presidential majority was constituted by a coalition whose coherence was fragile, for example during the presidency of Giscard d'Estaing, governments have largely proved able to mobilise political appeals to ensure the passage of their legislation. Between 1978 and 1981, for example, the Gaullist party within the National Assembly caused a number of problems for President Giscard d'Estaing and Prime Minister Barre, but never went so far as to risk a possible dissolution and general election. The governments of the second Mitterrand presidency, under Michel Rocard and Edith Cresson, have also managed to put together majorities for the legislation they wished to carry. One factor which explained this was a marked decrease in the amount of legislation introduced. In 1988 only 37 government bills were introduced in the National Assembly and between 1989 and 1993 an average of 56 a year, but this was still below the average of 74 bills a year for the first 30 years of the Fifth Republic (Elgie, 1991, p. 12; Maus, 1995, p. 180).

From the government's point of view the legislative function of the Parliament of the Fifth Republic has worked well. In all Western countries legislative activity seems to be increasing. In the first 30 years of the Fifth Republic some 3000 laws were passed. Very few governmental policies have been stymied by activity within Parliament, although presidents have been inhibited in the initiatives they might otherwise have taken (see Chapter 3). Where the government has ceded and withdrawn a bill it has usually been in response to intense pressure of public opinion, manifest for example in demonstrations like those concerning university reform in 1986. The incidents which occurred in 1984, when the carefully worked out balance of the government's school reform bill was disturbed by parliamentary amendments and consequent demonstrations forced its withdrawal, were very unusual.

The legislative role of the member of Parliament may seem reduced, by a combination of constitutional mechanisms and political pressures, to a purely formal one. Methods do exist, however, for members to influence legislation. One of the dilemmas within parliament is the balance that has to be struck between the largely political function of supporting – or opposing – governmental policy on a broad base, and the more technical function of going through proposed legislation with an eye to improving it technically, to some extent regardless of the policy that it embodies. There is some scope for members to fulfil this latter function, for example in acting as *rapporteurs* for a bill as it moves through a committee or by proposing amendments. In the last decade or so, however, the sharpness of much political debate has penetrated even to the committees, to the detriment, in the eyes of some commentators, of their function as places where the privacy of the proceedings allowed at least some partisan cleavages to be set aside. Floods of amendments, largely tabled by the opposition (500 were put down for Chirac's 1986 law giving employers greater rights to sack workers, and 1123 for the highly controversial and ultimately abortive university reform bill) frequently result in little change. For example, in 1989–90 5181 amendments were tabled, of which 2285 were adopted, 396 of them originating from the government, and 1477 from the committees, where the government usually has a majority. Eight bills were the subject of more than 100 proposed amendments, but the government was in fact able to maintain its legislative programme largely intact. Equally, of a total of 12 499 amendments tabled in 1994, 575 of them originating from the government and 1 684 from the committees,

4 379 were withdrawn and only just over one-sixth (2 364) eventually adopted.

Private members may introduce bills, though only if they will have no effect upon public resources or taxation. The time available for the discussion of private members' bills is very limited, so many such bills are never discussed at all. In some cases the government will support the proposal or incorporate it into a bill of its own. This happened in six cases during the Spring session of 1990. In that session six laws which stemmed solely from private members' bills were promulgated. This was a rather high number for a single session, deriving in part from the desire of the minority government to be more open to initiatives coming from outside its own ranks in the hope of enlarging its majority and strengthening parliamentary support. Exhibit 7.4 shows the proportion and the source of private members' bills passed between 1978 and 1988.

Members' perception of their role in the legislative process is emphasised by the fact that often very few actually turn up to take their part in the debates or even to vote in person. On one notorious occasion in the autumn of 1987, when the National Front members of Parliament created a considerable disturbance in the chamber partly in protest at such absenteeism, there were, for an afternoon and evening debate on a law about drug abuse, only 25 members out of 577 present. It is sometimes suggested that it is their work within the committees, where much of the real legislative detail is considered, that keeps them out of the plenary debates – every member is a member of one of the committees – but *le Monde* reported in April

---

EXHIBIT 7.4

Private members' bills (PMBs) (*propositions de loi*) passed

	PMBs as % of all laws passed	Introduced in National Assembly by				Introduced in Senate
		Soc	RPR/UDF	Comm	FN	
1978–81	16	3	26	1	0	6
1981–6	9	13	18	6	0	5
1986–8	24	1	28	1	1	12

Source: Frears (1990, p. 43).

1987 that out of 73 members of the committee on constitutional laws, legislation and general administration, only 36 were present at a major discussion of an important bill on the status of the French Melanesian territory of New Caledonia.

Votes are taken in the National Assembly by electronic means. All the members have their own places in the semicircular chamber, and each place is equipped with an electronic gadget which registers a vote when a key is turned in it. Until 1993 it was possible for a party representative to turn the keys of a large number of absent colleagues when a vote was taken. The Constitutional Council on 23 January 1987 decided that even when the constitutional provision that a member's vote is 'personal' and Parliament's own standing order limiting proxy voting had manifestly been flouted during the vote on a bill, the law so passed was valid. Dissatisfaction with the abuses to which the system could give rise led to a reform of the procedure in 1993 (see Exhibit 7.5).

The Focus of Political Conflict

Every vote in favour of a measure proposed or supported by the government is implicitly a confirmation of that government's position and right to govern. The constitution provides, in Articles 49 and 50, for that legitimacy to be formally and explicitly confirmed or disavowed. The prime minister may present his programme to Parliament, or make a general policy statement. If he makes that programme or statement an issue of confidence and is defeated in the National Assembly the government must resign. Motions of censure may also be proposed, and if they are successful, the government's resignation must follow. But the conditions for the tabling and voting of a motion of censure are tight. Such a motion must be proposed by one tenth of the members of the Assembly, and members whose motion has been unsuccessful may not propose another during that parliamentary session.[12] A majority of all members must actually vote in favour of the motion for it to pass. Abstentions consequently count as votes against the motion. The votes have sometimes been close. In May 1992 Prime Minister Bérégovoy survived a vote of censure over the reform of the common agricultural policy of the European Community by only 3 votes out of 577. But during the Fifth Republic only one motion of censure has succeeded, in October 1962. Prime Minister Pompidou resigned, de Gaulle dissolved the Assembly,

---

EXHIBIT 7.5

Electronic Voting

The 'turn key' method of voting in the National Assembly could have unintended consequences, which contributed to the pressure for change. Two incidents which occurred in April 1990 illustrate some of these consequences. During the debate of a fairly uncontroversial text a vote was taken. There were few members in the chamber, and the two Socialists who were turning all the keys for their absent colleagues had not finished doing so when the member who was chairing the session (one of the National Assembly's bureau (organising committee) – an opposition member) closed the vote. The result was found to be a defeat for the government. The Socialist members protested vigorously and asked for the vote to be repeated. This was eventually done, despite opposition disapproval.

Three weeks later an all-night debate on a proposal to revise the constitution came to the vote at seven in the morning. Many members were absent, and those who turned the keys for the opposition members did so to vote in accordance with the known general views of the various political groups, unless very precise instructions had been left in the member's place. In consequence fourteen opposition members found that they had voted against the proposal when they wished to support it or abstain. The result was a flood of press releases explaining their position, and a rather sour comment from one of their colleagues that those who wished to be certain of recording the right vote should have made the effort to be present in order to do so.

The reform introduced in the autumn of 1993 limits the number of absent colleagues for whom a member may turn the key to one. On 28 September 1993 Philippe Séguin, the president of the National Assembly, announced that the electronic system had been altered to implement the new limit. The first vote on this basis occurred later on the same day. It was called only five minutes before it was due to be taken and lasted only a few seconds, during which time the member had to hold the key in the turned position. Of the 235 members out of 577 who were present, eleven failed to operate the mechanism correctly.

Source: See Maus (1991, pp. 81–2) and *Pouvoirs* 68 p. 185).

Pompidou stayed in office until the elections, and was immediately reappointed as prime minister after the Gaullist electoral success.

Parliament under the Fifth Republic has not been the place where sharp political debate has been focused. There are a number of reasons for this: the reduced powers of Parliament; the rate of absenteeism, the limitations on questions, the existence of coalition governments, the fact that ministers are not actually members of the house, all these factors undoubtedly contribute to the absence of intense and adversarial conflict. Probably even more important has been the extent of presidential government for much, though not all, of the Fifth Republic. The general orientation of government policy could be attacked only through proxies in the Assembly, and presidents have responded to the political climate through press releases, interviews or press conferences, speeches, visits and television appearances. Governments have not normally thought it necessary to make statements to the National Assembly about issues of political concern. There was no statement about the sinking of the Greenpeace boat *Rainbow Warrior* in Auckland harbour by agents of the French security services in 1985, despite massive press speculation and the eventual resignation of the Minister of Defence. The Gulf crisis of 1990 did, however, provoke the recall of Parliament in August as, in February 1992 did the furore surrounding the admission to France for hospital treatment of the Palestinian George Habash. That media attention to the proceedings of Parliament is limited is both cause and effect of a perception that important politics happens elsewhere.

During and after the first period of *cohabitation* the National Assembly gained a slightly higher profile, and not just because of the rowdy tactics adopted by the end of 1987 by the National Front *députés*. Since governmental policy at that period was largely determined by the prime minister, who does appear in the Assembly, and in a situation where the government could not necessarily be sure of a majority, parliamentary debates might be seen as having some point. The minority government of 1993 and the second period of *cohabitation* reinforced this trend. Conversely, the prime minister could hope to rally support for his personal position. Chirac sought the National Assembly's confidence on a statement of general policy no fewer than three times. This was not a tactic adopted by his successors, for the Socialists, governing with a minority, needed to construct parliamentary majorities for every measure, and only risked a vote of confidence on general policy twice, once (under Rocard) over policy on the Middle East, and once (under Bérégovoy) over the GATT (General Agreement on Tariffs and Trade) negotiations. Balladur, during the second period of cohabitation, had the support of a much stronger majority and, after an initial vote on a statement of general policy in the first month of his government, only sought one further such vote, again in the very fraught circumstances of the GATT negotiations. However, since 1993 there has been an increased opportunity for the National Assembly to consider the general trends of government policy, in the shape of a weekly statement from the government. Since 1994 this has been replaced once a month by a debate on a European Union issue. The extension of the length of the parliamentary session will allow for a more continuous scrutiny of the general trends of policy than has previously been possible, and may contribute to ensuring that Parliament's role as a forum for political debate does not again diminish.

Political Education and the Expression of Grievances

Members of the French Parliament have access to a very large amount of information.[13] In 1981, each *député* received not only 120 reports from the bodies which officially report to Parliament, and strictly parliamentary documentation amounting to an average of 80 pages for every day of the year, but also documentation produced by pressure groups, press materials, and a steadily rising volume of daily correspondence. In 1973, one *député* estimated the average number of letters he and his colleagues received at 25 a day. Almost all *députés* hold periodic surgeries in their constituencies, and may also hold working meetings with the mayors and local councils of each *commune* in the constituency. In addition, computerised databases are now available to all members, through the computer equipment installed within the National Assembly and the Senate, and the Minitel terminal which was installed for all members within their constituencies in the Spring of 1984. French members of Parliament are assisted in dealing with this flood of information by the secretary and the personal assistant, paid for from Parliament's funds, to whom they have been entitled since the early 1970s. The efficacy of Parliament as a place of political education and information depends chiefly, however, not on the quantity and quality of information available, but mainly on the nature and level of debate and the extent to which Parliament is perceived, by government, members and media, as a major forum for such activities. The TV cameras are now present within the National Assembly. Perhaps more importantly, since 1989 some of the meetings of the parliamentary committees have been open to the press. On the whole the committees have chosen to open up those of their meetings which are concerned with the gathering of information rather than those in which draft legislation is discussed. This development nevertheless suggests that members of Parliament are becoming increasingly aware of a potentially wider role for parliamentary activity.

Members of Parliament may also be a channel through which citizens can express their grievances. A study of written questions to ministers showed that over half of them sought a decision in a matter affecting an individual or a particular group. Nearly a quarter of the questions requested further explanations of legal or taxation provisions or administrative decisions. The members can pass complaints of maladministration to the *médiateur de la république* (see Chapter 5).

Supervision and Control

The annual debates on the budget, when each ministry's spending plans for the coming year are discussed within Parliament, provide an opportunity for members to scrutinise policy intentions. Debate is limited by the brief time available – usually one day's debate is devoted to each part of the budget – and the issues concern future expectations more than past performance. Recent changes in the debate procedure have, however, increased the ability of *députés* to put direct questions to the minister during the debate.

Parliament's functions of supervision and control are carried out essentially through the procedures of questions and committee enquiries. Not only does question time engender very little interest in the Assembly, apart from the televised Wednesday session of questions to the government, but there is no evidence that questions are taken very seriously by the government and its officials. Some 15 per cent of the questions tabled between 1986 and 1988, both oral and written, remained unanswered when the National Assembly was dissolved; in the autumn of 1989 more than 30 per cent of written questions went unanswered. A senior British official was once staggered to hear his French opposite number say of a certain topic 'My Minister has been asked a question about that. We don't propose to answer it.'[14] Even when questions are answered, and the average proportion to which a response is eventually forthcoming has been rising to around 90 per cent during the 1990s, replies may be delayed long after the official time limit.

Committees of enquiry may also be set up. Since 1977 such committees of enquiry have held legal powers to call for witnesses and documents, and to undertake visits of enquiry. Proposals to set them up have often seemed like an opposition device to exploit government embarrassment and been opposed by the majority, so no committee of enquiry was set up at all before 1970 (Dreyfus and D'Arcy, 1989, p. 121). Their impact was until the late 1980s limited by the fact that all evidence was taken in secret, and no very embarrassing conclusions were likely to be forthcoming when, as was the case, governmental supporters formed the majority in any committee. Committees of enquiry were set up in both Senate and

National Assembly in late 1986 to enquire into the causes and consequences of the student demonstrations that year but were hampered by the ability of the police to refuse to provide information on national security grounds. In the National Assembly this committee was the only one to be set up during the first period of *cohabitation*. The Senate proved initially to be the less inhibited of the two houses in the matter, producing, for example, a notable report on the consequences of the oil spillage following the wreck of the *Amoco Cadiz* in 1978, but has more recently been less active than the National Assembly. The National Assembly began to develop its activities in this area later, and in the context of the greater freedom of manoeuvre provided by a minority government. In May 1990 for the first time the Assembly put into effect a new agreement that each parliamentary political group may once a year call for a debate on the merits of setting up a committee of enquiry into some topical issue. Clearly such a proposal is more likely to be defeated than not, but in 1990 the outcome was the creation of two such committees, one on water pollution and water resources, and one on the operation of the public agency that has the task of assisting immigrant workers. Indeed, since 1990 from two to four such committees have been set up each year. Even when reports are produced their impact tends to be very muted. They have not normally attracted press or television interest (Frears, 1990, p. 37).

In 1983 what amounts to a standing committee on science and technology was created, the Office for the Evaluation of Science and Technology Policy. This consists of eight *députés* and eight senators, with an advisory council of 15 scientists, charged with the task of explaining to Parliament the choices that have been made within science and technology policy. The result has been a number of solid reports on major technological and environmental issues, such as the semiconductor industry and the management of domestic and industrial waste, but as with the reports of the committees of enquiry, they have had a minimal impact.

The European Dimension

The relationship of France to the European Community has from the beginning been perceived principally as a matter of foreign relations (see Chapter 11). These are explicitly a matter for governmental and indeed presidential action and, in contrast, for example, to their Danish, British and Irish counterparts, French governments have resisted any suggestion that they should be bound by parliamentary opinion in their negotiations within the Council of Ministers.[15] Parliament has necessarily been associated with the implementation of EC measures, especially in the relatively rare cases where the application of a directive has involved the passage of a law. In general, however, very little attention was paid to European Community matters until the 1990s. In 1976, as it became more apparent that the Parliaments of the newer member states were finding means of ensuring for themselves a role in these matters, attention was focused on the relations between the Parliaments of the member states and the European Parliament by the need to legislate to fix the arrangements for the first direct elections to the European Parliament in 1979. At this point the Constitutional Council held that, in order not to infringe the principle of national sovereignty laid down in the constitution, the law must provide for election to a body which neither had nor would acquire real legislative powers. In this context, and as fears grew of increasing erosion of the role of the French Parliament, a successful private member's bill established small groups (*délégations pour les Communautés européennes*) of members in each House, with the task of reporting on proposals for EC legislation. They were limited in their effectiveness by the difficulties they experienced in obtaining adequate information from the French government, and by the jealousy with which the standing committees of both houses guarded their own rights. The *délégations* were little more than diffusers of information and occasional intermediaries between the political process and the various interests or groups who were liable to be affected by proposed EC legislation and sought to draw attention to its potential impact.

The creation of the single European market and the prospect of further institutional reform reopened the debate about the appropriate role for a national Parliament. In May 1990, after a prolonged negotiation between Senate and National assembly, a new law, again based on a private member's bill, reinforced the *délégations*. They were doubled in size, from 18 to 36 members, members of National Assembly who were also members of the European Parliament were permitted to be appointed to them, they were given more formal powers to hear ministers and representatives of the EU institutions, the government was obliged to transmit European Commission proposals to them at the point when they are passed to the Council of Ministers, and the Committees of the two houses may consult them on any law which touches on areas subject to EU policy. In 1990 the practice of occasional debates on European community affairs was also instituted and this has, as noted above, been extended to a monthly session in the National Assembly since 1994. The debates around the ratification of the Maastricht Treaty raised the stakes. The amendment to the constitution which was made to provide for the implementation of the Maastricht Treaty contained a provision which incorporated into the constitution the government's obligation (which already existed under the 1990 law) to communicate European Community legislative proposals to the National Assembly and allowed the houses, either in a plenary debate or through the *délégations*, to give their opinions. This constitutional amendment, proposed by a Socialist member of parliament, raised the status of European Community business and resulted, in 1993 and 1994, in the tabling of over twenty resolutions on Community legislative proposals in each year. Members of all the parliamentary political groups except the Communists had supported the constitutional amendment. It was clear that there was increasing concern amongst its members that Parliament should not lose any powers as European integration deepened, indeed they were determined that it should increase the European dimension of its activity. The need to do this was one of the motives that underlay the extension of the session by the constitutional amendment of 1995.

A Nursery of Political Talent

The role of the French Parliament as a nursery and reservoir for the political leadership of the country is much more limited than that, for example, of the British Parliament. It remains a feature of the political system of the Fifth French Republic that it is possible to make a political career very largely outside Parliament. A politician such as President Giscard d'Estaing's minister of health, Simone Weil, has never stood for election to the French Parliament. Of the prime ministers of the Fifth Republic only Chaban-Delmas, Mauroy and Rocard have spent much time as members of the National Assembly. Election as a *député* may, nevertheless, for leading politicians, be a necessary confirmation of democratic legitimacy, and if they have never been elected they may, as Pompidou and Barre did, seek a safe seat after arriving in a prominent position. Neither Pompidou nor Barre immediately served as members, since their ministerial post was incompatible with doing so. Both did eventually enter the Assembly, following dismissal or defeat, Pompidou in 1968, and Barre after the Socialist victory in 1981.

The fact that governmental teams may be drawn from a far wider arena than just Parliament may in part be both cause and effect of the fact that the French Parliament is not the pre-eminent location for political conflict and debate. Reputations as politicians are not to any great extent made or lost within Parliament.

Conclusion

Un Député, pour quoi faire? – what use is a member of Parliament? – was the title of a book published in 1982 (Masclet, 1982). In the light of the constraints illustrated above it seems a pertinent question. Yet Parliament is essential in all the main roles discussed above. Governments simply cannot get legislation passed if they cannot carry Parliament with them, as President Giscard d'Estaing discovered when he was forced to rely on the votes of the opposition in order to get his abortion law reform through and again when his plans for a capital gains tax had to be mitigated in order to make them acceptable. President Mitterrand had a similar experience when his government accepted amendments to his education reform bill in 1984 in order to get it through only to find that these changes made it much more broadly unacceptable.

After 1988 it became apparent that when the government is based upon a party or coalition that does not hold a parliamentary majority the scope for Parliament to play an active role increases. The Rocard government was obliged to change, amend or even drop bills – for example in June 1990 the proposed reform of the French legal profession – in order to ensure the passage of their legislative programme. Finding a coalition within the Parliament to support each individual measure became a major task for the prime minister, though one in which he was aided by continuing habits of rather weak party discipline and the presence in the National Assembly of nearly a score of members who were not formally attached to any of the parliamentary political groups.

Private members, even the *rapporteurs* on specific items in parliamentary committees, may not have enormous influence, but they do have some, and while the proportion of private members bills and amendments passed is not large, nor is it insignificant. The scope for action produced by the absence of a substantial and fairly disciplined majority such as characterised the first 30 years of the regime has resulted in a number of developments, for example the growing role for committees, and although a change in the political context could result once again in an acquiescent and subservient Parliament, some of the pattern of activity, especially the enhanced European dimension, is likely to endure.

Parliament in France has been, to an extent that may seem to observers from certain other traditions scandalous, apathetic about insisting upon its rights. It has not managed to harass the government over answering questions. The Senate where the sense of independence is greater, if only because senators serve guaranteed nine year terms, was initially willing to use committees of enquiry to a greater extent than the National Assembly, which has now followed suit, but neither house has established any kind of mechanism for regular examination of ongoing public policy issues. Parliament has been content to see the implementation of laws it has passed greatly delayed when the administration has proved unable or unwilling to issue the necessary implementing regulations, and even to see its wishes anticipated or frustrated, as when in 1981 the Minister of Justice issued instructions to magistrates to take into account the anticipated reform of the very controversial law and order (*sécurité et liberté*) bill before Parliament had discussed its repeal or replacement.

Before 1986 it was sometimes argued that the apparent powerlessness of Parliament concealed a latent power which might be revealed if and when the political balance changed and the President no longer commanded an acquiescent majority within the National Assembly. Even before 1986, as Presidents Giscard d'Estaing and Mitterrand discovered, that acquiescence could no longer be regarded as completely certain, although between 1981 and 1986 the personal loyalty and party discipline of the Socialist majority greatly assisted Mitterrand's programme.

In 1978 President Giscard d'Estaing made a speech at Verdun sur Le Doubs in which he said that if the forthcoming election produced a majority in the National Assembly of a party that was not a member of his coalition he would not be able to prevent the implementation of that party's programme. In 1978 that did not occur: the governing coalition was returned to power. In 1986, and again in 1993, when the President was a Socialist, it did happen. What proved to be crucial in 1986, however, was not the National Assembly's actual ability to thwart the President, but his recognition that the result required him to offer the post of prime minister to the leading figure of the successful coalition. So it proved, in the event, that the political and procedural devices which had before 1986 largely assisted the President to ensure the implementation of his programme could also be used by a prime minister with an adequate backing. The President could, and did, force the prime minister back onto the mercy of Parliament, but the government found there the support which it required. Parliament may occasionally have displayed a mind of its own, as for example in the election of Mitterrand's close associate and former Foreign Affairs Minister Roland Dumas to the chair of the influential foreign affairs committee, but it was not obstreperous nor apparently inclined to exploit the situation for its own ends. Although the person chiefly responsible for the governmental programme could now be present at debates and in theory be called to account, which had not been the case when that person was the President, neither in 1986 nor in 1993 did the accountability of the government notably increase.

Ironically, it was the advent in 1988 of a government which shared the President's political orientation but did not enjoy a majority which most encouraged the assumption of a rather more assertive role by Parliament. This followed the experience, during the 1980s, of genuine changes in the political orientation of the government, and hence also of the opposition. There is now a sense that the opposition of today, which has its place within Parliament, may indeed constitute the government of tomorrow. This perception, and the scope and importance of the issues with which legislation has recently dealt – nationalisation, decentralisation, privatisation, nationality and citizenship amongst many other things – may gradually be producing a somewhat more lively and active institution than during the 1960s and 1970s. A sense of the need to ensure a prominent role for the national Parliament in the face of the growing ambitions of the European Union and the European Parliament has also contributed to a higher profile for Parliament. The constitutional amendments of 1995 mark a further stage in the rehabilitation of Parliament. At the same time, however, it has become apparent that, even within a more parliamentary interpretation, the constitution can and does provide a framework which permits a government, if with effort, bargaining and occasional concessions, to carry out its programme in a way that the governments of the Fourth Republic could not.

8

The Nature of Party Politics in France

This chapter is the first of two concerned with the aspects of French politics that are most immediately and obviously visible to the observer, whether that observer is French, or an outsider. It is in the act of voting that citizens in democratic countries are most conscious of their role as individuals in political life. France has for most of the period since the war had a high rate of participation in voting, despite the multiplicity of types of election – for local councils at *commune*, *département* and since 1986 regional level, for the National Assembly, the European Parliament, and the Presidency and, from time to time, in referenda. It has been said that French political life exists in a state of permanent campaigning, and indeed there seem to be few months when an election is neither forthcoming, and the subject of debate and campaigning, nor just completed and hence the subject of analysis and associated triumph and recrimination. In this respect the early 1990s was highly unusual, for there were no elections in 1990 or 1991.

Electoral campaigning nowadays requires funds and organisation. It is rare, at levels above the most purely local, for an individual to stand for, let alone win, an election on the strength on his or her own personality and ideas alone. Electoral success tends to depend upon a party organisation. Shared convictions, ideas and approaches about the shape which society should take and the policy approaches required to bring into reality a common vision of a better future normally hold together the adherents of any particular party. Theorists regard them as a means by which the desires, preferences and aspirations of citizens can be aggregated into a form which will

215

enable them to be transformed into action. In France, however, there are important qualifications to be made to the general theories. Individuals may have important parts in political life because of who they are, not what they believe or which organisation they belong to. Political parties may arise principally out of shared support for a particular leader rather than out of strongly held and coherently formulated beliefs. Loyalties to particular party groupings may not be seen as very compelling or constraining. Political debate revolves around discussion of moral principles and broad ideas, and also around very specific personalities. Party programmes and manifestos are often, though not always, slight and vague.

The origins of many of these characteristics lie in the developments and cleavages described in Chapter 1. This chapter goes on from there to consider in more detail the ideological and personal factors that lie at the root of the structure of political parties that is found in France. The way in which this structure developed in the post-war years is then considered. The final section of the chapter is concerned with the way in which the development of the Fifth Republic has shaped the present party system. Chapter 9 discusses the fortunes of the individual parties within the Fifth Republic.

Types of Political Parties in France

During the first half of the twentieth century the overall structure and nature of the French party system was distinctive. Not only was the party system a multi-party system, as opposed to the broadly two-party systems of Britain and the United States,[1] but there was a great variety of internal organisation and structures within the parties themselves.

Hague and Harrop argue that there are five normal functions for parties in liberal democratic states:

- to provide links between the rulers and the ruled, especially to facilitate the flow of political communication;
- to aggregate interests, by transforming 'a multitude of specific demands into more manageable packages of proposals';
- especially when in government, to set and implement collective goals for society;
- to provide the mechanism through which the political elite, especially the top political leadership, emerges;

- to be 'objects of powerful emotional attachment (or antagonism), exerting a powerful influence upon the opinions and behaviour of their supporters' (Hague and Harrop, 1982, p. 102). This process is known as 'partisan identification'.

The failure of the French political parties of the Third and Fourth Republics to fulfil these functions was widely recognised. Indeed the constitution of the Fifth Republic was, as we have seen, partly shaped to provide institutional mechanisms that would compensate for the absence of parties that could do these things.

Byron Criddle argues that a number of causes explain this failure.[2] The first lay in the fact that the French party system was a multi-party system with too many parties competing for support. The origins of this plethora of parties lay in the various divisions of opinion within France identified in Chapter 1, and the fact that the lines of division within society did not coincide. These cleavages included those originating from the Revolution, such as those between republicans and anti-republicans, and between clerical and anti-clerical opinion. There were also the cleavages originating from the industrial revolution, such as those between working classes and bourgeoisie, and those between groups that favoured an interventionist state acting to promote social welfare, and those that wanted a minimal liberal state. In a situation where no compromise is possible between opposing points of view, and where there is no agreement on which cleavage is the most crucial one, the result will be a range of different parties or groups – see Exhibit 8.1 and Figure 8.1. These parties were almost all too small to bring together and articulate within a single programme the demands and desires of large numbers of the voters. They tended therefore to concentrate upon the issues that were most important to their own particular voters, and could not provide support and endorsement for a broad programme of government.

A second reason why the French political parties of the Fifth Republic failed to fulfil the functions performed by parties elsewhere was the weakness of their internal structures. In terms of Duverger's classic categorisation of political party structures (1964, pp. 17–22) many of the parties were 'caucus parties' – loose networks of local leaders, which came together to form electoral committees when there were elections, but made no attempt to organise mass support or produce national programmes. Many members of Parliament under the Fourth Republic, including two future Presidents, Giscard d'Estaing and Mitterrand, were elected on the basis of their personality or local roots, without national support or genuine party affiliation, though they might come together with other members of Parliament to form loose and undisciplined parliamentary groups. Only the Communist and the Socialist Parties differed significantly from this model. There was consequently no real concept of party discipline.

EXHIBIT 8.1

**Maurice Duverger's analysis of 'overlapping cleavages'
and the multi-party system**

In his classic work *Political Parties* (1964) Maurice Duverger described the ways in which overlapping cleavages could lead to a multi-party system, and took his example from France in the Fourth Republic. He took three major cleavages – between those sympathetic to Communism and the Soviet Union and those who were not, which he called the 'East–West' cleavage; between clerical and anti-clerical views; and between liberal and social-democratic views of the role of the state, which he called the 'freedom–planning' cleavage. His diagram (Figure 8.1) identified the six groups or parties which resulted and could be found in the Fourth Republic.

FIGURE 8.1
Overlapping cleavages and the multi-party system

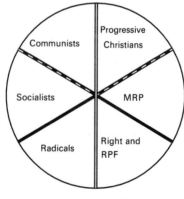

	Line of demarcation 'East–West'
	Line of demarcation 'Clerical–Anti-Clerical'
	Line of demarcation 'Freedom–Planning'

Note: Figure 8.1 is not scaled to represent the strength of the different groups.

The absence of the notion of a disciplined party organised around a coherent and credible programme helps to explain the third cause suggested by Criddle for the inability of the parties under the Third and Fourth Republics to achieve the normal functions of parties. The parties were unable to provide adequate support for any governmental programme especially since the electoral systems made it difficult for any one party to dominate (see Exhibit 8.2). No party was strong enough to govern alone, and those parties that were able to make working coalitions – after 1947 for over 20 years the Communist Party ceased to be an acceptable coalition partner – could not ensure that their supporters would uphold the coalitions for any length of time. In these very fragmented conditions politics could become strongly personalised, with debate and loyalties focusing around the personality and approach of particular leaders. One consequence was a certain distrust of powerful and attractive leaders, and when it seemed possible that Pierre Mendès France might develop as such a leader he ceased to be acceptable to Parliament as a prime minister.

Ideological Divisions

The divorce between party structures and the functions of government described above has tended to mean that ideological debate in French politics has tended to be lively and fierce, if at times remarkably abstract. The language of politics in France is still often more ideological and abstract than is usually the case in neighbouring countries such as the United Kingdom or Germany.

The Left

The parties of the Left find their ideological roots in the debates and formulations of the nineteenth century. There was a powerful tradition of indigenous French socialism expressed in the writings of Saint-Simon, Fourier and Proudhon and Blanqui, for example. Common to all these strands of thought were visions of a society in which workers would be freed from oppression and exploitation. 'Utopias are plentiful in the history of French socialist thought. The goal is nothing so limited or mundane that it could be achieved here and now; it is an absolute, a picture of perfection. Any compromise seemed a betrayal' (Ridley, 1970, p. 13). However, the dreadful

EXHIBIT 8.2
French parliamentary electoral systems since 1945

1. 1945: Proportional representation by *département* lists	2. 1946: Proportional representation by *département* lists	3. 1951 and 1956: Hybrid majority/proportional system – by *département* list in Paris regions, and elsewhere by *département* list with alliances	4. 1958 to 1993, except 1986: Two-ballot 'first past the post' system	5. 1986: Proportional representation by *département* lists
Constituencies: Each *département* except the seven largest constituted a single constituency. The seven largest were each divided into two or more constituencies	**Constituencies**: As in 1945	**Constituencies**: Single constituency in each *département* except eight (now including the largest (Gironde) which were divided into two	**Constituencies**: 1958 New constituencies were drawn up with roughly equal numbers of inhabitants and no *département* having less than two Modifications ensued subsequently Boundaries were comprehensively redrawn after 1986 election (see p. 000).	**Constituencies**: Each *département* constituted a single constituency
Representation: Multi-member constituencies One member for every 100 000 inhabitants A minimum of two members in each constituency. 522 seats for mainland France, 66 for Algeria and colonies	**Representation**: As in 1945 but 544 seats for mainland France, 66 for Algeria and colonies	**Representation**: As in 1946	**Representation**: Single-member constituencies In 1958 there were 465 metropolitan constituencies In 1981 there were 491 and in 1988 550. Including the overseas *départements* there are 577 members.	**Representation**: Multi-member constituencies with one seat for approximately every 108 000 inhabitants Minimum of two seats in each constituency 577 members

Candidates: Candidates were obliged to stand as members of a list which was as long as the number of seats in the constituency

No Candidate could appear on more than one list

Votes had to be cast for the list

Distribution of seats: In proportion to votes through the quotient and highest average method

Candidates: As in 1945, except that voters could express a preference between candidates on their chosen list

Preference would only be taken into account if over half the voters for a particular list altered it, which never happened

Distribution of seats: By highest average, without quotient

Candidates: Candidates were obliged to stand as members of a *département* list

Outside the Paris region (8 constituencies, 75 members) alliances could be made between lists from parties presenting such lists in at least 30 constituencies

Distribution of seats: In Paris region by proportional representation using the quotient and highest remainder system

Elsewhere any list or alliance with an absolute majority of votes cast took all the seats, with distribution within alliances by highest average

If no absolute majority were attained, distribution was to all lists or alliances gaining over 5 per cent of the total vote, by highest average

Candidates: Each candidate must designate a replacement – *suppléant*.

Candidates may withdraw between the two rounds of voting

Distribution of seats: Candidates gaining an absolute majority are elected at the first ballot

Otherwise those gaining over a minimum proportion of the total votes cast (1958 5 per cent, 1967 10 per cent, 1978 12.5 per cent) go on to second ballot, where candidate gaining the highest number (plurality) of votes is elected

Candidates: Candidates obliged to stand as members of a list as long as the number of seats in the constituency plus two, to provide replacements if required

Votes are cast for the list with no expression of preference between candidates

Distribution of seats: Proportionately between all lists gaining over 5 per cent of the votes cast by the quotient and highest average system.

experience of the attempt in 1870 to organise a revolutionary workers' government in Paris – the Paris Commune – which resulted in the death, imprisonment or exile of many socialists delayed the development of organised political parties of the Left.

When socialist political organisation began to re-emerge at the very end of the 1870s, Marxism emerged as the dominant ideological influence. However, although this period saw the development of organised political parties which clearly claimed to represent the working class, and although the influence of Marxism predominated, the early years of socialist political organisation were marked by the formation of numerous small parties, often largely associated with a single political leader. It is also important to note that a trade union movement was developing alongside the socialist political organisations, but was never closely linked to them. The proliferation of socialist parties was one cause of this, as was the strong anarchist tendency within the trade unions. In this respect the development of the French socialist and labour movements contrasted sharply with developments in the United Kingdom.

In the period leading up to the First World War this disunity was overcome, and from 1905 a unified Socialist Party existed led, until his assassination just before the war broke out, by Jean Jaurès. The party was anti-capitalist, and committed to a broadly Marxist approach. Disputes continued within it over the extent to which it should co-operate with bourgeois governments, and with measures that would ameliorate the situation of workers without undermining the capitalist system. It was not willing to participate in government by providing ministers.

This period of unity turned out to be relatively brief, lasting from 1905 to 1920. The Socialist Party split again over reactions to the 1917 Revolution in Russia, and particularly to the pressure that the Soviet Communists put upon socialist parties elsewhere to join the Communist International to support and protect the revolution achieved in the Soviet Union. The structure and objectives of the Communist International were set out in the Twenty One points of the Communist International; the result was a split in the French party, which occurred at the 1920 Congress of the party in Tours. The majority of the party accepted the Twenty One points, and became the French Communist Party. The minority refused, being especially unwilling to accept the insistence that revolution rather than reform should be the party's only aim, and that co-operation with bourgeois governments should cease. This minority became the French Section of the (Second) Workers' International (*Section française de l'internationale ouvrière* – SFIO), the name it retained until 1969.

This split in the Left had long-lasting and bitter consequences. The Communist Party became, and remained, determinedly Leninist, and subsequently Stalinist also. It adopted the tightly pyramidal structures of Leninist democratic centralism. It quite rapidly became 'a malleable instrument of the Soviet Union'(Bell and Criddle, 1988, p. 131) always accepting that the international priorities of the Soviet Union should override any strategy which the French domestic political situation might suggest. The Soviet Union has been seen by the PCF as the exemplar and model of a socialist state and the birthplace of the workers' revolution to which all workers aspire. Even in the mid-1970s, when the PCF had come reluctantly to admit that some criticism of the USSR, for example over human rights issues, might be possible, PCF leader Georges Marchais famously asserted that the overall record of the Soviet Union was *'globalement positif'* – generally positive. When changes in the political strategy of the PCF have occurred – for example, when Communists began to collaborate with the socialists in the 1930s in the anti-fascist popular front movement, and when they withdrew from government in 1947 – they did so because the policy of the Soviet Union changed.

If the roots of the PCF's approach lie firmly in uncompromising loyalty to the principles of Marxism–Leninism and the Soviet Union, at least until the rapid and traumatic collapse of Eastern European communism between 1989 and 1991, there is no single simple explanation of its role and influence. Two important aspects can be noted. First, the PCF gave a very high priority to its role as a working-class party. Most of its leaders have had working-class origins, and it has sought to ensure that its parliamentary candidates are also from such backgrounds. This gave it a particular strength in those areas where the traditional working-class were strongly present, such as the industrial suburbs round Paris, the so-called 'red belt' or '*banlieues rouges*', and in which the PCF were solidly entrenched, in municipal government and in a whole network of party organisations which provided a virtual party sub-culture, out of which the faithful adherent need never stray. Analysts have seen it as pre-eminently a party of 'protest' (Lavau, 1981, pp. 34–44). It allowed those groups who had traditionally felt alienated from social and political developments to express their sense of conflict.

Secondly, especially just before and, even more importantly, in the first decade or two after the Second World War, the PCF was for many intellectuals – academics, writers, students and others – the political expression of the Marxism that they felt represented a coherent intellectual system that responded to the problems, inequities and injustices of the world around them. Marxist discourse dominated intellectual debate. Many such people joined the party: others, such as the philosopher Jean-Paul Sartre were close to it but not members. In his autobiography *Paris–Montpellier* the historian Emmanuel le Roy Ladurie (1982) describes the generous impulses and idealism which led to his membership of the party in the late 1940s, and the disillusion and dismay, especially after the Soviet suppression of the Hungarian revolt in 1956, that caused him to leave the party – a departure which he nevertheless experienced almost as bereavement. Intellectuals were always distrusted by the PCF leadership, and did not on the whole achieve prominent positions within the party, but they did undoubtedly contribute to the image of the party and helped to account for the importance of its position within the Left until the 1980s.

The Socialist Party which constituted itself as the SFIO in the aftermath of the Tours congress split retained its essentially Marxist ideological base. It was led throughout the inter-war period by Léon Blum, and succeeded quite quickly in overtaking the Communists, in votes cast and in parliamentary seats. It firmly refused any form of collaboration with the Communists, and indeed bitterly opposed them, until the threats from fascism prompted the creation of the joint programme for a Popular Front in the mid-1930s. The success of the supporters of this programme brought Blum into power as Prime Minister between 1936 and 1938. The Communists would not join the government. However, the Fifth Republic provided a much less congenial context for it, and its fortunes were at a very low ebb by the end of the 1960s. The period between 1969 and 1971 saw a major reconstruction symbolised by a new name – the *Parti Socialiste* (PS) (see Chapter 9).

In the immediate post-war period the SFIO found itself again in government, alongside Communists and Christian Democrats. In May 1947 the Communists left the government, but the SFIO continued to be a key component in the shifting alliances that provided the Fourth Republic's governments.

The party retained its broadly Marxist rhetoric, at least until it came into power in 1981, but its ideological base was wide and fragmented. According to John Gaffney, the Socialist Party, whilst sharing the broad aims of all Socialist parties, such as the emancipation of working people, the use of the state to secure, or at least facilitate, these aims, and the redistribution of wealth, has also added other, specifically French emphases, notably a commitment to a strong national defence policy, a tendency to Jacobin centralism which co-exists within the party in a good deal of tension with strong support for decentralisation, a traditional hostility to the Catholic church, and the continued use of the Marxist-inspired rhetoric of liberation.[3]

The Socialist Party contained within it members who looked to the traditions of Socialist anarchism, others who drew upon the more structured and authoritarian Marxist views, others whose main background was in the organised socialism of some of the large Socialist town councils, and others again whose approach was close to that of modernising reformist social democratic parties elsewhere, with an emphasis on equality and fraternity. The party organisation has consequently been obliged to recognise organised minorities and provide for the regular expression of their points of view (Pickles, 1972, p. 185). The factions tend to be associated with particular leaders, and during the 1980s they became increasingly identified with particular leaders jostling for position in the hopes of becoming the next presidential candidate for the party after Mitterrand.

Other West European socialist parties with a background similar to that of the French party, and most notably the West German Social Democratic Party, a party with an even longer tradition than that of the French party, found themselves obliged, during the post-war period, to jettison some of their most traditional ideological formulations. The German party formally renounced both Marxism and anti-clericalism in 1959. The French party did not feel able to do this, reflecting perhaps the extent to which ideological opposition to the dominant political strands of the Fifth Republic was important to it in the first three decades of that regime. However, its evolution since, in 1981, it came into government for the first time since the Fourth Republic, has been rapid and marked, and is described in Chapter 9.

Christian Democracy

Politically, the centre is an uneasy and uncomfortable place, and the parties of the Centre in France, which flourished briefly in the political space left by the discrediting of the Right in the post-war years, have dwindled, trapped by the features of the Fifth Republic's party system, described below, which have tended to force all parties to identify either with a governing coalition, or with the opposition. As in many European countries (except the United Kingdom) after the Second World War a Christian Democratic party (the *Mouvement républicain populaire* – MRP) developed in France. French Christian Democratic ideas originated in the ideas of social Catholicism, arguing for a middle way between liberal capitalism and Marxism (Irving, 1973, p. 55). This led to support for state intervention in the economy, and for the institutions of the welfare state. Suspicion of unchecked central power caused the party to oppose the proposals for the direct election to the presidency when they were introduced in 1962, whilst support for the Catholic church, and particularly for the role and status of church schools divided the party from the Socialists. Like other Christian Democratic parties, the MRP was a firm advocate of European integration. Despite the MRP's criticism of de Gaulle, it could not survive the competition from the Gaullists in the Fifth Republic. Christian Democratic ideas continue to be represented in French politics, however. A successor party, the *Centre des démocrates sociaux* (CDS) formed part of President Giscard d'Estaing's governing coalition during the 1970s, and continued within that grouping – the *Union pour la démocratie française*, UDF – in opposition during most of the 1980s. Whilst it remains strongly committed to the ideals of European integration, its emphasis on state intervention has diminished. 'Perhaps the two areas where the CDS remains wedded to its Christian Democratic past is in its continued espousal of the importance of the family as the source of social solidarity, and its adherence to the traditional moral norms of society' (Rizzuto, 1991, p. 17). The discomfort and ambiguity of a centrist position is emphasised by the fact that although nominally part of the opposition in the period of the minority socialist government after 1988 the CDS frequently voted for government measures, and some of its members became ministers.

The Right

Gaullism

Gaullism is one of the few political creeds to be identified by the name of a single individual. De Gaulle, despite the strength of vision that constituted so powerful a part of his charismatic personality, never produced a specific or coherent political statement. His most important published works are his memoirs. His complex and ambiguous personality provided scope for a range of interpretations of what loyalty to his vision might actually mean. Jean Charlot interprets Gaullism in terms of the generations of followers of de Gaulle – those of the first period of the wartime resistance, those of the political organisation of the late 1940s, and those who flocked to support him on his return to power in 1958, and who formed the nucleus of a party for whom the voters could, and did, vote to express their support for de Gaulle himself. In supporting him his followers were generally expressing rather unfocused aspirations for the unity and standing of France.[4]

The 'certain idea' or, in another translation, the 'precise image',[5] of France which de Gaulle evoked at the start of his memoirs meant a commitment to the international status and independence of France. This involved overcoming the fragmentation of France internally. De Gaulle's ideological rejection of the politics of party and, for example, his commitment to linking workers into the activities of their enterprises through works' councils and profit sharing, stemmed from his desire to override conflict and division arising from the pursuit of individual, narrow interest, which weakened France internally. A respected, legitimate, strong and effective state was required to provide the firm government which a potentially fragmented society required. 'To French voters the Gaullist party offered a charismatic leader; the heroic aura of the resistance; loyalty to institutions that offered a stable government for the first time in the twentieth century; *gloire*; a sure barrier against communism, and economic prosperity'.[6]

The departure of de Gaulle in 1969 and his death in 1970 did not immediately deprive Gaullism of its force. The adjective 'Gaullist' has remained attached to the *Rassemblement pour la république* founded, in 1976, and still led, by Jacques Chirac. However, having lost the presidency in 1974 and moved into opposition in 1981 the Gaullists have redefined their approach. In the 1960s the defence of the institutions which de Gaulle had imposed was the central Gaullist concern. As these institutions became embedded and uncontested this essential element of Gaullist identity became irrelevant. This has permitted an 'ideological slippage'[7] in response to the political needs of the time. Gaullism, Andrew Knapp asserts (1994, p. 185) has no core ideology, although it is always right-wing, nationalist and relatively authoritarian. Nor does it have a core area or territory in France where it is unshakeably implanted. Its survival has resulted from the strengths of its party organisation, the development of a system of local leaders (*notables*) who can rely on their local power and their local record, and on Jacques Chirac's own strong and determined leadership. The nature and consequences of this survival are discussed in Chapter 9. As Chirac claimed 'No one knows what the General would have said today.'

The non-Gaullist Right

Throughout the Fifth Republic a number of political groups have maintained the political traditions of the French Right outside the Gaullist organisations. Two features are important. First, the rapid rise of Gaullism after 1958 swept up many of the voters who might previously have supported political groups of this type; not only the Christian Democrats, but the other loose political formations, such as the National Council for Independents and Peasants, and the Radical Party found themselves enfeebled within the new rules of the political game. Secondly, the organisations concerned would not describe themselves as belonging to the Right wing in politics. They use the term 'centre', or even 'centre-right', but the concept of the Right in politics was so thoroughly discredited by the experiences of war-time collaboration that it has been generally repudiated. Nowadays the term is firmly attached to the extreme Right. Nevertheless, the development of the party system under the Fifth Republic has set these groups firmly within political coalitions with the Gaullists that, like comparable coalitions and parties elsewhere in Europe, fall within a broad European classification of right-wing parties and governments.

Under the Fifth Republic the non-Gaullist right was brought together by Valéry Giscard d'Estaing in a federation that was intended to support his presidency in the general election of 1978 and in the presidential election in 1981. The *Union pour la démocratie française* has always been a fragile confederation, highly dependent upon individual leaders whose rivalries and jockeying for position have placed great strains upon its cohesion. Consisting, as it does, of a number of political formations, some of which are little more than a power base for the ambitions of an individual, a consistent ideological approach is perhaps not to be expected. Analysts[8] have argued that it can best be seen as the continuation of the moderate conservatism embodied in the nineteenth century constitutional monarchy of Louis-Philippe (see Chapter 1) and continued amongst the moderate republicans of the late nineteenth century. Whilst the UDF (like the

British Conservative party) embraces a very wide spectrum of conservative opinion, its emphases are largely anti-collectivist, meritocratic, and liberal, in the sense of favouring market competition and de-regulation.

The extreme Right

In his taxonomy of the traditions of the Right in France Rémond (1982) includes the counter-revolutionary right. Amongst the traditions allied to this strand of political ideology he included monarchists, extreme nationalists, and fervent supporters of the traditional elements of the Roman Catholic church, the so-called *intégristes*. These largely anti-democratic strands have long been present in French political life; the Vichy regime incorporated a number of them. In the aftermath of the Liberation their importance in French political life waned, though the fervent anti-communism that accompanied them found some refuge in the strident anti-communism of the Gaullism of the late 1940s.

Other manifestations of extreme right politics flared briefly during the Fourth Republic and the early years of the Fifth Republic. In the mid-1950s Pierre Poujade led a movement based largely upon the rejection by shopkeepers and small businesses of the modernising trends of capitalism and their resentment of the impact of economic development (see Exhibit 8.3). The Poujadists denounced technocracy and bureaucracy – especially the tax collectors. It was essentially a party of protest and rejection rather than of forward vision, and did not survive the advent of de Gaulle in 1958, but it captured a wave of discontent, especially in the South and West. But not all its success was there, and amongst the Poujadist members of Parliament returned in 1956 from Paris was Jean-Marie Le Pen.

The cause of retaining a French Algeria was the other issue that mobilised the extreme right in the late 1950s and early 1960s. Here nationalism, extreme patriotism, defence of the army and military values came together. Bitter opposition to de Gaulle's moves which led to independence for Algeria took violent and clandestine forms in the bombing and assassination attempts of the clandestine *Organisation de l'armée secrète* (OAS).

In 1972 Jean-Marie Le Pen (see Exhibit 9.3, p. 268) set out to create a political organisation that would federate the many and varied ideological strands of the extreme right in France. For nearly a decade his political group could be dismissed as a minor and irrelevant aspect of the fringe of political life. The reasons for the rise of the National Front are discussed below. Here it is appropriate to note the extent to which the National Front has attracted a wide range of extreme right-wing opinion. Nationalists, those who supported French Algeria and especially French colonists resettled in France after Algerian independence, traditional Roman Catholics, and neo-fascists are all to be found amongst Le Pen's supporters. Himself a former Poujadist member of Parliament, some of his support springs from the same roots. Although Le Pen himself denies personal anti-semitism, that long-standing aspect of the French extreme right is clearly visible alongside the virulent xenophobia of his party.

EXHIBIT 8.3

Poujadism

In 1953 Pierre Poujade, the owner of a stationery shop in a small town in the *département* of the Lot in South West France organised his neighbours to resist an attempt by a tax inspector to inspect a fellow shopkeeper's accounts. The movement burgeoned rapidly, attracting many small shopkeepers and tradesmen who were struggling in an era of increasing competition and inflation, and who resented the exactions of the tax authorities.

Poujade founded the *Union de défense des commerçants et artisans* (UDCA). The movement attracted support rapidly, mostly in the centre and south west of France, especially from shopkeepers, and from small farmers, including those whose traditional home-distilled spirits were threatened by official campaigns against alcoholism. The movement drew its initial strength from protest against technocrats and officials, notably the tax officials, and a rejection of economic progress. Initially encouraged by the Communist Party, the Poujadists became increasingly right-wing in their themes and extravagant rhetoric.

The UDCA fought the 1956 election with a campaign that Williams (1972, p. 164) describes as 'slanderous, violent and utterly negative'. They won over 2.5 million votes, about 11.5 per cent of the poll. 53 members were returned, but eleven of them were unseated for breaches of the electoral law.

The Poujadist members, who included the future leader of the National Front, Jean-Marie Le Pen, did not prove effective within the National Assembly, lacking any programme for positive action or reform, and failing to hold together as a parliamentary group. In 1958 Poujade himself would not support de Gaulle, but his followers did. The movement was crushingly defeated in the 1958 election.

Poujade himself returned to business, and was active during the 1980s in promoting the cultivation of the jerusalem artichoke as a potential source of fuel to replace petrol. He did not entirely leave political life, appearing as a candidate for election to the European Parliament in 1979 and 1984 on lists that attracted a tiny proportion of the vote. He supported Mitterrand's presidential candidacy in 1981. He is a member of the Economic and Social Council (see Exhibit 2.5).

The diversity of ideological approaches found within and between the various political parties and groups in France reflects the continued salience of cleavages along intellectual and philosophical lines. However, political vision also has direct political outcomes. The discussion of the ideological roots of French politics has revealed the extent to which the political debate has been influenced, sometimes crucially, by the impact of individual personalities. External influences may also affect internal approaches – models both of social democracy and of liberal market-oriented policies from elsewhere in Europe have clearly had an impact upon French political thinking in the last two decades. French political debate is particularly lively, aided by the marked tendency of leaders and groups in all the parties to reinforce their power-bases by setting up political think tanks or clubs as a forum for debate and policy formulation. Examples include the well-known *Club Jean Moulin* which was a focus for the formulation of policy in opposition to the Gaullist government in the 1960s, the *Clubs perspectives et réalités*, founded by future President Giscard d'Estaing in 1966, the right-wing *Club de l'Horloge* and the *Témoin* club set up by Jacques Delors. All the parties, however, operate within a system of electoral competition and the space which they occupy within the political spectrum is determined by a range of institutional and social factors. It is to the pattern of these interrelationships that the next section of this chapter turns.

The Post-war Party System

In 1945 the first post-war election in France marked something of a turning point, for three-quarters of the votes cast went to parties which had a distinct political programme, and were organised upon the basis of local membership – the PCF, the SFIO and the MRP.

The 1945 elections had taken place while General de Gaulle was Prime Minister. He continued as prime minister whilst the Constituent Assembly which had been set up by these elections attempted to elaborate a constitution, and it was when he realised that the outcome was unlikely to be one which he could accept that, in January 1946, he resigned as prime minister. It may seem strange that there was no party within the National Assembly at that time specifically committed to upholding de Gaulle's point of view and, despite holding strong and clear views about the future shape of

French government, he had made no attempt to organise political support for himself – though the strength of the MRP vote probably reflected the fact that for many it was the party closest to de Gaulle. De Gaulle was dismayed by what he saw as a resurgence of the pre-war parties. His concept of political life, described above, envisaged a strong and direct link between the citizen and the state, expressed by voting, but a voting that should support a broad view of the general national interest. Political parties, for him, inevitably represented narrow and sectional interests, which engendered conflict, rather than producing national unity.

In 1947 the Communist Party was turned out of the government, and from that time onwards throughout the Fourth Republic maintained a general stance of opposition to the government of the day and to co-operation with any other party. Also in the Spring of 1947 de Gaulle launched what he saw as a political movement, not a party, the *Rassemblement du peuple français* (RPF). Large rallies and meetings were held, and the municipal elections in the autumn of that year resulted in a marked success for candidates with the RPF label. The movement was strongly anti-communist, and also reflected de Gaulle's opposition to the other political parties and to the constitution which a Constituent Assembly dominated by them had produced. De Gaulle was, however, never able, nor indeed likely, to achieve his ambition of drawing together a huge movement of people of all political persuasions in support of his own view of the general interest. Inevitably, his movement came to look ever more like one of the traditional parties which he so despised. It drew its support largely from the Right, especially at the expense of the MRP, the Radicals, and the smaller groups of conservative independents.

Party politics in France during the 1950s presented a complicated picture. To the left was the Communist Party led by Maurice Thorez, who had spent the war in Moscow and was resident there for medical reasons from 1950 to 1953. The party backed the twists and turns of Soviet policy and approaches, frequently finding itself in the ironic position of voting against the government alongside the Gaullists, but retaining a steady and high level of support amongst the electorate, for it gained over a quarter of the vote in the general elections of both 1951 and 1956. Much of this support came from the urban working class. In 1951 over 40 per cent of PCF voters were under the age of 35, and the 1950s was also the period in which Marxist, indeed PCF, influence over intellectual life in France was pervasive and powerful.

The SFIO was also well organised and strongly entrenched in certain regions, such as the North and the region of Marseilles. It too drew support from the industrial working class, but also, importantly, from amongst schoolteachers, and junior officials and public servants. Within the Fourth Republic the Party was committed to the constitution of which it had been one of the architects.

The MRP declined steadily throughout the Fourth Republic, as the right-wing voters for whom it had been a safe haven immediately after the war found more congenial representatives. It certainly suffered from the brief rise of the Gaullists. To the right of the MRP were the looser groupings of more conservative politicians. The Radical Party had, as Maurice Larkin points out, never been very radical (Larkin, 1988, p. 39). Discredited after the war for the part they were perceived as having played in the events which brought about the fall of France in 1940, the Radicals re-emerged as a moderate right party, attracting a traditional following – in 1951 65 per cent of their voters were over 65 – held together essentially by periodic congresses and by participation in many of the coalition governments of the Fourth Republic. The party provided a number of very well known ministers and prime ministers, of whom the charismatic Pierre Mendès France was the most notable, but with virtually no local or constituency organisation. Even more loosely grouped and further to the right were the various members of Parliament who described themselves as independents or as representatives of the peasants, and in 1951 a parliamentary group known as the *Centre national des indépendants et paysans* (CNIP) came into being – a group which really acquired any sort of national identity only at election time.

De Gaulle's disillusion with the inability of his RPF to function in any mode other than that of a traditional party led him to withdraw steadily from it. In 1953 he dissolved the parliamentary branch of the party, leaving members who had been elected under the RPF label to join other parliamentary parties, or to form a disavowed rump of their own. In 1955 de Gaulle announced that he was withdrawing from politics altogether, and the RPF organisation withered and virtually disappeared. In the 1956 election Gaullists took less than 5 per cent of the vote. But as Gaullism declined as a political phenomenon, Poujadism flared up briefly, drawing partly on disillusioned Gaullists, but also on the Radical Party's clientele and upon a somewhat wider protest vote that might otherwise have been expressed in a vote for the PCF. Poujadism managed to take over 11 per cent of the vote in the 1956 election, winning 55 parliamentary seats.

The 1956 election was the last election of the Fourth Republic and, as Jean Charlot has pointed out (1989, p. 32) the results showed a pattern of one genuinely large party – the PCF – able to take a quarter of the votes, but politically ineligible to participate in government and five medium-sized parties. Three of them – the SFIO, the Radicals (already showing signs of major splits within the party over the appropriate choice of allies) and the Conservative Independents – each attracted around 15 per cent of the vote and two – the Poujadists and the MRP – gained somewhat over 11 per cent. Finally the demoralised and almost moribund Gaullists took 4 per cent whilst de Gaulle himself stayed firmly at home at Colombey-les-Deux-Eglises and wrote his memoirs.

After 1958: The Evolution of the Party System

The political experiences of the Fifth Republic radically transformed the Fourth Republican parties. In 1988 and 1993 the general election revealed five main party groupings, only one of which had existed with largely unchanged name and structure since before 1970. Three of these parties attracted enough votes to be described as 'major' parties – the PS with 36 per cent in 1988 and 20 per cent in 1993 and the RPR and the UDF with around 20 per cent each on both occasions (see Exhibit 9.2). The other two parties, the FN and the PCF were medium size as vote catchers, attracting between 9 and 13 per cent of the vote. In 1993 the ecologists registered their presence, with nearly 8 per cent of the vote. Earlier in the Fifth Republic, in 1978, the result had been strikingly symmetrical: four major parties in two blocs, the PCF and the PS on the left and the RPR and the UDF on the right. Each received between 20 and 23 per cent of the vote at the first ballot of the general election. Clearly a number of factors have shaped and reshaped the party system since the advent of the Fifth Republic.

The most important of these features are the emergence of the Gaullist party, the institutional developments that produced a clear-cut distinction between the parties of government and opposition, and the persistence of multi-partyism, albeit nowadays of a limited, rather than extremely fragmented type (Bartolini, 1984, p. 122).

The Emergence of the Gaullist Party

The emergence of the Gaullist Party was of crucial importance to the political development of the Fifth Republic for two major reasons:

- First, it provided for the first decades of the regime a solid parliamentary basis for the entrenchment of the Fifth Republic's institutions. The framers of the Constitution had not expected the power of the President and government to be based upon the existence of a largely disciplined governing majority. But such a majority existed, and the Gaullist Party was the dominant element in it. Political practice and expectations shifted to accommodate this fact.
- Secondly, the Gaullist Party was the first mass-based disciplined party of the French right. It did not (at least initially[9]) look just to the local standing of its candidates as a basis for electoral support nor, unlike the earlier RPF, and much to the surprise of some commentators, did it depend solely upon the charisma of de Gaulle himself, for it survived his resignation and his death. Modern techniques of central organisation, of the selection and briefing of candidates, of attracting voters and marketing the party's appeal were developed. The effect of this, which was, of course, partly a result of the institutional factors discussed below, was to provide a haven for a large right-wing electorate, putting great pressure upon fragmented parties of the centre, and encouraging the formation of alliances and larger groupings both on the Right and between the parties of the Left who needed to ensure their own defence, indeed survival.

Electoral Systems and the Development of an Opposition

The development of political coalitions of parties constituting a clear opposition to the incumbent governing coalition was a relatively slow process. De Gaulle's return to power in 1958 was not totally unopposed. In the National Assembly in June 1958, despite the evident urgency of the situation, 224 members voted against his appointment as Prime Minister. De Gaulle's political opponents were the French Communist Party, left-wing socialists, and a number of prominent political personalities, including ex-Prime Minister Pierre Mendès France and future President François Mitterrand. Such opposition was not generally popular and those who campaigned against the new Constitution at the referendum paid for their actions in the general election. The PCF's first ballot vote declined to 18.9 percent, a loss of some half a million votes compared to the previous election in 1956. The effect on the PCF share of the seats was (as the authors of the system had probably intended) catastrophic, for there were only ten PCF members (just over 2 per cent) in the new National Assembly. Moreover, Mendès France and Mitterrand both lost their seats.

By 1962 the situation had changed. The National Assembly had passed a vote of censure, the resolution of the Algerian problem had removed the main consideration holding together a solid parliamentary majority, and many non-Gaullist politicians wished to see a return to what they held to be a more normal political life. Election of the President by universal suffrage would, they felt, decisively alter the balance of the institutions. A number of the non-Gaullist parties, from both left and right, grouped together to oppose the amendment and the referendum, an opposition shared by the PCF. There was thus, briefly, an opposition coalition, albeit a rather weak one. This, combined with the operation of the two-ballot system in the general election of 1962 and the presidential election of 1965 began to illustrate the changes which the new electoral system would impose upon the parties and to force them to consider appropriate strategies.

Under the two-ballot system any candidate who had gained above a certain minimum proportion of the vote could stand in the second ballot, but there were clear advantages in avoiding too much fragmentation of the vote. Whilst at the first ballot voters can and do express their personal convictions, at the second ballot they can frequently be persuaded to vote for the candidate most likely to win amongst those whom they find not unacceptable. In the presidential election such a situation is forced upon the voters by the provision that only two candidates may stand at the second ballot. The outcome has been what was frequently, in the late 1960s and 1970s, described as the 'bipolarisation' of French politics. Such a term is misleading in so far as it suggests that France has moved towards a two-party system. It is much less misleading if it serves to indicate that what emerged was a much more clear-cut notion than had existed before 1962 of the existence of a government and an opposition.

The notion of 'the opposition' had not developed before, for under most of both the Third and Fourth Republics the shifting coalitions which formed the governments, of which particular political groups might or might not at any time be members, had been flanked by 'outsider' groupings who represented not alternative governments but alternative regimes – a monarchy, a workers revolution, a Gaullist constitution (see Exhibit 1.1, p. 12). In these circumstances any notion of a 'loyal opposition' was virtually impossible. Its development in France depended, first, upon the existence of a relatively clear-cut choice, such as was presented especially by the presidential elections. Despite much speculation in 1995 about the possibility of the two second-round candidates emerging from the same party, all the presidential elections (except 1969) have resulted in a clear-cut choice between Left and Right. A second factor was the acceptance by all the parties of the nature of the Fifth Republic's institutions, and the withering away of serious proposals to overthrow the whole constitutional settlement. A further dimension was added to this latter factor after the presidential election campaign of 1974, when the possibility and consequences of having president and government of different political persuasions, as eventually happened in 1986, began to be discussed.

When party blocs which are clearly filling the roles of a governing coalition and an opposition coalition develops, then the possibility of a decisive change of government also exists. The first signs of such a trend came in the run-up to the 1967 general election, when Mitterrand persuaded the parties and groups of the non-Communist Left that had supported his presidential candidacy in 1965 (see Chapter 9) not only to make an electoral agreement not to put up candidates against each other on the first ballot but also to designate a Shadow Cabinet. The politics of relations between coalition partners and of the formation of governments in France (see Chapter 4) have proven too complicated to permit the continued existence of shadow cabinets, but the brief experience of 1967 was a pointer to the future. *Alternance* – the complete replacement of one governing coalition with another – first occurred in 1981, when the electoral success of the 'opposition' in the presidential election was confirmed by an overall majority for the new President's party in the general election. There were further complete changes of government (though not President) in 1986, 1988 and again in 1993. In 1988 the re-election of President Mitterrand was not followed by a clear majority victory for his party in the subsequent general election (see Exhibit 9.2). The Socialist Party was the largest party in the National Assembly, however, and the three Socialist prime ministers between 1988 and 1993 were able to maintain a majority for the government's programme. Some dissident members of the UDF were included as ministers in both the Rocard and Cresson governments. The boundaries between government and opposition had shifted a little and become slightly blurred, but the main outlines were still clear.

Alternance has thus become a regular and accepted feature of the operation of the French political system – a fact that can with hindsight be seen largely as a consequence of the institutional framework, but one which the authors of that framework scarcely anticipated, and a fact with which the administrative and governmental machinery, after the surprise and confusion of 1981, has now learnt to reckon.

The Survival of Multi-partyism

The emergence of potentially alternating governing and opposition coalitions has not, however, led to the development of a two-party system. Within the coalitions the individual parties persist, and struggle for dominance, place and influence. There are a number of explanations for the survival of multi-partyism. First, the varied and conflictual ideological heritage of the different parties, described above, makes some combinations unthinkable, even if in fact many ideological differences have lessened almost to disappearing point.[10] Secondly, existence as a separate entity may mean that a party can exact at least a share of the spoils in return for support, at either first or second ballot, of the coalition candidates. The two-ballot system has encouraged the formation of alliances before the election, as occurred in 1993 when a single candidate for the RPR–UDF alliance stood in 494 out of 577 seats. The alliance, under the title *Union pour la France*, published a joint programme, though each of the constituent parties also published its own. The two-ballot system also allowed for a system of 'primary' elections (*désistement*), so that the partners within the coalition can put up individual candidates in the first round and agree that the best placed candidate from the coalition should go forward to the second round. In 1993 this occurred with a reasonably good grace in many of the seats where both Communist and Socialist candidates were still confronting each other after the first round. Thirdly, new parties have emerged outside the major alliances. Two such parties emerged in the 1980s, first the National Front and subsequently the Greens. The National Front was much assisted by the adoption, for the 1986 general election, of a proportional representation electoral system. The return to the two-ballot system in 1988 did not, however, result in its diminution as a national political force, even if it lost all but one of its parliamentary seats in 1988 and failed to gain any in 1993.[11]

The party system of the Fifth Republic is a weak and fragmented system. The paucity of organisational and financial resources available within the parties, and the importance of local roots rather than party identification for political success, reduce the incentives for party loyalty.[12] In addition, the lure of the presidency encourages jockeying for position and personal rivalries and may split and weaken parties. This was true of the UDF in the run up to the 1988 elections and of the Socialist Party in the early 1990s. It was starkly illustrated by the emergence of two RPR candidates in 1995. It fosters the obsession of the French media with the personal relationships between politicians not their policies (Laughland, 1994, p. 94). Since presidential candidates feel that they must transcend party it encourages the erosion of ideological difference which Mény argues has already reached the point where 'party labels constitute convenient indications of the orientation of the [politician] on the political landscape, but tell little about real allegiances, programmatic orientations or indeed ideological choices'.[13] Moreover, it may be that the major cleavages of the 1990s, for example over the progress of European integration, now run within and across parties rather than between them. Nevertheless, the party system has provided governmental stability and a mechanism for the transition of power from governments of one broad ideological persuasion to those of another. It has not proved fixed or static and the political landscape has undergone steady and continuing change. The next chapter explores the strategies and fortunes of the various parties.

9

Parties, Voters and Elections

The ideological heritage and the institutional structures described in Chapter 8 have provided the broad context within which the party political contests of the Fifth Republic have been fought out. The parties' fortunes have fluctuated, and their approach, strategy and tactics have varied. The first decade of the Fifth Republic was dominated by the emergence of the Gaullist Party, and the development of a governing coalition. The 1970s were the period in which the Socialist party was building up the position and support that led to its victory in 1981. During the 1980s the political pattern shifted again, as the Communist party declined, the extreme right National Front began to be prominent on the political scene and the Ecologists also started to attract votes (see Exhibits 9.1 and 9.2).

This chapter analyses the fortunes of the parties since 1958, arguing that they have undergone a process of adaptation to the institutions of the Fifth Republic. As Colette Ysmal (1990) argues, the old social and ideological cleavages still shape parts of the political structure, but they no longer suffice fully to explain shifts in voting preferences and the emergence of new political forces. A whole range of other considerations come into play, including the credibility of the different parties, their strategies, the impact of their leaders, especially the presidential candidates, and the force of the issues before the voters at the moment of the election. The consequence over the period has been an unprecedented mobility in electoral choices and party political fortunes.

240

EXHIBIT 9.1

The results of the presidential elections, 1988 and 1995

24 April 1988: first ballot
Valid votes: 79.4 per cent of registered voters

Candidate	Votes	Valid votes (%)
F. Mitterrand	10 367 220	34.10
J. Chirac	6 063 514	19.54
R. Barre	5 031 849	16.54
J-M Le Pen	4 375 894	14.40
A. Lajoinie	2 055 995	6.76
A. Waechter	1 149 642	3.78
P. Juquin	639 084	2.10
A. Laguiller	606 017	1.99
P. Boussel	116	0.38

8 May 1988: second ballot
Valid votes 81.02 per cent of registered voters

Candidate	Votes	Valid votes (%)
F. Mitterrand	16 704 279	54.02
J. Chirac	14 218 270	45.98

23 April 1995: first ballot
Valid votes: 75.56 per cent of registered voters

Candidate	Votes	Valid votes (%)
L. Jospin	7 097 786	23.30
J. Chirac	6 348 375	20.84
E. Balladur	5 658 796	18.58
J-M Le Pen	4 570 838	15.00
R. Hue	2 636 460	8.64
A. Laguiller	1 615 552	5.30
P. de Villiers	1 443 186	4.74
D. Voynet	1 010 681	3.32
J. Cheminade	84 959	0.28

7 May 1995: second ballot
Valid votes: 73.71 per cent of registered voters

Candidate	Votes	Valid votes (%)
J. Chirac	15 766 658	52.63
L. Jospin	14 191 019	47.37

EXHIBIT 9.2

The results of the general elections, 1988 and 1993

	1988				1993			
	Votes at first ballot	Percentage of first ballot votes	Seats in National Assembly *	**	Votes at first ballot	Percentage of first ballot votes	Seats in National Assembly *	***
Extreme Left	89 065	0.36			448 784	1.77		
Communists	2 765 761	11.32	27	26	2 323 437	9.21	23	23
Socialists and allies	9 176 708	37.53	277	272	5 063 930	20.06	70	57
Ecologists	86 312	0.35			1 944 578	7.70		
RPR	4 687 047	19.14	129		5 133 870	20.35	247	257
UDF	4 519 459	18.50	130		4 849 489	19.22	213	215
Other moderate Right	697 272	2.85	13		1 164 377	4.61	24	23
Unaffiliated				15				2
National Front	2 359 528	9.65	1	1	3 158 843	12.52		
Other	50 493	0.13			1 132 668	4.47		

Notes:

* Seats attributed at the election.
** Parliamentary groups, June 1988; includes associated members.
*** Parliamentary groups, Autumn 1993; includes associated members.

The Emergence of the Gaullist Party

When General de Gaulle came to power as prime minister in 1958 Parliament contained only a handful of avowed Gaullists (see Figure 9.1). His first government contained ministers from each of the main parliamentary parties except the Communists, and of his ministers only the distinguished author André Malraux and the future Prime Minister Michel Debré were strongly identified with Gaullism as a political movement. Following the referendum which accepted the constitution, a new electoral system was introduced in October 1958 (see Exhibit 8.2, p. 220) and a general election under the new rules was called for November. This election produced the first clear message that the new constitution had altered the shape of French party politics. An electoral organisation distinguished by its loyalty to de Gaulle had sprung up in an extremely short time. De Gaulle steadfastly refused ever to have his own name officially associated with any kind of political movement, so another title had to be found – 'Union for the New Republic' (*Union pour la nouvelle république* – UNR) – though for general convenience the label 'Gaullist' was popularly used.

Aided by the new two-ballot electoral system the movement's success was spectacular: with just under 20 per cent of the first ballot vote they gained 199 out of 546 seats in the National Assembly. Together with his allies, de Gaulle was assured of a majority in the National Assembly, at least until the Algerian crisis which had brought him into power was settled, not as a result of the political arithmetic of party allegiance in the Assembly, but because sufficient members were not prepared to jeopardise the success of what was seen as the only possible solution to France's plight. The Gaullist members provided a solid basis for the majority which de Gaulle could command.

Once the crisis in Algeria receded disagreement with de Gaulle quickly began to be openly expressed. The SFIO, which had avoided action which could result in the overthrow of the government, and the MRP, whose ministers had left the government because of their disagreement with de Gaulle's policy on European integration, were both prepared to contribute to the majority which passed a motion of censure against the government over de Gaulle's plans for constitutional amendments. The consequence was the dissolution of Parliament and a general election in November 1962. The result was again striking. The Gaullists gained 35.5 per cent of the first-ballot vote,

FIGURE 9.1
**Votes and National Assembly seats taken by the Gaullists and their
allies, general elections, 1958–93**

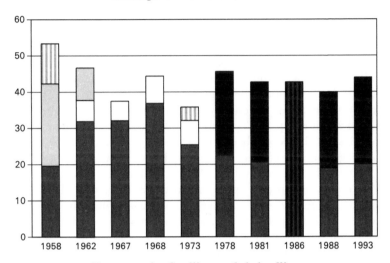

**Votes cast for Gaullists and their allies
as percentage of valid votes at first ballot**

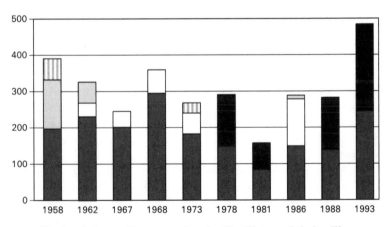

National Assembly seats taken by Gaullists and their allies

and between the ballots cemented an alliance with Valéry Giscard d'Estaing and his followers that ensured an overall majority of seats – 256 out of 465 – for Gaullists and their allies.

Gaullism, it was now evident, was not merely a rapid reaction to a dramatic crisis. It was clearly a solid political force upon which a political programme could be built. It was less clear whether it was a durable force, and even more doubtful whether it could in any sense survive de Gaulle – the RPF had not long outlasted his retreat from politics.

The RPF, itself based to some extent on the old Resistance personnel and contacts, had provided a national organisation that could be revived. Congresses of the new party were held from 1959 onwards, but the Gaullist Party was initially effectively a parliamentary party devoted largely to unconditional support of de Gaulle. It could have no specific manifesto, beyond loyalty, but that it sought to ensure, trying to maintain discipline amongst its members and prepared to expel those who dissented. After 1962 Prime Minister Georges Pompidou recognised that, if the President was to maintain a solid presidential majority within Parliament and mobilise an adequate vote in the presidential election, an organised, mass-based party would have to be created to provide the necessary support. De Gaulle himself continued to pitch his appeal to all the French people, on a national basis. Pompidou, however, as prime minister, became the effective leader of the Gaullist Party, overseeing its parliamentary programme and its organisation, and becoming involved in the choice of candidates for the 1967 elections.

The Gaullists and their allies retained their majority in the 1967 elections, though by a very narrow margin, but the backlash against the Left following the events of May 1968 assured them a healthy majority within the assembly between 1968 and 1973. As President, following de Gaulle's resignation in 1969, Pompidou was much more clearly identified than de Gaulle himself was ever willing to be as the leader of the party, even though the careful rhetorical distancing of the presidency from any particular party was maintained. The Gaullist party survived: it had succeeded in establishing itself firmly as a broadly-based party of the centre-right. Its electoral successes and its long-term role as a party of government, linked with the effects of the Fifth Republic's institutional structures, had favoured its emergence as a modern party.

The 1970s saw the emergence of a number of tensions. In 1972 the conflict between the progressive stance of the governmental programme of Jacques Chaban-Delmas and the recognition by Pompidou and other powerful party leaders (the so-called 'barons' of Gaullism such as Debré, Guichard and Foccart) of the need to retain the support of the more conservative back benchers and electorate resulted in Chaban-Delmas' dismissal as prime minister. In 1974 a section of the Gaullists led by Jacques Chirac deserted Chaban-Delmas in the presidential election campaign and helped to ensure the victory of Giscard d'Estaing. The Gaullist Party thus lost the presidency, having lost its overall majority in the National Assembly in 1973, although it remained the dominant partner in the governing coalition. It now had to adjust to a President from another political organisation, so that while unconditional support of the Fifth Republic and of the presidency remained one of its crucial tenets, support for the individual who was President was no longer automatic.

Chirac's services in the campaign were rewarded by his appointmentas prime minister, and from this position he was able to take over as secretary general of the Gaullist party, the first time since 1958 that a prime minister had formally been also a party leader. As a factor in the complex relationship between presidential and prime ministerial power within a governing coalition (see Chapter 4) the experiment was not a success. Following his resignation Chirac undertook a profound remodelling of the Gaullist Party. He relaunched it, gave it a new name (the *Rassemblement pour la république* – RPR), entrenched his own leadership within a new organisational structure, launched a membership drive, and consolidated his personal position by winning election in 1977 as the first mayor of Paris under the reformed local government arrangements. He continued as mayor of Paris until his election as President in 1995.

The Gaullists had thus weathered the crisis after 1974, overcoming the split at the time of the 1974 election, the loss of the presidency in 1974, and the premiership in 1976, and growing electoral competition from the Giscardian UDF. The party emerged with a reformed organisation, an uncontested leader and an electoral pact with the UDF for the general election of 1978. However, its structural position was weakened by the loss of the major offices of state. By the early 1980s the RPR was still able to win more votes in local and national elections than any other right-wing party, although its electoral support had narrowed from the broad base which General de Gaulle's personal appeal had attracted.[1] Between 1981 and 1993, except for the period between 1986 and 1988, it ceased to be the largest single party in the National Assembly.

The RPR had emerged from under the shadow of General de Gaulle, and established itself as a modern, mass-based, organised party of the centre-right. It made ritual references to the Gaullist inheritance but, since in the early 1980s it 'formally adopted a neo-liberal and relatively Europhile programme, marking a break with its statist and nationalist traditions (despite vain resistance from several of the old guard)'[2] it pursued policies and approaches which did not differ greatly from those of other such parties in Europe. It may be more accurate to refer to its stance in the 1980s and 1990s as 'neo-Gaullist'. Chirac's return to power as prime minister between 1986 and 1988, as the leader of the dominant party in a governing coalition under a Socialist president (*cohabitation*) was marked by policies of privatisation and deregulation, a tighter law and order and immigration policy, and a rhetoric of 'rolling back the state'. This approach was sustained in 1993 if rather more cautiously.

Between 1988 and 1995 the RPR faced another period of crisis. First, the defeat of 1988 led to internal dissent and challenges to Chirac's leadership from younger 'reformist' politicians such as Michel Noir, the mayor of Lyons who was eventually expelled from the party. Secondly, the growing electoral successes of the National Front posed acute dilemmas of political alliance, especially at local level, and of policy orientation. The law and order and anti-immigration policies of Charles Pasqua, minister of the interior in both 1986–8 and 1993–5, were aimed at accommodating this section of the electorate. Thirdly, although the party leadership stuck to support for the ratification of the Maastricht Treaty in 1992, prominent members of the party, notably Philippe Séguin and Charles Pasqua, campaigned for a 'no' vote. RPR members of Parliament (72 out of 127), senators (70 out of 90) and members of the European Parliament (3 out of 13) supported a 'no' vote despite the leadership's position (Buffotot, 1993, p. 280). Finally, the landslide victory in the 1993 general election and the appointment of an RPR prime minister encouraged, rather than prevented, the emergence of two plausible Gaullist candidates in the 1995 presidential election. Charles Pasqua, most prominently, appealed for the organisation of nationwide 'primary' elections on the United States model to ensure that there would be only one candidate of the moderate Right. But the legal and practical difficulties proved insurmountable. However, each candidate needed to find a distinctive appeal. Chirac's was, much more than before, based on notions of a mitigated and social market. He was unable, once in office, to keep the contradictory promises of his campaign. He had promised to deal with high unemployment and low wages without at the same time raising taxes; in fact, taxes were raised, public sector pay was frozen and unemployment fell very slowly. The result was a vertiginous drop in public approval (see Figure 3.1). Chirac's message was reformist and populist, and in that sense could latch onto some of the themes of Gaullism in the past (Cole, 1995, p. 332) However, these themes throughout the 1980s and 1990s have proved flexible enough to accommodate considerable change in orientation without the alienation of a substantial core of voters. Moreover, the rhetoric of French *grandeur* and independence persists and was used in 1995 to justify the resumption of nuclear testing in the face of widespread international opprobrium. But it too is capable of divergent interpretations, as the division in the Gaullist party over the ratification of the Maastricht Treaty revealed. Despite the retention of a number of distinctive features the neo-Gaullists are now clearly a flexible, pragmatic, centre-right party.

Coalitions, Blocs and the Demise of the Centre

The earliest consequence of the factors described above was the development of a governing coalition in the period after 1962. The Gaullist Party did not enjoy an absolute majority in the 1962–7 Parliament, and was dependent upon a group of allies, chiefly a number of conservative members who had been elected under the 'independents and peasants' label, and looked to the young Valéry Giscard d'Estaing as their leader. He had taken over a parliamentary seat from his grandfather in 1956, and had thus depended for his first steps in politics on his personal, local and family connections, rather than on party organisation. As one who had demonstrated enormous success in moving through the succession of the most selective academic hurdles that in France leads initially to a civil service career – from the Ecole Polytechnique to the Ecole Nationale d'Administration and on to the finance inspectorate (see Chapter 5) – his ability was uncontested, and in 1959 he became a junior minister in the Finance Ministry. By early 1962 he had become minister of finance – one of the most important posts within the government (see Chapter 4). The Independents and Peasants group with which he was associated was divided over the constitutional reform of 1962, but Giscard d'Estaing with some of the other members of the group supported de Gaulle, and clearly identified themselves as allies of the Gaullists.

After the 1962 general election Giscard d'Estaing retained his post as finance minister, and also began to set about fashioning a political power-base for himself. Initially this took the form of a parliamentary 'study group' of the Independents and Peasants' members who had followed him, plus a number of young politicians, some of whom had come like him through the elite civil service recruitment and training process and shared his rather technocratic style. This group he called the Independent Republicans (*Républicains indépendents* – RI). His group supported de Gaulle in the 1965 presidential election, but Giscard d'Estaing lost his ministerial job in the subsequent reshuffle. De Gaulle was shocked that he had been forced into a second ballot at that election by a failure to gain over 50 per cent of the vote on the first ballot, and felt that some of the government's unpopularity was due to its economic mismanagement, for which Giscard d'Estaing provided a convenient scapegoat. Giscard d'Estaing regained the parliamentary seat that he had renounced on taking up ministerial office, maintained a high public profile, and turned the RI into a fully-fledged political party. This party remained part of the governing coalition in the sense that its parliamentary members would never vote to bring the government down, but Giscard d'Estaing was careful to preserve a certain critical distance from Gaullism and de Gaulle, epitomised in the famous phrase by which he characterised his position during the final years of de Gaulle's presidency 'Oui mais . . .' – 'yes but . . .'.

In the 1969 presidential election Giscard d'Estaing supported Pompidou, and was rewarded by returning to the Ministry of Finance. His victory in the 1974 presidential election campaign was due to a well-conducted campaign, to his success in presenting himself as a competent, modern, progressive, forward-looking candidate, who was nevertheless firmly within the safe framework of the coalition that had governed France since 1958, and also to the disunity of the Gaullists and the defection of a good number of them to his cause. His party base was still relatively weak; in the 1973 general election the Giscardians had taken only just over 10 per cent of the first-ballot vote and 54 out of 490 seats. Giscard d'Estaing continued to govern with the parliament elected in 1973 in which the Gaullists dominated the majority, but his political relationship with Chirac became increasingly difficult and led to Chirac's replacement in 1976 by the academic economist Raymond Barre as prime minister. The

Gaullist party regrouped under Chirac, and was then relaunched as the RPR, maintaining a critical and separate position within the coalition.

The efficacy of presidential government had depended since 1958 upon a loyal and dependable parliamentary majority. With the approach of the 1978 general election and following the local elections in Paris, where Chirac had defeated Giscard d'Estaing's candidate, Giscard d'Estaing needed a political backing upon which he could depend and which could counterbalance the Gaullists. This he succeeded in creating, first by the relaunch of the Independent Republicans as the Republican Party (*Parti Républicain* – PR) in 1977, and then by the creation of a federation of the PR with other non-Gaullist elements of the majority.

Giscard d'Estaing had thrown in his lot with de Gaulle from the beginning, and brought with him a group that originated from the conservative right. Increasingly, and especially through the creation, in the 1960s, of a network of political debating clubs, he had attracted civil servants and professional and business people interested in liberal economics, a lessening of state intervention, the development of European integration and progressive social policies. Giscard d'Estaing looked, however, to enlarge his support not only within the conservative right, but also within the centre. Within his federation, created shortly before the 1978 election, whose title, the Union for French Democracy (*Union pour la Démocratie Française* – UDF) echoed that of the book he published during his presidency – *Démocratie Française* (1976) – he successfully provided a home for those remaining parties of the centre who, having been forced to choose, had opted for the governing majority.

The Christian Democratic MRP and the Radicals had both been medium-sized parties with 10 to 15 per cent of the vote each before the demise of the Fourth Republic. They carried with them the taint of their identification with that discredited regime, and suffered from the inroads into their electorate made by the Gaullists and, especially in the case of the Radicals, from their division over the Algerian question. As support for actual or potential presidential candidates became an increasingly important part of the political game centre parties found themselves obliged to take sides, and their struggles to resist this imperative during the 1960s were rewarded by falling votes and the loss of parliamentary seats.

The MRP disappeared into a broader centre group before the 1967 general election; that group itself fragmented between those who rallied to Pompidou in 1969, and those who remained in opposition until 1974. In 1976 the *Centre des démocrates sociaux* brought the parts together again, and the CDS became and has remained one of the main constituent elements of the UDF which, in addition to the *Parti Républicain* also embraces a large part of what remains of the Radical Party, the *Parti Social-Démocrate*, various political clubs and a small number of individual members.

The UDF is a weakly organised group, an uneasy confederation that remains close to the classic formula of a cadre party. It is consequently susceptible to rivalry amongst its leading personalities and to dissidence amongst its constituent groups. During the 1980s the UDF just succeeded in surviving the disruptive effects of the ambitions of some of its leaders, such as François Léotard, and of intense rivalry between ex-President Giscard d'Estaing and ex-Prime Minister Barre in the run up to the 1988 presidential election; in the event there was only one UDF candidate, Barre, who came in third. In the subsequent general election, unlike previous elections, the RPR and the UDF put up only one candidate in each constituency for the first round, under a joint label. However, once the successful candidates reached Parliament, division occurred, not only between RPR and UDF, but within the UDF, for the CDS members and other 'Barrists' split from the rest of the 'Giscardian' UDF to form a separate Parliamentary group. The split then took electoral form in the 1989 European elections when the CDS put up a separate list against a joint list backed by the RPR and the remains of the UDF and headed by Giscard d'Estaing.

These divisions, combined with the minority Rocard government's courtship of the centre – his government actually included four UDF members – and need to find parliamentary majorities for its measures, led at that time to renewed speculation about the possibility of a renewed role for Centre parties along Fourth Republican lines. By the end of 1991, however, most of the dissident CDS had been driven back to the UDF. A degree of unity within the party and the alliance with the RPR were both patched up in time for the 1993 elections, when a single UPF (RPR–UDF alliance) candidate was agreed upon for most seats. The strains were still evident, however, for Philippe de Villiers, originating in the UDF, was a vociferous campaigner for a 'no' vote in the 1992 Maastricht referendum, despite the generally strongly pro-integration stance of the UDF. He went on to head a list of his own for the European Parliament elections in 1994, which gained 13 per cent of the vote and 13 MEPs.

The UDF is important in government, with a strong representation in Juppé's Cabinet (see Exhibit 4.2) and also in local government – providing the mayors for two major towns, Toulouse and Marseilles – and in the Senate (see Table 9.3). It has, for general elections in 1988 and 1993, and European Parliament elections in 1989 and 1994, continued to be linked to the RPR in a difficult marriage of convenience from which it draws the benefit of a higher level of parliamentary representation than it could expect if it were confronted by direct electoral competition with the RPR. In 1995, in the absence of a candidate of its own, its leaders divided their support between Balladur and Chirac, with the bulk of the support going to Balladur who was 'transformed by default into a UDF candidate' (Cole, 1995, p. 330). His fate and Lionel Jospin's unexpected success seems to confirm the view that voters are still looking for a choice between Left and Right (Cole, 1995, p.339) and reinforce the sagacity of Frank Wilson's observation that 'few voters are willing to abstain from the choice between the Right and the Left by voting for a centrist movement.'[3] The fact that choice between Left and Right can now be seen in such stark terms is also a comment upon the development of the Left during the Fifth Republic.

The Left in the Fifth Republic

The Fortunes of the Socialist Party

The 1960s were a dispiriting decade for the Socialist Party. The SFIO was largely discredited by its association with the Fourth Republic and, although it endorsed the new constitution, by 1962 it was clearly opposing de Gaulle and the way in which he was shaping the Fifth Republic. Parts of the party favoured alliance with the Communists, and others retained the party's earlier profound anti-Communism. After an abortive attempt by the leader of the party's powerful section in the Bouches-du-Rhone (Marseilles area), Gaston Defferre, to unite the non-Communist Left in support of his presidential candidacy in 1965, he dropped out and the party supported Mitterrand, who was then the leader of a small group of left-wing clubs, and joined in his Federation of the Left for the elections of 1967 and 1968. The tactics of the 1960s had not proved conspicuously successful; the performance of the Left had been creditable in 1967, but the after-math of the May 1968 events brought a surge of Gaullism and, after the election, the collapse of the Federation. Defferre could only attract a humiliating 5 per cent of the votes in the 1969 presidential election.

In 1969 a reconstructed party, the *Parti Socialiste*, replaced the SFIO. The movement towards the PCF which was to lead to the 1972 common programme made a tentative beginning, and the new party began to install younger and more diverse local party officials within its organisation, and to recruit new members. But the new First Secretary, Alain Savary, was not an electorally appealing figure, nor a charismatic leader, and the absence from the party of François Mitterrand who clearly did possess the necessary qualities seemed increasingly senseless (Bell and Criddle, 1988, p. 60). In July 1971 Mitterrand joined the new party, and three days later became its First Secretary.

Between 1971 and the end of the 1980s the story of the Socialist Party was one of a steady gain in credibility and electoral solidity, confirmed by its winning of an absolute majority in the National Assembly elected in 1981 (see Figure 9.2). The 1986 election reduced its share of the vote, and put it into opposition. Mitterrand's victory in 1988 did not entirely fulfill expectations of success, for in the general election that followed the PS failed to attract the votes of over a million of those who had voted for Mitterrand. Nevertheless, within most European contexts a score of between 30 and over 37 per cent, which the Socialist Party achieved in three general elections between 1981 and the end of the decade, seems respectable, especially since party support is increasingly spread across the whole of France (Hanley, 1989, p. 19).

One of the chief factors which helps to explain this rise and consolidation over a period of two decades was the impact of Mitterrand himself. When he took over the leadership of the party he already had a solid and prominent standing as the candidate who had united the Left and taken de Gaulle to a second ballot in 1965. His ministerial posts under the Fourth Republic and his initial resistance to the institutions of the Fifth Republic were not necessarily an asset, but his presence, style – both in speeches and in his accessible writings – and experience lent weight and credibility to his leader-ship, which was reinforced by his strong performance in the 1974 presidential campaign. His political astuteness, indeed cunning, was never in question. 'Sphinx' and 'enigma' are epithets that have

FIGURE 9.2
Votes and National Assembly seats taken by the Left,
general elections, 1958–93

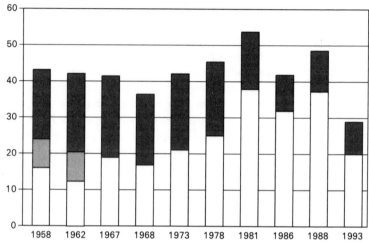

Votes cast for Radicals, Socialists and their allies
as percentage of valid votes at first ballot

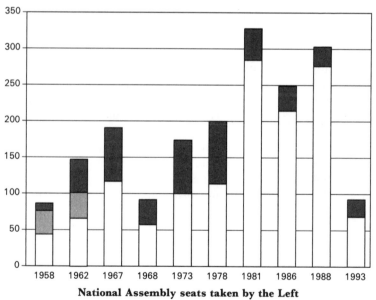

National Assembly seats taken by the Left

▓ Communists   ▒ Radicals   ☐ Socialists and their allies

regularly been applied to him. His 1981 presidential campaign, benefitting from expert and highly effective professional advice, presented him as a *force tranquille*, promising determined, but non-disruptive change. The political structures of the Fifth Republic impose the support and promotion of a presidential candidate as perhaps the major preoccupation of any major political party. Despite the manoeuvres of potential successors, there was no challenge from within the party to Mitterrand's right to the presidency. Mitterrand gathered and retained party members and voters behind him. This unifying effect was particularly evident in the mid-1970s, when Michel Rocard brought his small left-wing party, the *Parti Socialiste Unifié* into the PS, and other new members included Jacques Delors, with his Roman Catholic and trade union background, who went on to be minister of finance in the 1981 government, and then President of the Commission of the European Community.

During his presidency Mitterrand held together a party in which the existence of rival factions was institutionalised. Within the party different *courants* or tendencies exist, usually associated with the leading personality within them. Before each PS congress, lengthy political motions are circulated, each sponsored by a group of like-minded members of the party. Seats on the party executive – the *Comité Directeur* and the party's executive bureau – are allocated to each group whose motion receives the votes of more than 5 per cent of the delegates in proportion to the support gained. In this way the range of opinions within the party is represented at the centre.[4] Clearly it is in the context of a contest for party leadership and for the position of a Socialist candidate as presidential candidate that most of the rivalry within the party is likely to occur, and Mitterrand's dominance largely stifled this for 20 years, despite both Rocard's active campaigning for the candidacy should Mitterrand have decided not to stand in 1988, and also the jockeying for position amongst the leading contenders, including Rocard, Lionel Jospin and Jacques Delors, in advance of the 1995 presidential election.

The impact of Mitterrand, whilst a very major factor, did not by itself explain the changed fortunes of the PS after 1971. A second part of the explanation lies in a number of interlinked social and organisational factors. After 1971 the party 'had much of the same internal structure, and local implantation, and many of the same second rank leaders as it had before [Mitterrand] became its leader'.[5] Nevertheless, party membership climbed steadily through the 1970s; in 1971 before Mitterrand and his followers joined, the PS counted some

61 000 members. By 1979 there were 170 000 (Bell and Criddle, 1988, p. 200). The membership was increasingly drawn from the educated, professional middle class,especially those in state employment, a tendency that was even more marked amongst the party's activists, for example congress delegates and *deputés*.[6] Despite the long Socialist traditions of anti-clericalism, the party at its leadership level was also increasingly drawing upon Roman Catholics. This reflected changes in the Roman Catholic church during the 1960s and 1970s as much as changes in the PS, but it brought the PS some support from new sources,[7] whilst at the same time the decline of religious practice helped the PS to expand its electorate, especially in traditionally strongly Catholic areas. The proportion of women members and activists also rose.

During the 1980s the PS seems to have been 'in tune with the times' (Frears, 1991, p. 81; Bell and Criddle, 1988, p. 208). It built upon changes in the social, professional and employment structures of France in the last two decades. It benefited both from changes in the Roman Catholic Church and from the increasing secularisation of society. It attracted women in a period when they have become increasingly conscious of their position within society and politics. It also, during the 1980s, proved able 'through social and political "networking", to adapt to changing ideological and social conditions within the electorate and to adopt new social movements'.[8] Howard Machin suggests that the PS was, more than any other party, able to establish sympathetic links with the anti-racism movement, and particularly with the young generation of French-born children of parents of North African origin. Similar links were also established with the student movement (see Exhibit 10.3). It is, Machin argues, the ability of the PS to be attractive to these new movements that has prevented it from being outflanked by other groups, and enabled it to remain the largest single party throughout the 1980s and early 1990s.[9]

A third factor that has affected the PS's place within the political system has been its role as a party of government. The Socialists had long-standing and deep roots at local and municipal level. These local bases provide opportunities for patronage, and hence encourage clientilism, but also corruption especially where the party is in control of the local administration. However, following Mitterrand's election in 1981 which was not widely or confidently forecast, and the sweeping success of the Socialist Party which achieved an overall majority in the National Assembly, the party had to find its place, in government at national level, in a presidential system which suited Mitterrand well enough – not, he said, made to measure for him, but fitting him nonetheless – but whose rhetoric allowed for no special place for the President's party. Indeed, some politicians and commentators expressed themselves as shocked when a seminar was held early in the presidency so that the government could discuss policy with PS backbenchers.

The consequences were, as John Gaffney points out, that the party had to shift from a perception of itself as concerned chiefly with largely rhetorical and ideological left-wing support for a charismatic leader whose success would almost automatically herald major social change and progress to realising that it must be 'a party representative of a huge grouping of French citizens and providing rational, competent and incrementalist government. The realities of government were to be the motor of this change'.[10] The constraints of the domestic and international economic situation meant that the priorities and the language of the Socialist government had, from 1983, to shift, under the influence of ministers such as Delors and Bérégovoy, to an emphasis on rigour, on the value of the *entreprise*, on the need for nationalisation to provide not a motor for the transformation of industry but rather an opportunity for firms to restructure and return to profit. The President and the government carried the party with them, and it went into opposition in 1986 having established its credentials as a moderate and legitimate party of government, with a number of real achievements to its credit, including an economic record that was at least as good as that of most of the other members of the European Community, and major change, stemming from the decentralisation programme, in local government.

In 1988 the PS became again the party of government, even though it had not been able to take a majority of seats in the National Assembly. Mitterrand in his 1988 campaign distanced himself much more sharply from the PS than he had done in 1981, and some party leaders blamed his equivocal attitude for their failure to gain a clear majority. Nevertheless the PS again provided the Prime Minister, the leading ministers, and many ministerial advisers. By the early 1990s the PS had moved a long way since 1981. It had clearly become a progressive but moderate social-democratic party.

These three interlinked factors – the effect of Mitterrand, the adaptation of the party to the changing social and political context, and its reshaping of itself as a pragmatic, centre-left, social-democratic party of government – helped the PS to create and sustain for itself, for a decade after 1980, a place as the major single party within the French party system. However the PS's position proved far from secure.

The decline in the fortunes of the Socialists in the 1990s was rapid and steep. A series of elections since the end of the 1980s has seen tumbling scores for the Socialists and their allies (see Figure 9.2). After 14 years of the presidency and ten of government they are no longer a governing party. Jospin's showing in the 1995 election was surprisingly good, but only served to emphasise that new strategies and approaches will be needed if the Socialists are to repeat the rise of the 1970s.

A number of reasons can be suggested for the decline.[11] First, much of the electoral success of the Socialists had depended upon the personal success and standing of François Mitterrand. The party's main electoral achievements followed directly upon his successes, and his appeal went wider than that of the party. In dreaming, as they did, of a Delors candidacy for 1995 the Socialists were no doubt hoping that the effect could be reproduced with another charismatic candidate. But Jacques Delors finally declined to stand, and Jospin's appeal, although better than was feared, proved inadequate.

Second, the Socialists have suffered the disadvantages of an incumbent party in a period of difficulty. Although GDP per capita grew in France between 1988 and 1993, inflation was held down, the commitment to the EC exchange rate mechanism (ERM) strengthened and much industrial adjustment achieved, the unemployment rate in the late 1980s and early 1990s was well above the OECD average and rising. At the same time the adjustment and deregulation that had begun under the Chirac government, the Single Market and the reforms of the Common Agricultural Policy were adversely affecting several hitherto rather sheltered groups within the economy. The Socialist government failed to produce a convincing strategy to deal with unemployment. The issue is one on which social democratic governments are particularly vulnerable, since the improvement of the material well-being of all of society is one of their most specific missions.

Third, the Socialists were particularly hard-hit by revelations of scandal and malpractice. Presidential staff, Socialist ministers and their associates were implicated in allegations of financial corruption, the framing of innocent people on terrorism charges, insider trading and in the contaminated blood scandal (see above, page 126). Such problems were by no means confined to the Socialists, but they bore particularly hard upon an incumbent government.

Fourth, the party was unable to sustain a coherent strategy of alliances with other political groups to complement or replace the alliance with the Communists, whose results by the early 1980s were so poor that they could no longer provide sufficient support to enable the Socialists to sustain a majority of the Left. As Figure 9.2 demonstrates, the collapse of the Communist vote has had a critical impact upon the results of the traditional left. Michel Rocard's 'big bang' approach – a proposal for some sort of merger between ecologists, dissident Communists and Socialists, which he had talked of during the 1993 election campaign, failed to prosper. At the 1994 European elections the Socialists found themselves in competition not only with ecologists and a 'Sarajevo' list put together to protest against inaction over the war in Bosnia, but also with a list headed by a former Socialist minister, Jean-Pierre Chevènement, and, much more seriously, a list put up by their erstwhile allies in the *Mouvement des radicaux de gauche*. This list attracted 12 per cent of the vote, compared with the Socialists' 15 per cent. The poor score fatally damaged Rocard's position as leader of the Socialists and ended his hopes of a presidential candidacy in 1995. Some have seen in the apparent encouragement offered by Mitterrand to Bernard Tapie, the media hero, business tycoon, football club owner and ultimately bankrupt leader of the MRG list, a deliberate ploy to ruin Rocard's chances and ensure thereby that an old adversary would never occupy the Elysée. Be that as it may, the outcome was an isolated and strategically incoherent Socialist party.

Fifth, the party itself had been riddled by in-fighting and dissension. In 1989 Mitterrand's hostility to Michel Rocard led him to try to prevent his taking over as party leader, but Mitterrand himself failed to impose his own preferred candidate. The battle for the succession reached 'epic proportions' between Fabius and Rocard after the latter ceased to be prime minister. Even though it seemed to have been resolved in Rocard's favour in 1993, by the end of 1994 his leadership was over. In the event the relatively smooth adoption of Jospin as 1995 presidential candidate at a late stage after Delors' withdrawal papered over some cracks. There had, however, already been one secession. In 1992 Jean-Pierre Chevènement, who had resigned as minister of defence in protest at the Gulf War, campaigned actively against the party line for a 'no' vote in the Maastricht referendum and in 1993 he created his own group, the *Mouvement des citoyens*, and put up some candidates against the Socialists in the election of that year, and a separate list for the European election in 1994.

Sixth, the 1990s revealed in sharp form new cleavages within society which the Socialists seemed incapable of addressing. Mitterrand in the 1970s and 1980s had succeeded in bringing together the traditional left-wing vote with a more middle-class, educated, professional, modernising electorate. But that synthesis could not be sustained and was finally blown away by the Maastricht referendum. The opposition at that point between those social groups who viewed the future with optimism, and those who felt that their interests and security were threatened, 'was a catastrophe for the Socialist Party, costing it more than any other party' since a 'no' vote in the referendum by a voter who had previously voted Socialist was in nearly half the cases translated into a vote for a different party in 1993.[12]

Seventh, a further threat came from the Ecologists (see below). Although the Ecologists have not been able to repeat at national level their success at the regional elections of 1992, there has been some coming and going of voters between Ecologists and the Socialists.[13] The Socialists' active attempts to win over both voters and leaders from the Ecologists (Sainteny 1994) have met with limited success, and the competition with the Ecologists has certainly contributed to the Socialists' weakness.

The Demise of French Communism

The first general election of the Fifth Republic sent the Communist vote plunging to just under 19 per cent – a figure that was for a long time thought to represent the bedrock of PCF support. The party relied upon a number of traditional sources of support: the traditional industrial working class, located, for example, in the Communist districts around Paris; an equally traditional protest vote, found in the areas and amongst those groups that had long taken an 'anti-establishment' stance, which gave the PCF, for example, a rather surprising vote amongst the small peasant farmers of the South West; the young, especially the educated young, for whom a Communist vote was part of an assertion of rebellious identity; and those intellectuals for whom the PCF was the concrete expression of their Marxist belief system. After the Second World War the party's support was strengthened by the undeniably heroic and leading role it had played in the Resistance.

The party was closely controlled by its leader and its central politburo, secretive and disciplined, faithfully following the twists and turns of Soviet policy, earning thereby Socialist leader Guy Mollet's celebrated gibe that it was not to the left of the Socialists, but to the East of them. As the Cold War intensified through the 1950s the PCF, following its expulsion from government in 1947, held itself grimly apart from the governmental process, denouncing the Fourth Republic, and equally vehemently refusing de Gaulle, his constitution of 1958 and his amendment of 1962. Some of the Fifth Republic's institutional arrangements, for example the two-ballot electoral system, were quite clearly designed to disadvantage the PCF.

The PCF, however, were in an ambiguous position in relation to the governmental system. They had formed part of the government until 1947, continued to campaign in parliamentary elections to seek to win seats in the National Assembly, and to support, or even put up, candidates for the presidential election. They also played an important role in local government. So the party has consistently been part of the political system which it has consistently denounced.

During the 1960s the party began slowly to reconsider its position and tactics. In the election of 1962 it improved its share of the vote (see Figure 9.2), although it was never again to return to the levels it had always attained between 1945 and 1956. Its representation in parliament went up sharply from 10 to 41, largely because of Socialist *désistement*. The party noted the logic of this, at the same time as it was slowly coming to terms with 'destalinisation' in the East and with the development of detente.

In 1965 the PCF rallied behind Mitterrand's bid for the presidency and did not put up a Communist candidate, and in the general elections of 1967 and 1973 an electoral agreement within the Left ensured that only the best placed candidate of the Left went forward to the second ballot in each constituency. In 1971 the arrival of Mitterrand at the head of the Socialist Party on the basis of a commitment to seeking an alliance with the Communists coincided with the impetus towards alliance on the part of the PCF. The consequence was the negotiation of the Common Programme of the Left, adopted in 1972.

Mitterrand was quite clear from the beginning that the main aim was to reduce the PCF's influence and poach its electorate, whilst the

PCF central committee asserted that 'l'union est un combat' (Portelli, 1987, p. 166). Faced with the mounting gains of the Socialists, the PCF found itself simultaneously trying to assert its own identity and credentials, for example through attacks on Socialist policy proposals, and through support for the Portuguese Communist Party, and trying to open itself up to wider support. But unlike the Italian Communist Party (PCI) the PCF proved unable to chose between eurocommunism and orthodoxy, nor between reliance upon a narrowly defined working class or a broader social alliance, nor between strategies of close alliance with the socialists or isolated sectarianism, and, as Portelli says, it fell back upon an unsatisfactory middle way (Portelli, 1987, p. 171).

The union of the left resulted in important local electoral gains for both the Socialists and Communists in 1976 and 1977. In the run-up to the 1978 general election, however, the PCF had to face the stark fact that it was no longer the dominant partner in the alliance. The result was a sharp, brutal, public breach between the two. This split is usually held to have resulted chiefly from a refusal, by the PCF, to contemplate coming into power in a subordinate position (Portelli, 1987, p. 174).

Mitterrand's presidential victory in 1981, and the overall majority for the Socialist Party in the National Assembly which followed posed acute dilemmas for the PCF, and marked a stage in the party's electoral decline which at the time seemed surprising, but could, with hindsight, be interpreted as part of a longer-term trend. A score of less than 16 per cent of votes cast in the first ballot brought the party below the so-called bedrock level of 1958. Four Communist ministers entered the government after the general election, all of them senior figures within the party, although the most prominent members of the leadership were not offered ministerial posts.

Both the 1983 local elections, and the European elections of 1984 showed continued decline, and at the government reshuffle that followed those elections, in which the general unpopularity of the Mitterrand government had been demonstrated, the Communists left the government and the party returned to outspoken criticism of the Socialists. The shifts of policy and the party's apparent inability to restore its fortunes produced marked dissent within the traditionally disciplined ranks of the party members and even its leadership. Georges Marchais succeeded in retaining until retirement in January 1995 the position as a party leader he had held since 1972, but the party deemed it expedient that he should not be the presidential candidate in 1988. The party managed to save a little face in the general elections of 1988 (11.31 per cent at the first ballot, and 27 seats) largely, it has been suggested, because it was able to call upon the long-standing strengths of the party at local municipal level (Bridgford, 1988, p. 44; Hanley, 1989, p. 19) but even these have in recent years been considerably eroded. Apart from this, in every electoral contest it faced from the mid-1970s the pattern was one of accelerating decline which seems to have stabilised between 1993 and 1995 at around 6 to 9 per cent of the vote.

The collapse of East European Communism has further under-mined the party's credibility, reinforcing the discrediting of Marxism that began amongst the intellectuals of the 1970s. It finally lost the remnants of the place it had enjoyed, most notably in the 1940s and 1950s, as a dominant force in much academic and intellectual life. Other factors contributing to its electoral decline include its failure to adapt to societal changes such as the disappearance of traditional heavy manufacturing industry, greater social and geographical mo-bility and the decline in trade unionism (see Chapter 10). Moreover, its internal structures remained very rigid, and only at the Congress in 1994 which elected Robert Hue as the next leader did it formally abandon 'democratic centralism'. A strongly left-wing, Marxist strand has not completely disappeared from French politics: the veteran Trotskyist, Arlette Laguiller, fighting her fourth presidential election, scored her highest ever vote, 5.3 per cent, in the first ballot in 1995, and the PCF retains some local strength, but nationally it now plays a relatively minor role.

Politics and the Ecology Movement

The 1970s, in France as in other countries, saw a rising level of public concern about environmental issues and of mass action and demon-strations in protest against developments or policies suspected of causing environmental damage (see Chapter 10, p. 295). The ecology movement which grew out of the general concerns for conservation and ecological problems that emerged particularly after 1968 initially consisted largely of fragmented and often locally based groups. These were largely peopled by grass-roots activists with very little central or political organisation. Indeed, the movement was characterised by a distrust of leadership. A presidential candidate in 1974 attracted only a minuscule vote, although a Paris-based group achieved 11 per cent of the vote in the Paris municipal elections in 1977. There was an ecologist list in the European elections of 1979, which gained 4.39 per cent of the vote, and an ecology candidate (Brice Lalonde) in 1981, though neither had an organised political base. In general their electoral performance was very modest throughout the 1970s and 1980s, in contrast to the Greens of West Germany, for example, who were aided by the German electoral system.

At the time of the European election in 1984 a confederation of ecology movements was created as a unifying political force, linked to the transnational ecology party grouping.[14] It came to be known as *Les Verts* (the Greens) a shortened version of the full title, *Les Verts confédération écologiste – parti-écologiste*. It was the outcome of dissent about political strategy within the ecology networks. By 1984 Lalonde had opted for co-operation with more established political forces and, partly in reaction to this *Les Verts* emerged as an organised party, though it proved able to attract little more than 3 per cent of the vote and Lalonde's rival list scored much the same. In 1988 the Green presidential candidate, Antoine Waechter improved this score slightly, achieving just under 4 per cent.

A high point for *Les Verts* came in 1989. The party set its sights principally upon winning seats at local and regional levels, and did not even present candidates at the general elections in 1988. In the 1989 municipal election it averaged over 9 per cent of the vote in the 94 towns of over 20 000 inhabitants in which its candidates stood (Cole, 1989, p. 27) and altogether 1400 Green councillors were elected. At the 1989 European elections later that summer the party probably benefited from the increased credibility provided by its good municipal election results, and from the appearance of its leader, Antoine Waechter, on television. It achieved over 10.5 per cent of the votes and nine seats. The party's performance in 1989 was a considerable surprise, although well in line with general political trends throughout Europe: in the United Kingdom there was a 15 per cent vote for the Greens in the European election. The high hopes engendered by these results, and by favourable opinion polls, were soon disappointed. There were several reasons. The first was undoubtedly the apparently ineluctable tendency of the Ecologists to fragment, engendered in part by the 'somewhat anarchic individualism' (Frears, 1991, p. 108) of their activists and also by disagreements over strategy. Whilst *Les Verts* under Waechter refused all alliances, Brice Lalonde in 1992 set up a rival party, *Génération ecologie* (GE), intended largely to capture the ecological protest vote in the forthcoming regional and general elections and deliver it to the Socialists at the second ballot. The consequence was that a high score in the regional elections for the Ecologists taken together (nearly 14 per cent) was split almost equally between the two contenders. However, this was sufficient to win a number of seats at regional level, and hold the balance of power in the Nord–Pas de Calais region, where a coalition between Ecologists and Socialists resulted in a female councillor from *Les Verts* becoming president of the Regional Council.

The two ecology parties managed to patch up an agreement for the 1993 general election, but the result was profoundly disappointing. With under 8 per cent of the vote between the two parties on the first ballot only two candidates even went through to the second ballot and both were defeated. Further splits and dissension followed. *Les Verts* evicted Waechter from the leadership in favour of Dominique Voynet, who had emerged as a media personality during the campaign. Under her the party moved more clearly in favour of a strategy of alliance with the alternative Left, such as dissident Communists and left-wing former Socialists while also being wooed by Rocard as part of his 'big bang' approach. Waechter left *Les Verts* and set up an independent ecologist movement. Similar disputes flared up in *Génération ecologie*. Fragmentation was all too visible at the European elections of 1994, when *Les Verts* presented one list, *Génération ecologie* another, and a former GE leader figured prominently on Tapie's list. Neither ecology list achieved more than 3 per cent of the votes. In 1995 neither Lalonde nor Waechter stood, the latter failing to do so because he fell 30 signatures short of the 500 needed for nomination. Voynet was the sole ecologist candidate but her results, at 3.32 per cent, were back to the levels of a decade previously. Nor was this poor performance redeemed at local level in the municipal elections a month later.

Fragmentation, strategic incoherence and infighting have all wreaked havoc on the Ecologists' electoral fortunes. Their ideology and political approach, incorporating a rejection of most contemporary ideas about economic development and eschewing materialism, have not proved sufficiently robust to capture and hold a large and stable group of followers, especially in a climate of economic difficulty and unemployment. For some they provide an opportunity for a protest vote, but such support is always liable to be fickle. Those who perhaps share some of their ideals do not necessarily vote for them.[15] The electorate for the Greens has been predominantly young, with an average age of 38, highly educated, drawn from the professional middle classes and more female than male. Especially when they seemed to be flourishing and opinion polls were encouraging the mainstream parties shaped parts of their strategy to combat them (Sainteny 1994). This effect seems likely to continue.

The National Front

Local and European elections proved, briefly, to be a springboard from which the Greens could launch themselves into a national role. In this they were comparable to the National Front (*Front National –* FN) which, however, managed also to establish itself much more strongly at a national level.

The rise of the National Front through the 1980s was the most striking development within French political life in that decade (see Figure 9.3). Unlike the Greens, the extreme Right was not a new phenomenon within the French political spectrum. By the early 1970s Jean-Marie Le Pen, (see Exhibit 9.3) managed to bring together into a single political organisation – the National Front – a wide variety of strands of extreme Right opinion. A good deal of support for the FN, at least initially, came from those who were still bitterly resentful of the French abandonment of Algeria. Many of these were former French settlers in Algeria (the so-called *pieds-noirs*) repatriated when Algeria achieved independence. This resentment had probably helped to achieve a 5 per cent first-ballot score for the extreme Right candidate in the presidential election of 1965. Support also came from some remnants of the anti-modernisation, anti-state movement amongst small shopkeepers, farmers and small businessmen known, after the name of its leader Poujade, as Poujadism (see Chapter 8). This had flared briefly in the 1950s, and Le Pen had been one of the Poujadist deputies in the National Assembly. As the credibility of the FN grew during the 1980s support came also from some intellectuals critical of marxist influence and what they saw as western decadence. Some monarchists were attracted to the FN, as were some Catholics who disliked the liberal changes that had occurred in the Roman Catholic church since the 1960s. Thuggish and violent elements also found an outlet in the FN.

The initial impact of the National Front was minimal. In the 1974 presidential election Le Pen gained 0.7 per cent of the first ballot. No extreme Right candidate managed to muster enough nomination

FIGURE 9.3
Votes cast for the National Front, 1974–95
(selected elections, percentage of valid votes cast)

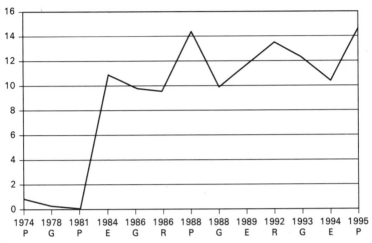

Key:
P = Presidential election (first ballot)   R = Regional council election
G = General election (first ballot) ,   E = European Parliament election

signatures to stand in the 1981 presidential election, and in the general election that followed the FN took 0.18 per cent of the vote. The first sign of a change in the fortunes of the FN came when Le Pen himself took over 11 per cent of the vote in a Paris *arrondissement* in the municipal elections of spring 1983, though nationally the FN secured only 0.3 per cent of first-ballot votes. In November and December that year the FN list spectacularly scored over 16 per cent in a municipal by-election in Dreux – a town with a large immigrant population – and made a pact with the local Gaullists which resulted in the election of an FN member on the second ballot. Scores in another town by-election and in a parliamentary by-election in which Le Pen himself stood that autumn confirmed a dramatic rise in votes. In 1984 elections to the European Parliament took place, with a voting system that obliged the parties to present a national list of candidates for all 81 seats. Seats were allocated to each list in proportion to the number of votes cast for that list nationally. The FN took 11 per cent of the national vote, and gained 10 seats in the European parliament, a score and representation which they retained at the 1989 European Parliament election.

EXHIBIT 9.3

Jean Marie Le Pen

Jean-Marie Le Pen was born in Brittany in 1928. His experience in the Resistance as an adolescent fuelled a virulent anti-Communism, and he became involved in right-wing student groups while registered as a law student in Paris. He then joined the army, and was sent to Indo-China as a parachutist. He subsequently returned to his law studies, but quickly became involved in Pierre Poujade's movement (see Exhibit 8.3) and in 1956 was elected to Parliament by a Paris constituency as a Poujadist, becoming its youngest member.

He almost immediately left his parliamentary duties to rejoin his regiment, and whilst serving in Algeria was suspected of being involved in torturing an Algerian prisoner. He has never been convicted for this, though the accusation continues to haunt him. At this period he lost one eye in a brawl at an electoral meeting. He left the Poujadists and was re-elected to Parliament in 1958 as an independent, losing his seat in 1962.

He continued to be active in politics, supporting the 1965 presidential campaign of the extreme Right candidate, Tixier Vignancourt. In 1972 he founded the National Front. Towards the end of the 1970s he inherited a fortune bequeathed to him by one of the earliest members of the FN.

He stood as a candidate in the presidential election of 1974 gaining less than 1 per cent of the vote, and took only just over 3 per cent of the vote in his Paris constituency in 1978. In 1981 he could not assemble the necessary signatures for a nomination as a presidential candidate.

In 1983 in a number of local and by-elections, and especially at the 1984 elections to the European Parliament, the FN's share of the vote began to increase substantially, and Le Pen, having been a very marginal and little known political figure, acquired a degree of media notoriety, which he exploited fully. A scandalous divorce in 1987 – his ex-wife sought to embarrass him by being photographed wearing nothing but an apron – had no noticeable impact upon his political prospects. His crude outspokenness has resulted in much litigation. He has managed to rebut charges of personal anti-semitism, but his 1987 reference to the Holocaust as 'detail' of history was certainly damaging, whilst in 1988 an extremely offensive pun again alluding to the Holocaust provoked the departure from the party of the only FN member elected to Parliament in the 1988 election.

The 1986 general election in France was also conducted under a proportional representation system, so a vote for the FN of just under 10 per cent brought the party 35 parliamentary seats. However, with the return to the previous ballot system in 1988 an only slightly diminished proportion of the votes produced only one *député*, who was subsequently expelled from the party. A parliamentary by-election in December 1989 returned the FN candidate, so the party continued to be represented in the National Assembly until 1993, when a higher proportion of the vote failed to yield any seats. In contrast to the Ecologists and the Communists, voting support for the National

Front has been sustained at above 10 per cent, with peaks in the first ballot of presidential elections.

The reasons for the rapid rise in the fortunes of the FN are undoubtedly complex, but a number may be suggested. They are closely interlinked and interdependent, and explanations have to be sought in the conjunction of a number of factors rather than in any single or dominant cause. For the purposes of analysis the factors can be divided into three groups: those related to the issues around which Le Pen focuses his programmes; those related to the structure of the electorate and the electoral system; and those related to legitimacy, credibility, respectability and publicity.

Amongst the factors that relate to issues are:

- The FN has latched on to certain issues which have found a considerable echo in parts of the electorate, and has found a style of expression, based on alleged plain speaking and the supposed common sense of the ordinary person, in posters, party political broadcasts and other campaigns, that has proved attractive (see Table 9.1).
- Among the main issues on which the FN has successfully campaigned have been those which appeal to feelings of insecurity amongst the electorate in times of economic and social change, recession and restructuring (Hargreaves, 1988, p. 35). The theme

TABLE 9.1

Issues which influenced voting decisions in the 1988 Presidential elections and the 1993 general elections. Selected issues by percentages of electorate.

	1988		1993	
Most influential issues	**Total**	**Le Pen**	**Total**	**FN**
Law and order (*insécurité*)	31	55	34	57
Social inequality	31	18	32	26
Unemployment	45	41	68	64
Immigrants	22	59	31	72
Rising prices	15	13	n.a.	n.a.
The construction of Europe	21	15	25	11
The environment	11	6	22	10
Education and training	29	20	42	23
Economic competitivity	23	21	11	6

Source: Compiled from CSA exit polls quoted in Ysmal (1990, p. 99) and Habert *et al.* (1993, p. 155).

of the need for security, in the sense of the repression of crime and the enforcement of law and order, has been closely linked to the much stronger and simpler theme of hostility to immigrants and immigration. There is also a general theme of protest against the evils of modern society, with denunciations of drug addiction and the spread of AIDS.

- The initial impact of the FN came soon after France had experienced the major political upheaval of *alternance*, and the advent of a left-wing government. France had been experiencing a recession and a rising rate of unemployment throughout the 1970s. The centre-right governments of the 1970s had attempted to combat this through austerity measures and restructuring. They had also responded with law and order legislation to concerns about crime and hooliganism. Equally, there was nothing new about an undercurrent of hostility to immigrants, which had produced tougher immigration controls and repatriation schemes during the 1970s. The advent of the Socialist government produced, in the early years, some liberalisation of policy on illegal immigrants, and of law and order and penal policy, thus enabling the extreme right to make political capital out of attacking the government's approach. The Socialist government, however, failed to achieve the hoped-for transformation of the economy and the unemployment situation. For some, the change of government in 1981 had not produced the radical social transformation for which they had hoped. For them a vote for the FN was a protest vote against the failure of past hopes. For others the new government, allied with the Communists, looked like the first step on a dangerous road towards Communist totalitarianism, which the traditional right had not been strong enough to resist.
- The referendum on the ratification of the Maastricht Treaty demonstrated a growing cleavage in France between relatively affluent, optimistic, educated voters who voted 'yes' to the Treaty and more disadvantaged, less educated, more peripheral voters who constitute a strong populist strand in French politics. The National Front articulates the fears and desires of an important section of these voters. The 'anti-European' stance of the National Front appeals to them. The National Front attacks the European Union's provision for freedom of movement and the abolition of frontier controls. It opposed the extension of voting rights at local and European elections to citizens of the Union who are not

French nationals, which they saw as the thin end of a wedge which would lead to voting rights for all immigrants. The National Front, although almost entirely devoid of any explicit economic ideology, has consistently rejected the competition-oriented, globalist logic which the parties that are, or have been, in government see as inescapable in a world of increasing economic interdependence.

- The National Front has exploited a growing sense of disillusion with traditional politics and mainstream parties. The perceived inability of the Left to effect radical change, discussed above, was mirrored by disillusion with the Right in the mid-1980s. The Chirac government after 1986 recognised the force of the issues which the National Front was raising. Charles Pasqua, as minister of the interior, both then and in 1993, took a tough line on law and order and immigrant issues. But in 1988 the Right failed to hold on to power, and after 1993 could do little to ease unemployment or lift the burdens which economic adjustment placed on the unskilled and disadvantaged. At the same time politicians of all the mainstream parties became increasingly mired with the stains of corruption and illegality (see above p. 125). The result was increasing disaffection of the voters and refusal to support the mainstream parties, a refusal from which the National Front undoubtedly benefited.

The factors that relate to the structure of the electorate and of the voting system include the following:

- The National Front continues to attract a higher level of support from the under 35 age group than from older voters. National Front candidates in the general election of 1993 and Le Pen in the first round of the 1995 presidential election were supported by industrial workers, a higher proportion of whom vote for the National Front than for any other party. Support has also been growing amongst lower clerical workers, small shopkeepers and tradespeople, and farmers. Geographically, the National Front attracts voters from the eastern half of France, especially from those more urbanised areas in which both high crime rates and a substantial foreign population occur. 'The National Front has no electoral strongholds in which either a population of foreigners and/or a high crime rate is not present.'[16] In some of the areas where it is important, such as the Provence-Alpes-Côte d'Azur area the FN could from the beginning exploit certain traditional extreme Right sympathies.

- Proportional representation, both for the European elections and for the 1986 general election, gave the FN its crucial point of entry into the political institutions. Once represented in the European Parliament and the National Assembly the party acquired, in public and media perception, the status of a legitimate part of the political scene that had to be treated seriously. Even when the return to the two-ballot system in 1988 all but eliminated the FN's representation in the National Assembly, it retained its members within the European Parliament, and this representation continued at the same level after the European Parliament elections in 1989. A vote for the FN could not be regarded as wasted or marginal.

- It is notable that the peaks of the FN's electoral appeal have occurred in the first ballot for the presidential elections (see Figure 9.3). The personal appeal of Le Pen, especially in circumstances where there is truly no likelihood of the FN actually taking power, is undoubtedly a crucial factor. However, the other electoral contests of the first half of the 1990s have proved that the FN can sustain a vote of over 10 per cent of the electorate. In the 1995 municipal elections three towns, one of them a major one (Toulon), fell to the FN.

The growth of the legitimacy and credibility of the FN was of crucial importance to its rise. Amongst the factors involved were:

- The FN made its first impact in by-elections, when the scrutiny of large parts of the national media tends to be closely focused upon political conflict in a single small area. This certainly resulted in an exposure that the FN could not have expected in other circumstances.

- Le Pen proved to have a personality and demeanour that parts of the electorate found reassuring and not threatening. Despite occasional horrific and revealing lapses – for example his reference to the holocaust as 'a mere detail of history' – he distanced himself from the wilder and more overtly anti-semitic and racist statements of some of his followers. As Jean Charlot points out (1994, p. 120), he has contrived to draw together, partly within his own life history (see Exhibit 9.1), many of the traditional themes of the far Right – the nationalism of the 1930s, the anti-Gaullism of Vichy, Poujadism (see Exhibit 8.3), Algérie française, and tradi-

TABLE 9.2

Age, sex, profession and voting behaviour in the general election of 1993 and the first ballot of the presidential election in 1995 by percent of each category

		NF 1993	Le Pen 1995	Moderate Right 1993	Chirac and Balladur 1995	Socialists and allies 1993	Jospin 1995	PCF 1993	Hue 1995
Sex	Male	14	M 19	45	M 42	20	M 19	9	M 7
	Female	13	F 10	44	F 37	20	F 29	10	F 6
Age	18–24	18	M 17 / F 16	36	M 39 / F 30	18	M 21 / F 29	9	M 9 / F 10
	25–34	10	M 17 / F 13	38	M 35 / F 33	21	M 24 / F 27	10	M 10 / F 8
	35–49	13	M 17 / F 12	41	M 44 / F 46	19	M 21 / F 23	8	M 8 / F 8
	50–64	13	M 15 / F 9	50	M 51 / F 56	21	M 19 / F 20	10	M 10 / F 8
	65+	13		51		20		9	
Profession	Farmers	13	14	59	53	12	13	3	5
	Small business/self-employed	15	21	56	55	14	8	5	5
	Executive and professional	6	6	53	45	27	26	7	5
	Middle management	8	10	31	36	28	31	6	7
	White-collar worker	18	19	35	32	18	23	10	10
	Blue-collar worker	18	27	37	25	19	21	12	15
	Inactive/retired	12	n.a.	50	n.a.	20	n.a.	11	n.a.

Source: Habert (1993) and Buffotoot and Hanley (1996).

tionalist Roman Catholicism. He has always, however, known exactly where to draw the line between legitimacy and illegality. The FN has contrived to make many of the themes of these ideologies admissible within general political discourse (Birenbaum, 1992, p. 310).

- The presence of FN members in the National Assembly and in the European Parliament and their largely respectable behaviour (with only occasional outbreaks such as the occasion in October 1987 when they created a virtual riot in the chamber of the National Assembly in protest against the absenteeism of members of the established parties) gave the party the public status of a legitimate participant in the political system, with the accompanying press and television exposure. It was clear that in the period from 1986 to 1988 the policies of the Chirac government were influenced by their presence in Parliament. In these circumstances a vote for the extreme Right became an act which an increasing number of voters were prepared to contemplate.

The FN has been described as the party of discontent and fear (Mayer and Perrineau, 1989). The economic and social crisis of the 1990s has threatened many long established certainties. Farmers find themselves exposed to change through the reform of the European Community Common Agricultural Policy and the new GATT agreement. Shopkeepers suffer from increases in competition. Unemployment looms for both the underqualified workers whose jobs are disappearing and for the middle manager and white collar worker whose qualifications are no longer an automatic passport to stable and respectable existence. To all these groups, as Pascal Perrineau points out,[17] the FN offers a utopian vision of the retrieval of a (mythical) national past and national identity. Only the educated upper professional classes seem to be largely immune to these blandishments. The FN is not merely a party of protest, but also the outcome of the emergence of an important new cleavage that runs not so much between Left and Right as between the 'establishment' and those who are profiting, or at least not suffering, from change, and the 'anti-establishment' disadvantaged groups.

The FN is not a Fascist party. It does not reject the regime. It is not particularly bellicose. It tries hard, if not totally successfully,[18] to maintain its credibility and respectability. But it is a party of the extreme Right, and in 1994 nearly three quarters of the respondents in an opinion poll agreed that Le Pen and his party represented a danger to democracy. It has, however, established itself firmly within the political spectrum, and whilst its place at national level may be marginal, except when it is boosted by a system of proportional representation, at local levels it can pose dilemmas for the parties of the moderate Right. They must decide whether to try to avoid splitting the right-wing vote by making pacts with the FN, especially for local elections. For a number of moderate Right politicians such a course of action is intolerable. The extent to which anti-immigrant rhetoric has crept into the discourse of politicians of the Right, such as ex-President Giscard d'Estaing, and even of the Left, for Mme Cresson opened her premiership with fierce statements about the repatriation of illegal residents, is a measure of the concern induced by the electoral appeal of Le Pen's themes.

Conclusion

The party political landscape of France has changed markedly over the period of the Fifth Republic. Parties have in general become larger, more firmly organised, even if their financing, despite efforts to bring some openness and order, remains a matter for mystery and scandal. The parties act, within Parliament, in general, in a disciplined way. There is no longer a plethora of small parties, grouping like-minded local worthies, but fewer, larger, genuinely national organisations (see Table 9.3). In this sense the scene has, since 1958, become much simpler. The nature of election campaigns, with a concentration of media attention upon the leaders, and especially the demands of the presidential campaigns, has increased the focus of politics upon personalities.

Some commentators have even noted a decline in political extremism.

Certainly the massive decline of the PCF has been a marked feature of the 1980s, and despite the rise of the FN 'the political extremes, which under the Fourth Republic represented nearly half the electorate, account, even today, for no more than one fifth' (Charlot, 1989, p. 34). The dominant parties – PS, RPR, UDF – are situated firmly within the centre ground of political life. It is perhaps the major achievement of the Fifth Republic's institutions, and of two leaders in particular – de Gaulle and Mitterrand – to have produced in France a system of political representation and change that is taken for granted, stable and effective.

TABLE 9.3

The political balance in France, 1995

		1	2	3	4	5
Left	PCF and allies	23	15	2	2	1
	Socialists and allies	67	75	3	22	16
	Total Left	90	92	5	24	19[a]
Right	RPR	255	94	7	24	6
	UDF	206	105[b]	11	45	8
	Total moderate Right	461	221[c]	18	71[d]	14
	FN					1
	Other/unattached	26[e]	8	1[f]		1
	Total	577	321	26	95	35

Note:
1. National Assembly groups, October 1995; includes members and allies.
2. Senate groups October 1995; includes members and allies.
3. Presidents of regional councils after March 1992 elections.
4. Présidents of metropolitan *département* councils after March 1992 elections (excluding Paris).
5. Mayors of metropolitan *communes* of more than 100 000 inhabitants after June 1995 elections.
[a] Includes two 'other Left'.
[b] Split into two groups: *Union Centriste*, 59 members; *Républicains et Indépendants*, 46 members.
[c] Includes 22 members of centre-left group, *Rassemblement Démocratique et Social Européen*.
[d] Includes two 'other Right'.
[e] All 'other Right'.
[f] Ecologist (*Les Verts*).

The 1970s and 1980s were marked by the massive decline of the Communist Party. Despite the rise of the FN at the end of the 1980s it could be argued that 'the political extremes which under the Fourth Republic represented nearly half the electorate, account[ed], even [then] for no more than one-fifth' (Charlot, 1989, p. 34). In the 1990s the parties of the centre ground of political life continue to dominate. The crucial electoral choice still seems to be perceived as being between moderate Right and moderate Left, as Lionel Jospin's unexpectedly good performance in 1995 demonstrated. All the mainstream parties have adapted to the institutions and practices of the Fifth Republic and to the *alternance* they have made possible. But the 1990s have begun to provide evidence of a new phenomenon – a considerable disaffection towards the processes of political representation. The turnout at elections, although still high, has dropped (see Figure 9.4). There has been a growth in the levels of spoiled or blank votes, although they remain at under 3 per cent. It is always possible for a voter to turn out in order to put nothing into the envelope which should contain the voting slip as a gesture of protest. Jean-Marie Le Pen ostentatiously did this at the second ballot of the presidential elections in 1995. The 1990s have also seen a marked rise in the number of votes for the smaller groups, the extremes and the anti-establishment parties, which together now amount to over one-third of all votes cast. In this context the rhetoric of the mainstream parties, as they seek to address the causes of 'social fracture' and 'exclusion' takes on a particular urgency.

FIGURE 9.4
Voter protest in the 1980s and 1990s
(Abstentions, Communist, National Front
and other anti-system party votes)

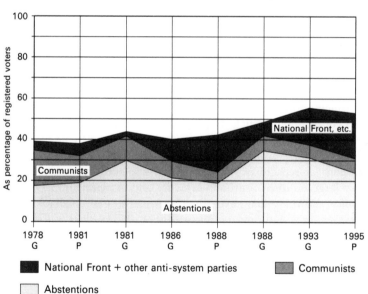

Key: P = presidential election.
     G = general election.

10

The State and Civil Society: Pressure and Interest Groups

The French constitution proclaims the sovereignty of the people. It is from this sovereignty that the legitimacy and authority of the government derives. The tradition of direct suffrage, dating back to the French Revolution firmly locates the exercise of this sovereignty in the casting of a vote. Political parties have developed as the means by which voting choice can be organised, channelled and expressed. The constitution (Article 4) recognises their right to exist and their role in voting choice. Political parties, however, are by no means the only channels through which citizens may choose to voice their opinions or seek to express their interests, needs and demands. A very large number of groups, societies and associations exist within France and they, too, have important roles to play in shaping both policy-making and policy implementation. Many clubs and societies exist for purely social recreational and cultural reasons, but even they may occasionally be stirred to more political action, as when representatives of the local anglers' societies began, in Brittany during the 1980s, to take legal action against farmers whose agricultural activities polluted the water.

It has sometimes been argued that the French are not 'joiners'; that the strength of family ties, and of individualism within French society has meant that there has not been a strong social tradition of membership of associations or clubs of any sort. However, a poll taken in 1951 found that 41 per cent of the respondents were members of a voluntary association (Wilson, 1987, p. 14). Recent decades have seen a marked change. The Ministry of the Interior records the number of new groups registered at the prefectures. In 1965 nearly 17 500 new groups were formed (Wilson, 1987, p. 15). By the end of the 1980s the figure was some 45 000.[1]

Nevertheless, there has long been a strand in French political life and thought which has deplored the existence of such groups, or at least any propensity they may have for involvement in public activity. There have been those, like General de Gaulle, for instance, who have felt that the expression of popular sovereignty ought not to involve any intermediate groupings between the citizen and the result of the vote (Wilson, 1987, p. 13). This tradition is rooted in the views of the eighteenth century philosopher, Jean-Jacques Rousseau, who saw the state, in its role as the organiser and guarantor of society, as embodying a general will which ought directly to express the interests of all. 'It is therefore essential,' he wrote, 'if the general will is to be able make itself known, that there should be no partial society within the State and that each citizen should express only his own opinion' (Rousseau, 1762).

In 1791 a law was passed, in the interests of an unconstrained expression of the general will and of revolutionary equality, which dissolved the old guilds and other associations and prevented the formation of any group which would represent a special or particular interest or need. This *Loi le Chapelier* was repealed in 1884 and in 1901 a further law recognised citizens' rights to freedom of association and provided a legal basis upon which an association or society could exist.

In much French thinking the state, as the overall custodian and guarantor of the organisation of society, has a clear role in relation to any formal grouping of citizens. While it is not illegal to form a purely private club, any group which wants protection or legal status, for example to protect its funds against embezzlement, must register its existence and its aims and objectives with the local prefecture (see Exhibit 10.1). The role of the state in relationship to clubs and associations in general frequently extends beyond mere legal recognition. Almost all clubs will expect to get some financial assistance or subsidy, even if only of a very modest amount. This largesse is most frequently distributed by local government, usually at the level of the *commune*, although the other levels of local government and even central ministries may also produce funds. This phenomenon reflects one aspect of French political culture. Politicians are not in general expected to be as active in pursuing the individual problems and

EXHIBIT 10.1

La vie associative

Many French thinkers, politicians, lawyers and officials hold a concept of the state as the body through which power is legitimated and organised; as such the state exercises public power with the task of ensuring the peacefulness, security and good order of society. The state therefore maintains a general oversight over all activities within society, providing the necessary legal and administrative frameworks. The 1901 law on associations was intended to do this chiefly for cultural and religious associations, clubs and societies. It continues to provide the means through which any association, club or society can have an existence before the law, giving it, for example, the right to own money or property.

Any group of people has the right to found an association. However, if the association wishes, for example, to open a bank account or obtain premises, then it must set out its aims and objectives, provide itself with a constitution on an approved model, and declare these at the office of the local prefect. Its existence will be announced in the daily government publication, the *Journal Officiel*. If the association wishes to extend its legal capacity – for example, to receive legacies – it must obtain from the Minister of the Interior a declaration that it is "of public utility". It then becomes subject to "supervision" – *tutelle* – of its finances by the authorities. The government may abolish any association whose aims are held to be a threat to public order.

This official oversight of associations, clubs and societies means that it is possible to have a fairly clear view of the number and type of associations that exist. It engenders a feeling that associations are in some ways a part of public, rather than private, life, and that the activities of associations – *la vie associative* – constitute a special sector of the life of society as a whole. This has a double effect. First, many associations look to the authorities to provide them with subventions and financial support. Secondly, the authorities often look to associations as the channel through which desirable activities can be undertaken, for example, the care of the handicapped or the promotion of cultural activities.

In 1987 there were estimated to be between 500 000 and 600 000 associations in France, and just under half of all French people over the age of 18 belonged to at least one. Between 1984 and 1986 estimated membership was as follows:

Type of association	Membership as % of over-18 age-group	Type of association	Membership as % of over-18 age-group
Sporting	18.9	Religious	4.7
Cultural, leisure interest	11.6	Political	3.1
		Youth	2.8
Over sixties	8.5	Family	2.6
School parents	8.2	Consumers	2.4
Professional	7.1	Conservation	2.0
Trade Union	6.8	Student	1.7
Welfare, charitable	6.6	Women's	1.1
Local, amenity	6.0		

Source: Data from Institut National de la Statistique et des Etudes Economiques, *Données Sociales* (Paris, 1990, p. 369).

grievances of their constituents as are those in the United Kingdom. On the other hand, they are expected to be diligent in seeking to advance the material and economic interests of the area that they represent (Pickles, 1972, p. 159). Whilst mayors may recognise that handing out a few hundred francs annually to the local anglers may not greatly enhance their electoral fortunes, on the whole they prefer not to put this to the test by refusing, and the associations expect it.

In many cases a voluntary group, often a small one, demonstrates a social need, and the state will then take over the action necessary to meet the need, sometimes continuing to use the association as its agent, but effectively providing a very large part of the necessary resources. A notable exception to this process was the family planning movement. The *Mouvement français pour le planning familial* was founded in 1956. Since the promotion of contraception was strictly speaking illegal until 1967 the state could not become involved, and so in its early years the movement was, in John Ardagh's words 'a remarkable and rare example in France of effective unofficial civic action on a national scale' (Ardagh, 1988, p. 344).

> The relationship between the state and the various groups, at all levels, is thus very complex. The state has always maintained ambiguous relations with the interest groups. On the one hand, it rejects them in the name of its own theoretical sovereignty; on the other, it establishes such close relations with them that it is some-times difficult to distinguish between public and private interests or institutions. (Mény, 1989, p. 391)

Whilst these features characterise large numbers of groups, they do differ in their role and their impact upon the making and implementation of policy. The next section of this chapter describes the main categories into which groups may be divided.

The Nature of the Interest Groups

It is possible to consider the nature of pressure and interest groups in France under different headings. First it may be appropriate to categorise them in terms of their own internal structure, objectives and functions. Secondly, they may be considered in the light of their relationship to the state, and the types of impact that they have upon public policy and functions. Clearly these two types of description overlap, but for the sake of clarity they may be taken in turn. This section considers the functions of the groups under four headings:

- parastatal groups,
- social partners,
- pressure and lobbying movements and groups,
- clubs and societies.

Parastatal Groups

There are, in France, a number of groups of which membership is compulsory for certain individuals or enterprises, and which are entitled to levy dues. They are controlled by elected representatives, not government officials, and they have the functions of organising certain aspects of economic life, often undertaking essentially public functions as agents of the state. They may also serve, however, to represent the functional interests of their membership to the state, and may be consulted and conferred with. The main organisations of this type are the various 'chambers': chambers of commerce (*chambres de commerce*), chambers of agriculture (*chambres d'agriculture*) and chambers of trades (*chambres de métiers*). These bodies may have important roles in the implementation of government policy. For example, the chambers of agriculture act as government agents in the management of various types of agricultural grant and subsidy such as the funds available to assist in the restructuring of agricultural holdings. Chambers of Commerce may have a very wide range of activities, financed through government subsidy, levies on their members, and income generated. They often run local facilities, such as airports. They may contribute subsidies to the local business schools, which they have often helped to create and on whose governing bodies they are almost always well represented (Chafer, 1988, p. 18). The larger chambers of commerce run extensive export advisory service for local business, dispensing state funds for export support. Thus in 1990 the Chamber of Commerce in Besançon was employing 180 staff members to assist local firms and businesses 'to prepare for the competitive challenges of the single European market' and specifically to provide information and identify sources of subsidies.

The essence of these groups is that although they are organised as private groups membership is in fact compulsory, and they are legally assimilated to the public sector.

These chambers, ... are real corporate organisations in the traditional sense of the term. They enjoy fiscal advantages and disciplinary or regulatory powers and play a semi-public role in matters such as public investment and the organisation of the profession. Integration and the overlap of public and private roles have been pushed furthest in these institutions. (Mény, 1989, p. 394).

Indeed, some definitions of public sector employment include the figures for their employees: around 38 000 at the beginning of 1985 (De Singly and Thélot, 1988, p. 48).

Social Partners

These groups do not have the characteristic of compulsory membership. They, too, however, have recognised roles in certain public functions, although they also have a clearer role in the representation and defence of the economic interests of their members, not only in relation to the state, but also in dealings with other groups. They were largely born out of the political and ideological background of the class struggle.

The most important of these groups are the trade unions and the employers' organisations. Given their conflictual relationships, both with the state and with each other, it may seem perverse to describe them as social partners, although that is the terminology increasingly used, perhaps more in hope than belief, within the European Community, and it does reflect the recognised roles that such groups may play, for example, in some social security organisations.

The level of trade union membership is low (see Exhibit 10.2). Recent estimates of a figure that is extremely difficult to ascertain with any accuracy suggest that between 8 and 11 per cent of the work force may be unionised.[2] The French trade union movement has always been characterised by fragmentation. As Jack Hayward has pointed out, notions of democracy and socialism had developed in France before the emergence of an industrial workforce on a large scale. The consequence was that workers' groups did not develop as part of a labour movement concerned broadly with the amelioration of the conditions of workers within the current political system, largely through collective bargaining. Rather they emerged as 'weak and fragmented ... unions whose prime function was that of ideological mobilisation outside and against the liberal democratic system' (Hayward, 1986, p. 57).

EXHIBIT 10.2

Trade unions in France (principal union confederations)

Name	Leader 1991	Approx. membership claimed*	Estimated effective membership**	Political orientation
Confédération générale du travail (CGT)	Louis Viannet (Secretary General)	800 000	600 000	Close to the Communist Party
Confédération française démocratique du travail (CFDT)	Nicole Notat (Secretary General)	558 000	470 000	Close to the Socialist Party
Confédération française des travailleurs chrétiens	Guy Drilleaud (President)	250 000	100 000	Catholic
CGT-FO (Force ouvrière)	Marc Blondel (Secretary General)	1 100 000	500 000	Moderate left-wing
Confédération française de l'encadrement	Paul Marchelli (President)	400 000	Less than 100 000	White collar
Confédération générale des cadres (CGC)				
Fédération de l'education nationale	Guy Le Néouannic (Secretary General)	350 000	300 000	Teachers at all levels of education
Fédération nationale des syndicats d'exploitants agricoles	Raymond Lacombe (President)	700 000	n.a.	Farmers

Notes:
* Early 1990s.
** 1989; estimations from Noblecourt (1990).

Source: Europa Yearbook (1995); *Quid* (1995); Mouriaux and Bibès (1990); Noblecourt (1990).

The oldest and largest of the French union confederations is the *Confédération générale du travail* (CGT). This confederation groups together some 18 000 (Mouriaux, 1983, pp. 16, 22) individual unions, organised through local federations in each *département* and through 44 functional federations. It has an explicitly Marxist analysis of industrial relations, and a general ideological commitment to the bringing about of a socialist society. It was traditionally strong in the steel, construction and chemical industries, in the ports and the mines, and in the public sector gas, electricity and railway undertakings. In 1947, in the atmosphere of the developing cold war, the union came under Communist control. Thereafter the relationship between the leadership of the CGT and that of the French Communist Party (PCF) was very close, though not formal. The CGT was long regarded as the instrument of the PCF's industrial relations policy. Not all members of the CGT are members of the PCF, or even particularly committed to the Communist line; 'workers join the CGT not because of its political position . . . nor because of its pugnacious stance, but because in much of French industry it has been the only visible union' (Wilson, 1987, p. 75). The union, like all other unions in France, experienced, during the late 1970s and the 1980s, a very sharp decline in membership. According to Réné Mouriaux, it probably lost half its membership between 1976 and 1989.[3] In the 1990s the decline and fragmentation of the PCF posed particular problems for the CGT. Internal disputes ensued about how far the CGT should distance itself from the PCF. There must be a question-mark over the long-term survival of the PCF (Mouriaux, 1994, p. 117).

After the assertion of Communist control over the CGT in 1947, a non-Communist element broke away and set up a rival confederation, the *Force ouvrière*. Noted for its virulent anti-Communism, and attracting a relatively high proportion of white-collar workers, from banking, insurance, the health services and the middle to lower ranks of the civil service, it has attempted to maintain its distance from all the political parties and from any specifically political objectives. Its stance in relation to issues such as worker participation has been fairly radical, and it has included a Trotskyite wing, but it has on the whole concentrated upon collective bargaining procedures and eschewed political strikes. Its membership held up well until 1985 (Headlam, 1989, p. 32) (though it has been declining since) and during the 1980s it may well have become the second largest union confederation and possibly even have overtaken the CGT. In so doing the FO overtook the *Confédération française démocratique du travail* (CFDT). This union emerged in 1964 out of the Roman Catholic *Confédération française des travailleurs chrétiens* (CFTC). This union owed its origins to late nineteenth century Catholic social movements, developed by the Roman Catholic Church to attempt to combat the influence of Marxist socialism amongst the workers. In 1964 a large proportion of the union elected to break its formal links with the church, and this group renamed and reformed itself, developing also a more political analysis of society and moving quite rapidly towards the left. Many of its leaders continued to be left-wing Catholics, and in the period after the end of the 1960s when the Socialist Party was reforming itself, and attracting increasing support from left-wing Catholics, amongst other groups, the CFDT also moved quite close to the Socialist Party. It did not, however, benefit markedly from the accession of a Socialist government to power in 1981. The CFDT attempted to maintain a generally supportive but nonetheless clearly distinct relationship with the Socialist governments, but this did not succeed in preventing a decline in membership numbers.[4]

These union confederations consist of individual unions representing workers and employees across the whole spectrum of occupations. They are not, however, the only unions or union confederations. There are major groups representing particular occupational sectors. They include the middle-class white-collar union representing middle management and executives, the *Confédération générale des cadres,* and the unions which represent teachers at all levels of state education, traditionally a sector in which levels of unionisation could reach two-thirds. Most teaching unions were for most of the post-war period federated in the very large and influential *Fédération de l'education nationale* (FEN). With a total of perhaps half a million members its strength could give it an important voice in some professional matters. The move by the Socialist government in 1984 to change the status of church schools (see Exhibit 10.3) was partly a result of FEN pressure. The defeat of the changes was a blow to the FEN which found itself unable thereafter to oppose further reforms. An attempt to reform the union structure in 1992 by making it a much more federal body resulted in the expulsion of some of its component groups and a schism. In 1993 a new education union, the *Fédération syndicale unitaire* was founded, which claims 150 000 members, leaving about the same number in the residual FEN, but the FSU's overall influence, measured by the success of its candidates in elections to the various professional bodies, seems greater (Mouriaux, 1994, p. 114).

In the education sector, as elsewhere, fragmentation and division is a major characteristic of the unions, whose influence is certainly weakened thereby.

Farmers also have a separate unions, of which the largest and by far the most influential is the *Fédération nationale des syndicats d'exploitants agricoles* (FNSEA) although there are other smaller rival groups.

In addition there are a wide range of small independent professional associations and unions concerned to defend the professional interests of their members. These may be the independent unions, often of workers within a particular enterprise, which are often accused of being the creatures and tools of management, although they have become important in the car industry, for example. They may also be the associations of those with a particular background or job; for example those which unite the former students of an elite educational institution. These might not recognise themselves as a union, nor do they necessarily have a recognised status as a representative body, but they do act in the defence of their members' material interests.

Employers, too, have their own organisations. The representation of business is much less fragmented than is that of labour. The principal organisation is the *Confédération nationale du patronat français* (CNPF). The organisation was founded in the post-war period as a response both to a militant workforce, and to the *dirigiste* tendencies of the state in the face of industrialists and employers who had been discredited by the failure of many of them to rally to de Gaulle and the Resistance during the war. De Gaulle famously remarked to a gathering of industrialists soon after the Liberation that he had not seen many of them in London. The CNPF is a federal body, based both upon the trade associations, of which the most powerful within the CNPF has been the *Union des industries metallurgiques et minières* and upon local associations of employers (Lefranc, 1976, p. 174). It combines within itself both commerce and industry. Its representative role has always been particularly important in general matters such as social security and taxation.

Although the CNPF manages to combine within itself a surprisingly wide range of industrial and commercial employers (Headlam, 1989, p. 34), the owners of small businesses are grouped within the *Confédération générale des petites et moyennes entreprises* (CGPME). In the early 1980s the response of the Mitterrand government to what was seen as the hostility of the *patronat* was to encourage a rival organisation, the *Syndicat national de la petite et moyenne industrie* (SNPMI) which

EXHIBIT 10.3

Educational change and direct action

The success of the Socialist party in 1981 brought into power a party with a very long tradition of commitment to a secular education system and hostility to the role of the church in schools. Mitterrand's programme for the election had advocated a single, unified, secular system of national education. A bill was introduced into Parliament in 1984 which fell considerably short of this, but provided that teachers in Catholic schools might if they wished be absorbed into the state education service, and that places in church schools would be taken into account in determining the distribution of school places in any area. The Ministry of Education had cleared the ground by undertaking negotiations with the authorities of the Roman Catholic church to ensure that a carefully balanced compromise was arrived at which largely satisfied both sides. However, when the bill was before Parliament, some of the Socialist backbenchers succeeded in persuading their colleagues to pass various amendments which overturned some of the elements of the compromise.

At the same time political forces on the Right were regaining strength after the division and demoralisation of the Socialist victory. The slogan that the Socialists were attacking fundamental freedoms, including parental choice, was an appealing one. The schools issue was an immediate rallying point and a massive march which attracted possibly as many as a million demonstrators was organised in Paris in July. This coincided with a very poor performance by the Left in the European Parliament, and the result was the withdrawal of the bill, a governmental crisis, a reshuffle and a new prime minister.

The experience of 1993 was almost a mirror image. With a strong majority of the Right in Parliament, a backbencher, Bruno Bourg-Broc, introduced a bill to amend one of the remaining provisions of the 1850 *loi Falloux*, which had regulated parts of the relationship between the state and private (church) schools for nearly 150 years. Since the *loi Debré* of 1959, the state has paid the salary costs of private school staff, but the *loi Falloux* still prevented local authorities from subsidising more than 10 per cent of capital costs. Bourg-Broc's law sought to remove this ceiling. The consequence would have been competition between public and private schools for public funds, and a greater diversity of provision as regions or *départements* fixed their subsidy policies according to their ideological orientation (Firth, 1994, p. 390). The law was referred by the Socialist members of both houses to the Constitutional Council, which annulled its main article as contrary to the constitutional principles of equality and *laïcité*. At the same time 112 different organisations – parties of the Left, trade unions, associations – organised a march in defence of state education in Paris in which 260 000 people participated, according to the police. The organisers claimed one million. The government promulgated the truncated law, but announced that it would not put forward a replacement for the main provision which had been annulled.

In addition to these major episodes of direct action concerning schools policy there were, between 1984 and 1995, three instances of the withdrawal of proposals which affected students and young people. In 1986 Chirac's minister of education, M. Devaquet proposed a bill to reform university entrance. This bill would have allowed universities greater freedom to determine their own curriculum, to set fees (within a low ceiling) and to select students at entry. It was perceived as 'placing new administrative and social barriers in an already obstacle-strewn course leading from school to the first job' (Knapp, 1994, p. 94).

Large student demonstrations against the bill ensued in Paris, and one student died as a result of police action against the protesters. The fact that the victim was of Arab extraction linked the uproar which followed to the cause of anti-racism at a time when the racist extreme Right was becoming increasingly vociferous. The withdrawal of the bill which followed was prompted in part by disagreements within the government, where several ministers threatened resignation if it were pursued. The result was a weakened government and a diminished position for the prime minister. The subsequent withdrawal of a bill to reform the nationality laws was also a consequence of a fear of protest and of another damaging retreat.

In the spring of 1994 the protests of students and young people widened again, into a movement of mass demonstrations and protests against regulations made by the Balladur government to encourage the employment of young people through a *contrat d'insertion professionnelle* at only 80 per cent of the legal minimum wage. Students and unions again made common cause against the law. The Balladur government backed down, withdrawing the regulations not much more than a month after they had been published.

In December 1994 the minister for higher education, François Fillon, issued a ministerial circular setting a reform programme for the technological higher education institutions, the *Instituts universitaires technologiques*. In January 1995 a report (the Laurent report) on the future of higher education was published. Strikes and demonstrations, initially in higher education and subsequently in schools, followed. In the middle of February 1995 the Balladur government withdrew the circular and repudiated the report.

would challenge both the CNPF and the CGPME. The attempt misfired, and the SNPMI produced anti-government protest which led, in 1983, to violence.[5] At the same time, as the government began to discover the virtues of the *entreprise* as the key to economic recovery, it moved back to reliance upon the CNPF to organise the general relationship between government and industry.

Pressure and Lobbying Movements and Groups

Trade unions and employers' associations are, of course, very largely concerned with pressure and with lobbying to further the interest of their members. However, they are regarded as having a broader general interest in the organisation of relationships within society, reflected, for instance, in the specific right of union membership granted by the constitution. Nevertheless, the boundary between them and pressure groups is hard to establish. Indeed, in the sense that any particular group may at some time seek to influence the decision-making process, the definition of a pressure group becomes very wide indeed. This section considers two types of group which influence the determination of political priorities and the making of detailed administrative decisions: first the large national movements that seek to have an effect upon broad policy areas; and secondly groups with narrow sectoral interests which become involved in the making of specific decisions.

France seems to lack the large, national voluntary 'public interest' associations with interests in particular policy areas that characterise some aspects of interest group politics in some other countries; there is no French equivalent of the United States' Association that campaigns for the right to carry arms or the British Royal Society for the Protection of Birds whilst French consumers' organisations developed much later than, and were partly modelled upon, the British Consumers' Association. The voluntary civic action undertaken by the *Union fédérale des consommateurs* which has 160 local branches and some 45 000 active members is still unusual in France (Ardagh, 1988, p. 386).

Nevertheless such 'non-occupational' groups (Wilson, 1987, pp. 48ff) do exist; Wilson categorises them as either 'advocacy groups', concerned with advancing the cause of those who seek services from the state, or as 'public interest' groups. Amongst the advocacy groups he includes the organisations representing former servicemen which were very influential during the Fourth Republic, and have continued to ensure that there is a government minister with special responsibility for them, the student groups, the family associations, the parent–teacher associations, and the women's movement. The groups representing the former French settlers in Algeria, the so-called *pieds-noirs*, who returned to France after Algerian independence and who succeeded in extracting concessions from the government during the late 1980s would be another example. Wilson discusses the consumers' associations and the environmental movement under the category of public interest groups, though one could certainly argue that, for example, the nature of the interests of women and of consumers are very similar; and both depend upon public policy action as well as upon social change and changes in attitudes by individuals and companies to achieve their objectives. Four major movements are discussed below; if their categorisation is problematic, they have in common the breadth of their impact and their effect upon political attitudes in a wide sphere. They are the 'regional' movements, for example in Brittany, the students' movement, the women's movement and the ecological and anti-nuclear movement.

Breton regionalism was fired by two principal motives. One was a rejection of the policy of cultural assimilation that for so long prevented the encouragement and development of the Breton language and culture. Secondly, the economic development of a backward and agricultural region seemed slow, neglected, and likely to be further marginalised as increased European integration shifted the balance of economic advantage still further away from peripheral areas.

The movement took a number of forms; within Brittany local academic groups began to lobby and plan for increased economic development and local economic autonomy for Brittany. This proved to be a slow process, and for some the Breton regional movement was translated into direct, clandestine and violent action. Whilst a tradition of violent demonstrations has by no means disappeared, government response to the movement (see below) has lessened the relevance and appeal of terrorism in Brittany. The Breton movement is a particularly well documented example of an ethnic regional movement, but the movement in Corsica was not dissimilar.

Students are by definition a changing and transient population. Student generations are short and may not share the goals, aims, or degree of commitment to activism of their predecessors. Nevertheless, they do constitute a definable group of which large sections have at various times during the Fifth Republic been mobilised in ways which have had important effects, although there have always been minority groups amongst the students opposed to the majority. Students very often have dual concerns, both for those issues which most directly affect the nature and quality of their education, and for much broader and more general political issues. In 1968 these two concerns fused, under the leadership not of the more established student or political organisations, but of various ad hoc groups, some more or less inspired by Trotskyite or Maoist views, and of a few charismatic individuals, to bring about what is variously known as the student revolt, or the student uprising, or simply the events of May 1968 (see Exhibit 10.4).

The strength of the student protests, directed initially at the shortcomings of the French educational system, but rapidly widened into criticisms of almost every aspect of French social, political and cultural life, and revulsion at the brutal police repression acted as the catalyst for a general strike, fuelled by discontent at working conditions and wage levels. Secondary school children, broadcasting journalists, civil servants and many others became involved in

EXHIBIT 10.4

May 1968

Chronology

March – April	Student agitation at the Nanterre campus calling for improved conditions
2 May	Nanterre campus closed by university authorities
3 May	Students occupy courtyard of Sorbonne
Police called to clear courtyard
Violent clashes and numerous arrests.
5 May	Four students given prison sentences as a result of 3 May clashes
6 May	Riots in Latin quarter (university area) of Paris
422 students arrested, about 600 injured
Extent of police violence causes much adverse comment
7 May	Student strike throughout Paris and in universities throughout France
10–11 May	Further demonstrations and riots, demanding release of detained students
11 May	Prime Minister Pompidou returns from visit to Afghanistan, promises re-opening of the Sorbonne and university reform
11 May	Two major unions, CGT and CFDT, call for a general strike on 13 May
13 May	Strike including state radio and TV
14 May	Students occupy the Sorbonne and set up revolutionary committees and discussion group
President de Gaulle arrives in Romania for state visit
16 May	Renault workers take over factories at Boulogne–Billancourt (Paris) and elsewhere demanding better wages and conditions
17 May	Workers' strikes spread
18 May	De Gaulle returns from Romania
24 May	Further disorders in Paris
CGT organises march in Paris
Number of strikers has risen to over 9 million
Broadcast by de Gaulle.
26–27 May	Negotiations between unions and government
27 May	Grenelle agreement between unions and government
Workers offered 7 per cent general pay rise
29 May	De Gaulle makes secret visit to General Massu at French base in Baden, Germany

30 May	Second broadcast by de Gaulle
	General election called
	Demonstration in Paris in support of the government
31 May	Government reshuffle
Early June	Workers returning to work
10–11 June	Some student rioting
14–16 June	Students abandon occupation of the Sorbonne and the Odéon theatre
17–24 June	Car workers return to work
23 and 30 June	Two rounds of the general election
	Gaullists win overall majority in the National Assembly
12 July	Strike at state radio and TV ends

Causes

A wide range of causes have been suggested for these events. Bénéton and Touchard (1970) enumerate eight major explanations that were offered at the time, ranging from psychological disturbance to deliberate subversion. Some are patently far-fetched. Those who took part certainly had many varied motives. The events acted as a catalyst for the expression of a huge range of grievances and discontents that had found no other outlet. The marginalisation of the trade unions and the weakness and fragmentation of political opposition in the first decade of the Fifth Republic all contributed. The violence of the police and the vacillations of the government were also key factors in turning student protest into a major "event", indeed an uprising.

Effects

The immediate outcome of the events was the Gaullist victory in the June general election, and a general wage rise that fuelled inflation and contributed to the 1969 devaluation of the franc. Over a longer term, the idealism of May 1968 fed into the revival of the Socialist Party during the 1970s. Some commentators have seen a number of the new movements that emerged during the 1970s, such as the women's movement, as owing some of their initial impetus to the questioning of prevailing values that was a marked feature of the student movement. Mendras and Cole (1991, p. 229) see May 1968 as an important turning point in the development of French society, symbolising the rejection of austerity and narrowly constraining moral codes, but they also take the view that the areas in which nothing has changed are probably more important than those in which there has been substantial change. The events of May 1968 were vivid and dramatic; their legacy is obscure and ambiguous.

impassioned discussions of what working conditions, social relations, and the shape of society and politics should be. The art of the poster and the slogan blossomed. The effects of the general strike were far-reaching and uncomfortable; no-one was unaffected. The government seemed briefly to waver, and for a little while it was possible to believe that the times were truly revolutionary. And then the government reached an agreement with the main unions – the Grenelle agreement – and wage levels were raised. The calling of a general election, which eventually produced a strong right-wing backlash, defused the political situation. The students went on holiday.

The crisis was diagnosed by some as the outcome of a blocked and stagnant society, where genuine opposition was difficult, and channels for the effective expression of grievances inadequate or non-existent, where management was distant, personal and patriarchal, and relationships within families and within the educational system rigid formal and old-fashioned. In such a society, it could be argued, pressure builds up until a gasket blows; a violent upheaval releases the pressures, and the system settles back, relatively unaltered.

Certainly throughout the 1970s and the first half of the 1980s student activism was virtually non-existent. When students again began to play a more prominent role it was over educational matters, but in the 1980s student protests very rarely spilled over into more general issues. In 1983 right-wing students protested at the Mitter-rand government's plans for higher education in the context of a broader wave of protests against the Socialist government's policies by professional groups, including farmers, nurses and civil servants. More seriously, in 1986 students were strongly opposed to a bill for the reform of higher education introduced by the higher education minister in the Chirac government, Devaquet. The withdrawal of the Devaquet bill (see Exhibit 10.3) increased the confidence of the students in their ability to achieve some of their goals. Students became more active in the following years in strikes and protests against the extremely poor material conditions which prevail in many French universities and, in 1994, against proposals to reduce the minimum wage for those under 26.

The women's movement as it exists today in France is also often traced back to the events of May 1968 (see Duchen, 1986). Certainly that period, with its general questioning of the established order, alerted an increased number of women to the disadvantages of their status within society, at the same time as the women's movement was reviving and advancing in Britain and the United States. As in other countries, the women's movement in France does not take a clear or easily definable institutional form. A number of groups exist, concerned with various areas of concern to women. The French term for women's liberation, *Mouvement de libération des femmes*, was, in the 1970s, adopted and registered as a trade mark by one particular group, of a distinctive intellectual, psychoanalytical and separatist persuasion, thus preventing its formal use by others. This not unnaturally caused consternation and resentment amongst other women's groups.

The women's movement in France has been notable for its intellectual, literary and cultural character, and the influence of psychoanalytical theory. However, there have also been campaigns around specific areas of special concern, such as the liberalisation of laws on contraception and abortion. For example, in 1972 the writer Simone de Beauvoir, whose 1947 book *The Second Sex* was so influential in the women's movement outside France, and the lawyer Gisèle Halimi founded an organisation called *Choisir* to campaign for legislative reform. The movement continues fragmented, concerned both with the philosophical and intellectual discussion of the nature and role of women, and with influencing government policy, and existing also in the small local groups, not all of whom would necessarily recognise themselves as belonging to the women's movement as such, who concern themselves with issues such as the welfare of immigrant women or of battered wives.[6]

The environmental or ecology movement is also often traced back to the events of 1968. In fact groups and associations concerned with the conservation of nature had existed since the nineteenth century, but they were small, fragmented, and largely ineffectual. During the 1970s a number of campaigns began which attracted national attention. The long-running dispute over the attempt by the army to extend its firing ranges in the remote Larzac plateau, which began in 1971, and continued until one of the first acts of the Mitterrand government in 1981 was to cancel the proposals, was one example. Similarly, following examples in West Germany and the United Kingdom, in the mid-1970s objections to the civil nuclear programme, previously unheard of, began to be voiced. It is worth noting that, unlike the case of the United Kingdom, there has never been, in France, any significant movement against nuclear weapons, so there was no linkage between the issues of civil and of military nuclear use. In 1977 a large demonstration against a fast breeder reactor near Lyons resulted in one death and a number of injuries but not in any change to the programme for the reactor's construction. At the end of the 1970s a campaign against the construction of a nuclear power station on the Breton coast also attracted national attention. President Mitterrand cancelled those plans immediately he came to power, but the rest of the extensive nuclear programme went ahead under the Socialists.

The environmental movement has continued fragmented and ineffectual. A plethora of small local naturalists and conservation groups exists, now federated in the *Fédération française des societés de la protection de la nature* but there are no large and powerful national groups. During the 1970s some of the ecologist groups, like their counterparts elsewhere in Europe, began to develop political strategies (see Chapter 9).

Clubs and Societies

'*La vie associative*' is the collective French term used to describe the activities of all sorts of associations and clubs (see Exhibit 10.1). The traditional stereotype portrays the French as generally highly attached to life within the rather narrow confines of family and perhaps business contacts, and wary and suspicious of involvement in voluntary, cultural or recreational activity within the community. There is much anecdotal evidence to support this stereotype (Ardagh, 1988, pp. 290–305). Equally, however, during the 1970s and 1980s changes occurred (see p. 279, above). Most clubs and associations are small and local, even if, as noted above in the case of local naturalists' and conservationists' societies, they may be loosely federated at national level. Secondly, all clubs, if they are to enjoy legal protection, have to be registered within the bureaucratic framework of the 1901 law on associations. Thirdly, a great many clubs request and expect a measure of public subsidy, which may come from the local *commune*, the *département*, the region or central government. There is no vigorous culture of fund-raising to support such local activities; it is hard to identify the French equivalent of the jumble sale or coffee morning. Fourthly, many cultural and recreational activities are largely run by salaried employees, working as *animateurs* of the various activities. It has sometimes been said that the expansion of such activities during the 1970s produced, in those working in this sphere, a noticeable new group of potentially influential voters for the Socialist Party, attracted, partly as a result of the type of work they did, with its emphasis on the collective good and public provision, to a party of the moderate left. Certainly Socialist governments sought explicitly to encourage *la vie associative*, undeterred by the paradox of state action in pursuit of what must be essentially voluntary and personal activities.

The Role of the Groups: Context, Tactics and Responses

Many of the groups described above explicitly do, and all potentially may, play a political role, in the sense that they will seek to influence decisions, finding solutions to problems that will be to the liking and benefit of their members, or more generally seeking to contribute to the shaping of society in ways they find congenial. In determining the scope of the groups' influence their relationship with the political authorities becomes crucial. Various attempts have been made to apply to the relationships between the French groups and the state the theoretical models which are in general use to describe patterns of state–group relations in other Western liberal democracies. Those who have done so have tended to find the exercise rather unsatisfactory. Wright contrasts four theoretical ways of describing relationships between the state and the groups with what he calls 'the untidy reality' (Wright, 1989, pp. 254–93). Frank Wilson also discusses various theoretical formulations and whilst he finds some features from each of them present in French interest group politics, he also concludes that 'none of the four models . . . is sufficient to describe the reality of group/government relationships in France' (Wilson, 1987, p. 241). Wilson insists upon the importance of idiosyncratic factors such as the nature of the personalities involved on both sides, and the salience of any particular issue within public opinion at any time. He notes that whilst there is a temptation for analysts of politics to regard the groups' relationship with the authorities as their most important priority at any one time, they do in fact all have a multiplicity of other tasks which will affect their overall behaviour. Jack Hayward remarks (Hayward, 1986, p. 46) that in considering the relationship between the state and the groups the state is often regarded as monolithic; in fact, much recent research has shown the administrative authorities to be highly fragmented, so that different parts of the administration are likely to maintain very different styles of relationships with the groups.

The Groups in Context: The Role of the State

There are, however, a number of specific statements that can be made about the role of interest and pressure groups in France. First, the role of the administrative authorities in shaping the ways that groups can operate and the success that they may have in advancing their cause is a very powerful one. There are a number of reasons for this. A constant theme throughout the description of the nature of the groups above has been the dependence of many of the groups upon state determined legal frameworks, upon state subsidies, and sometimes upon publicly financed personnel. Secondly, the structure of the Fifth Republic's institutions has resulted in a strong political–administrative executive. There is a very large scope for administrative discretion and the work of Parliament is largely dominated by governmental priorities (see Chapters 3, 5 and 7 above). Groups which are seeking to achieve specific goals are most likely to do so through contacts within the administration. This, combined with the growth of organised and disciplined parties (see Chapter 8) means that Parliament is not a place where competition occurs between lobbies and groups with conflicting interests. In this respect the Fifth Republic differs from the Fourth Republic, which was sometimes described as a *régime des intérêts*. Then the shifting and unstable nature of the political coalitions within Parliament and the relatively weak status of the government within it meant that a lobby which could muster adequate support amongst individual parliamentarians could at least exercise a veto power over proposed policies which it saw as adversely affecting its interests, even if it could not so readily advance new policies. Wilson cites the example of the move of the wholesale fruit and vegetable market from the centre of Paris to the suburbs. Although the desirability of doing so had been recognised since the early years of the century, only through the operation of Fifth Republican institutions was it possible to overcome the blocking veto of various vested interests (Wilson, 1987, p. 216).

Thirdly, the notion of the state as being above conflicting, partial interests and their special pleading persists in the rhetoric of ministers and of administrators. The 'pluralist' notion that democracy involves unfettered competition between the various interests, within a relatively 'free-market' and de-regulated framework has little place within the institutional ideology of the Fifth Republic, where the notion of the general interest is important. In France the mainstream ideas that have determined the attitudes of many political actors have regarded the notion of the individual or group as capable of acting outside the state as definitely radical. At least since 1945 the state has been expected to play a major strategic role within society. To stress that the rhetoric and ideology of the state implies a kind of moral aloofness and authoritarianism is not to suggest that the state actually succeeds in being very powerful or effective. No perception of the public interest really provides much guidance as to where, or indeed whether, to run a motorway or site a nuclear power station. But the rhetoric does provide the state with a weapon against the groups if it chooses to use it (see Holmes and Stevens, 1986, p. 11). Wilson says, 'This is still a democratic state . . . In its actual policy process, however, it is not a participatory state . . . It is in this difficult political context that contemporary interest groups must operate in France' (Wilson, 1987, p. 220).

Whilst the groups operate within a context that gives the state a pre-eminent role, it is also true that the state, in its various manifestations, also needs the groups. Some groups are needed, first, to assist in the process of the implementation of policy. Indeed, the parastatal groups described above may carry out the disbursement of state funds and subsidies, and the state also relies upon some trade associations for the disbursement of state funds and the collection of statistics. The trade unions have a much larger role in society than their size and fragmentation might warrant because of the part they play in running the social security system.

Secondly, some parts of the state need the groups as their allies in the process of competition and conflict within the administration. The relationship may in effect be a patronage relationship[7] but the size and importance of any patron's client groups will enhance the patron's standing and influence within the administration. For example, in the early 1970s the French government appointed a Minister for the Environment, in response to a number of pressures that had come from the environmental movement, but equally from the developing international concern with environmental issues, and in 1973 a free-standing ministry was created, though for most of the period since then it has been attached as a junior ministry to other departments. One of the ministry's greatest weaknesses has been its lack of adequate links into a powerful and cohesive pressure group. As noted above, the environmental movement is very fragmented, lacks a coherent peak organisation, includes a political wing with a highly radical and conflictual approach, and has little influence at either local or national level. The ministry could not therefore link into ideas that had been given prominence and priority at either national or local levels, or utilise public opinion sensitised by powerful non-governmental sources.

In contrast, the Ministry of Agriculture, whose priorities are frequently sharply different from and opposed to those of the Ministry of the Environment, is strongly linked into such a network of contacts with the farmers' unions, especially the FNSEA. Close linkages may act a brake as well as a support. Edith Cresson, first Minister of Agriculture of the Socialist government in 1981, fearing this, made attempts to promote rival organisations to the FNSEA, for the government distrusted a body that had co-operated very closely with the policies of its predecessors. What resulted was virulent confrontation with the FNSEA which the rival groups were not sufficiently powerful or at home with the new status accorded to them to counteract. Within a few years the government had moved back into a closer relationship with the FNSEA.

Similar relationships have developed in other sectors. In formulating a policy for any particular sector of social or industrial activity a good deal of specialised information and advice is required. Research into the relationships between the administration and industry has revealed the extent to which the bodies actually involved in the industry concerned enjoy what has been described as a 'monopoly of legitimate expertise'.[8] In many cases those bodies are the individual firms, which effectively act as pressure groups in the pursuit of their own interests. 'The information available to governments concerning costs, technology and future prospects tends to come from the industry itself. In an uncertain world it is difficult to test wisdom by first principles, and the critical element of strategic judgement is based on information which cannot easily be queried by civil servants' (Cawson *et al.*, 1990, p. 361).

The state needs some groups, but it is important to be clear about the limitations of this assertion. First, whilst the French administration may develop detailed policies in collusion with certain groups and on the basis of information and expertise supplied by them, the relationship does not amount to the kind of partnership between the state and the main interest organisations for the determination of major political goals for which the term 'corporatism' is sometimes used. 'Corporatism . . . involves a process of bargaining between actors representing monopolistic organisations and (because we are speaking here of "public" policy) actors representing the state' (Cawson *et al.*, 1990, p. 6). This simply does not occur in France as a way of determining the very broad strategies of public policy – the choice between privatisation and nationalisation, for example, or the approach to be taken in relation to closer European integration.[9] Where such bargaining does occur is in relation to very specific policies and goals. What emerges may be called a 'policy community'. Within that community individuals, both politicians and administrators and those representing functional interests, and groups of various kinds will co-operate, bargain, negotiate, and conflict.

> The policy-making process is conceived as operating within semi-pluralistic, elitist decision-making communities, which in the case [for instance] of economic and industrial policy give pride of place to the discretion of actors in the major business firms, to the public and private bankers and to the politico–administrative leaders, exercised within a framework of domestic and international constraints. (Hayward, 1986, p. 38)

A second qualification to the statement that the state needs some groups is that the state does not need any and every group, and may exercise a great deal of choice as to those groups with whom any part of it may choose to interact. A common distinction made by those who analyse the groups is that between 'insider' groups and 'outsider' groups. 'Insider' groups are those deemed to be useful and supportive, given particular official recognition, consulted, included in the membership of the vast range of consultative and joint committees which various parts of the administration sponsor or run. These groups are regarded as *interlocuteurs valables*, respected and responsible. A group's status is not necessarily fixed and invariable but may relate to the issue at hand, and may change over time. It has been observed, for example, that one of the features of the French industrial policy community in the 1970s and 1980s was its ability to exclude the trade unions from influence in that area (Hayward, 1986, p. 66). Nor, even under a Socialist government, did the unions play a determinant role in formulating the laws reforming the shape of industrial relations passed in the early 1980s (the *lois Auroux*). On the other hand in 1991 all the confederations except the CGT signed the collective agreement with the employers' federation on vocational training that was forthwith translated almost verbatim into law. Moreover, they have a formal place in the determination of conditions of service, disciplinary matters and promotion procedures within the civil service and belong to the tripartite bodies which run the social security system.[10]

Yves Mény has noted that policy communities may be fragile, and alter as external constraints change, the most striking source of change being the European Community. The EC provides opportunities for 'outsider' groups to go over the head of the French government, as happened when a supermarket chain took action in the European court to force the abandonment of a fixed retail price for petrol. Moreover, the EC's competition rules, with the coming of the single European market, may lessen the ability of some groups to use a position buttressed by state regulations to protect themselves against competition, as has occurred with the auctioneers (Mény, 1989, pp. 395–6) and the legal profession.

Thirdly, it should be noted that the power and legitimacy of the state in relation to the groups, discussed above, is such that it has not proved possible in France for any group, however close and collusive its relationship with the state, unequivocally to 'capture' parts of the state and impose its own priorities unconditionally. There is no doubt that groups with interests of their own – and even the civil servants who on the one hand seek to enforce the political and administrative priorities of the political executive may on the other have professional interests of their own which they defend, sometimes ferociously, as a group – seek to deploy their relationships with the state as a resource in their activities. The farmers, organised in the FNSEA, and always very close to the Ministry of Agriculture, have not been able to capture total control over agricultural policy, or even to dictate the French stance in Common Agricultural Policy discussions on Brussels. In industrial sectors pressure led to the massive subsidisation of the steel industry, and French manufacturers of consumer electronics have benefited from the protection conferred through state measures to impose idiosyncratic standards (the SECAM TV system, for instance) or deter competing imports. Some areas have enjoyed considerable freedom of manoeuvre as a result of their particular position within the state. Thus Electricité de France, as a nationalised industry, has been in a strong position to pursue its own interests and impose them and has done so effectively. But the state has not been a totally acquiescent or compliant partner and cannot necessarily continue such protection against the pressure of external forces, for example, EC policies.

The Groups and Politics: Pre-emption and Incorporation

One of the ways in which pressure groups contribute to the political life of France is by the contribution of ideas and concerns to the general flow of political debate and competition, and by alerting public opinion to specific issues. The contribution of the groups to the political development of the country in this way may seem indirect, but it can nevertheless be substantial. This is particularly true of the broader groupings of interests that described above as 'movements'. What occurs is a process familiar in relatively pluralist democracies: as an issue grows in salience and attracts public attention it may, though not necessarily without conflict, attract the attention of one or more of the organised political groups. The role of the group or movement is often to mobilise initial support and public interest. In some cases the issues will be sufficiently broad and radical to ensure that the movement continues, even after the issue has been incorporated within the political and administrative structures. In other cases the group or movement may dwindle as the issue moves into the mainstream political agenda. The ecology movement is an example of a movement that has faced the dilemmas of this process in a particularly visible and acute form throughout Europe. It is the case that for many of the movements their relative distance from the more structured and perhaps rigid institutions may result in greater scope for the expression of radical and creative ideas. Jack Hayward (1978) remarked in the late 1970s that the most interesting developments in French politics were taking place outside the specifically 'political' structures and institutions.

The regional groups discussed above, such as the Breton movement, were one of the forces that influenced the decentralisation reforms of the early 1980s. They were not the predominant factor, but the fact that Corsica was the first region to be created and was given a special status indicates the priority given to certain regional demands. Corsican nationalism still manifests itself in feuding and violence on the island, but the Breton movement has faded in importance as the place of the Breton language and culture has been increasingly recognised and the region has developed economically.

The women's movement was not the only influence upon the social reforms of President Giscard d'Estaing's presidency, but those reforms included a number of measures taken in response to the post-1968 women's movement and a new sensitivity in government circles to 'women's issues'.[11] The divorce laws were liberalised and abortion legalised. In 1974 President Giscard d'Estaing invited the centre-left journalist Françoise Giroud to become junior minister for *la condition féminine*. In 1981 under Mitterrand what had, after 1976 been demoted to a *délégation* was replaced by a ministry for the rights of women, under an energetic woman, Yvette Roudy. The cabinet status of the ministry did not survive the advent of the right-wing Chirac government and it has not since regained the high profile which it had under Roudy. A highly cynical view would see the whole tale of government attention to women's issues as symbolic or opportunistic, an attempt to woo an increasingly politically aware group in society. Siân Reynolds points out that it would be naive to suppose that women's rights had ever been a major priority with the Socialist Party, and that overtly feminist groups, by 1986, felt that "going official" had rather demobilised independent feminism'.[12] Less cynical would be the observation that the high profile and energetic efforts of Yvette Roudy did result in women's issues coming more firmly onto the Socialists' agenda, and that recognition of the genuine, if unspectacular, achievements of 'institutional feminism',[13] including, for example, the 1992 law against sexual harassment at work, may have assisted in 'the rallying of the feminists to the Socialist banner' of which 'the PS and Mitterrand reaped the electoral fruits'.[14]

The decision of some of the ecological groups to take an overtly political stance and field electoral candidates certainly produced a challenge to the established parties, despite the limited success of the 'green' candidates. Again, the result has been the adoption of a more ecological rhetoric, especially by the Socialist Party. For the ecologists this posed a classic political dilemma: was it wise to risk the purity of a single-minded approach and possibly alienate some supporters, by alliance with another group, which might however result in reforms along the lines they advocated? In the mid-1980s Brice Lalonde, who had been the Ecology candidate in the presidential election campaign of 1981, opted for the alliance strategy, and subsequently became minister for the environment after Mitterrand's 1988 victory, while other ecologists refused alliance, and supported an Ecology candidate, Waechter. Differing strategic approaches and personal rivalries continued to contribute to the political disarray of the ecologists. Combined with the pressures of continuing recession, when economic issues tend to dominate, this has limited their influence upon political debate in the 1990s.

Contestation and Direct Action

Collusion with the political authorities, or co-option into the traditional political structures are not the only ways in which groups may
seek to have political effects. There is a long tradition in France of
direct action and confrontation with the authorities. Such action may
be organised by relatively established groups, as for example the
demonstrations and protests against the run down of the steel
industry in Lorraine organised there and Paris in 1978–9 by the
CGT. Strikers at Air France in 1993 caused the withdrawal of drastic
restructuring plans and precipitated the resignation of the chairman
of the company. In October 1995 a massive one-day strike by public
sector workers against a public sector pay freeze brought France to a
virtual standstill, and this was followed in November and December
by much more extensive strikes in the public sector (see Exhibit 3.5)
But protests and strikes may also be the result of small autonomous
committees or local groups. This was the case with the railway strike
of the winter of 1986–7. Such action is frequently at least potentially
violent, as for example with the repeated hijackings of lorries of
British sheep and sheep meat by groups of local farmers in protest at
what was seen as unfair competition from the British, which produced
an outcry in Britain when one such episode resulted in the burning of
the animals. The results of direct action may be spectacular, as in the
almost countrywide traffic jam along the main *autoroutes* which
resulted from a lorry drivers' protest in 1983.

Direct action is noisy, causes inconvenience and may catch the
headlines. It is very infrequently clearly politically effective. However, there have been notorious occasions when action has followed
such tactics, which tends to encourage those who resort to them. This
has been particularly true where the issues have related to education
and young people (see Exhibit 10.3). But the effects of direct action
are frequently less apparent. The largest strike and demonstration
movement of the Fifth Republic, the events of May 1968, whilst it
may have had far-reaching effects upon social and cultural expectations, and provided an impetus for later social movements, had very
limited long-term political effects. Where the French government is
strongly constrained by other political factors, especially those which
arise from the interdependence of modern nation states, results may
be particularly limited; the violence of the steelworkers in 1978–9
may have improved the redundancy terms they were offered, but did
nothing to halt the re-structuring of the French industry.[15] Air

France's restructuring plans will take effect over a rather longer period than had been intended before the strike, but the airline cannot be indefinitely sheltered from the need to adapt to changing conditions and to conform to European Community policy. Similarly pelting the Minister of Agriculture with eggs, as French farmers did in 1982, or blocking roads with farm animals, as in 1993, have had very little effect upon the overall trends of the EC Common Agricultural Policy.

Nor should the phenomenon be exaggerated. The numbers of working days lost through strikes declined through the 1980s. Violent direct action, although always newsworthy, is sporadic and isolated.

Conclusion

Despite the constitutional rhetoric of indivisibility, France is a highly fragmented and pluralistic society, with a wide range of organisations that bring together people with a shared interest, and that may seek, persistently, or from time to time, to influence the political and administrative decision-making processes. Very many such groups are fragmented, divided along ideological or territorial boundaries, often very small, and frequently in conflict with other groups. There are very few large national level organisations or lobbies.

Nevertheless, one of the main roles of such groups is to place issues of concern to important groups of the population firmly upon the political and administrative agenda. Paradoxically, the fulfilment of such a role may often weaken the groups. Mendras and Cole (1991, *passim*, but esp. p. 228) argue that the large social movements of the 1970s which took their impetus from May 1968 are almost extinct. Their causes have been absorbed either by governmental action – decentralisation, the creation of the Ministry of Women's Rights – or by co-option into the programmes of the political parties. Howard Machin points out the role of the Socialist party in incorporating the priorities and in some cases the leaders of the movements into its structures.[16]

Similarly the trade unions have found themselves in a position that was both more prominent and yet weaker as a result of the industrial relations reforms of the early 1980s (the *lois Auroux*). The Socialist government wished to strengthen the 'social partnership' element of industrial relations. In an industrial environment where many French firms are still strongly dominated by a relatively authoritarian boss, and 'French workers correctly perceived the process of decision-making within the firm as essentially unilateral' (Gallie, 1983, p. 98) many of the improvements in working conditions that in other countries are likely to be the results of collective bargaining have traditionally been the result of political agitation and action by the state. For this reason both the conditions under which redundancies could be declared, which are always monitored by the state officials of the *Inspection du Travail* and the introduction of flexible working hours were matters for political controversy and legislative action through the 1980s and 1990s, by both Socialist and right-wing governments. In an attempt to alter this climate – and also possibly to weaken the Communist dominated CGT – the *lois Auroux* set up extensive consultative procedures within firms on matters such as training and health and safety. Employee representatives are directly elected by all employees, rather than nominated by the unions. The unions may, and do, field lists of candidates, but they have lost any monopoly of representation, and may be serious stretched by the need to find enough *militants* to fulfil these functions. Moreover, the size of the vote for each union's list gives a ready and relatively public measure of the extent and limits of its influence, whereas membership figures remain a deliberately murky area.

Despite apparent fragmentation and weakness the interest groups and lobbies thus continue to play a crucial and lively role in the formulation and implementation of political programmes and the administration of policies. In this area, as in others, the role of the state as a key actor, both in constituting the framework within which these activities occur, and in the activities of its own different parts within the complex pattern, is a distinctive feature of the French system.

Part IV

France and Europe

11

France and Europe: Policy Making and Politics

France is a member of the European Union. France's relations with the European Union and until 1993, the European Community are in part shaped by factors which reach back to the very early years of the Community. Indeed, the original impetus for the creation of an international body with supranational powers came from Jean Monnet and the Commission of the French Plan for Reconstruction and Modernisation which he headed. The founding of the earliest Community authority, the European Coal and Steel Community, arose from a French initiative devised by him and propounded by the then Foreign Minister, Robert Schuman. The objective was to solve political and economic problems relating to the rehabilitation of Germany and the organisation of the coal and steel industry that were of great concern to France. The structures that were set up then, and those which followed for the European Economic Community and Euratom, were strongly influenced by French models and patterns of administration, and tended initially to provide a milieu into which French administrative assumptions meshed rather easily. As the European Community institutions have gradually developed a life of their own, so French administrators and politicians have been obliged, sometimes painfully, to come to terms with new methods and approaches.

A subsequent plan for the creation of a European Defence Community involved too great a surrender of control over national defence forces for many French politicians to accept, and was defeated in the French Parliament in 1954 by an unlikely alliance involving both Communists and Gaullists. The European Coal and Steel Community was the forerunner of the European Economic Community and the European Atomic Energy Community. When the European Economic Community was set up an important part of its political base was in effect a bargain between Germany and France, that involved the opening of the very large West German market to French agricultural produce in return for freer access for the products of German manufacturing industry to what had been a very protected French market. Some of the officials and politicians involved also hoped that the EEC would increase and accelerate the operation of the market forces that were forcing the French economy into becoming more competitive and acquiring modernised capitalist structures, a transformation which the 1945 nationalisation of about half the French banking system and the creation of the Planning Commission (which was able, in its early years, to deploy large Marshall Aid funds) had only begun.

De Gaulle came into power just as the EEC and Euratom were being set up. He had been opposed to French participation in them, but he did not repudiate them. Instead he attempted to shape the Communities and French participation within them to accord more closely with his view of French national interest. He was willing to accept the economic advantages of the Community, but would have preferred a looser political structure allowing the Community to develop into a more intergovernmental forum for co-operation in fields such as foreign and cultural policy – both areas in which, at that time, French pre-eminence amongst the six founder members was likely to be uncontested. His attempts to promote this, through a set of proposals known as the Fouchet plan, foundered on the resistance of the other member states. He was, however, successful in preventing British membership of the Community during his lifetime. He wished to prevent the shift in emphasis within the Community, the opening up of the Community to greater American influence, and the challenge to French leadership that he thought British membership would bring.

Following a major confrontation between France and the other member states of the Community in 1965, during which the French representatives withdrew from the main decision-making bodies of the Community – though not from some of the day to day management bodies – de Gaulle succeeded in establishing the so-called Luxembourg Compromise of 1966. This was the principle, that endured until the late 1980s, that a member state had the right to veto proposals that it regarded as contrary to its vital national interests. France was also able to cut back some of the ambitions of the Commission of the European Community for faster movement towards a more federalist approach, and to ensure a shift in the balance of power within the Community institutions towards the Council of Ministers where national interests were most fully represented.

However, the period of confrontation during 1965 also made it clear that the pressures upon the French government were not solely political. Economic interests were clearly involved. French farmers were benefiting in important ways from the Common Agricultural Policy (CAP); this helps to explain why the CAP, which scarcely figures in the Treaty of Rome, took so high a priority in the early years. It has been suggested that it was the unpopularity of a confrontation which might have jeopardised these gains that helped to force de Gaulle to a second ballot in the 1965 presidential election.

De Gaulle's rhetoric was the rhetoric of national independence and the importance of the nation state – a sharp contrast to the earlier vision of Monnet and Schuman whose concern with the practical politics of economic interdependence was linked to a grander vision of the redundancy of the nation state within Europe. None of de Gaulle's successors has felt able to jettison the Gaullist language about the status and role of France, a language that was linked to a view about the need for a European identity and role that would counterbalance what would otherwise be the absolute domination of the superpowers. If some of France's fellow member-states suspected that talk of the interest of Europe essentially covered a concern for French national interests simply and solely, such language nevertheless allowed successive French governments to claim the status of 'good Europeans'.

The complexity of the French approach to the European Community has stemmed from the fact that it has always included elements both of Jean Monnet's vision of the inevitable logic of greater European co-operation, and of Gaullist rhetoric.[1] Each successive President since 1958 has encouraged and developed progress in certain areas. For de Gaulle the Common Agricultural Policy and the customs union were key economic factors that were of crucial importance to France. The Community therefore had a useful role to play in these rather technical areas.

After de Gaulle's resignation and death President Pompidou encouraged the admission of the United Kingdom, the Republic of

Ireland and Denmark to the Community. He was seen to be a leading influence over the summit at the Hague in 1969 which set a renewed agenda for the Community, involving enlargement, and also proposing (as it turned out rather prematurely) progress towards economic and monetary union.

Over the next decade France retained a leading role in the development of the Community. The partnership between President Giscard d'Estaing and Chancellor Helmut Schmidt of West Germany built upon the privileged relationship between their two countries which had begun with the relationship between German Chancellor Adenauer and de Gaulle in the early 1960s. Franco-German initiatives were responsible for a number of the advances made by the Community during the second half of the 1970s, especially the development of the European Monetary System (EMS) and of the political co-operation machinery, which again echoed the Gaullist emphasis on intergovernmental machinery, and on the primacy of political – that is, foreign policy – considerations. In institutionalising the summit meetings of the heads of government of the Community into a regular European Council Giscard d'Estaing also emphasised the importance France placed upon political impulsion for the Community deriving from the member-states rather than primarily from the Commission.

'De Gaulle, generally viewed as a foe of the EEC, enthusiastically used the Community's free-trade provisions to modernize French industry and its agricultural policy as a lever on West Germany. Mitterrand also [saw] the EEC as an essential tool of French modernisation, but in thoroughly different circumstances.'[2] During the 1980s the French supported the development of a single European market, and the signing of the Single European Act which provided the institutional basis for the single market and for further movement towards integration. The need for energetic action and preparation for the challenges of the new structures were seized upon by the political parties as a slogan and a legitimising argument that could support their particular programmes. The appointment of Mme Cresson as Prime Minister in 1991, for example, was vigorously explained by President Mitterrand as providing the dynamic leadership that France would require in order to prepare for the coming of the single market after 1993.

However, the optimism which this rhetoric implied was tempered and sobered during the 1990s by a number of further factors. First, the end of the cold war and the unification of Germany had a major impact in several areas. The balance within the founding bargain upon which the European Community had been based was unsettled by the creation of a German state which was much enlarged and with a population which considerably exceeded that of France. Moreover, as the German economy struggled to absorb the costs of unification, the French economy suffered alongside it, because the French franc was, within the European Monetary System and under the 'franc fort' policy pursued by governments of both political persuasions since 1983, closely linked to the Deutschmark. The result was relatively low inflation in France but, by the mid-1990s, a high and intractable unemployment rate. President Mitterrand was far from enthusiastic initially about the speed and nature of the unification process. France subsequently accepted it with a good grace and continued to insist that the Franco-German axis must remain the pivot about which the Community – or rather, after 1993, the European Union – would continue to turn.

The end of the cold war also, quite quickly, produced a queue of Central and East European countries applying to join the European Union. During the period when France held the presidency of the European Union in 1995, a period which spanned the presidential election, France made clear statements in favour of the enlargement of the European Union up to, but not beyond, the borders of the former Soviet Union. However, the enlargement of the European Union to 15 members at the beginning of that year, and the prospect of further enlargement to the East, caused considerable concern. The Chirac government was anxious lest the balance tip too far away from the Mediterranean countries, and wished to promote the cause both of the southern member states and of other Mediterranean countries, notably in North Africa.

The end of the cold war also raised serious questions about appropriate defence policy. The Maastricht Treaty provided for the development of a common foreign and security policy. In addition to participation in this France was also much involved in setting up joint arrangements with neighbours and allies. These included the Euro-corps, a multinational infantry force, as well as, for example, the joint Franco-British rapid reaction force deployed in Bosnia. In December 1995 France rejoined the military committee of NATO, a decision which marked a turning point in French defence relationships but which seemed a logical continuation of French participation in joint operational arrangements, such as a Franco-British air headquarters inaugurated in October 1995, which had gone so far as to lead many

commentators to the conclusion that France had already operationally rejoined NATO's military structures.

A second factor was the difficult conclusion of the Uruguay round
of negotiations of the General Agreement on Tariffs and Trade. These
negotiations were linked with reforms to the Common Agricultural
Policy of the European Community, since one of the preconditions for
American agreement to the new treaty was a reduction in subsidy to
European farmers. The EC was in any case undertaking such reforms
in attempts to restrain and rationalise expenditure and prevent the
production of shamefully large agricultural surpluses. These reforms
hit many French farmers, who felt that their incomes were threatened. A second major issue in the negotiations related to a French
attempt to find ways in which American film and television imports
could legally be curbed. More generally, and more disturbingly
perhaps for French public opinion, given the extent to which
European integration had been seen as a vehicle for French interests,
the underlying question was the extent to which France could, or
would, if necessary stand out against her European Union partners.

The reform of the CAP was one of the issues which mobilised
opinion at the time of the Maastricht Treaty ratification debate,
which preceded the final stages of the GATT negotiations. The
ratification debate awoke much French public opinion to the potential impact of the European Union. Partly because of the ease with
which French political and administrative working practices fitted in
with a Community system that had been devised broadly along
French lines, and because of the experience and skill of French
negotiators and the relatively unchallenged leading role France was
able to play in the EC for its first three decades, the implications of
the supranational aspects of the EC and then the EU were only slowly
recognised amongst many politicians and officials. The French elite
had regarded it largely as a matter for foreign policy and remote from
domestic concerns. Surprisingly, perhaps, relatively few French high
fliers had occupied senior posts in the Brussels administrations. Until
the appointment of Jacques Delors, French commissioners of the
European Communities had gained little prominence, even if one
them (Raymond Barre) subsequently went on to become prime
minister. The ministries in Paris had not been much concerned to
acquaint themselves with the procedures and law of the Communities, and it had been notoriously difficult to ensure the implementation of rulings by the European Court of Justice in France. The
French Parliament has never developed a sophisticated system of

parliamentary scrutiny of European legislation, and only in the 1990s did it even begin to take steps in this direction (see Chapter 7). The debate over the ratification of the Maastricht Treaty brought many of these issues into the open. It also served as a rallying point for many other forms of discontent. The consequence was political division that not only separated the mainstream parties from the parties of protest, but also ran right through the mainstream. Risk of exacerbating divisions within the mainstream parties meant that European issues were played down in the presidential election campaigns. President Chirac, once elected, reasserted his views of the primacy of French national interest, resuming nuclear testing against vociferous protest within the European Parliament and most of the member states, though the Commission declined to arraign the French government before the European Court of Justice. He made it clear that, while France remained committed to the goal of economic and monetary union by 1999, and would take the necessary internal fiscal measures to achieve the prerequisites, all the conditions which the German government and the Bundesbank were seeking to attach to the single currency would not necessarily be acceptable. In general the theme of French national interest was restated after 1995 with resumed vigour.

Opportunities and Constraints

The theme of French national interest was never absent from France's approach to Community policy. From the beginning it was acknowledged by those who supported French membership of the Community that it was clearly in the national interest that the economy should be modern and competitive. During the 1980s France, despite the Socialist government's espousal in 1983 of a more liberal approach to the economy, and its recognition of the value of competitive enterprise, was not prepared to embrace the deregulatory and privatising approach of Thatcherite Great Britain, which saw the single market largely as a yet wider zone of deregulation and unfettered competition. Privatisation in France, begun by the 1986 Chirac government, had lost most of its impetus after the stock market crash of the autumn of 1987. Measures had to be found to defend European specificity against increasing pressure especially from Japanese technology and this, the French government felt, should be the aim of the single market. A purely national industrial policy was no longer proving adequate to promote and defend French national industry against the competition of multinational firms, and indeed some of the major French companies, even those in state ownership, such as the electronics and defence group Thomson, were increasingly behaving as multinationals in determining their competitive strategies. The scope for national initiatives was dwindling as, for example, French government assistance to French car manufacturers came under critical scrutiny from the EC Commission, and it became less possible to repeat the measure that, in November 1982, briefly required all imported video recorders to pass through customs at the small inland town of Poitiers, thus effectively confining that year's Christmas sales to products made in France.

In these circumstances the calculation of the national interest becomes complex. The development of the Community has provided opportunities for progress and development in France. The CAP provided the clearest example in the 1950s and 1960s. If the major benefits of the policy were felt by affluent and efficient farmers in the north of France, the structure of the policy was also seen to increase the welfare of more marginal farmers elsewhere.

The 1980s' initiative that led to the 1992 programme, the Single European Act and the Maastricht agreements also involved a complicated balance. The French government had long argued the need for a European industry that could compete with American and Japanese technology and competitivity. Some French businessmen, such as Jacques Calvet, the head of the Peugeot car company, argued loudly for reinforced European subsidies and protection. President Mitterrand was, in the early 1980s, consistently hostile to the American Strategic Defence (star wars) Initiative not least because of the American domination of the programme and the likelihood that the major part of the benefits of the technological developments that could stem from it would fall to US industry. He took a leading part in promoting a European scheme for an advanced technology initiative, EUREKA, in response. The European Single Market programme seemed to offer greater scope for European industry and for the development of a European industrial policy.

Similarly, proposals for the development of the European Monetary System towards a European central bank and perhaps a common currency could entail the loss of autonomy for the Bank of France and the disappearance of the Franc. But if the alternative were the *de facto* domination of the European economy by the Deutschmark and the German central bank, the Bundesbank then, in the French government's view, it might be preferable to have a European central bank where a French representative would have an equal voice. The Maastricht summit in December 1991 gave the French government much of what it wanted. President Mitterrand had been the most cautious of all the Western leaders about German unification. A firm timetable for economic and monetary union would, he hoped, ensure that Germany would be locked into a European process and not simply achieve domination by default, as a result of her economic and industrial strength. This was achieved. So was a agreement on ways of moving forward on the implementation of the social measures, even without British involvement, to ensure that almost all member states would bear the costs of progressive social policies equally. President Mitterrand had proposed a European 'social area' (*espace sociale*) in the early 1980s when the cost of Socialist social policies seemed to be having an adverse effect on French competitivity, and France had supported the European Commission's proposed social charter. The Maastricht Treaty also contained references to support for industrial development on which France had been particularly keen. The increased emphasis placed by the European Commission from 1993 on measures to combat unemployment was supported by France in the light of growing national unemployment, as was investment in Trans-European Networks which were expected to underpin growth and provide jobs.

These opportunities, however, are counterbalanced by constraints which challenge long-established habits of behaviour. The regulatory and dirigiste attitudes of the French state have been challenged. Examples of such challenges include the success of a chain of petrol stations – Leclerc – in using European Community law to challenge national price controls, and of the cut-price travel company Nouvelles Frontières in attempting to increase competition in air travel, a sector dominated by state regulation which certainly served to further the interests of the nationalised airline, Air France. French anger at the refusal of the Commission of the European Communities to permit the sale of the Canadian aircraft company De Havilland to the French company Aérospatiale on competition grounds was very evident in 1991: expectations that the presence within the Commission of two French commissioners should usually ensure the achievement of goals which the French thought desirable were abruptly dispelled. In the first half of the 1990s the French government increasingly found some aspects of its industrial policy open to question from Brussels. The sensitive issue of state subsidisation of French industry, both private and public sector, was another issue that began to come to the fore. Moreover, it was becoming increasingly clear that there would be considerable difficulty in developing the sort of Community-wide industrial policy which France favoured as a substitute for domestic policy.

This was not the only European policy area which led to disappointment. One of the developments which had parallelled the extension of European Union policy was the conclusion of the Schengen agreement covering co-operation on policing measures, and the abolition of border controls. This agreement was technically outside the Community framework. The French clearly hoped and expected that, although it would abolish frontier controls between the territories of the states involved, it would result in much tighter control at all the external frontiers with non-participant states. This proved not to be the case and, in the climate induced by a rise in terrorist activity, and citing the drug-trafficking problem which had burgeoned following the abolition of frontier controls between the Netherlands and the other Schengen partners, France withdrew from the arrangements only months after they had come into force.

In addition to constraints upon the content of policy the European Union also resulted in constraints upon the style of policy making. French politicians and officials are having to accommodate to a style of policy making in Brussels which is less 'top-down' than has been frequently the case in France. Those who formulate policy in Brussels are relatively open and may be receptive to lobbying. Political considerations play an important part in policy formulation, and a crucial one at the stage of negotiation within the Council of Ministers with which the legislative procedure culminates. It is expected that measures will be drawn up after a broadly consultative and consensual approach and will then be applied uniformly, whereas in France it frequently arises that measures are adapted to fit needs on the ground only after promulgation through a mechanism of dispensations. The administration of the European Commission and the secretariat of the Council of Ministers are fairly hierarchical organisations, with an immense range of nationalities in which networks of personal relationships like those upon which the French elite rely in Paris may be difficult or impossible to form, although Jacques Delors himself drove many of his policies forward in this way. It may not always be possible, as it more frequently was within a much smaller Community, and still is in Paris, to fix a matter by a well-placed telephone call. Nor, as the French most notably discovered in the de Havilland case, is there an equivalent to the prime minister to whom the two sides of a contradictory argument can be put and from whom a decision will descend. The French have only slowly discovered the necessity of lobbying, and experience it as constraint upon their policy making.

The development of the European Community throughout the period of the Fifth Republic thus involved both considerable opportunities for the assertion of French leadership and the pursuit of national interest, and a growing recognition that many of the distinctive features of French policy would be subject to constraint and change. The ways in which French policy towards the European Community has been developed and implemented thus continue to be of considerable importance, and these are examined in the next section of this chapter.

The Elaboration of European Policy

French policy towards the European Community epitomises the complexity of the shaping of public policy. The President and his staff, the prime minister, other ministers, the officials of the ministries, the French representative at the European Community in Brussels, Parliament, the political parties and the pressure groups all play a greater or lesser role.

The President and his staff at the Elysée have a major role in formulating the French approach. De Gaulle set the tone and the agenda of the French approach to the European Community during his presidency. He used all the means at the President's disposal, most spectacularly the press conference at which he announced his veto on British accession, to enunciate and expound his views, and in doing so shaped an area of activity that he regarded as clearly a field for presidential activity to his own individual mould. The decisions that provoked the crisis of 1965 were, like the decision in 1965 to withdraw from the military organisation of NATO, his personal decisions. All subsequent presidents have been influenced by his style. It is the President who attends meetings of the European Council, and consequently it is upon his staff that the main burden of the task of preparing for them falls. Under President Mitterrand the head of the government department dealing with the co-ordination of French relationships to the Community was also sometimes attached to his office.

Presidential activity and influence are particularly intense during the periods when France holds the presidency of the Council of Ministers. In both 1984 and 1989 President Mitterrand undertook visits to capitals of the other member states and was deeply engaged in pushing forward French priorities. In 1995 the French presidency spanned the presidential election, but following his victory Chirac also adopted a high profile. Outside these exceptional periods, and even under *cohabitation*, important policy decisions are taken at the *Elysée*. One of the reasons for the problems encountered in the ratification of the Maastricht Treaty may have been that it was negotiated well away from public attention by a small team of officials and ministers centred around the President (Lequesne, 1993, p. 180). The President has consistently dominated the policy-making process in relation to European integration.

The prime minister also plays a part in the formulation of policy relating to the European Community, especially at the more day to day level. As EC policy comes increasingly to involve a range of different aspects of policy, the co-ordinating role of the prime minister and his office described in Chapter 4 has become important in this sphere also. The government department responsible for co-ordinating policy towards the Community, the *Secretariat Général de la Comité Intérministerielle pour les questions de coopération économique européenne* (SGCI) is usually attached to the prime minister's office. During the first period of *cohabitation* European policy was a particularly delicate area in the relationship between prime minister and President; both men attended the meetings of the heads of government, causing difficult problems of protocol for the organisers.

The prime minister is most likely to be deeply involved in the making of policy towards the European Union when there are financial implications, or difficult choices concerned with the internal political impact of the policies. Edith Cresson during her short tenure of office tried to mobilise industrialists and bankers in support of a more active industrial policy for the European Community, an attempt which did not survive her period in office. French policy in relation to the longer-term plans for financing the EC (the so-called 'Delors packages') required prime ministerial intervention. Moreover, the prime minister has to undertake the task of justifying the outcome of EC decisions to Parliament, so that Pierre Bérégovoy was faced by a vote of censure over the reform of the CAP in 1992, and

Edouard Balladur also faced difficulties at the time of the conclusion of the GATT negotiations at the end of 1993.

The example of the Maastricht negotiations underlines the role played by officials in the development of the French approach to detailed matters within the Community. The SGCI serves as the main centre for the co-ordination of policy and for liaison with the French representation in Brussels. The SGCI was set up initially in 1948 to handle relationships with the newly emerging European bodies – such as the Organisation for European Economic Co-operation (OEEC), which is now the Organisation for Economic Co-operation and Development (OECD). This was set up as a body that would transcend and overcome the fierce interministerial rivalries between the Finance Ministry, the Foreign Ministry and the Planning Commission. These rivalries continued and were indeed complicated by the creation of the European Economic Community and Euratom in 1958, which markedly increased the number of domestic ministries involved with Community policy. It was de Gaulle's concern with European policy in the mid-1960s, and a fear that French officials involved in relationships with the Community were tending to become unduly 'pro-European', that prompted Prime Minister Pompidou to insist that the SGCI must take charge of all contacts between Paris and Brussels. The prime minister would maintain a firm overall co-ordination.

This system has essentially survived up to the present day. The SGCI transmits the EC proposals as they arrive from Brussels to the appropriate ministries, asking for their comments. The line to be adopted is then settled at a meeting – there are often as many as five a day – called by the SGCI. If agreement cannot be reached the matter may be passed on to the Prime Minister's personal staff for the Prime Minister's decision. But such prime-ministerial intervention occurs only in about 10 per cent of cases. Quite often the political clout of the Secretary General of the SGCI – who is an official – is sufficient to allow decisions to be taken within the SGCI that all will accept. This is particularly true since the Secretary General has almost always combined the post with that of being a close personal advisor either, as in the early 1960s, of the prime minister or, as has been the case ever since then, of the President. Elizabeth Guigou, who subsequently became minister of European affairs, was a noted holder of both positions under President Mitterrand. This illustrates the complex overlapping of official, personal and political factors in the ways in which decisions are taken.

Much of the detailed negotiation in Brussels is undertaken by the staff of the permanent representation there. Observers who are familiar with the Brussels machinery note that the French officials who negotiate are normally well briefed and well prepared on the principles underlying any proposed course of action. Their tendency is to formulate a logical and thoroughly well-thought-through case often derived from the principles at stake and then to press it on the basis of rational and tenacious argument. Although they will act on the basis of in instructions from the SGCI these instructions are not always written and formal. On technical details French negotiators are perceived as often less well-supported by back-up staff than other delegations.

A former French Permanent Representative in Brussels commented upon the scope which he enjoyed to act autonomously and to exercise his own judgement. He would not necessarily expect to consult Paris for instructions at every point as the negotiations developed. This was a consequence of the autonomy of judgement and decision that senior French officials expect to enjoy (see Chapter 5) and of the continuity of French approach and policy towards the Community, which meant that the Representative had a context of long-standing and consistent policy within which to place his decisions. Contrasting his experience with that of the British, who have a notably more regular and formal requirement to report upon the progress of negotiations and seek written instructions, the former representative observed that whilst the French system enabled him to respond with greater rapidity and flexibility, it also meant that the maintenance of continuity and consistency was more heavily dependent upon a limited number of people, and a change in personnel could result in difficulties.

The political parties play a less obvious role in the formulation of policy towards the Community. Until the early 1990s they were largely able to avoid obvious internal disagreements over policy towards the EC. Throughout the 1980s the component parties of the UDF, especially the CDS with its Christian Democrat heritage and the Giscardian PR, steadily supported the development of the French role within the Community. The Socialist position was more ambiguous and qualified but, especially after 1981, very supportive of President Mitterrand's initiatives within the Community. Jacques Delors, who became President of the European Commission in 1985, had previously been the Socialist minister of finance in Mitterrand's first government, and remained a leading member of the PS and a possible contender for nomination as the party's presidential candidate to succeed President Mitterrand in 1995. In general the theme of '1992' was a 'mobilising myth' which most of the main parties used both to assert that the Community was the framework 'which would allow French values, ambitions and assertiveness to be in some measure preserved and imparted to others'[3] and to plead that their party would be best placed to do this.

The National Front and the Communists remained opposed to any development of the Community along the path of ever closer union. The National Front base their stand upon strongly patriotic and xenophobic sentiments, the Communists denounce a capitalist conspiracy. The Gaullist party, however, underwent the largest shift in attitude. Following de Gaulle, they were quick to denounce any tendency by the Community to extend the scope of its powers, or to move beyond a largely technical role. It was in order to satisfy the Gaullist component of the governing majority that President Giscard d'Estaing was obliged to insert into the legislation setting up the mechanisms for direct elections to the European Parliament when they first occurred in 1979 a proviso that this did not involve any extension of the powers of the European Parliament. However, The RPR under Jacques Chirac shifted its emphasis quite markedly during the early 1980s. They began to emphasise de Gaulle's role as a founding father of the Community, and a supporter of the customs union and the agricultural policy. They supported the single market and the aspects of deregulation involved. The referendum on the ratification of the Maastricht Treaty brought these underlying divisions to the surface and resulted in a major split between the two viewpoints.

The French Parliament is slowly developing a role in relation to EU matters. The fact that under the French constitution many EC directives can be implemented in France through governmental regulation and do not concern those areas where law must be made by Parliament (see Chapter 7) also limited the amount of public discussion. The Single Market proposals and the 1992 rhetoric were important factors in changing the situation (Maus, 1991, p. 77). Both houses of parliament set up 'delegations' for the European Communities – committees of members representing all the parliamentary parties – and in 1990 their powers were extended. They are entitled to receive information about proposals for EC legislation from the government. They may invite the French members of the European Parliament to join in their meetings. Increased provision has been made for questions and debates on EU matters. The French parliament is thus now attempting to ensure some national democratic scrutiny of EC legislation similar to that undertaken by the British, Irish and Danish parliaments. The impact is likely to be limited, but their existence is symptomatic of a growing public concern with the implications of the development of European integration. This concern is likely to be reflected in pressure from the French for national parliaments to play a greater role in the formulation and endorsement of European policy. The impact of the constraints discussed above has certainly contributed to this concern.

Some pressure groups have long been conscious of the impact of the Community, and most notably the farmers. French agriculture has benefited greatly from the CAP, and agriculture has been transformed in some areas, for example through the enormous development of the intensive production of pigs and poultry in Brittany over the last twenty years. Farmers have, however, been quick to demonstrate, sometimes quite violently, when the consequences of the CAP seemed threatening. The series of attacks that occurred during the late 1980s on lorries transporting British sheepmeat and even live animals are a particular example. British exporters complained bitterly that the French local and central authorities, whilst firmly denouncing such actions, seemed unprepared to take strong action to prevent or punish the perpetrators. From the French point of view this approach is more explicable. The authorities at local level, especially the prefect and the mayor, are accustomed to a situation where policy may be applied at local levels with a degree of discretion. Within French political culture an important and legitimate part of the role of the state is perceived as being the protection and enhancement of the economic and social interests of as wide a number of groups as possible, if necessary against the full effect of the competitive market. It may be politically more acceptable, and more conducive to social order, to allow some of the costs of the adjustment to be born by external actors – the British transporters – rather than by local groups.[4]

However, groups and interests have come slowly to realise that the state may no longer be in a position to offer the degree of shelter from the impact of the forces of European and global competition and change provided in past years. Multinational business has long been aware that effective lobbying – the timely acquisition and deployment of information and the advocacy of particular courses of action – in Brussels is an important way of influencing the shape of the

European environment. French business, and French interests in general, have not been noted for effective action in Brussels, although, for example, the farmers were represented in the European federation of farmers' organisations. One consequence has been that the implications of Brussels legislation are not always understood until the legislation is in place. The rules on the protection of migratory birds, which provoked the appearance of candidates supporting hunting and rural pursuits in local and national elections, especially in the south west, during the 1990s, can be seen as the result of a failure in lobbying by the interests affected. The role of lobbying is growing, however. An indication is that all the French regions now have offices in Brussels.

The French response to the European Community illustrates the combination of ideological rhetoric and pragmatic, almost opportunistic, management that tends to constitute the formulation of policy. It is a combination which operates within a fragmented political and administrative system, which is legally and formally rational and highly structured, but which works partly because complex and interlocking informal relationships constitute not only checks and balances, but also flexibility and opportunities. The closely interlinked Parisian elites facilitate communication. Most of the Secretaries General of the SGCI have been members of one of the *grands corps*, and although Elisabeth Guigou was not, she had served as an official in the very high status Treasury Directorate of the Ministry of Finance. Despite the effectiveness of French policy co-ordination on Community matters some, looking at the experience of decentralisation described in Chapter 6, and especially at the growing economic role of the regions, and at the arrival of the single European market, might conclude that the French state is at once too large and centralised, and too small.

12

Conclusion

The chapters of this book have described the frameworks that determine how the government acts. Politics and government play a crucial role in shaping the experiences, assumptions and expectations of those who life in a particular country, even in an age of increasing similarity, interdependence and integration between countries. They play a major part in causing any one country to be different from any other.

France's experiences and traditions of politics and government have given her a quite specific place in the political history of Western Europe. France stands firmly within the tradition of liberal democratic capitalist states. Indeed, as we saw in Chapter 1, the principles of the French Revolution, deeply anchored within French political culture, played a major part in defining, for the whole of Europe, what notions of democracy and a liberal view of human rights might mean. French state structures, developed as the nation state consolidated, incorporated within the revolutionary principles as the expression of the will not of the monarch but of the sovereign people, and refined by Napoleon, persisted alongside the revolutionary principles. The consequence was a basis for government and politics which, at least from the early modern period of history, differed quite markedly from that found in English-speaking countries.

France, then, cannot be characterised as a centrally-planned, not as a pluralistic, nor as a corporatist political system. Rather it is a mixed system in which market forces interact with civil society and with 'autonomous governmental preferences' (Safran, 1991, p. 147). These preferences are determined sometimes by partisan allegiance and ideology, sometimes by international or constitutional constraints, sometimes – and perhaps to a greater extent in France than, for example in the United Kingdom – by views about administrative rationality or desirability.

Because the state in France has played, and despite the changes considered below, continues to play a predominant role, governmental preferences have a particular force. This force derives from the tradition of state authority based upon the structures and presuppositions of Roman law, upon the emergence of the absolutist monarchy as the focus of the nation state's life, and upon the notion of political economy, which gave public power a predominant role in the control of economic activity. As Jack Hayward points out

> The normative weight of national tradition was tilted in favour of state force rather than market forces and it was taken for granted that governments could decide what they wanted to happen and were able to make it happen provided they had the will.
>
> However a governmental predilection to act as though it is sovereign is separated from its capacity to do so by the countervailing constraints that social and economic forces exert upon it (Hayward, 1986, p. xiii).

The liberal capitalist economy has its own autonomy and its own constraints. Governments develop ideas about the shape and balance of the national economy that they wish to see, but obliged, within a capitalist framework, in the end to leave not only the detail but also much of the broad strategy of economic activity to those whose livelihoods, whether as companies or as individuals, stand or fall by the economic decisions and choices that they make. Moreover, economic activity is less and less conscious of national boundaries. The state of the international economy, the movement of exchange rates, comparative levels of inflation and interest rates, the competitiveness of imports and exports and many other factors combine to affect the decisions of companies and investors in ways which governments may seek to influence but cannot control. This was clearly demonstrated in France in the early 1980s, when the effect upon the balance of payments of the expansionary social and economic policies of the Socialist government led quite rapidly to the introduction of more restrictive polices of austerity and the recognition of the importance of the market.

Although French policies in any specific context may be distinctive, international economic trends inevitably influence policy. For example, long-standing resistance to inward investment by foreign, especially Japanese, companies has slowly been lifting as such investment has grown in neighbouring countries. Equally the deregulation of the financial market of the City of London certainly influenced the subsequent deregulation of the Paris financial institutions in the late 1980s.

The study of European policy making in Chapter 11 illuminated the profound impact of the European context. The policy change of 1983, when the Socialist government chose to restrain public expenditure, force public sector companies to restructure and compete, and abandon some of its more heroic policy ambitions was a least as important a political change as any engendered by the outcome of elections during the 1980s and 1990s. It set the tone and approach for the economic policies, including the maintenance of the *franc fort*, for successive governments for over a decade.

The international context within which France is placed has, since the beginning of the 1990s, changed with bewildering rapidity, in Africa, in central and eastern Europe, and indeed within the European Union, for a united Germany constitutes a new type of neighbour in France, while the departure of Jacques Delors marked the end of an era in the EU. 'Sovereignty . . . is likely to be increasingly split between the different levels of government abroad as well as at home; it is shared between the French state (itself increasingly decentralised) the EC and the market itself. And what this complex structure guarantees is concern about and debates on French identity, on the ability of the French *nation* to define and defend its originality even when the *state* that used to be its straitjacket loses or gives up many of the powers it used to have'.[1] The governmental apparatus and political system of France will shape the responses to these new challenges. The values, priorities, concerns and traditions that have characterised French identity are carried within them as much as within the social life and civil society which they both shape and reflect.

Not only did administrative and political development differ in France, so did the shaping of the country's economic framework. French capitalism emerged in a country where the dominant, though not always the unchallenged, view was that the interest and prosperity of the country were best served by the subordination to state authority of the forces of private greed and profit-seeking that are the motor of capitalism (Hayward, 1986, pp. xiii). For complex social and economic reasons full-blooded capitalism developed relatively late in France, so that, again, assumptions, habits and practices differed from those of the English-speaking countries, even though the values and practices of capitalism are shared.

Although France is often described as having a strong and centralised state the strength of the countervailing forces means that the state is far from being overbearing or dictatorial. In the first place, as we saw in Chapters 3, 4 and 5, to take of 'the state' as if it were a single unified entity, with a clear and consistent purpose, is misleading. It is not only the case that political priorities and the sense of direction from the top can vary as governments change, but also that differences and conflicts exist throughout all levels of the state institutions. Moreover, there is considerable scope, as the discussion of local government structures in Chapter 6 showed, for varying interpretation and implementation of policies at local level.

Equally France is not a highly pluralistic political society (Safran, 1995, p. 298). Although, as Chapter 10 demonstrated, differing groups and economic interests make demands, and compete for the resources with which to satisfy them, even in recent years it has never been accepted in France that the task of the state should merely be to preside in a fairly neutral fashion over the interaction of competing demands. Presidential candidates offer, and voters expect, a vision of the future of society and, as Chapter 5 suggested, the tradition of legitimate and competent intervention by the state has enabled governments to act decisively. Finally, France is not a corporatist political system. The state is not merely an equal partner with the groups that perform the main social and economic functions in society. Nor is there general agreement as to what the nature of French society and the economy should be for the future. Even if, as was suggested in Chapter 8, some of the fiercest ideological cleavages in France are diminishing in their salience and force, and extremism is tending to decline, *alternance* in 1971, 1986, 1988 and 1993 proved that political change occurs and can make a difference.

Notes

1 France: An Introduction

1. For the patterns of housing and the distinctive ways of life developed around the textile industry in the Nord in the nineteenth century, see Hilden (1986).
2. Not women, who did not achieve political rights in France until 1944.
3. For the move away of the population, especially the male population, from church-going, see Dupeux (1976, pp. 168, 186–7).
4. For a discussion of women and the Republic see Siân Reynolds, 'Marianne's Citizens', in Reynolds (1986).

2 The Constitutional Framework

1. The concept of a loyal opposition, with recognised leaders who may even draw an official salary, and who take their places on state occasions as part of the formal constitutional structure, remains unknown in France.
2. The major biography has been translated into English: Lacouture (1990, 1991). For a brief, vivid pen portrait, see Wright (1989).
3. A resolution which would start the amendment procedure was approved by 408 votes to 165 in May 1958.
4. Réné Rémond, 'La création du système', in Duhamel and Parodi (1985).
5. Debré began his career with degrees in law and political science, and in 1935 joined the elite civil service *corps* of the Council of State, the main governmental legal advisory body. He distinguished himself in the Resistance, and in 1945 was brought back from a post as governmental representative in the provinces to undertake a major programme of administrative reform. A committed Gaullist, he became a senator and was a fierce critic of the political and constitutional system of the Fourth Republic.
6. They were the Socialist Guy Mollet, the Christian Democrat Pierre Pflimlin, Felix Houphouët-Boigny representing the parties of the French territories in Africa, and Louis Jacquinot, an independent. Mollet had been prime minister from January 1956 to May 1957 and Pflimlin had briefly held that office during the closing days of the Fourth Republic, from 13 to 28 May 1958.

7. George Ross, 'Adieu vieilles idées: the middle strata and the decline of Resistance–Liberation Left discourse in France', in Howorth and Ross (1986, pp. 57–83).
8. See Dreyfus and D'Arcy (1993, p. 158) on freedom of association.
9. Abraham Lincoln at the dedication of the National Cemetery at Gettysburg, 19 November 1863.
10. A similar provision appears in the Basic Law of (formerly West) Germany of 1949.
11. The procedure – provided for by Article 85 – was used once, in 1960.
12. One of the ministers at the time, Pierre Sudreau, resigned because in his view the government was acting unconstitutionally.
13. Quermonne (1980, p. 65), quoting Noel (1976, p. 223).
14. See Debré's speech to the Conseil d'Etat on 27 August 1958, printed in Quermonne (1980, p. 621).
15. Williams (1972, p. 438). See ch. 30 for a brilliant discussion of the IV Republican 'system' against which the framers of the V Republic were reacting.
16. *France Observateur* (7 August 1958), quoted in Claude Emeri, 'Les déconvenues de la doctrine', in Duhamel and Parodi (1985, p. 80).
17. Candidates for election must nowadays, since the Organic Law of 1976, be nominated by 500 sponsors, who must be elected mayors of communes, elected members of the council of a *département*, members of the Economic and Social Council, or members of Parliament. They must come from at least thirty different *départements* or overseas territories.
18. Odile Rudelle, 'Le général de Gaulle et l'élection directe du président de la République', in Duhamel and Parodi (1985, p. 117).
19. See François Goguel, 'Introduction', in Duhamel and Parodi (1985, p. 130).
20. A list of all the members of the Council from 1959 to 1992, with brief biographical details is given in Avril and Gicquel (1992, pp. 148–52).
21. Figures from Loic Philip, 'Bilan et effets de la Saisine du Conseil Constitutionell', in Duhamel and Parodi (1985).
22. Of the 45 referrals by members of Parliament between 1974 and 1981 all but one arose from members of the opposition. The exception was the referral of the law on abortion in 1975. In 1976 the finance bill was referred simultaneously by the opposition, the majority and the prime minister. See Avril and Gicquel (1992, p. 63).

3 The Presidency

1. Quoted in *The Guardian Weekend*, 6 May 1995, p. 13.
2. President Mitterrand, speech of 13 June 1990, quoted in Maus (1991, p. 40).
3. Quoted in Quermonne (1980, p. 176).
4. Quermonne (1980, p. 195) gives examples of a number of important issues on which de Gaulle and Giscard d'Estaing sought the views of each minister in turn. See also Giroud (1977, pp. 26–43). Schifres and Sarazin (1985, p. 194) say that President Mitterrand never did this.

5. The photograph published as Plate 33 in Horne (1977) shows young servicemen listening to the radio broadcast.
6. De Gaulle made eight such broadcasts in 1960 and six in 1961 as a result of the turbulence in Algeria. In 1962, which saw not only Algerian independence but also the referendum on the constitution, he made eleven, whilst the student disturbances of 1968 produced seven broadcasts. See André Passeron (*Le Monde*, 12 septembre 1991).
7. The President never appears before Parliament and there is no regular or formal equivalent of the Queen's speech or the State of the Union address. Compared with the United Kingdom, Parliament in France is much less able to insist on being told about important policy initiatives ahead of the press or on statements about major events being made to them. Consequently news of policy developments is often conveyed initally through the media.
8. M. Harrison, 'The President, Cultural Politics and Media Policy', in Hayward (1993).
9. The phrase was used by Massot (1987) as a chapter heading. See Anne Stevens, 'The Presidential Staff', in Hayward (1993).
10. In many ways Foccart and his secretariat operated as if they were an autonomous ministry, rather than a branch of an exective office. In 1974 the separate status of the secretariat was abolished, although African affairs have always had a somewhat individual position within the Elysée.
11. Jolyon Howorth, 'The President's Special Role in Foreign and Defence Policy', in Hayward (1993). See also Howorth (1991, pp. 3–16).
12. Not to be confused with the Secretary General of the Government, a senior official based in the Prime Minister's department with responsibilities not dissimilar from those of the British Cabinet Secretary.
13. Giesbert (1990, p.139). See also Favier and Martin-Roland (1990, p. 433).
14. Etienne Burin des Roziers in Pilleul (1979, p. 225). Interviews with former members of President Giscard's staff and with former ministerial *cabinet* members (Paris, September 1991).
15. The incumbents have all been male, although there has been a female deputy secretary-general.
16. Portelli (1987, pp. 114–15) and L. Hamon, 'Du Référendum à la Démocratie Continue', in Duhamel and Parodi (1985, pp. 504–21).
17. Quoted in Quermonne (1980, p. 181).

4 The Governmental Machine

1. Quoted in Quermonne (1980, p. 637).
2. In the 1988 Rocard government the Minister for the Civil Service, Michel Durafour, was a full cabinet minister, a status that has continued, reflecting the priority given to administrative reform and modernisation and also, under Balladur and Juppé, to reducing public spending.

3. Jean Massot, 'Le Président de la République et le Premier Ministre', in Chagnollaud (1991, p. 26).
4. Volkmar Lauber, 'Economic Policy', in McCarthy (1987).
5. In Jacques Chirac's 1986 government there were 43 ministers, in May 1988 Michel Rocard's government contained 49, and in Edith Cresson's 1991 government there were 45 (not including the prime minister).
6. Thus in 1991 such a title was held by Jean-Pierre Soisson, the leading non-Socialist minister in the Council of Ministers, no doubt to mark the government's desire to extend its support towards the political centre that Soisson represented. Alain Juppé did not use the title in either of his 1995 governments.
7. This pattern again contrasts with that of the United Kingdom. The number of ministers and junior ministers in the United Kingdom, at around 100, is approximately twice that in France. Partly, but not entirely, because of the need to have a spokesman in the House of Lords – French ministers can freely attend and speak, but not vote, in both houses of Parliament – most UK Cabinet ministers have a team of at least three or four junior ministers attached to them.
8. It is hard to believe that the existence of the President's mistress (housed for some of the time in official accommodation) and a daughter would have gone unremarked, or at least unreported, through two election campaigns and some thirteen years in office in most western countries.
9. In Hayward 1993 p. 216
10. Figures from Fournier (1987, p. 109).
11. Pascal Lamy, head of the cabinet of Jacques Delors during his time as President of the Commission of the European Communities, observed the difficulties of his compatriots in this respect: interview in *Esprit*, no. 10 October 1991, p. 70 cited in Pierre Muller, 'Le modèle français de l'administration face à la constitution d'un espace public européen' (Muller, 1992, p. 23).

5 The Administrative System in France

1. Danièle Lochak 'Les hauts fonctionnaires et l'alternance: quelle politisation?' in Muller (1992, p. 47).
2. Stephen E. Bornstein, 'The Politics of Scandal', in Hall, Hayward and Machin (1994, p. 270).
3. All the *médiateurs* up to the present have been male.
4. Jack Hayward, 'Mobilising Private Interests in the Service of French Policy Style?', in Richardson (1982).
5. Margaret Sharp and Peter Holmes 'The State: Captor or Captive?', in Sharp and Holmes (1989, p. 10).
6. Kevin Morgan, 'Telecom Strategies in Britain and France: The Scope and Limits of Neo-liberalism and Dirigisme', in Sharp and Holmes (1989, p. 54).
7. *L'Express*, 8–14 December 1989.

6 Local Government

1. These consortia take the form of intercommunal agreements. There are also 153 (1985) *districts* and nine (1985) *communautés urbaines*, essentially devised for large urban areas where the multiplicity of *communes* posed particular difficulties, which provided for joint operation of a number of services, for example the fire service, infrastructure development and town planning. *Communautés urbaines* were imposed upon Bordeaux, Lille, Lyons and Strasbourg by law in 1966.
2. There are also four overseas *départements*: Guadeloupe, Martinique and French Guyana in the Caribbean, and Réunion in the Indian Ocean.
3. Sonia Mazey, 'Decentralisation: *La Grande Affaire du Septennat*', in Mazey and Newman (1987, p. 123), see also Schmidt (1991, pp. 365–7).
4. Howard Machin, 'The Traditional Structures of Local Government in France', in Lagroye and Wright (1979).
5. Cathérine Grémion, 'Que reste-t-il des administrations déconcentrées?', in Muller (1992, p. 189).

7 Parliament

1. This penalty was quite widely used immediately after the war, as part of the punishment of those who had collaborated with the enemy occupation.
2. During the three weeks of the official campaign candidates may only display posters – of a uniform and rather small size – on the official noticeboards provided.
3. 68 out of 491 in 1978, 156 out of 491 in 1981 and 120 out of 577 in 1988. None in 1986 because of the use of proportional representation: Dreyfus and D'Arcy (1993, p. 83).
4. The system used was the 'highest average' system, with the elimination of lists achieving less than 5 per cent of the vote.
5. The number has increased by two in each of the three renewals of 1983, 1986 and 1989, the extra members being additional representatives of French citizens living abroad. As in the National Assembly, there is a replacement system rather than by-elections.
6. 28 out of 491 in 1981, 33 out of 577 in 1986, 33 out of 577 in 1988 and 32 out of 577 in 1993.
7. This concern is understandable. Although the holder of multiple offices was entitled to draw only half pay for some of them, Schmidt reports that in 1985 Jean Lecanuet was drawing some 61 500 francs (over £6000) a month from the combined tasks of member of the European Parliament, senator, regional councillor, *président* of the *conseil général* of the Seine Maritime and mayor of Rouen. The average basic salary of a senator or *député* was then about 33 000 frances a month: Schmidt (1991, p. 147).
8. Giscard d'Estaing was the second *député* to give up his seat for this reason. Alain Carignon, mayor of Grenoble and a former Gaullist

minister had resigned his seat in 1988 to concentrate on the affairs of Grenoble. Two other *députés* gave up their European Parliament seats at the same time.

9. For example, by Ashford (1982).
10. I am much indebted to Maus, 'Parliament in the Fifth Republic', in Godt (1989) for the ideas and information in this section.
11. The procedure may be used more than once during the passage of a bill. Thus the budget for 1990 required the use of the procedure five separate times in the autumn of 1989. Motions of censure were tabled and voted on on the first two occasions.
12. This disqualification does not apply in the cases where a motion of censure is proposed when the government has used the provision of the constitution's Article 49, paragraph 3 to make a law an issue of confidence.
13. The information in this paragraph is taken from Le Men (1984).
14. Personal communication.
15. I am much indebted to Christian Lequesne (1993, ch. 6) for the information and ideas in this section.

8 The Nature of Party Politics in France

1. See Duverger (1964, Book 2, ch. 1) for a classic statement of the contrasts.
2. Byron Criddle, 'France: Parties in a Presidential System', in Ware (1987, p. 137–8).
3. John Gaffney, 'The Emergence of a Presidential Party: The Socialist Party', in Cole (1990, p. 63).
4. Robert Poujade, quoted in Charlot (1971, p. 67).
5. Translated, by Monica Charlot and Marianne Neighbour, in Charlot (1970, p. 168).
6. Andrew Knapp, 'Un parti comme les autres: Jacques Chirac and the Rally for the Republic', in Cole (1990, p. 140).
7. This phrase, translated from Pascal Perrineau, is quoted by Martin Schain in 'Toward a Centrist Democracy? The Fate of the French Right', in Hollifield and Ross (1991, p. 79).
8. Alistair Cole, 'The Union for French Democracy', in Cole (1990, p. 120), following Réné Rémond's classic formulation in Rémond (1982).
9. See Yves Mény, 'The Reconstruction and Deconstruction of the French Party System', in Flynn (1995) and Knapp (1994) for the argument that in this respect the Gaullist Party is now no different from most of the others.
10. Mény 'Reconstruction', p. 191.
11. The member then elected subsequently left the party, but another member of the party was returned to Parliament in one of France's rare parliamentary by-elections, at Dreux in December 1989.
12. Mény 'Reconstruction', pp. 182–7.
13. Mény 'Reconstruction', p. 184.

9 Parties, Voters and Elections

1. Frank L. Wilson, 'The Evolution of the Party System', in Godt (1989, p. 58).
2. Howard Machin, 'Changing Patterns of Party Competitition', in Hall, Hayward and Machin (1994, p. 41).
3. Wilson, 'The Evolution of the Party System', p. 67.
4. Bell and Criddle (1988, p. 213, 215–16) for most of these details.
5. John Gaffney, 'The Emergence of a Presidential Party: The Socialist Party', in Cole (1990, p. 62).
6. For this paragraph, see Bell and Criddle (1988, pp. 197–209).
7. Thus in 1967 only 8 per cent of regular churchgoers voted Socialist, whilst in 1988 16 per cent did so. Since the proportion of the electorate who were regular churchgoers had in this period declined from 25 to 14 per cent the gain was not large in absolute terms: Frears (1991, p. 81).
8. Machin, 'Changing Patterns', p. 51.
9. Machin, 'Changing Patterns', p. 51.
10. Gaffney, 'The Emergence of a Presidential Party', p. 66.
11. This section owes much to the unpublished paper presented to the Political Studies Association Conference of 1995 by David Bell and Byron Criddle on 'The "crisis" of social democracy, the French case' and to Peter Holmes 'France: Economy', in *Europa Yearbook Western Europe* (1993).
12. Gérard Grunberg, 'Que reste-t-il du parti d'Epinay?', in Habert *et al.* (1993, p. 214)
13. Daniel Boy, 'Ecologistes; Retour sur terre', in Habert *et al.* (1993, p. 179)
14. These paragraphs are largely drawn from Frears (1991, ch. 9), Hainsworth, 'Breaking the Mould', Hainsworth, 'France', in Lodge (1990).
15. H. Machin and A. Guyomarch, '1990–1994', in Hall, Hayward and Machin (1994, p. 304).
16. Pascal Perrineau, 'Le Front National: Le force solitaire', in Habert *et al.* (1993, p. 144).
17. Perrineau, 'Le Front National' p. 152.
18. See *Le Monde* 14 September 1995, for the refusal of consultancy and accountancy firms in France to accept the newly elected FN town councils as clients, because it would put them beyond the pale in the eyes of all their other clients.

10 The State and Civil Society: Pressure and Interest Groups

1. Peter Hall, 'Pluralism and Pressure Politics', in Hall, Hayward and Machin (1994, p. 79).
2. Mouriaux (1994, p. 108) says that in 1993 about 8 per cent of the workforce was unionised. In 1989 he was quoted (Headlam, 1989, p. 32) as estimating 9 to 11 per cent unionisation.
3. Reported in Headlam (1989, p. 33).

4. A minority section of the CFTC retained its church links, and the old name, but remained a very small group.
5. Suzanne Berger, 'The Socialists and the *Patronat*: the dilemmas of coexistence in a mixed economy', in Machin and Wright (1985, pp. 231–2).
6. Siân Reynolds, 'The French Ministry of Women's Rights 1981–86: Modernisation or Marginalisation?', in Gaffney (1988, pp. 149–69); see also Reynolds (1988).
7. Wilson (1987, p. 242) likens it to clientilism as found in Italy.
8. The phrase is from Bauer and Cohen (1981).
9. See Wilson (1987, pp. 244ff) for a good explanation of why not.
10. For an extensive discussion of the resources available to groups which may determine the role they can play, see Wright (1989, pp. 279–89).
11. Reynolds, 'The French Ministry of Women's Rights', p. 150.
12. Reynolds, 'The French Ministry of Women's Rights', p. 159.
13. Reynolds, 'The French Ministry of Women's Rights', p. 159.
14. Howard Machin, 'Changing Patterns of Party Composition', in Hall, Hayward and Machin (1994, p. 49).
15. John Eisenhammer, 'Longwy and Bagnoli: A Comparative Study of the Trade Union Response to the Steel Crisis in France and Italy', in Mény and Wright (1987, p. 609).
16. Howard Machin, 'Changing Patterns', pp. 49–50.

11 France and Europe: Policy Making and Politics

1. Philippe Moreau Defarges, 'France and Europe', in Godt (1989, p. 227).
2. Stanley Hoffman, 'Mitterrand's Foreign Policy of Gaullism by any other name', in Ross, Hoffman and Malzacher (1987, p. 301).
3. Jack Hayward, 'Ideological Change: The Exhaustion of the Revolutionary Impetus', in Hall, Hayward and Machin (1994, p. 28).
4. This analysis echoes some of the themes suggested by Dupuy and Thoenig (1985).

12 Conclusion

1. Stanley Hoffmann, 'Thoughts on Sovereignty and French Politics', in Flynn (1995, p. 258)

Guide to Further Reading

General

Two short books in French – Charlot (1994) and Mény (1993) – condense within them the extensive knowledge and considerable insights of two of the major figures in contemporary French political science and cover the themes of many of the chapters of this book. Both assume some background familiarity with the French situation. So do Wright (1989), which is comprehensive, lively to the point of being provocative, and very clear, and Hollifield and Ross (1991) which deals with a range of political and policy themes. Morris (1994) provides a more basic but stimulating introduction in English. Hall, Hayward and Machin (1994) and Flynn (1995), by providing up to date analysis of current developments, would enable readers to build upon the foundations which this study seeks to lay. *Pouvoirs* and *Modern and Contemporary France* are amongst the most useful periodicals.

1 France: An Introduction

Pinchemel (1987) and the two volumes of Braudel (1989, 1990) provide comprehensive and wide ranging surveys of many aspects of French physical, social, economic and historical structures. Price (1993) is a great deal more concise. Thomson (1969) still provides an interesting political viewpoint on the Third Republic. Agulhon (1993), McMillan (1992) and Larkin (1988) are invaluable for the historical background of the twentieth century, and the latter two both have useful indications of further reading. For more detailed history, the eighteen volumes of the *Nouvelle Histoire de la France Contemporaine*, published by Seuil and becoming available in English translation through the Cambridge University Press (for example Rioux 1987) are an indispensable starting-point. Hazareesingh (1994) provides a detailed analysis of the intellectual and political traditions discussed in this chapter. On the Vichy period Paxton (1972) is the classic and still outstanding study and no book on the Fourth Republic has surpassed, or even equalled Williams (1972). Flockton and Kofman (1989) in English and Parodi (1981) in French are clear introductions to the post war economy of France. Vesperini (1993) is up-to-date and comprehensive, but less accessible to the non-economist. Dupeux (1976) covers a very broad span of social development. Bell *et al.* (1990) is an essential work of reference, for it provides a biographical sketch of many of the political leaders mentioned in this book. The regularly updated editions of *L'Etat de la France* (Paris: La Découverte) provide a well documented overview of many political, policy, social and economic issues.

2 The Constitutional Framework

The text of the constitution as amended to the beginning of 1995 is published in a bilingual edition in French and English by the Ministère des affaires étrangères. Maus (1995) provides an extensive array of supporting texts and statistics. Andrews and Hoffman (1981) include a useful discussion of the constitution which is comprehensively considered in Duhamel and Parodi (1985). Documentation Française (1991) is concise. Dreyfus and D'Arcy (1993) and Quermonne and Chagnollaud (1996) provide clear descriptions of its institutional impact. Wahl (1959) and Debré in Andrews and Hoffman (1974) illuminate its origins. Barillon (1986) is a useful work of reference. Constitutional developments are chronicled each quarter in *Pouvoirs* and the *Revue française de droit constitutionnel*.

3 The Presidency

The institution of the presidency is comprehensively covered by Massot (1987). See also *Pouvoirs*, 41 (1987). The reading suggested for Chapter 2 also covers the role of the President. Hayward (1993) and Wahl and Quermonne (1995) are very comprehensive studies of many aspects of the presidency. Insights into the working of the Elysée are given in both these works and in Schifres and Sarazin (1985). On the presidents themselves, see Shennan (1993), Lacouture (1990, 1991), Roussel (1994), Giesbert (1990), the two volumes of Favier and Martin-Roland (1990, 1991), Northcutt (1993) and Cole (1994). On the Constitutional Council, see Avril and Gicquel (1993) and Stone (1992) and, on the Conseil d'Etat as well, *Conseil Constitutionnel et Conseil d'Etat* (1988).

4 The Governmental Machine

On the earlier years of the Fifth Republic see Anderson (1970), Andrews (1982) and Institut Charles de Gaulle (1990). Claisse (1972), Antoni and Antoni (1976), Long (1981) Massot (1979) and Fournier (1987) are all basic sources. Wright (1989), Godt (1989) and Chagnollaud (1991) include discussions of the themes evoked in this chapter. On *cohabitation* see Tuppen (1991) and Cohendet (1993).

5 The Administrative System in France

Suleiman (1974, 1978) still provides the major outline of political–administrative relationships available in English. In French see Dupuy and Thoenig (1985) and Muller (1992). De Baecque and Quermonne (1981) is a mine of information and reflects the concerns of the 1970s. On the effect of *alternance*, see Cerny and Schain (1985) and Lochak and Chevallier(1986).

6 Local Government

There are two valuable studies of the local government system before the 1983 decentralisation laws: Lagroye and Wright (1979) and Machin (1977). Grémion (1976) provides a masterly and very influential study of local–central relations. Ashford (1982) makes a stimulating comparative argument, while Schmidt (1990) sets a thorough study of the decentralisation reforms in a clear historical context. Ten years of regionalisation are comprehensively discussed in Loughlin and Mazey (1995). In French, Rémond and Blanc (1989) is the standard comprehensive textbook, whilst Rondin (1985) takes a refreshingly sceptical view. On local politicians, see Garraud (1989).

7 Parliament

The chapter on parliament in Wright (1989) is a concise and very comprehensive discussion. On electoral systems and elections, Cole and Campbell (1989) is the standard work, usefully complemented by Frears (1991). On the early years of the Fifth Republic, see Williams (1968) and, for a more recent overview, Kimmel (1991) and Camby and Servent (1994). On the Senate, see Cluzel (1990).

8 The Nature of Party Politics in France

and

9 Parties, Voters and Elections

The political development of the Fifth Republic is well described in most of the general works on French politics. For a lively survey of the political history of the Fifth Republic, see Portelli (1990). On the party system, see especially Hall, Hayward and Machin (1994) and Hollifield and Ross (1991) and also Wright (1989) Machin (1989) and Wilson in Godt (1989). Ysmal (1989, 1990) are indispensable general works and Cole (1990) contains extensive bibliographies. Charlot (1970) and Duhamel (1980) are classic studies of Gaullism and the Left, respectively, in the first decade or two of the Fifth Republic. On the Right in historical context, see Rémond (1982), on the Gaullists Knapp (1994), on the Socialists Bell and Criddle (1988) and Bergonioux and Grunberg (1992), on the Communists the fascinating insider study by Jenson and Ross (1985) and Bell and Criddle (1994). On the National Front, see Mayer and Perrineau (1989), Birenbaum (1992) and Marcus (1995) and on the ecologists, see Sainteny (1991). Laughland (1994) and Mény (1992) are forceful denunciations of the corruption of the system.

10 The State and Civil Society: Pressure and Interest Groups

Wilson (1987) is a comprehensive study. On the trade unions, see Mouriaux and Bibès (1990), Noblecourt (1990) and Mouriaux (1994). Weber (1986) is a study of the CNPF and Keeler (1987) of the farmers. Mendras with Cole (1991) ranges widely over the changing aspects of civil society in France. On the events of 1968, see Hanley and Kerr (1989). On the women's movement, see Jenson and Sineau (1995).

11 France and Europe: Policy Making and Politics

There is no general study of this topic. Christian Lequesne's major study (1993) considers the institutional framework in illuminating detail. Moreau Desfarges' chapter in Godt (1989) treats it broadly and the underlying attitudes are analysed in Cerny (1980) and in Lacouture (1991). Dyson (1994) covers the key topic of economic and monetary relations. The chapters on France in Lodge (1986, 1990) are revealing. See also *Pouvoirs*, 48 (1989).

Bibliography

Agulhon, Maurice (1993) *The French Republic 1879–1992* (Oxford and Cambridge, Mass.: Blackwell).

Anderson, Malcolm (1970) *Government in France* (Oxford: Pergamon).

Anderson, R. D. (1977) *France 1870–1914* (London: Routledge & Kegan Paul); (1984) (New York: Routledge, Chapman & Hall).

Andrews, William (1982) *Presidential Government in Gaullist France* (Albany, NY: State University of New York Press).

Andrews, William and Stanley Hoffman (1981) *The Fifth Republic at Twenty* (Albany NY: State University of New York Press).

Antoni, Jean-Dominique and Pascale Antoni (1976) *Les Ministres de la Ve République* (Paris: Presses Universitaires de France).

Ardagh, John (1988) *France Today* (Harmondsworth: Penguin and New York: Penguin USA).

Ashford, Douglas (1982) *French Pragmatism and British Dogmatism* (London: Allen & Unwin and New York: HarperCollins).

Avril, Pierre and Jean Gicquel (1993) *Le Conseil Constitutionel*, 2nd edn (Paris: Montchrestien).

Barillon, R. (ed.) (1986) *Dictionnaire de la Constitution*, 4th edn (Paris: Cujas).

Bartolini, Stefano (1984) 'Institutional Constraints and Party Competition in the French Party System', *West European Politics*, 6(3) (October).

Bauer, Michel and Elie Cohen (1981) *Qui Governe le Groupes Industriels?* (Paris: Seuil).

Bell, D. S. and Byron Criddle (1988) *The French Socialist Party: The Emergence of a Party of Government*, 2nd edn (Oxford and New York: Clarendon Press).

Bell, D. S., Douglas Johnson and Peter Morris (eds) (1990) *Biographical Dictionary of French Political Leaders since 1870* (London and New York: Harvester Wheatsheaf).

Bell, David S. and Byron Criddle (1994) *The French Communist Party in the Fifth Republic* (Oxford: The Clarendon Press).

Bénéton, P. and J. Touchard (1970) 'Les interprétations de la crise de mai–juin 1968', *Revue Française de Science Politique*, XX(3) (June).

Bergonioux, Alain and Gérard Grunberg (1992) *Le Long Remords du Pouvoir: Le Parti Socialiste Français 1905–1992* (Paris: Fayard).

Birenbaum, Guy (1992) *Le Front National en Politique* (Paris: Balland).

Bodiguel, Jean-Luc and Jean-Louis Quermonne (1983) *La Haute Fonction Publique* (Paris: Presses Universitaires de France).

Bornstein, Stephen (1994) 'The Politics of Scandal', in Hall, Hayward and Machin (1994).

Braudel, Fernand (1989) *The Identity of France: Vol. 1, History and Environment* (London: Fontana and New York: HarperCollins).

Braudel, Fernand (1990) *The Identity of France; Vol. 2, People and Production* (London: Fontana and New York: HarperCollins).

Bridgford, J. (1988) 'Back from the Brink: the French Communist Party and the 1988 Elections', *Modern and Contemporary France*, 35 (October).

Brown, L. and J. F. Garner (1983) *French Administrative Law*, 3rd edn (London: Butterworth).

Buffotot, Patrice (1993) 'Le Référendum sur l'union Européenne', *Modern and Contemporary France*, NS1 (3).

Buffotot, Patrick and David Hanley (1996) 'Chronique d'une victoire annoncée: les élections présidentielles de 1995', *Modern and Contemporary France*, NS4 (1).

Camby, Jean-Pierre and P. Servent (1994) *Le Travail Parlementaire sous la Ve République* (Paris: Montchrestien).

Cawson, Alan, Peter Holmes, Kevin Morgan, Anne Stevens and Douglas Webber (1990) *Hostile Brothers: Competition and Closure in the European Electronics Industry* (Oxford and New York: Oxford University Press).

Central Statistical Office (1990) *Economic Trends* (London: Her Majesty's Stationery Office).

Cerny, Philip (1980) *The Politics of Grandeur; Ideological Aspects of de Gaulle's Foreign Policy* (Cambridge and New York: Cambridge University Press).

Cerny, Philip and Martin Schain (1985) *Socialism, the State and Public Policy in France* (London: Pinter and New York: Routledge, Chapman & Hall).

Chafer, Tony (1988) 'Business Education in France: an expanding sector', *Modern and Contemporary France*, 34 (July).

Chagnollaud, Dominique (ed.) (1991) *Bilan Politique de la France 1991* (Paris: Hachette).

Chapsal, Jacques and Alain Lancelot (1979) *La Vie Politique en France depuis 1940* (Paris: Presses Universitaires de France) 5th edn.

Charlot, Jean (1970) *The Gaullist Phenomenon* (London: Allen & Unwin).

Charlot, Jean (1989) 'Les Mutations du Système des Partis Français', *Pouvoirs*, 49.

Charlot, Jean (1994) *La politique en France* (Paris: Le Livre de Poche).

Chirac, Jacques (1995) *La France pour tous* (Paris, election brochure).

Claisse, A. (1972) *Le Premier Ministre de la Ve République* (Paris: LGDJ).

Clark, David A. (1984) 'The Ombudsman in Britain and France: a comparative evaluation', *West European Politics*, 7(3) (October).

Cluzel, J. (1990) *Le Sénat dans la Société Française* (Paris: Economica).

Cohendet, Anne-Marie (1993) *La Cohabitation* (Paris: Presses Universitaires de France).

Cole, Alistair (1989) 'The French Municipal Elections on 12 and 17 March 1989', *Modern and Contemporary France*, 39 (October).

Cole, Alistair (1994) *François Mitterrand: A Study in Political Leadership* (London: Routledge).

Cole, Alistair (1995) 'La France pour tous? – The French Presidential Elections of 23 April and 7 May 1995', *Government and Opposition*.

Cole, Alistair (ed.) (1990) *French Political Parties in Transition* (Aldershot and Brookfield, Vermont: Dartmouth).

Cole, Alistair and Peter Campbell (1989) *French Electoral Systems and Elections Since 1789* (Aldershot: Gower).

Collard, Sue (1992) 'Mission impossible: les chantiers du Président', *French Cultural Studies*, ii, pp. 97–132.

Colombani, J. M. and J.-Y. Lhomeau (1986) *Le Marriage Blanc* (Paris: Grasset).

Conseil Constitutionnel et Conseil d'Etat (1988) (Paris: LGDJ Montchrestien).

De Baecque, François and Jean-Louis Quermonne (eds) (1981) *Administration et Politique sous la Cinquième République* (Paris: Presses de la Fondation National des Sciences Politiques).

De Gaulle, Charles (1959) *Mémoires de Guerre: le salut* (Paris: Plon).

De Singly, F. and C. Thélot (1988) *Gens du Privé, Gens du Public* (Paris: Bordas).

Debbasch, Charles (1982) *L'Elysée Dévoilé* (Paris: Albin Michel).

Debbasch, Charles *et al.* (1985) *La Ve République*, 2nd edn (Paris: Economica).

Documentation Française (1991) *Institutions et Vie Politique: Les Notices* (Paris: Documentation Française).

Dreyfus, Françoise and François D'Arcy (1993) *Les Institutions Politiques et Administratives de la France*, 4th edn (Paris: Economica).

Duchen, Claire (1986) *Feminism in France From May '68 to Mitterrand* (London: Routledge & Kegan Paul).

Duhamel, Olivier (1980) *La Gauche et la Cinquième République* (Paris: Presses Universitaires de France)

Duhamel, Olivier and Jean-Luc Parodi (eds) (1985) *La Constitution de la Cinquième République* (Paris: Presses de la Fondation Nationale des Sciences Politiques).

Dulong, Claude (1975) *La Vie Quotidienne à L'Elysée au temps de Charles de Gaulle* (Paris: Hachette).

Dupeux, Georges (1976) *French Society 1789–1970* (London: Methuen and New York: Routledge, Chapman and Hall).

Dupuy, François and Jean-Claude Thoenig (1985) *L'Administration en Miettes* (Paris: Fayard).

Duverger, Maurice (1964) *Political Parties* (London: Methuen and New York: Routledge, Chapman & Hall).

Duverger, Maurice (1987) *La Cohabitation des Français* (Paris: Presses Universitaires de France).

Dyson, Kenneth (1994) *Elusive Union: The Process of Economic and Monetary Union in Europe* (London and New York: Longman).

Elgie, Robert (1991) 'La Méthode Rocard Existe-t-elle?', *Modern and Contemporary France*, 44 (January).

Elgie, Robert (1993) *The Role of the Prime Minister in France 1981–1991* (London: Macmillan and New York: St Martin's Press).

Elgie, Robert and Howard Machin (1991) 'France: The Limits to Prime Ministerial Government in a Semi-presidential System', *West European Politics*, 14(2) (April).

Elgie, Robert and Moshe Maor (1992) 'Accounting for the Survival of Minority Governments: An Examination of the French Case', *West European Politics*, 14 (4).

Favier, Pierre and Michel Martin-Roland (1990) *La Décennie Mitterrand: Tome 1, Les Ruptures* (Paris: Seuil).

Favier, Pierre and Michel Martin-Roland (1991) *La Décennie Mitterrand: Tome 2, Les Epreuves* (Paris: Seuil).

Favoreu, Louis and Löic Philip (1988) *Le Conseil Constitutionnel, principes directeurs* (Paris: Editions STH).

Firth, Kevin (1994) 'Towards Diversity – Developments in French Secondary Education since 1980', *Modern and Contemporary France*, NS2 (4).

Flockton, Christopher and Eleonore Kofman (1989) *France* (London: Paul Chapman Publishing and New York: Taylor & Francis).

Flynn, Gregory (ed.) (1995) *Remaking the Hexagon: The New France in the New Europe* (Boulder, Colorado and Oxford: Westview Press).

Fourastié, Jean (1979) *Les Trentes Glorieuses* (Paris: Fayard).

Fournier, Jacques (1987) *Le Travail Gouvernmentale* (Paris: Presses de la Fondation Nationale des Sciences Politiques).

Frears, John (1990) 'The French Parliament: Loyal Workhorse, Poor Watchdog', *West European Politics*, 13(2) (July).

Frears, John (1991) *Parties and Voters in France* (London: Hurst and New York: St Martin's Press).

Gaffney, John (ed.) (1988) *France and Modernisation* (Aldershot: Avebury and Brookfield, Vermont: Ashgate).

Gallie, Duncan (1983) *Social Inequality and Class Radicalism in France and Britain* (Cambridge and New York: Cambridge University Press).

Garraud, Philippe (1989) *Profession: Homme Politique* (Paris: l'Harmattan).

Gaxie, Daniel (1986) 'Le Ministre', *Pouvoirs*, 36.

Genevois, Bruno (1989) 'L'Influence du Conseil Constitutionnel', *Pouvoirs*, 49.

Giesbert, F. O. (1990) *Le President* (Paris: Seuil).

Giroud, Françoise (1977) *La Comédie du Pouvoir* (Paris: Fayard).

Giscard d'Estaing, Valéry (1976) *Démocratie Française* (Paris: Fayard).

Giscard d'Estaing, Valéry (1988, 1991) *Le Pouvoir et la Vie*, 2 vols (Paris: Cie 12).

Godt, Paul (ed.) (1989) *Policy Making in France* (London: Pinter and New York: Columbia University Press).

Grémion, Pierre (1976) *Le Pouvoir Périphérique* (Paris: Seuil).

Habert, Philippe, Pascal Perrineau and Colette Ysmal (1993) *Le Vote Sanction: les élections législatives des 21 et 28 mars 1993* (Paris: Département des études politiques du Figaro & Presses de la Fondation Nationale des Sciences Politiques).

Hague, Rod and Martin Harrop (1982) *Comparative Government: An Introduction* (London: Macmillan and Atlantic Highlands N.J.: Humanities Press).

Hall, Peter, Jack Hayward and Howard Machin (1994) *Developments in French Politics*, 2nd edn (London: Macmillan and New York: St Martin's Press).

Hanley, D. (1989) 'Waiting for the President: the political year in retrospect, September 1987 to August 1988', *Contemporary France*, Vol. 3 (London: Pinter).

Hanley, D. L. and A. P. Kerr (1989) *May '68: Coming of Age* (London: Macmillan and New York: International Specialised Book Services).

Hanley, David (1993) 'Socialism Routed? The French legislative elections of 1993', *Modern and Contemporary France*, NS1 (4).

Hargreaves, Alec (1988) 'Le Pen's Paradoxes', *Modern and Contemporary France*, 35 (October).

Hayward, J. (1978) 'Dissentient France: The Counter Political Culture', *West European Politics*, 1(3) (October).

Hayward, J. (1986) *The State and the Market Economy* (Brighton: Harvester Wheatsheaf and New York: New York University Press).

Hayward, Jack (1993) *De Gaulle to Mitterrand: Presidential Power in France* (London: Hurst and Company).

Hazareesingh, Sudhir (1994) *Political Traditions in Modern France* (Oxford and New York: Oxford University Press).

Headlam, Allan (1989) 'Le Paysage Industriel Français: Les syndicats et l'emploi', *Modern and Contemporary France*, 37 (April).

Hilden, Patricia (1986) *Working Women and Socialist Politics in France 1880–1914* (Oxford and New York: Clarendon Press).

Hollifield, James and George Ross (eds) (1991) *Searching for the New France* (New York and London: Routledge).

Holmes, Peter and Anne Stevens (1986) *The Framework of Government–Industry Relations and Industrial Policy Making in France*, Working Paper Series on Government–Industry Relations, University of Sussex.

Hooghe, Liesbet and Michael Keating (1994) 'The Politics of European Union Regional Policy', *Journal of European Public Policy*, 1 (3).

Horne, Alistair (1979) *A Savage War of Peace: Algeria 1945–1962* (Harmondsworth: Penguin and New York: Penguin USA).

House, J. W. (1978) *France: An Applied Geography* (London: Methuen; (1979) New York: Routledge, Chapman & Hall).

Howorth, Jolyon (1991) 'France and the Gulf War: From Pre-war Crisis to Post-war Crisis', *Modern and Contemporary France*, 46 (July).

Howorth, Jolyon and George Ross (eds) (1986) *Contemporary France, Vol. 1* (London: Pinter and New York: Columbia University Press).

Institut Charles de Gaulle (1990) *De Gaulle et ses Premiers Ministres 1959–1969* (Paris: Plon).

Institut International d'Administration Publique (1991) *Enquête sur les Fonctions Publiques de l'Europe des Douze* (Paris: IIAP).

Irving, R. E. M. (1973) *Christian Democracy in France* (London: Allen & Unwin).

Jenkins, Brian and Peter Morris (1993) 'Political Scandal in France', *Modern and Contemporary France*, NS1 (2).

Jenson, Jane and George Ross (1985) *The View from Inside: A French Communist Cell in Crisis* (Berkeley CA: University of California Press).

Jenson, Jane and Mariette Sineau (1995) *Mitterrand et les Françaises* (Paris: Presses de Sciences Po).

Jobert, Bruno (1989) 'The Normative Frameworks of Public Policy', *Political Studies*, 37(3) (September).

Jobert, Bruno and Pierre Muller (1987) *L'Etat en Action* (Paris: Presses Universitaires de France).

Keeler, John (1987) *The Politics of Neo-corporatism in France* (Oxford and New York: Oxford University Press).

Keeler, John T. S. (1985) 'Confrontations Juridico–politiques: Le Conseil Constitutionnel face au Gouvernement Socialiste comparé à la Cour Suprême face au New Deal', *Pouvoirs*, 35.

Kimmel, Adolph (1991) *L'Assemblée Nationale sous la Ve République* (Paris: Presses de la Fondation Nationale des Sciences Politiques).

Knapp, Andrew (1991) 'The *cumul des mandats*, Local Power and Political Parties in France', *West European Politics*, 14(1) (January).

Knapp, Andrew (1994) *Gaullism Since De Gaulle* (Aldershot: Dartmouth).

Kuisel, Richard (1979) *Capitalism and the State in Modern France* (Cambridge and New York: Cambridge University Press).

Lacouture, J. (1981) *Pierre Mendès-France* (Paris: Seuil).

Lacouture, J. (1986) *De Gaulle. Tome 3 Le Souverain* (Paris: Seuil).

Lacouture, J. (1990) *De Gaulle, Vol. 1 The Rebel 1890–1944* (London: Collins–Harvill and New York: W. W. Norton).

Lacouture, J. (1991) *De Gaulle, Vol. 2 The Ruler* (London: Collins–Harvill and New York: W. W. Norton).

Lagroye, Jacques and Vincent Wright (eds) (1979) *Local Government in Britain and France* (London: Allen & Unwin).

Larkin, Maurice (1988) *France Since the Popular Front: Government and People 1936–1986* (Oxford and New York: Clarendon Press).

Laughland, John (1994) *The Death of Politics: France under Mitterrand* (London: Michael Joseph).

Lavau, Georges (1981) *A Quoi Sert Le Parti Communiste Français?* (Paris: Fayard).

Le Men, Jean François (1984) 'L'Information de Parlementaire Français', *Notes et Etudes Documentaires*, 4758 (Paris: Documentation Française).

Le Roy Ladurie, Emmanuel (1982) *Paris-Montpellier: PCF–PSU 1945–1963* (Paris: Gallimard).

Lefranc, G. (1976) *Les Organisations Patronales en France* (Paris: Payot).

Lequesne, Christian (1993) *Paris-Bruxelles: comment se fait la politique européenne de la France* (Paris: Presses de la Fondation Nationale des Sciences Politiques).

Leyrit, Claude (1995) *Les Partis Politiques et l'Argent* (Paris: Le Monde editions).

Lochak, Danielle and Jacques Chevallier (1986) *La Haute Administration et la Politique* (Paris: Presses Universitaires de France).

Lodge, Juliet (ed.) (1986) *Direct Elections to the European Parliament* (London: Macmillan and New York: St Martin's Press).

Lodge, Juliet (ed.) (1990) *The 1989 Election to the European Parliament* (London: Macmillan and New York: St Martin's Press).

Long, Marceau (1981) *Les Services du Premier Ministre* (Paris: Economica/Presses Universitaires d'Aix-Marseille).

Loughlin, John and Sonia Mazey (1995) *The End of the French Unitary State: Ten Years of Regionalisation* (London: Frank Cass).

Luchaire, François, Gérard Conac and Gilbert Mangin (1989) *Le Droit Constitutionel de la Cohabitation* (Paris: Economica).

Machin, Howard (1977) *The Prefect in French Public Administration* (London: Croom Helm and New York: St Martin's Press).

Machin, Howard (1989) 'The Evolution of the French Parties and the Party System', *West European Politics*, 12 (3) (October).

Machin, Howard and V. Wright (eds) (1985) *Economic Policy and Policy Making under the Mitterrand Presidency* (London: Pinter and New York: St Martin's Press).

Marcus, Jonathan (1995) *The National Front and French Politics* (London: Macmillan).

Masclet, J.-C. (1982) *Un Député, pour quoi faire?* (Paris: Presses Universitaires de France).

Masclet, J.-C. (1989) *Le Droit Electorale Français* (Paris: Presses Universitaires de France).

Massot, Jean (1979) *Le Chef du Gouvernement en France* (Paris: Documentation Française).

Massot, Jean (1987) *L'Arbitre et le Capitaine* (Paris: Flammarion).

Maus, Didier (1991) *La Practique Constitutionelle Française 1 octobre 1989–30 septembre 1990* (Paris: Presses Universitaires de France).

Maus, Didier (1995) *Les Grands Textes de la Pratique Institutionnelle de La Ve République* (Paris: Documentation Française).

Mayer, Nona and Pascal Perrineau (eds) (1989) *Le Front National à Découvert* (Paris: Presses de la Fondation Nationale des Sciences Politiques).

Mazey, Sonia and Michael Newman (1987) *Mitterrand's France* (London: Croom Helm and New York: Routledge, Chapman & Hall).

McCarthy, P. (ed.) (1987) *The French Socialists in Power* (Westport, Conn.: Greenwood Press).

McMillan, James (1992) *Twentieth Century France: Politics and society 1898–1991*, 2nd edn (London: Edward Arnold).

Mény, Yves (1989) 'The National and International Context of French Policy Communities', *Political Studies*, 37(3) (September).

Mény, Yves (1992) *La Corruption de la République* (Paris: Fayard).

Mény, Yves (1993) *Le système politique français* (Paris: Montchrestien).

Mény, Yves and V. Wright (eds) (1987) *The Politics of Steel: Western Europe and the Steel Industry in the Crisis Years* (Berlin: De Gruyter).

Mermet, G. (1994) *Francoscopie 1995* (Paris: Larousse).

Ministère de la Culture et de la Communication (1980) *Des Chiffres pour la Culture* (Paris: Documentation Française).

Mollet, Guy (1973) *Quinze Ans Après* (Paris: Albin Michel).

Monnet, J. (1978) *Memoirs* (London: Collins and New York: Bantam Books).

Morris, Peter (1994) *French Politics Today* (Manchester: Manchester University Press).

Mouriaux, René (1983) *La CGT* (Paris: Seuil).

Mouriaux, Réné (1994) *Le Syndicalisme en France depuis 1945* (Paris: La Découverte).

Mouriaux, René and Geneviève Bibès (1990) *Les Syndicats Européens à l'Epreuve* (Paris: Presses de la Fondation Nationale des Sciences Politiques).

Muller, Pierre (1992) *L'Administration Française est-elle en crise?* (Paris: L'Harmattan).

Noblecourt, Michel (1990) *Les syndicats en questions* (Paris: Les Editions Ouvrières).

Noel, Léon (1976) *De Gaulle et les Débuts de la Ve République 1958–1965* (Paris: Plon).

Northcutt, Wayne (1993) *Mitterrand; a Political Biography* (New York: Holmes and Meier).

Parodi, Maurice (1981) *L'Economie et la Société Française depuis 1945* (Paris: Colin).

Paxton, Robert (1972) *Vichy France: Old Guard and New Order* (New York: Columbia University Press).

Pickles, Dorothy (1972) *The Government and Politics of France, Vol. 1* (London: Methuen and New York: Routledge, Chapman & Hall).

Pilleul, G. (ed.) (1979) *L'Entourage et de Gaulle* (Paris: Plon).

Pinchemel, Philippe (1987) *France: A geographical, social and economic survey* (Cambridge and New York: Cambridge University Press).

Portelli, Hugues (1987 and 1990: 2nd edn) *La Politique en France sous la Ve République* (Paris: Grasset).

Price, Roger (1993) *A Concise History of France* (Cambridge: Cambridge University Press).

Quermonne, Jean-Louis (1980) *Le Gouvernment de la France sons le Ve République* (Paris: Dalloz).

Quermonne, Jean-Louis and D. Chagnollaud (1996) *Le Gouvernement de la France sous la Ve République*, 5th edn (Paris: Dalloz).

Rémond, Bruno and Jacques Blanc (1989) *Les Collectivités Locales* (Paris: Presses de La Fondation Nationale des Sciences Politiques/Dalloz).

Rémond, Réné (1982) *Les Droites en France* (Paris: Aubier).

Reynolds, S. (1988) 'Whatever Happened to the French Ministry of Women's Rights?', *Modern and Contemporary France*, 33 (April).

Reynolds, S. (ed.) (1986) *Women, State and Revolution* (Brighton: Wheatsheaf and Amberst: University of Massachusetts Press).

Richardson, Jeremy (1982) *Policy Styles in Western Europe* (London: Allen & Unwin).

Ridley, F. R. (1966) 'French Technocracy and Comparative Government', *Political Studies*, 14(1).

Ridley, F. R. (1970) *Revolutionary Syndicalism in France* (Cambridge: Cambridge University Press).

Rioux, Jean-Pierre (1980) *La France et la Quatrième République, Tome 1. L'Ardeur et la Nécessité* (Paris: Seuil).

Rioux, Jean-Pierre (1987) *The Fourth Republic 1944–1958* (Cambridge and New York: Cambridge University Press).

Rizzuto, Franco (1991) 'The Parties of the Mainstream Right: evolution and adaptation', *Modern and Contemporary France*, 47 (October).

Rondin, Jacques (1985) *Le Sacre des Notables* (Paris: Fayard).

Ross, George, Stanley Hoffman and Sylvia Malzacher (1987) *The Mitterrand Experiment* (Cambridge: Polity Press).

Rousseau, J.-J. (1762) *The Social Contract*, Book 2, Ch. 3 (trans. G. D. H. Cole, revised edn) (London: Dent, 1973).

Roussel, Eric (1994) *Georges Pompidou*, 2nd edn (Paris: Lattès).

Safran, William (1995) *The French Polity*, 4th edn (London and New York: Longman) 3rd edn.

Sainteny, Guillaume (1991) *Les Verts* (Paris: Presses Universitaires de France: Que Sais-je?).

Sainteny, Guillaume (1994) 'Le Parti Socialiste face à l'écologisme', *Revue Française de Science Politique*, 44 (3) June.

Scargill, Ian (1995) '*L'amenagement du territoire:* The Great Debate', *Modern and Contemporary France*, NS3 (1).

Schifres, Michel and Michel Sarazin (1985) *L'Elysée de Mitterrand* (Paris: Alain Moreau).

Schmidt, Vivien A. (1990) *Democratising France* (Cambridge and New York: Cambridge University Press).

Sharp, Margaret and Peter Holmes (eds) (1989) *Strategies for New Technology* (London: Philip Allan and Atlantic Highlands, N.J.: Humanities Press).

Shennan, Andrew (1993) *De Gaulle* (London and New York: Longman).

Social Change in Modern France (Cambridge: Cambridge University Press).

Stewart, J. H. (1951) *A Documentary Survey of the French Revolution* (New York: Macmillan).

Stone, Alec (1992) *The Birth of Judicial Politics in France: The Constitutional Council in Comparative Perspective* (Oxford and New York: Oxford University Press).

Suleiman, Ezra (1974) *Politics, Power and Bureaucracy in France* (Princeton, N.J.: Princeton University Press).

Suleiman, Ezra (1978) *Elites in French Society: The Politics of Survival* (Princeton, N.J.: Princeton University Press).

Terrazzoni, André (1987) *La Décentralisation à la Epreuve des Faits* (Paris: LGDJ).

Thomson, David (1969) *Democracy in France Since 1870*, 5th edn (Oxford: Oxford University Press).

Tournier, Fréderique (1995) 'François Mitterrand et l'affaire Bousquet', *Modern and Contemporary France*, NS3 (3).

Tuppen, John (1983) *The Economic Geography of France* (London: Croom Helm and New York: Barnes & Noble).

Tuppen, John (1991) *Chirac's France 1986–1988* (London: Macmillan and New York: St Martin's Press).

Vesperini, Jean-Pierre (1993) *L'Economie de la France sous la Ve République* (Paris: Economica).

Wahl, N. (1959) 'The French Constitution of 1958: the initial draft and its origins', *American Political Science Review*, 53 (June).

Wahl, Nicholas and Jean-Louis Quermonne (1995) *La France Présidentielle* (Paris: Presses de Sciences Po).

Ware, Alan (ed.) (1987) *Political Parties: Electoral Change and Structural Response* (Oxford and New York: Basil Blackwell).

Weber, Eugen (1979) *Peasants into Frenchman: the modernisation of rural France* (London: Chatto & Windus and Stanford, CA: Stanford University Press).

Weber, Henri (1986) *Le Parti des Patrons* (Paris: Seuil).

Wilcox, Lynne (1994) 'Coup de Langue: The amendment to Article 2 of the Constitution', *Modern and Contemporary France*, NS2 (3).

Williams, Philip (1968) *The French Parliament 1958–1967* (London: Allen & Unwin and New York: HarperCollins).

Williams, Philip (1970) *Wars, Plots and Scandals in Post War France* (Oxford: Oxford University Press).

Williams, Philip (1972) *Crisis and Compromise: Politics in the Fourth Republic,* (paperback edn) (London: Longman).

Wilson, Frank L. (1987) *Interest Group Politics in France* (New York: Cambridge University Press).

Wright, Vincent (1989) *The Government and Politics of France*, 3rd edn (London: Unwin Hyman).

Ysmal, Colette (1989) *Les Partis Politiques sous La Ve République* (Paris: Montchrestien).

Ysmal, Colette (1990) *Le Comportement Electoral des Français*, 2nd edn (Paris: La Découverte).

Index